Contents

Chapter I
Convergence criteria

‡ Each country sub-section deals in turn with: price developments; fiscal developments; exchange rate developments; long-term interest rate developments; and ends with a concluding summary.

2 Examination of the key aspects of convergence in 1998 (continued)

Chapter II
Compatibility of national legislation with the Treaty

CONVERGENCE REPORT

Report required by Article 109j of the Treaty establishing the European Community

March 1998

© **European Monetary Institute, 1998**
   Postfach 16 03 19, D-60066 Frankfurt am Main

ISBN 92-9166-057-4

Printed by Kern & Birner GmbH + Co., D-60486 Frankfurt am Main

5   Country assessments

List of Boxes, Tables and Charts *

Boxes

Tables

Charts

---

* **Convention used in the tables:**
"-" Not applicable
"." Not available
"..." Nil or negligible

Relate to the tables and charts in the "Introduction and summary" part of the Report. The tables and charts relating to Chapter I, section 2 of the Report are listed in the respective country parts of that section.

Abbreviations

Countries *

BE	Belgium
DK	Denmark
DE	Germany
GR	Greece
ES	Spain
FR	France
IE	Ireland
IT	Italy
LU	Luxembourg
NL	Netherlands
AT	Austria
PT	Portugal
FI	Finland
SE	Sweden
UK	United Kingdom

Currencies

BEF/LUF	Belgian/Luxembourg franc
DKK	Danish krone
DEM	Deutsche Mark
GRD	Greek drachma
ESP	Spanish peseta
FRF	French franc
IEP	Irish pound
ITL	Italian lira
NLG	Dutch guilder
ATS	Austrian schilling
PTE	Portuguese escudo
FIM	Finnish markka
SEK	Swedish krona
GBP	Pound sterling

---

* In accordance with Community practice, countries are listed in the Report using the alphabetical order of the national languages.

Introduction and summary

Introduction and summary

This Report examines the achievement of a high degree of sustainable convergence (see Chapter I) as well as compliance with the statutory requirements to be fulfilled for national central banks ("NCBs") to become an integral part of the European System of Central Banks ("ESCB"), with particular emphasis on central bank independence (see Chapter II). In producing this Report, the EMI fulfils the requirement of Article 109j (1) of the Treaty establishing the European Community (the "Treaty") to report to the EU Council "on the progress made in the fulfilment by the Member States of their obligations regarding the achievement of economic and monetary union". The same mandate has been given to the European Commission and the two reports have been submitted to the EU Council in parallel. Both reports represent the starting-point of the procedure according to Article 109j (2) and (4), which will entail the following *additional steps*:

- the European Commission shall submit to the EU Council a *recommendation*, for each Member State, on whether it fulfils the necessary conditions for the adoption of a single currency;

- the EU Council, acting by a qualified majority on that recommendation, shall *assess*, for each Member State, whether it fulfils the necessary conditions for the

adoption of a single currency and *recommend* its findings to the Council, meeting in the composition of the Heads of State or Government;

- the European Parliament shall be consulted and *forward its opinion* to the Council, meeting in the composition of the Heads of State or Government; and, finally,

- the Council, meeting in the composition of the Heads of State or Government, shall (on 2 May 1998) *confirm* which Member States fulfil the necessary conditions for the adoption of a single currency, acting by a qualified majority and on the basis of the recommendations of the EU Council, and taking into account the two reports and the opinion of the European Parliament.

Denmark, in accordance with the terms of Protocol No. 12 of the Treaty, has given notification that it will not participate in Stage Three of Economic and Monetary Union. The United Kingdom, in accordance with the terms of Protocol No. 11, has also notified the EU Council that it does not intend to move to the third stage in 1999. As a consequence, neither Member State will participate in the single currency at the start of Stage Three. Nevertheless, both countries' progress towards convergence is examined in detail in this Report.

I Convergence criteria

1.1 Framework for analysis

In this year's Report under Article 109j (1), the EMI makes use of a common framework for analysis and examines the state of convergence on a country-by-country basis.

The common framework for analysis is outlined in Chapter I of the Report (under "Key aspects of the examination of convergence in 1998"). It is based, first, on the Treaty provisions and their application by the EMI with regard to the developments of prices, fiscal deficit and debt ratios, exchange rates and long-term interest rates, also taking into account other factors; and, second, on a range of additional backward and forward-looking economic indicators which are considered to be useful for examining the sustainability of convergence in greater detail.

The common framework is subsequently applied individually to all fifteen Member States. These country reports, which focus on each Member State's performance, should be considered separately, in line with the provisions of Article 109j.

In this Report and the ensuing interpretation of the convergence criteria the EMI has to take into account the principles laid down by the European Council. The Council has emphasised many times the need for a high degree of sustainable convergence and, in that context, the need for a strict interpretation of the convergence criteria to make EMU work. In December 1996 the European Council meeting in Dublin stated in respect of its decision to be taken under Treaty Article 109j (4): "The Council takes this opportunity to stress that the four criteria of sustainable convergence and the requirement of central bank independence must be strictly applied. This is essential if the coming completion of monetary union is to have the essential quality of stability and the euro is to be assured of its status as a strong currency. It

is equally important that, when the criteria are applied in early 1998, they are applied with a view to ensuring that government financial positions in particular are sustainable and not affected by measures of temporary effect".

This Report builds on principles set out in previous reports published by the EMI, especially the first EMI report prepared under Article 109j (1), entitled "Progress Towards Convergence 1996", which was issued in November 1996, and the November 1995 report prepared under Article 7 of the EMI Statute, entitled "Progress Towards Convergence". In particular, a number of guiding principles are used by the EMI in the application of the convergence criteria. Quoting from the 1995 and 1996 reports: "First, the individual criteria are interpreted and applied in a strict manner. The rationale behind this principle ... is that the main purpose of the criteria is to ensure that only those Member States which have economic conditions that are conducive to the maintenance of price stability and the viability of the European currency area should participate in it. Second, the convergence criteria constitute a coherent and integrated package and they must all be satisfied; the Treaty lists the criteria on an equal footing and does not suggest a hierarchy. Third, the convergence criteria have to be met on the basis of current data. Fourth, the application of the convergence criteria should be consistent, transparent and simple." Moreover, it is emphasised again that compliance with the convergence criteria is essential, not only at a specific point in time, but also on a sustained basis. In this vein, the country reports elaborate on the sustainability of convergence.

The statistical data used in the application of the convergence criteria have been provided by the Commission (see also Annex 2). Convergence data on price and long-term interest rate developments are presented up to the period ending in January 1998, the latest month for which data on Harmonised Indices of Consumer Prices ("HICPs") were available. For exchange rates, the period considered in this Report ends in February 1998, the latest full month before the examination by the EMI was concluded.[1] Data for fiscal positions cover the period up to 1997. These data were judged by EUROSTAT to be in accordance with the rules laid down in the European System of Integrated Economic Accounts (ESA, second edition). However, this does not prejudge the assessment of whether fiscal positions are to be regarded as sustainable. Account is also taken of the latest Commission projections for 1998, together with national budgets for 1998 and the most recent Convergence Programmes, as well as other information which is considered to be relevant in the context of forward-looking considerations concerning the sustainability of convergence.

1.2 The state of convergence

Since publication of the EMI's report entitled "Progress Towards Convergence 1996" in November 1996, major improvements in terms of convergence have been seen in the Union. Between the last quarter of 1996 and January 1998 the EU average rate of HICP inflation has fallen from 2.2% to 1.3%; all Member States with the exception of Greece recorded rates of HICP inflation of around 2% or less in January 1998, and the standard deviation, as a measure of convergence, has decreased from 1.6% in the last quarter of 1996 to 0.9% in January 1998. In parallel, long-term interest rates have been falling throughout the Union to reach low EU-average levels of around 5½% at the end of the reference period and differentials between most EU countries' bond yields have been virtually eliminated. Over the two-year reference period up to February 1998, bilateral ERM exchange rates have in general remained broadly stable. Countries outside the ERM have tended to trade above average March

1996 bilateral exchange rate levels, although to differing degrees. In addition, in 1997 significant reductions have been achieved in fiscal deficits across the Union, and in a few countries budgetary positions were in surplus. The EU-wide fiscal deficit ratio has fallen to 2.4% of GDP, which represents a decline of 1.8 percentage points compared with 1996. Furthermore, for the first time during the 1990s, the debt-to-GDP ratio for the EU as a whole declined in 1997. Overall conditions necessary to maintain an environment conducive to non-inflationary growth have thus improved. However, the average debt ratio still stands at 72.1% of GDP and is much higher in three Member States. In addition, the decline in deficit ratios below the reference value and the fall in debt ratios in many countries have only recently been realised. Furthermore, the recent reductions in deficit and debt ratios have partly been related to one-off measures.

Within the context of a single monetary policy, the adjustments seen over the recent past need to be carried substantively further. Indeed, decisive and sustained corrective policies of a structural nature are warranted in most countries. These requirements for lasting policy adjustments result from the combined burden arising from (i) high and persistent unemployment, which according to the analysis conducted by the EMI and other international organisations is largely of a structural nature; (ii) demographic trends, which are expected to place a heavy burden on future public expenditure; and (iii) the high level of public debt, which will weigh on current budgets of many Member States until debt levels are reduced.

---

[1] *On 14 March 1998, i.e. after the reference period applied in this Report, the previous bilateral central rates of the Irish pound against the other currencies of the exchange rate mechanism were revalued by 3%. On the same day, the Greek drachma was incorporated in the exchange rate mechanism of the EMS. Both measures were effective from 16 March 1998.*

Clearly, as regards developments in labour markets, it will be crucial to strengthen national policies which enhance their functioning by means of reducing structural impediments. This will be paramount in reducing high levels of unemployment, which cannot be regarded as sustainable over the long term. Such policies would also contribute to increasing the ability of Member States' economies to respond quickly and effectively to country-specific developments in Stage Three, as well as to ensure competitiveness.

Insufficient progress in structural adjustment will severely complicate sustainable fiscal consolidation, which is needed in order to be able to cope effectively with the other main challenges which need to be addressed - the ageing of the population and high debt ratios. Against this background, it is emphasised that further consolidation is required in most Member States in order to reduce high ratios of general government debt relative to GDP and bring them down to 60% within an appropriate period of time. The need for stronger fiscal positions contrasts with substantial actual deficits in many countries. Progress is also required with respect to the Stability and Growth Pact effective from 1999 onwards. A forceful debt reduction within an appropriate period of time is warranted, first, in order to diminish vulnerability to changes in interest rates, which is aggravated if a larger share of debt matures within the short term, and, second, to make it easier to cope with future budgetary challenges, such as the increasing fiscal burden arising from the ageing of the population, in particular in the context of unfunded public pension systems, as well as the medium-term challenges arising from the need to reform unprofitable public enterprises and reduce structural unemployment. Third, reducing budgetary imbalances is necessary to re-establish a degree of flexibility for fiscal policies which enables countries to respond to adverse cyclical developments, i.e. low fiscal deficits or surpluses are needed under normal circumstances to allow automatic

stabilisers to work during periods of weak economic activity.

Evidently, in order to ensure sustainable fiscal consolidation, it is not sufficient to have recourse to measures with a temporary effect. In 1997 such measures were used to varying degrees in a number of Member States, which has complicated the assessment of the structural stance of fiscal policy. They need to be replaced by durable measures in order to avoid an increase in net borrowing requirements in 1998, or in subsequent years if they have given rise to future expenditure obligations or future shortfalls in revenues. Evidence available so far suggests that policies have been moving in the right direction, generally reducing the impact of temporary measures on public finances in 1998, a year for which budget outcomes are expected to be better than those recorded in 1997 in nearly all countries, and in a number of Member States more favourable than planned in medium-term Convergence Programmes.

Consistent with the aim of fostering sustainable economic growth, fiscal consolidation in recent years does appear to have been increasingly based on bringing down expenditure ratios, thereby counteracting the upward trend which had been observed in the early 1990s. However, as a result of falling interest rates, many countries have also benefited from lower interest payments relative to GDP and consolidation was focused in part on reducing investment expenditure. In the future, more emphasis needs to be placed on lowering current expenditure items. In addition, in a number of countries revenue ratios have approached levels which are detrimental to economic growth.

The criterion on price stability

Focusing on the performance of individual countries, over the twelve-month reference period ending January 1998 fourteen Member States (Belgium, Denmark, Germany, Spain,

France, Ireland, Italy, Luxembourg, the Netherlands, Austria, Portugal, Finland, Sweden and the United Kingdom) had average HICP inflation rates of below the reference value. This reference value was calculated by using the unweighted arithmetic average of the rate of HICP inflation in the three countries with the lowest inflation rates, plus 1.5 percentage points. These three countries' inflation rates were 1.1% for Austria, 1.2% for France and 1.2% for Ireland, and, adding 1.5 percentage points to the average of 1.2%, the reference value is 2.7%. HICP inflation in Greece was 5.2%, considerably lower than in previous years, but still well above the reference value (see Table A and Chart A).

Looking back over the period from 1990 to 1997, the convergence of inflation rates can be explained by a variety of common factors. In the first place, as is indicated for each individual Member State, it reflects a number of important policy choices, most notably the orientation of monetary policy towards price stability and the increasing support received from other policy areas, such as fiscal policies and the development of wages and unit labour costs. In addition, in most Member States the macroeconomic environment, in particular during the period following the cyclical downturn of 1993, has contributed to the easing of upward pressure on prices. Finally, in many Member States broadly stable exchange rates and subdued import price developments have helped to dampen inflation. At the level of individual countries, it is apparent that a group of Member States recorded relatively similar inflation rates for most of the 1990s, while several others made particularly rapid progress in 1996-97. Among the latter, annual CPI inflation in Spain, Italy and Portugal fell from 4-5½% in 1995 to around 2% in 1997. These three Member States have had twelve-month average HICP inflation rates of below the reference value since mid-1997. In Greece, HICP inflation fell from 7.9% in 1996 to 5.4% in 1997, while remaining considerably above the reference value (see Chart A).

Looking ahead to the near future, in most countries recent trends and forecasts for inflation tend to indicate that there is little or no sign of immediate upward pressure on inflation. The risks for price stability are often associated with a narrowing of the output gap, a tightening of labour market conditions and increases in administered prices or indirect taxes; in several countries, for the most part those which are further ahead in the current cyclical upturn, the rate of inflation is generally forecast to rise to somewhat above 2% during the period 1998-99. This applies to Denmark, Spain, Ireland, the Netherlands, Portugal, Finland and the United Kingdom. These Member States need to exercise firm control over domestic price pressures with regard to, inter alia, wage and unit labour costs. Support is also required from fiscal policies, which need to react flexibly to the domestic price environment.

The criterion on the government budgetary position

With regard to the performance of individual Member States in 1997, three countries have recorded fiscal surpluses (Denmark, Ireland and Luxembourg) and eleven Member States have achieved or maintained deficits at or below the 3% reference value specified in the Treaty (Belgium, Germany, Spain, France, Italy, the Netherlands, Austria, Portugal, Finland, Sweden and the United Kingdom). Only Greece recorded a deficit of 4.0%, which is still above the reference value. For 1998, fiscal surpluses or further reductions in deficit ratios are projected by the Commission for nearly all Member States. The Greek deficit is expected to fall to 2.2% of GDP (see Table A and Chart B).

As regards government debt, in the three Member States with debt-to-GDP ratios of above 100%, debt has continued to decline in relation to GDP. In Belgium the debt ratio in 1997 was 122.2%, i.e. 13.0 percentage points lower than the peak in 1993; in Greece the debt ratio in 1997 stood at 108.7%, i.e. 2.9

percentage points below the latest peak in 1996; and in Italy the debt ratio was 121.6%, i.e. 3.3 percentage points below the peak of 1994. In the seven countries which in 1996 had debt ratios significantly above 60% but below 80% of GDP, debt ratios also declined. This was particularly the case in Denmark, Ireland and the Netherlands, where debt ratios in 1997 were 16.5, 30.0 and 9.1 percentage points respectively below their peak levels of 1993, and stood at 65.1%, 66.3% and 72.1% of GDP respectively; in Spain the debt ratio in 1997 declined by 1.3 percentage points from its peak level of 1996 to reach 68.8% of GDP; in Austria the corresponding reduction amounted to 3.4 percentage points, taking the debt ratio to 66.1% of GDP. In Portugal the debt ratio was 3.9 percentage points below its 1995 level, bringing the debt ratio to 62.0% of GDP. Finally, in Sweden the debt ratio was 2.4 percentage points below its peak level of 1994, reaching 76.6% of GDP in 1997. In Germany, which in 1996 had a debt ratio of just above the 60% reference value, the debt ratio continued its upward trend and in 1997 was 19.8 percentage points higher than in 1991, standing at 61.3% of GDP. In 1997 four countries continued to have debt ratios of below the 60% reference value (France, Luxembourg, Finland and the United Kingdom). In France the debt ratio continued its upward trend to reach 58.0% of GDP in 1997 (see Table A and Chart B).

For 1998 further reductions in debt-to-GDP ratios are projected by the Commission for all Member States which had debt ratios of above 60% in 1997. In the cases of Denmark, Ireland and Portugal, a reduction to a level at or below the reference value is forecast. As regards countries with debt ratios of 50-60% of GDP in 1997, Finland and the United Kingdom are anticipated to reduce their debt ratios further below 60%, whereas in France the debt ratio is expected to increase marginally.

Overall, progress in reducing fiscal deficit and debt ratios has generally accelerated. However,

as has been pointed out above, in a number of Member States measures with a temporary effect have played a role in reducing deficits. On the basis of the evidence available to the EMI, the effects of such measures have been quantified at between 0.1 and 1 percentage point, with the level varying by country. To the extent that evidence is available, the magnitude of temporary measures in 1998 budgets has generally been reduced; in addition, as mentioned above, forecasts for 1998 suggest in most cases a further decline in deficit ratios. Reductions in debt ratios have benefited in part from a number of financial operations and transactions, such as privatisation, which are reflected in the so-called "stock-flow adjustment" item as reported in the main body of the Report. Such transactions are expected to continue to play a role in several Member States.

Notwithstanding recent achievements, further substantial consolidation is warranted in most Member States in order to achieve lasting compliance with the fiscal criteria and the medium-term objective of having a budgetary position that is close to balance or in surplus, as required by the Stability and Growth Pact, effective from 1999 onwards. This applies in particular to Belgium, Germany, Greece, Spain, France, Italy, the Netherlands, Austria and Portugal, where deficits in 1998 are forecast to be between 1.6 and 2.9% of GDP. For most of these countries, these consolidation requirements also apply when comparing the fiscal deficit ratios as projected in the Convergence Programmes for 1999-2000 with the medium-term objective of the Stability and Growth Pact.

Taking a broader view on the sustainability of fiscal developments, the case for sustained consolidation over an extended period of time, requiring substantial fiscal surpluses, is particularly strong for those countries with debt ratios of above 100% (Belgium, Greece and Italy). This compares with significant overall deficits in 1997 and the years before. In countries with debt ratios of significantly above 60% but below 80% of GDP, keeping the deficit ratio at current levels would not bring down the debt ratio to below 60% within an appropriate period of time, which indicates the need for further, in some cases substantial, consolidation. Instead, realising the fiscal positions forecast for 1998 by the European Commission and maintaining a balanced budget from 1999 onwards would reduce the debt ratio to below 60% over appropriate periods (Spain, the Netherlands and Austria). Sweden could achieve the same result by realising the surplus position forecast for 1998 and maintaining it for several years thereafter. In Germany the debt ratio is forecast to be just above 60% of GDP in 1998, which could allow it to be reduced to below the reference value as early as 1999 if a balanced budget were achieved in that year. In Denmark, Ireland and Portugal current and forecast fiscal balances would allow the debt ratio to be reduced to a level equal to or just below 60% as early as 1998. Finally, in France, where the debt ratio is just below 60% of GDP, complying with the Stability and Growth Pact from 1999 onwards would also ensure that the debt ratio does not exceed the reference value.

It should be noted that in assessing budgetary positions of EU Member States, the impact on national budgets of transfers to and from the EC budget is not taken into account by the EMI.

The exchange rate criterion

During the two-year reference period from March 1996 to February 1998 ten currencies (the Belgian/Luxembourg franc, the Danish krone, the Deutsche Mark, the Spanish peseta, the French franc, the Irish pound, the Dutch guilder, the Austrian schilling and the Portuguese escudo) have been participating in the ERM for at least two years before this examination, as stated by the Treaty. The periods of membership for the Finnish markka and the Italian lira were shorter, as these currencies joined and rejoined the exchange rate mechanism in October 1996 and

November 1996 respectively. Three currencies remained outside the ERM during the reference period referred to in this Report, namely the Greek drachma[2], the Swedish krona and the pound sterling.

Each of the ten ERM currencies mentioned above, with the exception of the Irish pound, has normally traded close to its unchanged central rates against other ERM currencies, and some currencies (the Belgian/Luxembourg franc, the Deutsche Mark, the Dutch guilder and the Austrian schilling) virtually moved as a bloc. On occasion, several currencies traded outside a range close to their central rates. However, the maximum deviation, on the basis of 10 business day moving averages, was limited to 3.5%, abstracting from the development of the Irish pound. In addition, the deviations were only temporary and mainly reflected transient movements of the Spanish peseta and the French franc (in early 1996), the Portuguese escudo (at end-1996/early 1997) as well as the Finnish markka (in early and mid-1997) vis-à-vis other ERM currencies. An examination of exchange rate volatility and short-term interest rate differentials suggests the persistence of relatively calm conditions throughout the reference period.

The Irish pound has normally traded significantly above its unchanged central rates against other ERM currencies; at the end of the reference period the Irish pound stood just over 3% above its central rates.[3] In parallel, the degree of exchange rate volatility vis-à-vis the Deutsche Mark increased until mid-1997 and short-term interest rate differentials against those EU countries with the lowest short-term interest rates widened over the same period. More recently, the

---

[2] As noted above, the Greek drachma was incorporated in the exchange rate mechanism of the EMS, effective from 16 March 1998.

[3] As noted above, the previous bilateral central rates of the Irish pound against other currencies of the exchange rate mechanism were revalued by 3%, effective from 16 March 1998.

former decreased and the latter narrowed somewhat while remaining relatively high.

In the case of the Italian lira, at the beginning of the reference period, before rejoining the ERM, it initially experienced a small and temporary setback in its previous strengthening trend, reaching a maximum downward deviation of 7.6% below its future central rate against one ERM currency in March 1996. Thereafter, it resumed its appreciation and tended towards its later central parities, moving for most of the time within a narrow range. In the case of the Finnish markka, also at the beginning of the reference period, before joining the ERM, it initially continued its weakening movement apparent over the previous few months - which had interrupted the longer-term upward movement since 1993 - reaching a maximum downward deviation of 6.5% below its future central rate against one ERM currency in April 1996. Thereafter, it appreciated and generally traded within a narrow range around its later central parities. Since joining and rejoining the ERM in October and November 1996 respectively, both the Finnish markka and the Italian lira have normally traded close to their unchanged central rates against other ERM currencies. As was the case for other ERM currencies, on occasion the Italian lira and the Finnish markka traded outside a range close to their central rates, but such deviations were limited and temporary. In both cases the relatively high degree of exchange rate volatility against the Deutsche Mark observed in earlier periods declined to low levels over the reference period and short-term interest rate differentials against those EU countries with the lowest short-term interest rates narrowed steadily in the case of the Italian lira and were insignificant in the case of the Finnish markka.

The three currencies remaining outside the ERM, namely the Greek drachma, the Swedish krona and the pound sterling, have normally traded above their March 1996 average bilateral exchange rates against other EU currencies. Short-term interest rate differentials against those EU countries with the lowest short-term interest rates remained wide in Greece, having narrowed until mid-1997 and widened significantly since November 1997, whereas they have narrowed significantly in Sweden. In the case of the pound sterling the short-term interest rate differential tended to widen.

The long-term interest rate criterion

Over the twelve-month reference period ending January 1998, fourteen Member States (Belgium, Denmark, Germany, Spain, France, Ireland, Italy, Luxembourg, the Netherlands, Austria, Portugal, Finland, Sweden and the United Kingdom) had average long-term interest rates of below the reference value. This reference value was calculated by using the unweighted arithmetic average of the long-term interest rates in the three countries with the lowest rates of HICP inflation, plus 2 percentage points. These three countries' long-term interest rates were 5.6% for Austria, 5.5% for France and 6.2% for Ireland, and, adding 2 percentage points to the average of 5.8%, the reference value is 7.8%. Representative long-term interest rates in Greece, which have been comparable with yields in other countries since June 1997, were 9.8% and thus stood well above the reference value (see Table A and Chart C).

Looking back over the period from 1990 to 1997, long-term interest rates were broadly similar in a number of countries when considered over the period as a whole. This applies to Belgium, Germany, France, Luxembourg, the Netherlands and Austria. In Denmark and Ireland long-term rates were also relatively close to those in the above-mentioned countries for most of the period. In Finland and Sweden the process of yield convergence accelerated from 1994-95 onwards and both countries have recorded limited differentials since around 1996. In Spain, Italy and Portugal, where yields were significantly higher for most of the 1990s, long-term interest rates declined steeply from 1995 onwards and moved below the reference value in either late 1996 or early 1997. A significant reduction was also seen in Greece. In the case of the United Kingdom, reflecting a different position in the cycle vis-à-vis continental European countries, a broad trend has been observed since the early 1990s of, first, convergence with, and later divergence from the long-term interest rates prevailing in the countries with the lowest bond yields, although long-term interest rate differentials have narrowed more recently.

The broad patterns observed in member countries are closely related to the developments in inflation rates (see above), which have facilitated a general reduction in long-term interest rates and a particularly marked decline in the case of the formerly high-yielding currencies. Other factors underlying this trend were the stability of exchange rates in most cases and the improvement in countries' fiscal positions, thereby reducing risk premia. These underlying developments were seen by the markets as improving the prospects for participation in Stage Three of EMU - an element which may in turn have played an independent role in accelerating the narrowing of yield differentials, both directly and by further improving the prospects for price and exchange rate stability.

Other factors

In addition to the convergence criteria mentioned above, the Report also takes account of a number of "other factors" which are referred to explicitly in Article 109j (1) of the Treaty: the development of the ECU; the results of the integration of markets; the situation and development of the balances of payments on current account and an examination of unit labour costs and other price indices (see Table B).

The growth of nominal unit labour costs has generally decelerated in the course of the 1990s to levels consistent with low rates of inflation. In a number of countries, namely Belgium, Germany, Ireland, the Netherlands,

Austria and Finland nominal unit labour costs over the period 1996-97 either were broadly stable or declined, while in several other cases (Denmark, Spain, France, Luxembourg, Portugal and the United Kingdom) increases were clearly positive but for the most part moderate. The main exception was Greece, where, despite a significant deceleration during the 1990s, the increase in nominal unit labour costs was 7.5% in 1997. In Italy and Sweden the increase in unit labour costs picked up in 1996 to close to 5%, before slowing in 1997 to 3.1% in Italy and 1.2% in Sweden.

As regards the other relevant price indices considered in this Report, these generally confirm the trend observed in HICPs. In some countries one or more other measures of inflation are somewhat above the level of HICP inflation.

Recent figures for EU countries' current account positions point to surpluses in eleven countries in 1997. Among these, in Spain, France, Italy, Finland and Sweden deficits were recorded in the early 1990s but have subsequently been eliminated; in the United Kingdom a small surplus emerged in 1997. In others, surpluses have been maintained throughout the 1990s. Belgium and the Netherlands, in particular, have built up sizable net asset positions. In the remaining four Member States (Germany, Greece, Austria and Portugal) current account deficits have been more persistent, although in the case of Germany the deficit in 1997 was small.

With regard to the integration of markets, European Commission figures on the state of implementation of internal market directives (as of February 1998) show that the average transposition rate in the Union is approximately 94%. In a breakdown by sector, the Commission identifies public procurement as the sector in which the most technical barriers remain. Considering trade flows in goods and services, the share of intra-EU trade as a percentage of total trade is significant for all EU countries. In 1996 intra-EU exports as a proportion of total exports ranged from 52% in the United Kingdom to over 80% in Portugal. The average for all EU Member States is 61%. For intra-EU imports the corresponding figures range from 54% in Ireland to 76% in Portugal, while the average for all EU countries is approximately 61%.

As regards taxation issues, indirect taxation and capital income taxation are of particular importance to the integration of markets. There continue to be significant differences between EU countries both in terms of the indirect taxation of goods and services and, for the taxation of capital income, in terms of the rates applied and their precise application. The tax treatment of interest payments is an example: in some EU countries there is a withholding tax, whereby the tax is levied on residents, while in others the paying agent is required to inform the tax authorities and, in general, residents and non-residents are treated differently. No comprehensive measures have yet been taken to harmonise capital income taxation in order to promote the integration of financial markets.

The overall private ECU market contracted further in 1997, reflecting declines in bank assets and liabilities and international bonds outstanding. This contraction took place despite some favourable developments in 1997. In particular, some legal uncertainties were resolved and, partly in response to this, the spread between market and basket ECU exchange rates narrowed further between end-December 1996 and end-December 1997 from around 90 basis points to par; it was even at a premium for a short period towards the end of 1997.

2 Compatibility of national legislation with the Treaty

2.1 Introduction

Article 108 of the Treaty states that Member States shall ensure, at the latest at the date of the establishment of the ESCB, that their national legislation, including the statutes of their NCBs, is compatible with the Treaty and the Statute ("legal convergence"). This does not require the harmonisation of NCBs' statutes, but it implies that national legislation and statutes of NCBs need to be adjusted in order to make them compatible with the Treaty and the Statute. For the purpose of identifying those areas where the adaptation of national legislation is necessary, a distinction may be made between the independence of NCBs, the legal integration of NCBs in the ESCB and legislation other than statutes of NCBs.

Compatibility requires that the legislative process be completed, i.e. that the respective act has been adopted by the national legislator and that all further steps, for example promulgation, have been accomplished. This applies to all legislation under Article 108. However, the above distinction between different areas of legislation is important when it comes to determining the date on which legislation must enter into force. Many decisions which the Governing Council of the ECB and the NCBs will take between the date of the ESCB's establishment and the end of 1998 will predetermine the single monetary policy and its implementation within the euro area. Therefore, adaptations which relate to the independence of an NCB need to become effective at the latest at the date of the ESCB's establishment. Other statutory requirements relating to the legal integration of NCBs in the ESCB need only enter into force at the moment that the integration of an NCB in the ESCB becomes effective, i.e. the starting date of Stage Three or, in the case of a Member State with a derogation or a special status, the date on which it adopts the single currency. The entry into force of adaptations of legislation other than statutes of NCBs which are required to ensure compatibility with the Treaty and the Statute is dependent on the content of such legislation and therefore needs to be assessed on a case-by-case basis.

This Report provides, inter alia, an assessment on a country-by-country basis of the compatibility of national legislation with the Treaty and the Statute.

2.2 Independence of NCBs

Central bank independence is essential for the credibility of the move to Monetary Union and, thus, a prerequisite of Monetary Union. The institutional aspects of Monetary Union require monetary powers, currently held by Member States, to be exercised in a new system, the ESCB. This would not be acceptable if Member States could influence the decisions taken by the governing bodies of the ESCB.

The Statute contemplates an important role for governors of NCBs (via their membership of the Governing Council of the ECB) with regard to the formulation of monetary policy and for the NCBs with regard to the execution of the operations of the ESCB (see Article 12.1 of the Statute, last paragraph). Thus, it will be essential for the NCBs to be independent in the performance of their ESCB-related tasks vis-à-vis external bodies.

The principle of the independence of NCBs is expressly referred to in Article 107 of the Treaty and Article 14.2 of the Statute. Article 107 contains a prohibition on attempts to influence the ECB, NCBs or the members of their decision-making bodies, and Article 14.2 provides for security of tenure for such members.

The EMI has established a list of features of central bank independence, distinguishing between features of an institutional, personal and financial nature.[4]

As regards institutional independence, rights of third parties (e.g. government and parliament) to:

- give instructions to NCBs or their decision-making bodies;

- approve, suspend, annul or defer decisions of NCBs;

- censor an NCB's decisions on legal grounds;

- participate in the decision-making bodies of an NCB with a right to vote; or

- be consulted (ex ante) on an NCB's decisions

are incompatible with the Treaty and/or the Statute and, thus, require adaptation.

With respect to personal independence, statutes of NCBs should ensure that:

- governors of NCBs have a minimum term of office of five years;

- a governor of an NCB may not be dismissed for reasons other than those mentioned in Article 14.2 of the Statute (i.e. if he/she no longer fulfils the conditions required for the performance of his/her duties or if he/she has been guilty of serious misconduct);

- other members of the decision-making bodies of NCBs involved in the performance of ESCB-related tasks have the same security of tenure as governors;

---

[4] There is also a criterion of functional independence, but as NCBs will in Stage Three be integrated in the ESCB, this is being dealt with in the framework of the legal integration of NCBs in the ESCB (see paragraph 2.3 below).

- no conflicts of interest will arise between the duties of members of the decision-making bodies of NCBs vis-à-vis their respective NCB (and, additionally, of governors vis-à-vis the ECB) and other functions which members of the decision-making bodies involved in the performance of ESCB-related tasks may perform and which may jeopardise their personal independence.

Financial independence requires that NCBs can avail themselves of the appropriate means to fulfil their mandate. Statutory constraints in this field must be accompanied by a safeguard clause to ensure that ESCB-related tasks can be properly fulfilled.

2.3 The legal integration of NCBs in the ESCB

The full participation of NCBs in the ESCB necessitates measures in addition to those designed to ensure independence. In particular, such measures may be necessary to enable NCBs to execute tasks as members of the ESCB and in accordance with decisions taken by the ECB. The main areas of attention are those where statutory provisions may form an obstacle to an NCB complying with the requirements of the ESCB or to a governor fulfilling his/her duties as a member of the Governing Council of the ECB, or where statutory provisions do not respect the prerogatives of the ECB. Thus the EMI's assessment of the compatibility of the statutes of NCBs with the Treaty and the Statute focuses on the following areas: statutory objectives, tasks, instruments, organisation, financial provisions and miscellaneous issues.

2.4 Legislation other than the statutes of NCBs

The obligation of legal convergence under Article 108 of the Treaty, which is incorporated in a Chapter entitled "Monetary Policy", applies to those areas of legislation which are affected by the transition from Stage Two to Stage Three. The EMI's assessment of the compatibility of national legislation with the Treaty and the Statute focuses in this respect on laws with an impact on an NCB's performance of ESCB-related tasks and laws in the monetary field. Relevant legislation requiring adaptation is in particular found in the following areas: banknotes, coins, foreign reserve management, exchange rate policy and confidentiality.

2.5 Compatibility of national legislation with the Treaty and the Statute

All Member States except Denmark, whose legislation does not require adaptation, have introduced, or are in an advanced process of introducing, changes in the statutes of their NCBs, following the criteria laid down in the EMI's Reports and in the EMI's opinions. The United Kingdom, which is exempt from the obligations under Article 108 of the Treaty, is in the process of introducing a new statute of its NCB which, while providing a greater level of operational central bank independence, is not expressly intended to achieve the legal convergence as required by the EMI for full compliance with the Treaty and the Statute. Throughout the European Union legislators, with the above exceptions, have undertaken a legislative process intended to prepare NCBs for Stage Three of EMU.

3   Summaries country by country

3.1 Belgium

Over the reference period Belgium has achieved a rate of HICP inflation of 1.4%, which is well below the reference value stipulated by the Treaty. The increase in unit labour costs was subdued and low rates of inflation were also apparent in terms of other relevant price indices. Looking ahead, there are no signs of immediate upward pressure on inflation; forecasts project inflation to be around 1½% in 1998 and 1999. The Belgian franc has been participating in the ERM for much longer than two years. Over the reference period it remained broadly stable, generally close to its unchanged central parities without the need for measures to support the exchange rate. The level of long-term interest rates was 5.7%, i.e. well below the respective reference value.

In 1997 Belgium achieved a fiscal deficit ratio of 2.1% of GDP, i.e. below the reference value, and the outlook is for a further decline to 1.7% in 1998. The debt-to-GDP ratio is far above the 60% reference value. After having reached a peak in 1993, it declined by 13.0 percentage points to stand at 122.2% in 1997; the outlook is for a further decline to 118.1% of GDP in 1998. Notwithstanding the efforts and the substantial progress made towards improving the current fiscal situation, there is an evident ongoing concern as to whether the ratio of government debt to GDP will be "sufficiently diminishing and approaching the reference value at a satisfactory pace" and whether sustainability of the fiscal position has been achieved; addressing this issue will have to remain a key priority for the Belgian authorities. The maintenance of a primary surplus of at least 6% of GDP per year and the achievement of growing and sizable overall fiscal surpluses are needed in order to be able to forcefully reduce the debt ratio to 60% within an appropriate period of time. This compares with a recorded fiscal deficit of 2.1% of GDP in 1997, as well as the forecast deficit of 1.7% in 1998. The Stability and Growth Pact also requires, as a medium-term objective, a budgetary position that is close to balance or in surplus.

With regard to other factors, in 1996 and 1997 the deficit ratio exceeded the ratio of public investment to GDP, while Belgium has maintained large current account surpluses and a strong net external asset position.

The statute of the National Bank of Belgium was amended with Law No. 1061/12-96/97. Assuming that specific provisions thereof, for which progressive adaptation is envisaged, will enter into force on time, the Bank's statute will be compatible with Treaty and Statute requirements for Stage Three. The EMI takes note that adaptations of various other laws are envisaged.

3.2 Denmark

Denmark, in accordance with the terms of Protocol No. 12 of the Treaty, has given notification to the EU Council that it will not participate in Stage Three of EMU. Nevertheless, its progress towards convergence is examined in detail.

Over the reference period Denmark has achieved a rate of HICP inflation of 1.9%, which is well below the reference value stipulated by the Treaty. The increase in unit labour costs has picked up recently and some other relevant indicators of inflation exceeded 2% in 1997. Looking ahead, there are no signs of immediate upward pressure on inflation; forecasts project inflation will rise to somewhat above 2% in 1998 and slightly higher in 1999. The Danish krone has been participating in the ERM for much longer than two years. Over the reference period it remained broadly stable, generally close to its unchanged central parities, without the need for measures to support the exchange rate. The level of long-term interest rates was 6.2%, i.e. below the respective reference value.

In 1997 Denmark achieved a general government surplus of 0.7% of GDP, thus comfortably meeting the reference value, and the outlook is for a surplus of 1.1% in 1998. The debt-to-GDP ratio is above the 60% reference value. After having reached a peak in 1993, the ratio declined by 16.5 percentage points to stand at 65.1% in 1997. Regarding the sustainability of fiscal developments, the outlook is for a decrease in the debt ratio to 59.5% of GDP in 1998, i.e. just below the reference value. Looking further ahead, if current fiscal surpluses are maintained, Denmark should comply with the medium-term objective of the Stability and Growth Pact, effective from 1999 onwards, of having a budgetary position that is close to balance or in surplus, and the debt ratio would fall further below 60%.

With regard to other factors, in 1996 the deficit ratio was below the ratio of public investment to GDP. Moreover, Denmark has recorded current account surpluses, while continuing to have a net external liability position. In the context of the ageing of the population, Denmark benefits from a rapidly expanding private pension sector.

The statute of Danmarks Nationalbank does not contain incompatibilities in the area of central bank independence. The legal integration of the Bank in the ESCB does not need to be provided for and other legislation does not need to be adapted as long as Denmark does not adopt the single currency.

3.3 Germany

Over the reference period Germany has achieved a rate of HICP inflation of 1.4%, which is well below the reference value stipulated by the Treaty. Unit labour costs fell and low rates of inflation were also apparent in terms of other relevant price indices.

Looking ahead, there are no signs of immediate upward pressure on inflation; forecasts project inflation will stand at around 2% in 1998 and 1999. The Deutsche Mark has been participating in the ERM for much longer than two years. Over the reference period it remained broadly stable, generally close to its unchanged central parities, without the need for measures to support the exchange rate. The level of long-term interest rates was 5.6%, i.e. well below the respective reference value.

In 1997 Germany achieved a fiscal deficit ratio of 2.7% of GDP, i.e. below the reference value, and the outlook is for a further decline to 2.5% in 1998. The debt-to-GDP ratio is just above the 60% reference value. As of 1991, the first year after German unification, the ratio increased by 19.8 percentage points to stand at 61.3% in 1997, reflecting to a large extent the fiscal burden relating to unification. Regarding the sustainability of fiscal developments, the outlook is for a marginal decline in the debt ratio to 61.2% of GDP in 1998. Keeping the deficit ratio at current levels would not be sufficient to bring the debt ratio down to 60% of GDP within an appropriate period of time, thus pointing to the need for further substantial progress in consolidation. The Stability and Growth Pact also requires as a medium-term objective a budgetary position that is close to balance or in surplus. Given the current debt ratio of just above 60% of GDP, achieving the fiscal position forecast for 1998 and realising a balanced budget thereafter would reduce the debt ratio to below 60% as early as 1999.

With regard to other factors, in 1996 and 1997 the deficit ratio exceeded the ratio of public investment to GDP, and Germany recorded current account deficits as a consequence of unification, while maintaining a net external asset position.

The statute of the Deutsche Bundesbank was amended with the Sixth Act amending the Deutsche Bundesbank Act dated 22 December 1997, which made the Bank's statute compatible with Treaty and Statute requirements for Stage Three. The EMI takes note that adaptation of the Act on Coins is envisaged.

3.4 Greece

A clear trend towards lower inflation has been discernible in Greece, with the CPI rate falling from above 20% in 1990 to 5½% in 1997. HICP inflation was 5.2% over the reference period. At the same time, the increase in unit labour costs decelerated to 7½% in 1997, and the reduction in inflationary tendencies is also indicated by other relevant measures of inflation. Looking ahead, forecasts suggest a fall in inflation to 4½% in 1998 and to 3½% in 1999. Long-term interest rates have been on a broadly declining trend during the 1990s, with the exception of 1997; they averaged 9.8% over the reference period. Overall, notwithstanding the progress made, Greece has not achieved a rate of HICP inflation or a level of long-term interest rates which are below the respective reference values stipulated by the Treaty.

Greece did not participate in the ERM during the reference period referred to in this Report.[5] Over the reference period, the Greek drachma traded above its March 1996 average bilateral exchange rates against most other EU currencies, which are used as a benchmark for illustrative purposes in the absence of central rates.

Since 1993 the fiscal deficit ratio has been reduced by a total of 9.8 percentage points to stand at 4.0% of GDP in 1997, above the reference value stipulated in the Treaty; the outlook for 1998 is for a decline in the deficit ratio to 2.2%, i.e. a level below the reference value. The debt-to-GDP ratio is far above the 60% reference value. After having reached a peak in 1993, the ratio broadly stabilised, before decreasing by 2.9 percentage points to 108.7% in 1997; the outlook for 1998 is for a decline in the debt ratio to 107.7% of GDP. Notwithstanding the efforts and the substantial progress made towards improving the current fiscal situation, there must be an ongoing concern as to whether the ratio of government debt to GDP will be "sufficiently diminishing and approaching the reference value at a satisfactory pace" and whether sustainability of the fiscal position has been achieved; addressing this issue will have to remain a key priority for the Greek authorities. Substantial primary surpluses and persistent, sizable overall fiscal surpluses will be needed to be able to reduce the debt ratio to 60% within an appropriate period of time. This compares with a recorded fiscal deficit of 4.0% of GDP in 1997, as well as the deficit forecast of 2.2% in 1998. The Stability and Growth Pact also requires, as a medium-term objective, a budgetary position that is close to balance or in surplus.

With regard to other factors, in 1996 and 1997 the deficit ratio exceeded the ratio of public investment to GDP, Greece recorded current account deficits and had a net external liability position. In the context of the ageing of the population, Greece benefits from a partly funded pension system.

The statute of the Bank of Greece was amended with Law 2548 dated 12 December 1997. As a result, there are no remaining incompatibilities with Treaty and Statute requirements for Stage Three in the Bank's statute. There are, however, two imperfections which still require adaptation before Greece adopts the single currency. The EMI is not aware of any other statutory provisions which would require adaptation under Article 108 of the Treaty.

3.5 Spain

Over the reference period Spain has achieved a rate of HICP inflation of 1.8%, which is well below the reference value stipulated by the Treaty. The increase in unit labour costs was

---

5 As noted above the Greek drachma was incorporated in the exchange rate mechanism of the EMS, effective from 16 March 1998.

subdued and a general trend towards low rates of inflation was also apparent in terms of other relevant price indices. Looking ahead, there is little sign of immediate upward pressure on inflation; forecasts project inflation will rise to somewhat above 2% in 1998 and 1999. The Spanish peseta has been participating in the ERM for considerably longer than two years. Over the reference period it remained broadly stable, generally close to its unchanged central parities, without the need for measures to support the exchange rate. The level of long-term interest rates was 6.3%, i.e. below the respective reference value.

In 1997 Spain achieved a fiscal deficit ratio of 2.6%, i.e. below the reference value, and the outlook is for a further decline to 2.2% in 1998. The debt-to-GDP ratio is above the 60% reference value. After having reached a peak in 1996, the ratio declined by 1.3 percentage points to stand at 68.8% in 1997. Regarding the sustainability of fiscal developments, the outlook is for a decrease in the debt ratio to 67.4% of GDP in 1998. Given the current debt ratio of somewhat below 70% of GDP, achieving the fiscal balance forecast for 1998 and a balanced budget thereafter would reduce the debt ratio to below 60% in 2001. Instead, keeping the 1998 overall or primary balances constant in the following years would bring the debt ratio down to 60% of GDP not before 2007 and 2004 respectively, thus pointing to the need for further substantial progress in consolidation. The Stability and Growth Pact also requires as a medium-term objective a budgetary position that is close to balance or in surplus.

With regard to other factors, in 1996 the fiscal deficit ratio exceeded the ratio of public investment to GDP, but it fell below that level in 1997. Furthermore, Spain has recorded current account surpluses, while continuing to have a net external liability position.

The statute of the Banco de España was amended in the area of central bank independence with Law 66/1997 of 30 December 1997. The Bank's statute is in the process of being amended in the area of the Bank's integration in the ESCB. Assuming that a draft law to this effect is adopted as it stood on 24 March 1998 and that it will enter into force on time, the Bank's statute will be compatible with Treaty and Statute requirements for Stage Three. The EMI takes note that further adaptation of Law 10/1975 of 12 March 1975 on Coinage is envisaged.

3.6 France

Over the reference period France has achieved a rate of HICP inflation of 1.2%, which is well below the reference value stipulated by the Treaty and one of the three lowest inflation rates in the Union. The increase in unit labour costs was subdued and low rates of inflation were also apparent in terms of other relevant price indices. Looking ahead, there are no signs of immediate upward pressure on inflation; forecasts project inflation will stand at well below 2% in 1998 and 1999. The French franc has been participating in the ERM for much longer than two years. Over the reference period it remained broadly stable, generally close to its unchanged central parities, without the need for measures to support the exchange rate. The level of long-term interest rates was 5.5%, i.e. well below the respective reference value.

In 1997 France achieved a fiscal deficit ratio of 3.0% of GDP, i.e. a level equal to the reference value, and the outlook is for virtually no further improvement in 1998 (a decrease to 2.9%) in spite of the favourable conjunctural situation. In addition, the fiscal debt ratio, though increasing to 58.0% of GDP in 1997, remained just below the 60% reference value; the outlook is for a marginal increase to 58.1% in 1998. Regarding the sustainability of fiscal developments, keeping the deficit ratio at current levels would not be sufficient to keep the debt ratio below 60% of GDP, thus pointing to a need for further substantial progress in consolidation. The Stability and

Growth Pact also requires as a medium-term objective a budgetary position that is close to balance or in surplus. This would also imply a reduction in the debt ratio to further below 60% of GDP.

With regard to other factors, in 1996 and 1997 the deficit ratio exceeded the ratio of public investment expenditure to GDP. Furthermore, France has recorded current account surpluses and a net external liability position.

The statute of the Banque de France is currently being adapted. Assuming that a draft law to this effect is adopted as it stood on 24 March 1998 and that it will enter into force on time, the Bank's statute will be compatible with Treaty and Statute requirements for Stage Three. The EMI takes note that adaptations of various other laws are envisaged.

3.7 Ireland

Over the reference period Ireland has achieved a rate of HICP inflation of 1.2%, which is well below the reference value stipulated by the Treaty and one of the three lowest inflation rates in the Union. Unit labour costs declined, and low rates of inflation were also apparent in terms of other relevant price indices. Looking ahead, there are some signs of immediate upward pressure on inflation, which may rise towards 3% over the next two years. The level of long-term interest rates was 6.2%, i.e. below the respective reference value.

The Irish pound has been participating in the ERM for much longer than two years. During the reference period it has normally traded significantly above its unchanged central rates against other ERM currencies, reflecting an autonomous upward trend of the currency in the light of buoyant domestic economic conditions. This is also mirrored in relatively high exchange rate volatility and short-term interest rate differentials, both of which have

declined more recently as the Irish pound has moved closer to its bilateral central rates against other ERM currencies.[6]

In 1997 Ireland achieved a general government surplus of 0.9% of GDP, thereby comfortably meeting the 3% reference value, and the outlook is for a surplus of 1.1% of GDP in 1998. The debt-to-GDP ratio is above the 60% reference value. After having reached a peak in 1993, the ratio declined by 30.0 percentage points to stand at 66.3% in 1997, reflecting inter alia very strong real GDP growth. Regarding the sustainability of fiscal developments, the outlook is for a decline in the debt ratio to 59.5% of GDP in 1998, i.e. just below the reference value. Looking further ahead, if current fiscal surpluses are maintained, Ireland should comply with the medium-term objective of the Stability and Growth Pact, effective from 1999 onwards, of having a budgetary position that is close to balance or in surplus, and the debt ratio would fall further below 60%.

With regard to other factors, in 1996 the deficit position did not exceed the ratio of public investment to GDP. Moreover, Ireland has maintained current account surpluses. In the context of a relatively favourable demographic situation, the pension system relies on funded private pensions and unfunded social security pensions play a relatively minor role.

The statute of the Central Bank of Ireland was amended by the Central Bank Act 1998. With the adoption and entry into force of this Act, and assuming that specific provisions thereof (for which progressive adaptation through ministerial orders is envisaged) will enter into force on time, there will be no remaining incompatibilities with Treaty and Statute requirements for Stage Three in the Bank's statute. There are, however, two

---

[6] *With effect from 16 March 1998, i.e. after the reference period referred to in this Report, the bilateral central rates of the Irish pound against the other ERM currencies were revalued by 3%.*

imperfections, which will not jeopardise the overall functioning of the ESCB at the start of Stage Three and which will be addressed in the context of forthcoming legislative changes. The EMI takes note that the Decimal Currency Act has also been adapted.

3.8 Italy

Over the reference period Italy has achieved a rate of HICP inflation of 1.8%, which is well below the reference value stipulated by the Treaty. The growth of unit labour costs picked up in 1996, before slowing to 3.1% in 1997, and a general trend towards low rates of inflation was also apparent in terms of other relevant price indices. Looking ahead, there is little sign of immediate upward pressure on inflation; the most recent forecast projects inflation to stand slightly below 2% in 1998 and around 2% in 1999. The level of long-term interest rates was 6.7%, i.e. below the respective reference value.

The Italian lira has been participating in the ERM for around 15 months, i.e. for less than two years prior to the examination by the EMI. On the basis of the evidence reviewed in the Report, in an ex post assessment, the lira has been broadly stable over the reference period as a whole. Within the ERM it has remained generally close to its unchanged central parities, without the need for measures to support the exchange rate.

In 1997 Italy achieved a fiscal deficit ratio of 2.7% of GDP, i.e. below the reference value, and the outlook is for a further decrease to 2.5% in 1998. The debt-to-GDP ratio is far above the 60% reference value. After having reached a peak in 1994, the ratio declined by 3.3 percentage points to stand at 121.6% in 1997. The outlook is for a decline in the debt ratio to 118.1% of GDP in 1998. Notwithstanding the efforts and the substantial progress made towards improving the current fiscal situation, there must be an ongoing concern as to whether the ratio of government debt to GDP will be "sufficiently diminishing and approaching the reference value at a satisfactory pace" and whether sustainability of the fiscal position has been achieved; addressing this issue will have to remain a key priority for the Italian authorities. Significant and persistent overall fiscal surpluses are rapidly needed to be able to forcefully reduce the debt ratio to 60% of GDP within an appropriate period of time. This compares with a recorded fiscal deficit of 2.7% of GDP in 1997 as well as the deficit forecast for 1998 of 2.5%. The Stability and Growth Pact also requires, as a medium-term objective, a budgetary position that is close to balance or in surplus.

With regard to other factors, in 1996 and 1997 the deficit ratio exceeded the ratio of public investment to GDP, while Italy has recorded sizable and increasing current account surpluses which brought the net external liability position near to balance.

The statutory provisions governing the Banca d'Italia, which are contained in various laws and decrees, have been amended. Assuming that the amendments to the Bank's By-Laws adopted by the General Meeting of Shareholders are approved by a Presidential Decree and that they will enter into force on time, and assuming that the provisions referred to in Article 11.1 of Legislative Decree No. 43 dated 10 March 1998 will enter into force on the date of the establishment of the ESCB at the latest, the Bank's statute will be compatible with Treaty and Statute requirements for Stage Three. The EMI is not aware of any other statutory provisions which would require adaptation under Article 108 of the Treaty.

3.9 Luxembourg

Over the reference period Luxembourg has achieved a rate of HICP inflation of 1.4%, which is well below the reference value stipulated by the Treaty. The increase in unit labour costs was subdued and low rates of inflation were also apparent in terms of other relevant price indices. Looking ahead, there is little sign of immediate upward pressure on inflation; forecasts project inflation will stand at 1½-2% in 1998 and 1999. The Luxembourg franc, which is in a monetary association with the Belgian franc, has been participating in the ERM for much longer than two years. Over the reference period it remained broadly stable, generally close to its unchanged central parities without the need for measures to support the exchange rate. The level of long-term interest rates was 5.6%, i.e. well below the respective reference value.

Luxembourg achieved a general government surplus of 1.7% of GDP in 1997, thereby comfortably meeting the 3% reference value, and the outlook is for a surplus of 1.0% in 1998. In addition, the fiscal debt ratio was virtually stable at 6.7% of GDP in 1997, i.e. remaining far below the 60% reference value, and the outlook is for an increase to 7.1% in 1998. With regard to the sustainability of fiscal developments, looking ahead, if current fiscal surpluses are maintained for 1998, Luxembourg should comply with the medium-term objective of the Stability and Growth Pact, effective from 1999 onwards, of having a budgetary position that is close to balance or in surplus.

With regard to other factors, Luxembourg has maintained large current account surpluses.

The Law of 20 May 1983 establishing the Institut Monétaire Luxembourgeois as amended and the Law of 15 March 1979 on the monetary status of Luxembourg are currently being amended with Law No. 3862. Assuming that this law is adopted as it stood on 24 March 1998 and that it will enter into force on time, there will be no remaining incompatibilities with Treaty and Statute requirements in the IML's statute, although there are various imperfections, which will, however, not jeopardise the overall functioning of the ESCB at the start of Stage Three. Two of these imperfections should be corrected urgently

3.10 Netherlands

Over the reference period the Netherlands has achieved a rate of HICP inflation of 1.8% which is well below the reference value stipulated by the Treaty. The increase in unit labour costs was subdued and generally low rates of inflation were also apparent in terms of other relevant price indices. Looking ahead, there are some signs of immediate upward pressure on inflation; forecasts project inflation will rise to around 2½% in 1998 and 1999. The Dutch guilder has been participating in the ERM for much longer than two years. Over the reference period it remained broadly stable, generally close to its unchanged central parities, without the need for measures to support the exchange rate. The level of long-term interest rates was 5.5%, i.e. well below the respective reference value.

In 1997 the Netherlands achieved a fiscal deficit ratio of 1.4% of GDP, i.e. well below the reference value, and the outlook is for an increase to 1.6% in 1998. The debt-to-GDP ratio is above the 60% reference value. After having reached a peak in 1993, the ratio declined by 9.1 percentage points to stand at 72.1% in 1997. Regarding the sustainability of fiscal developments, the outlook is for a decrease in the debt ratio to 70.0% of GDP in 1998. Looking further ahead, keeping the deficit ratio at current levels would not be sufficient to bring the debt ratio down to 60% of GDP within an appropriate period of time, thus pointing to the need for further substantial progress in consolidation. The Stability and Growth Pact also requires as a medium-term objective a budgetary position that is close to balance or in surplus. Given the current debt ratio of above 70% of GDP, achieving the fiscal position forecast for 1998 and realising a balanced budget thereafter would reduce the debt ratio to below 60% in 2002.

With regard to other factors, in 1996 and 1997 the deficit ratio did not exceed the ratio of public investment to GDP, and the Netherlands maintained large current account surpluses as well as a net external asset position. In the context of the ageing of the population, the Netherlands benefits from a sizable funded occupational pension system.

The statute of De Nederlandsche Bank is currently being amended. Assuming that a draft law to this effect is adopted as it stood on 24 March 1998 and that it will enter into force on time, there will be no remaining incompatibilities with Treaty and Statute requirements for Stage Three in the Bank's statute, although there is one imperfection, which will, however, not jeopardise the overall functioning of the ESCB at the start of Stage Three. The EMI takes note that adaptations of various other laws are envisaged.

3.11 Austria

Over the reference period Austria has achieved a rate of HICP inflation of 1.1%, which is well below the reference value stipulated by the Treaty and one of the three lowest inflation rates in the Union. Unit labour costs were broadly stable over the reference period (having decreased in 1996) and low rates of inflation were also apparent in terms of other relevant price indices. Looking ahead, there are some signs of upward pressure on inflation. The Austrian schilling has been participating in the ERM for longer than two years. Over the reference period it remained broadly stable, generally close to its unchanged central parities, without the need for measures to support the exchange rate. The level of long-term interest rates was 5.6%, i.e. well below the respective reference value.

In 1997 Austria achieved a fiscal deficit ratio of 2.5%, i.e. below the reference value, and the outlook is for a decrease to 2.3% in 1998. The debt-to-GDP ratio is above the 60% reference value. After having reached a peak in 1996, it declined by 3.4 percentage points to stand at 66.1% in 1997. Regarding the sustainability of fiscal developments, the outlook is for a decrease in the debt ratio to 64.7% of GDP in 1998. Looking further

ahead, keeping the deficit ratio at current levels would not be sufficient to bring the debt ratio down to 60% of GDP within an appropriate period of time, thus pointing to the need for further substantial progress in consolidation. The Stability and Growth Pact also requires as a medium-term objective a budgetary position that is close to balance or in surplus. Given the current debt ratio of above 65% of GDP, achieving the fiscal position forecast for 1998 and realising a balanced budget thereafter would reduce the debt ratio to below 60% as early as the year 2000.

With regard to other factors, in 1996 the deficit ratio exceeded the ratio of public investment to GDP, while in 1997 the difference was close to zero. Austria has maintained current account deficits as well as a net external liability position.

The statute of the Oesterreichische Nationalbank is currently being adapted. Assuming that a draft law to this effect is adopted as it stood on 24 March 1998 and that it will enter into force on time, the Bank's statute will be compatible with Treaty and Statute requirements for Stage Three. The EMI takes note that adaptation of the Foreign Exchange Act is envisaged.

3.12 Portugal

Over the reference period Portugal has achieved a rate of HICP inflation of 1.8%, which is well below the reference value stipulated by the Treaty. The increase in unit labour costs has decelerated markedly over the 1990s and the general trend towards low rates of inflation was also apparent in terms of other relevant price indices. Looking ahead, there are no signs of immediate upward pressure on inflation; forecasts project inflation to stand somewhat above 2% in 1998 and 1999. The Portuguese escudo has been participating in the ERM for considerably longer than two years. Over the reference period it remained broadly stable, generally close to its unchanged central parities, without the need for measures to support the exchange rate. The level of long-term interest rates was 6.2%, i.e. below the respective reference value.

In 1997 Portugal achieved a fiscal deficit ratio of 2.5%, i.e. below the reference value, and the outlook is for a decrease to 2.2% in 1998. The debt-to-GDP ratio is just above the 60% reference value. After reaching a peak in 1995 the ratio declined by 3.9 percentage points to stand at 62.0% in 1997. Regarding the sustainability of fiscal developments, the outlook is for a decrease in the debt ratio to 60.0% of GDP in 1998, i.e. a level equal to the reference value. Looking further ahead, current fiscal deficit ratios exceed the medium-term objective of the Stability and Growth Pact, effective from 1999 onwards, of having a budgetary position that is close to balance or in surplus, thus pointing to a need for further substantial consolidation. This would also imply a reduction in the debt ratio to below 60%.

With regard to other factors, in 1996 and 1997 the deficit ratio did not exceed the ratio of public investment to GDP, and Portugal has recorded current account deficits and a net external asset position.

The statute of the Banco de Portugal was amended by means of the Constitutional Law 1/97 of 20 September 1997 and Law No. 5/98 of 31 January 1998, which made the Bank's statute compatible with Treaty and Statute requirements for Stage Three. The EMI takes note that adaptations of various other laws are envisaged.

3.13 Finland

Over the reference period Finland has achieved a rate of HICP inflation of 1.3%, which is well below the reference value stipulated by the Treaty. Unit labour costs declined in 1997 and low rates of inflation were also apparent in terms of other relevant price indices. Looking ahead, there are some signs of immediate upward pressure on inflation; forecasts suggest a rate of 2-2½% in 1998 and 1999. The level of long-term interest rates was 5.9%, i.e. below the respective reference value.

The Finnish markka has been participating in the ERM for around 16 months, i.e. for less than two years prior to the examination by the EMI. On the basis of the evidence reviewed in the Report, in an ex post assessment, the Finnish markka has been broadly stable over the reference period as a whole. Within the ERM, it has remained generally close to its unchanged central parities without the need for measures to support the exchange rate.

In 1997 Finland achieved a fiscal deficit ratio of 0.9% of GDP, i.e. well below the reference value, and the outlook is for a surplus of 0.3% in 1998. In addition, the fiscal debt ratio declined to 55.8% of GDP in 1997, thus remaining below the 60% reference value. Regarding the sustainability of fiscal developments, the outlook is for a further decline to 53.6% in 1998. Against this background, Finland should comply with the medium-term objective of the Stability and Growth Pact, effective from 1999 onwards, of having a budgetary position that is close to balance or in surplus, and the debt ratio would fall further below 60%.

With regard to other factors, Finland has recorded sizable current account surpluses while continuing to have a net foreign liability position. In the context of the ageing of the population, Finland benefits from a partly funded pension system.

The statute of Suomen Pankki was amended by means of a revised Act on the Bank of Finland. The revised law has, again, been adapted through a new law (the "new law") in order to bring the Bank's statute fully into line with the Treaty and the Statute. With the adoption of the new law, the Bank's statute will be compatible with Treaty and Statute requirements for Stage Three. The EMI takes note that adaptations of the Currency Act and the Act on Coins have been completed.

3.14 Sweden

Over the reference period Sweden has achieved a rate of HICP inflation of 1.9%, which is well below the reference value stipulated by the Treaty. The increase in unit labour costs was subdued in 1997 and low rates of inflation were also apparent in terms of other relevant price indices. Looking ahead, there is little sign of immediate upward pressure on inflation; forecasts project inflation will stand at 1½-2% in 1998 and 2% in 1999. The level of long-term interest rates was 6.5%, i.e. below the respective reference value.

Sweden does not participate in the ERM. Over the reference period, the Swedish krona traded above its March 1996 average bilateral exchange rates against most other EU currencies, which are used as a benchmark for illustrative purposes in the absence of central rates.

In 1997 Sweden achieved a fiscal deficit ratio of 0.8% of GDP, i.e. well below the reference value, and the outlook is for a surplus of 0.5% in 1998. The debt-to-GDP ratio is above the 60% reference value. After having reached a peak in 1994, the ratio declined by 2.4 percentage points to stand at 76.6% in 1997. Regarding the sustainability of fiscal developments, the outlook is for a decline in the debt ratio to 74.1% of GDP in 1998. Against the background of recent trends in the deficit ratio, Sweden should comply with the medium-term objective of the Stability and Growth Pact, effective from 1999 onwards, of having a budgetary position that is close to balance or in surplus. Given the current debt ratio of above 75% of GDP, achieving the overall surplus forecast for 1998 and maintaining it in subsequent years would reduce the debt ratio to below 60% of GDP in 2003.

With regard to other factors, the deficit ratio exceeded the ratio of public investment to GDP in 1996, while falling below that level in 1997. In addition, Sweden recorded current account surpluses, while maintaining a net external liability position. In the context of the ageing of the population, Sweden benefits from a partly funded pension system.

The Constitution Act, the Riksdag Act and the Sveriges Riksbank Act are currently being amended to meet Treaty and Statute requirements for the independence of Sveriges Riksbank. Assuming that a draft law to this effect is adopted as it stood on 24 March 1998, there will be two remaining incompatibilities with Treaty and Statute requirements for Stage Three in the Bank's statute.

3.15 United Kingdom

The United Kingdom, in accordance with the terms of Protocol No. 11 of the Treaty, has notified the EU Council that it does not intend to move to the third stage in 1999. As a consequence, it will not participate in the single currency at the start of Stage Three. Nevertheless, its progress towards convergence is examined in detail.

Over the reference period the United Kingdom has achieved a rate of HICP inflation of 1.8%, which is well below the reference value stipulated by the Treaty. The increase in unit labour costs was subdued and a general tendency towards low rates of inflation was also apparent in terms of other relevant price indices. Looking ahead, forecasts project inflation at 2-2½% in 1998 and 1999. The level of long-term interest rates was 7.0%, i.e. below the respective reference value.

The United Kingdom does not participate in the ERM. Over the reference period, the currency appreciated against other EU currencies, partly reflecting the differing position in the cycle and the associated monetary policy stance.

In 1997 the United Kingdom achieved a fiscal deficit ratio of 1.9% of GDP, i.e. a level well below the reference value, and the outlook is for a further decline to 0.6% in 1998. In addition, the fiscal debt ratio decreased to 53.4% of GDP in 1997, thus remaining below the 60% reference value and the outlook is for a further decline to 52.3% in 1998. Regarding the sustainability of fiscal developments, looking ahead, with fiscal balances as projected, the United Kingdom should comply with the medium-term objective of the Stability and Growth Pact, effective from 1999 onwards, of having a budgetary position that is close to balance or in surplus, and the debt ratio would fall further below 60%.

With regard to other factors, the United Kingdom has recorded a small current account surplus in 1997, and has a net foreign asset position. In the context of the ageing of the population, the United Kingdom benefits from a pension system which is heavily reliant on funded private pensions.

Since the United Kingdom has notified the Council that it does not intend to adopt the single currency, there is no current legal requirement to ensure that national legislation is compatible with the Treaty and the Statute.

Economic indicators and the Maastricht Treaty convergence criteria
(excluding the exchange rate criterion)

		HICP inflation[a]	Long-term interest rate[b]		General government surplus (+) or deficit (-)[c]		General government gross debt[c]
Belgium	1996	1.8	6.5		-3.2		126.9
	1997[d]	1.4	5.7	#	-2.1		122.2
	1998[e]	-	-	#	-1.7		118.1
Denmark[f]	1996	2.1	7.2	#	-0.7		70.6
	1997[d]	1.9	6.2	#	0.7		65.1
	1998[e]	-	-	#	1.1	#	59.5
Germany	1996	1.2	6.2		-3.4		60.4
	1997[d]	1.4	5.6	#	-2.7		61.3
	1998[e]	-	-	#	-2.5		61.2
Greece	1996	7.9	14.4		-7.5		111.6
	1997[d]	5.2	9.8		-4.0		108.7
	1998[e]	-	-	#	-2.2		107.7
Spain	1996	3.6	8.7		-4.6		70.1
	1997[d]	1.8	6.3	#	-2.6		68.8
	1998[e]	-	-	#	-2.2		67.4
France	1996	2.1	6.3		-4.1	#	55.7
	1997[d]	** 1.2	** 5.5	#	-3.0	#	58.0
	1998[e]	-	-	#	-2.9	#	58.1
Ireland	1996	2.2	7.3	#	-0.4		72.7
	1997[d]	*** 1.2	*** 6.2	#	0.9		66.3
	1998[e]	-	-	#	1.1	#	59.5
Italy	1996	4.0	9.4		-6.7		124.0
	1997[d]	1.8	6.7	#	-2.7		121.6
	1998[e]	-	-	#	-2.5		118.1
Luxembourg	1996	*** 1.2	*** 6.3	#	2.5	#	6.6
	1997[d]	1.4	5.6	#	1.7	#	6.7
	1998[e]	-	-	#	1.0	#	7.1
Netherlands	1996	1.4	6.2	#	-2.3		77.2
	1997[d]	1.8	5.5	#	-1.4		72.1
	1998[e]	-	-	#	-1.6		70.0
Austria	1996	1.8	6.3		-4.0		69.5
	1997[d]	* 1.1	* 5.6	#	-2.5		66.1
	1998[e]	-	-	#	-2.3		64.7
Portugal	1996	2.9	8.6		-3.2		65.0
	1997[d]	1.8	6.2	#	-2.5		62.0
	1998[e]	-	-	#	-2.2	#	60.0
Finland	1996	** 1.1	** 7.1		-3.3	#	57.6
	1997[d]	1.3	5.9	#	-0.9	#	55.8
	1998[e]	-	-	#	0.3	#	53.6
Sweden	1996	* 0.8	* 8.0		-3.5		76.7
	1997[d]	1.9	6.5	#	-0.8		76.6
	1998[e]	-	-	#	0.5		74.1
United Kingdom	1996	2.5	7.9		-4.8	#	54.7
	1997[d]	1.8	7.0	#	-1.9	#	53.4
	1998[e]	-	-	#	-0.6	#	52.3

Source: European Commission.

*,**,*** = first, second and third best performer in terms of price stability.

= general government deficit not exceeding 3% of GDP; general government gross debt not exceeding 60% of GDP.

(a) Annual percentage changes.

(b) In percentages. For further explanation of the Greek data, see note in Table 12 for Greece.

(c) As a percentage of GDP.

(d) Data for HICP inflation and long-term interest rate refer to the twelve-month period ending January 1998; European Commission (spring 1998 forecasts) for general government surplus or deficit and general government gross debt.

(e) European Commission projections (spring 1998 forecasts) for general government surplus or deficit and general government gross debt.

(f) See footnote (c) in Table 4 for Denmark.

CPI inflation, unit labour costs and current account balance
(annual percentage changes unless otherwise stated)

		1990	1991	1992	1993	1994	1995	1996	1997[a]
Belgium	Consumer price index	3.4	3.2	2.4	2.8	2.4	1.5	2.1	1.6
	Unit labour costs	3.8	6.8	4.0	5.7	0.3	1.2	-0.2	0.5
	Current account balance[b]	1.8	2.3	2.8	5.0	5.1	4.2	4.2	4.7
Denmark	Consumer price index	2.6	2.4	2.1	1.2	2.0	2.1	2.1	2.2
	Unit labour costs	2.0	1.9	1.9	-0.7	0.0	2.0	0.9	3.0
	Current account balance[b]	1.0	1.5	2.8	3.4	1.8	1.1	1.7	0.6
Germany[c]	Consumer price index	2.7	3.6	5.1	4.5	2.7	1.8	1.5	1.8
	Unit labour costs	2.0	3.3	6.2	3.7	0.2	1.6	-0.2	-1.8
	Current account balance[b]	3.2	-1.1	-1.0	-0.7	-1.0	-1.0	-0.6	-0.1
Greece	Consumer price index	20.4	19.4	15.9	14.4	10.9	8.9	8.2	5.5
	Unit labour costs	19.5	9.3	12.6	12.7	11.7	11.3	9.9	7.5
	Current account balance[b]	-4.3	-1.7	-2.1	-0.8	-0.1	-2.5	-3.7	-3.8
Spain	Consumer price index	6.7	5.9	5.9	4.6	4.7	4.7	3.6	2.0
	Unit labour costs	9.3	8.1	8.0	4.9	0.0	1.9	2.9	1.9
	Current account balance[b]	-3.4	-3.0	-3.0	-0.4	-0.8	1.2	1.3	1.4
France	Consumer price index	3.4	3.2	2.4	2.1	1.7	1.8	2.0	1.2
	Unit labour costs	4.1	3.6	2.7	3.1	-0.3	1.8	1.4	1.3
	Current account balance[b]	-0.8	-0.5	0.4	0.9	0.6	0.7	1.3	2.9
Ireland	Consumer price index	3.4	3.2	3.0	1.5	2.4	2.5	1.6	1.5
	Unit labour costs	0.0	2.2	3.1	3.8	-1.7	-4.1	-2.6	-1.3
	Current account balance[b]	0.0	2.1	2.6	5.5	3.6	4.1	3.2	2.8
Italy	Consumer price index	6.1	6.4	5.4	4.2	3.9	5.4	3.9	1.7
	Unit labour costs	9.3	8.5	3.7	1.4	-0.4	1.8	4.9	3.1
	Current account balance[b]	-1.5	-2.1	-2.4	1.0	1.4	2.5	3.4	3.1
Luxembourg	Consumer price index	3.7	3.1	3.2	3.6	2.2	1.9	1.4	1.4
	Unit labour costs	6.6	3.5	4.0	-2.2	1.4	2.2	0.7	1.1
	Current account balance[b]	17.0	13.5	15.4	13.7	14.0	18.1	15.9	15.9
Netherlands	Consumer price index	2.4	3.1	3.2	2.6	2.8	1.9	2.0	2.2
	Unit labour costs[d]	1.7	3.9	3.1	2.2	-1.3	1.2	0.2	0.1
	Current account balance[b]	3.2	2.6	2.3	4.4	5.3	5.9	5.2	7.3
Austria	Consumer price index	3.3	3.3	4.1	3.6	3.0	2.2	1.9	1.3
	Unit labour costs	2.8	4.5	4.8	3.5	0.8	1.1	-0.5	0.0
	Current account balance[b]	0.8	0.0	-0.1	-0.4	-0.9	-2.0	-1.8	-1.8
Portugal	Consumer price index	13.4	11.4	8.9	6.5	5.2	4.1	3.1	2.2
	Unit labour costs	15.7	15.1	13.3	6.5	4.2	2.0	2.9	2.8
	Current account balance[b]	-0.3	-0.9	-0.1	0.1	-2.5	-0.2	-1.4	-2.0
Finland	Consumer price index	6.2	4.3	2.9	2.2	1.1	1.0	0.6	1.2
	Unit labour costs	8.8	7.7	-1.8	-4.7	-2.2	0.7	0.6	-2.4
	Current account balance[b]	-5.1	-5.5	-4.6	-1.3	1.3	4.1	3.8	5.3
Sweden	Consumer price index	10.4	9.7	2.6	4.7	2.4	2.8	0.8	0.9
	Unit labour costs	10.6	6.4	0.4	1.9	0.5	0.0	4.6	1.2
	Current account balance[b]	-2.9	-2.0	-3.4	-2.0	0.3	2.2	2.3	2.7
United Kingdom	Consumer price index	8.1	6.7	4.7	3.0	2.3	2.9	3.0	2.8
	Unit labour costs	10.1	7.1	3.2	0.4	-0.4	1.4	2.1	1.9
	Current account balance[b]	-3.4	-1.4	-1.7	-1.6	-0.2	-0.5	-0.3	0.4

Source: National data; for explanatory notes see Table "Measures of inflation and related indicators" and Table "External developments".
(a) Partly estimated.
(b) As a percentage of GDP.
(c) Unified Germany from 1992 onwards; current account balance from 1991 onwards.
(d) 1997: market economy.

Chart A

Reference value and Harmonised Indices of Consumer Prices
(12-month moving average of annual percentage changes)

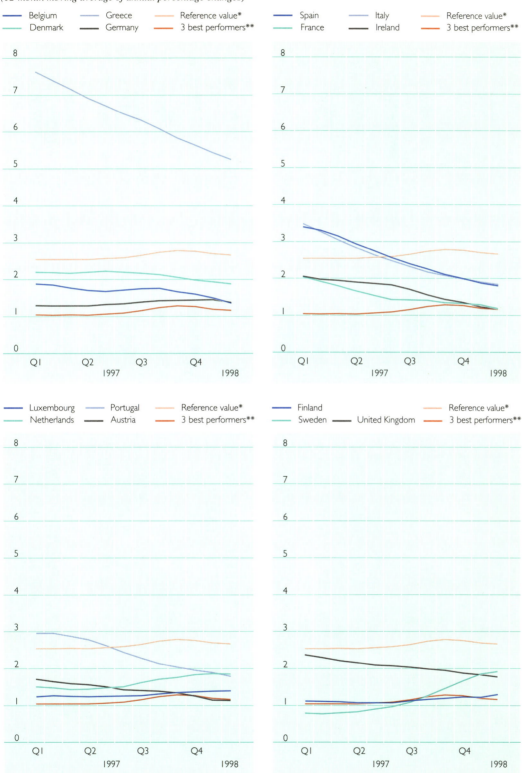

Source: European Commission.
* Unweighted arithmetic average of the three best-performing countries according to the price criterion plus 1.5 percentage points.
** Unweighted arithmetic average of the three best-performing countries according to the price criterion.

Performance in relation to Maastricht Treaty fiscal reference values
(as a percentage of GDP)

(a) General government surplus (+) / deficit (-)

■ 1996　■ 1997　■ 1998 (a)

(b) General government gross debt

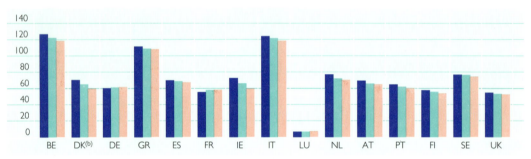

Source: European Commission (spring 1998 forecasts).
(a) Projections.
(b) See footnote (c) in Table 4 for Denmark.

Chart C

Reference value and long-term interest rates
(12-month moving average in percentages)

Source: European Commission.
(a) For further explanation of the data used see Table 12 for Greece.
*   Unweighted arithmetic average of the long-term interest rates of the three best-performing countries according to the price criterion plus 2.0 percentage points.
** Unweighted arithmetic average of the long-term interest rates of the three best-performing countries according to the price criterion.

Chapter I

Convergence criteria

1 Key aspects of the examination of economic convergence in 1998

This chapter aims at summarising, country by country, the evidence which is available from a comprehensive examination of economic convergence, referring to a number of economic criteria related to the development of prices, government financial positions, exchange rates and long-term interest rates, and taking into account other factors. In the following text, Boxes 1-4 briefly recall the provisions of the Treaty and provide methodological details which outline the application of these provisions by the EMI. Furthermore, the main text describes in greater detail the range of indicators which are considered for examining the sustainability of developments, most of which have already appeared in previous reports. First, the evidence of the period 1990 to 1997 is reviewed from a backward-looking perspective; this should help to better determine whether current achievements are primarily the result of genuine structural adjustments. Second, and to the extent appropriate, a forward-looking perspective is adopted. In this context it is highlighted that the sustainability of favourable developments hinges critically on appropriate and lasting policy responses to existing and future challenges. Overall, it is emphasised that ensuring sustainability depends both on the achievement of a sound starting position and on the policies pursued after the start of Stage Three of Economic and Monetary Union.

As regards *price developments*, the Treaty provisions and their application by the EMI are outlined in Box 1.

BOX 1

Price developments

1. Treaty provisions

Treaty Article 109j (1) requires:

"the achievement of a high degree of price stability; this will be apparent from a rate of inflation which is close to that of, at most, the three best-performing Member States in terms of price stability";

Article 1 of Protocol No. 6 on the convergence criteria referred to in Article 109j (1) of the Treaty, stipulates:

"The criterion on price stability referred to in the first indent of Article 109j (1) of this Treaty shall mean that a Member State has a price performance that is sustainable and an average rate of inflation, observed over a period of one year before the examination, that does not exceed by more than 1½ percentage points that of, at most, the three best-performing Member States in terms of price stability. Inflation shall be measured by means of the consumer price index on a comparable basis, taking into account differences in national definitions".

2. Application of Treaty provisions

- First, with regard to "an average rate of inflation, observed over a period of one year before the examination", the inflation rate has been calculated using the increase in the latest available twelve-month average of the Harmonised Indices of Consumer Prices (HICP) over the previous twelve-month average. Hence, with respect to the rate of inflation, the reference period considered in this Report is February 1997 to January 1998.

- Second, the notion of "at most, the three best-performing Member States in terms of price stability" which is used for the definition of the reference value has been applied by using the unweighted arithmetic average of the rate of inflation in the three countries with the lowest inflation rates, given that these rates are compatible with price stability and there are no outliers. At the time this Report was finalised, the three countries with the lowest HICP inflation rates observed over the reference period were Austria (1.1%), France (1.2%) and Ireland (1.2%); as a result, the average rate is 1.2% and, adding 1½ percentage points, the reference value is 2.7%.

Inflation has been measured on the basis of the data from HICPs, which were developed for the purpose of assessing convergence in terms of price stability on a comparable basis (see Annex 2 to this chapter).

To allow a more detailed examination of the sustainability of price developments, the average rate of HICP inflation achieved over the twelve-month reference period from February 1997 to January 1998 is reviewed in the light of the performance during the 1990s in terms of price stability. In this connection, attention is drawn to the orientation of monetary policy, in particular whether the focus of the monetary authorities has been primarily on achieving and maintaining price stability, as well as to the contribution of other areas of economic policy. Moreover, the implications of the macroeconomic environment for the achievement of price stability are taken into account. Price developments are examined in the light of demand and supply conditions, focusing inter alia on factors influencing unit labour costs and import prices. Finally, price trends across other relevant price indices (including the national CPI, the private consumption deflator, the GDP deflator and producer prices) are taken into account. From a forward-looking perspective, a view is provided on prospective inflationary developments in the immediate future, including forecasts by major international organisations, and structural aspects are mentioned which are relevant for maintaining an environment conducive to price stability after the start of Stage Three of Economic and Monetary Union.

Concerning *fiscal developments*, the Treaty provisions and their application by the EMI as well as procedural issues are outlined in Box 2.

BOX 2

Fiscal developments

1. Treaty provisions

Treaty Article 109j (1) requires:

"the sustainability of the government financial position; this will be apparent from having achieved a government budgetary position without a deficit that is excessive, as determined in accordance with Article 104c (6)". Article 2 of Protocol No. 6 stipulates that this criterion "shall mean that at the time of the examination the Member State is not the subject of a Council decision under Article 104c (6) of this Treaty that an excessive deficit exists".

Article 104c sets out the excessive deficit procedure. According to Article 104c (2) and (3) the Commission shall prepare a report if a Member State does not fulfil the requirements for fiscal discipline, in particular if

(a) the ratio of the planned or actual government deficit to gross domestic product exceeds a reference value (defined in the Protocol as 3% of GDP), unless:
   either the ratio has declined substantially and continuously and reached a level that comes close to the reference value;
   or, alternatively, the excess over the reference value is only exceptional and temporary and the ratio remains close to the reference value;

(b) the ratio of government debt to gross domestic product exceeds a reference value (defined in the Protocol as 60% of GDP), unless the ratio is sufficiently diminishing and approaching the reference value at a satisfactory pace.

In addition, the report prepared by the Commission shall take into account whether the government deficit exceeds government investment expenditure and all other relevant factors, including the medium-term economic and budgetary position of the Member State. The Commission may also prepare a report if, notwithstanding the fulfilment of the requirements under the criteria, it is of the opinion that there is a risk of an excessive deficit in a Member State. The Monetary Committee shall formulate an opinion on the report of the Commission. Finally, according to Article 104c (6), the EU Council, on the basis of the recommendation from the Commission, shall, acting by qualified majority, decide, after an overall assessment, whether an excessive deficit exists in a Member State.

2. Procedural issues and application of Treaty provisions

- First, with regard to the provision of Protocol No. 6, Article 2, that "the criterion on the government budgetary position... shall mean that at the time of the examination the Member State is not the subject of a Council decision under Article 104c (6) of this Treaty that an excessive deficit exists", it should be noted that the EU Council (ECOFIN) will officially revise the list of countries having an "excessive deficit" only after publication of this Report, on the basis of a recommendation of the Commission. Since it will be these forthcoming decisions by the EU Council which will precede the final decisions to be taken by the Heads of State or Government, the EMI Report does not comment further on the earlier decisions taken in June 1997.*

- Second, with regard to Article 104c, the EMI, in contrast to the Commission, has no formal role in the excessive deficit procedure.

- Third, for the purpose of examining convergence, and in advance of the decisions to be taken by Ministers in the excessive deficit procedure, the EMI expresses its view on fiscal developments. With regard to sustainability, the EMI examines key indicators of fiscal developments from 1990 to 1997, considers the outlook and challenges for public finances and focuses on the links between deficit and debt developments.

- Fourth:
   (a) in cases where a deficit ratio is considered by the EMI to have declined both "substantially and continuously", it provides its view with regard to the Treaty provision of the ratio having reached a level that comes "close to the reference value".

---

* According to the decisions of the EU Council in June 1997, all EU Member States currently have excessive deficits except Denmark, Ireland, Luxembourg, the Netherlands and Finland.

(b) with regard to the Treaty provision that the excess over the reference value is only "exceptional and temporary and the ratio remains close to the reference value", the EMI refers to the agreement reached in the Stability and Growth Pact.

- Fifth, with regard to the Treaty provision that a debt ratio of above 60% of GDP should be "sufficiently diminishing and approaching the reference value at a satisfactory pace", the EMI examines past and current trends, and, for countries in which the ratio exceeds the reference value, it provides a number of illustrative calculations. For countries with debt ratios of between 60% and 80% of GDP, these refer to the potential future paths of the debt ratio on various assumptions. For countries with debt ratios of above 100% of GDP, in addition to the above calculations, the overall and primary fiscal balances are shown which are consistent with a reduction of the debt ratio to 60% of GDP over five, ten and fifteen years, i.e. by 2002, 2007 and 2012 respectively.

The examination of fiscal developments is based on comparable data compiled on a National Accounts basis, in compliance with the European System of Integrated Economic Accounts (ESA 2nd edition; see Annex 2 to this chapter). The main figures presented in this Report became available from the Commission in March 1998 and include government financial positions in 1996 and 1997 as well as Commission estimates for 1998. Also, the relationship between the deficit ratio and government investment expenditure is reported for 1996 and 1997.

Concerning the closer examination of the sustainability of fiscal developments, the outcome in the reference year, 1997, is reviewed in the light of the performance during the 1990s. As a starting-point, the evolution observed in the debt ratio over the past is considered, and the factors underlying this evolution are examined, i.e. the difference between nominal GDP growth and interest rates, the primary balance, and the stock-flow adjustments. Such a perspective can offer further information on the extent to which the macroeconomic environment, in particular the combination of growth and interest rates, has affected the dynamics of debt; on the contribution of fiscal consolidation efforts as reflected in the primary balance; and on the role played by special factors as included in the stock-flow item. In addition, the structure of debt is considered, by focusing in particular on the share of debt with a short-term residual maturity and foreign currency debt, as well as their evolution. By linking these shares with the current level of the debt ratio, the sensitivity of fiscal balances to changes in exchange rates and interest rates is highlighted.

In a further step, the evolution of the deficit ratio is investigated. In this respect it is considered useful to keep in mind that the change in a country's annual deficit ratio is typically influenced by a variety of underlying forces. These influences are often sub-divided into "cyclical effects" on the one hand, which reflect the reaction of deficits to changes in the output gap, and "non-cyclical effects" on the other hand, which are often taken to reflect structural or permanent adjustments to fiscal policies. However, such non-cyclical effects, as quantified in the Report on the basis of Commission estimates, cannot necessarily be seen as entirely reflecting a structural change to fiscal positions, because they will also include any measures and other factors with only temporary effects on the budgetary balance. While complete and fully comparable data on such measures with a temporary effect do not exist, the available information for 1996-98 is provided when these measures have contributed to a reduction in deficit ratios. To the extent possible, a distinction is made between measures which improve the budgetary outcome in one year only and therefore require compensation in the following year ("one-off" measures), and measures which have the same implication in the short run but in addition lead to extra borrowing in later years, thereby first improving and later burdening the budget ("self-reversing" measures).

Past public expenditure and revenue trends are also considered in more detail. In the light of past trends, a view is put forward, inter alia, of the broad areas on which necessary future consolidation may need to focus.

Turning to a forward-looking perspective, 1998 budget plans and recent forecasts are recalled and account is taken of the medium-term fiscal strategy as reflected in Convergence Programmes. Thereafter, a number of illustrative calculations are presented (see Box 2). In respect of these calculations, a link between deficit developments and the prospective path of the debt ratio can be established, as well as a link to the objectives of the Stability and Growth Pact applicable from 1999 onward, of having a budgetary position close to balance or in surplus. Finally, long-term challenges to the sustainability of budgetary positions are emphasised, particularly those related to the issue of unfunded public pension systems in connection with aspects of demographic change.

With regard to *exchange rate developments*, the Treaty provisions and their application by the EMI are outlined in Box 3. For the currencies of Member States not participating in the ERM, performance is shown against each of the EU member currencies over the past two years.

BOX 3

Exchange rate developments

1. Treaty provisions

Treaty Article 109j (1) requires:

"the observance of the normal fluctuation margins provided for by the exchange-rate mechanism of the European Monetary System, for at least two years, without devaluing against the currency of any other Member State".

Article 3 of Protocol No. 6 on the convergence criteria referred to in Article 109j (1) of the Treaty stipulates:

"The criterion on participation in the exchange-rate mechanism of the European Monetary System referred to in the third indent of Article 109j (1) of this Treaty shall mean that a Member State has respected the normal fluctuation margins provided for by the exchange-rate mechanism of the European Monetary System without severe tensions for at least the last two years before the examination. In particular, the Member State shall not have devalued its currency's bilateral central rate against any other Member State's currency on its own initiative for the same period".

2. Application of Treaty provisions[*]

The Treaty refers to the criterion on participation in the Exchange Rate Mechanism (ERM) of the European Monetary System.

- First, the EMI examines if the country has participated in the ERM "for at least the last two years before the examination", as stated in the Treaty. In individual cases of a shorter period of participation, the EMI describes exchange rate developments over the full two-year reference period up to February 1998, the last full month before the EMI's report was adopted.

- Second, with regard to the definition of "normal fluctuation margins", the EMI recalls the formal opinion that was put forward by the EMI Council in October 1994 and its statements in the November 1995 Report on "Progress towards convergence":

   In the EMI Council's opinion of October 1994 it was stated that "...the wider band has helped to achieve a sustainable degree of exchange rate stability in the ERM...", that "...the EMI Council considers it advisable to maintain the present arrangements...", and that "...member countries should continue to aim at avoiding significant exchange rate fluctuations by gearing their policies to the achievement of price stability and the reduction of fiscal deficits, thereby contributing to the fulfilment of the requirements set out in Article 109j (1) of the Treaty and the relevant Protocol".

   In the November 1995 Convergence Report it was recognised by the EMI that "when the Treaty was conceived, the 'normal fluctuation margins' were ±2.25% around bilateral central rates, whereas a ±6% band was a derogation from the rule. In August 1993 the decision was taken to widen the fluctuation margins to ±15%, and the interpretation of the criterion, in particular of the concept of 'normal fluctuation margins', became less straightforward". It was then also proposed that account would need to be taken of "the particular evolution of exchange rates in the EMS since 1993 in forming an ex post judgement".

   Against this background, in the assessment of exchange rate developments the emphasis is placed on exchange rates being close to the central rates. When examining exchange rate developments within the ERM, reference is made to the currency's deviation from all bilateral central rates in the system as a neutral and transparent way of presentation.

- Third, the issue of "severe tensions" is generally addressed by examining the degree of deviation of exchange rates from ERM central parities, and by using such indicators as exchange rate volatility vis-à-vis the Deutsche Mark and its trend, as well as short-term interest rate differentials vis-à-vis the group of countries with the lowest money market rates and their evolution.

All bilateral exchange rates for the reference period from March 1996 to February 1998 are derived from ECU exchange rates which are quoted daily and published in the Official Journal of the European Communities (see Annex 2 to this chapter).

---

[*] *In the opinion of two members of the Council, the EMI should not base its Report on a particular interpretation of ERM participation, but should submit a thorough Report for the EU Council to assess de facto sustained exchange rate stability in the context of the economic fundamentals in all Member States. These members underline that the exchange rate criterion can no longer be applied straightforwardly because the form of the ERM which existed when the Treaty was prepared came to an end in August 1993 with the decision to widen the permitted fluctuation margins from ±2.25% to ±15%.*

With regard to a more detailed examination, apart from reviewing the performance of nominal exchange rates over the reference period from March 1996 to February 1998, evidence relevant to the sustainability of current exchange rates derived from real exchange rate patterns vis-à-vis ERM participating countries is briefly reviewed (for non-ERM members reference is made to real exchange rates against EU currencies), as well as the current account of the balance of payments, the degree of openness of the Member State and the destination of trade (i.e. the share of intra-EU trade), and net foreign asset positions.

With regard to *long-term interest rate developments*, the Treaty provisions and their application by the EMI are outlined in Box 4.

BOX 4

Long-term interest rate developments

1. Treaty provisions

Treaty Article 109j (1) requires:

"the durability of convergence achieved by the Member State and of its participation in the exchange-rate mechanism of the European Monetary System being reflected in the long-term interest-rate levels".

Article 4 of Protocol No. 6 of the Treaty stipulates:

"The criterion on the convergence of interest rates referred to in the fourth indent of Article 109j (1) of this Treaty shall mean that, observed over a period of one year before the examination, a Member State has had an average nominal long-term interest rate that does not exceed by more than 2 percentage points that of, at most, the three best-performing Member States in terms of price stability. Interest rates shall be measured on the basis of long-term government bonds or comparable securities, taking into account differences in national definitions".

2. Application of Treaty provisions

- First, with regard to "an average nominal long-term interest rate" observed over "a period of one year before the examination", the long-term interest rate has been calculated as an arithmetic average over the latest twelve months for which data on HICPs were available. Hence, the reference period considered in this Report is February 1997 to January 1998.

- Second, the notion of "at most, the three best-performing Member States in terms of price stability" which is used for the definition of the reference value has been applied by using the unweighted arithmetic average of the long-term interest rates of the three countries with the lowest inflation rates (see Box 1). At the time this Report was finalised, the long-term interest rates of these three countries observed over the reference period were 5.6% (Austria), 5.5% (France) and 6.2% (Ireland); as a result, the average rate is 5.8% and, adding 2 percentage points, the reference value is 7.8%.

Interest rates have been measured on the basis of harmonised long-term interest rates, which were developed for the purpose of assessing convergence (see Annex 2 to this chapter).

As mentioned above, the Treaty makes explicit reference to the "durability of convergence" being reflected in the level of long-term interest rates. Therefore, developments over the reference period from February 1997 to January 1998 are reviewed in the context of the path of long-term interest rates during the 1990s and the main factors underlying differentials vis-à-vis those prevailing in the EU countries with the lowest long-term interest rates.

Finally, Article 109j (1) of the Treaty requires the Report to take account of several *other factors*, namely "the development of the ECU, the results of the integration of markets, the situation and development of the balances of payments on current account and an examination of the development of unit labour costs and other price indices". These factors are reviewed in the country chapters under the individual criteria listed above, while the development of the ECU is discussed separately in Annex I to this chapter.

Each country chapter concludes with a summary.

2   Examination of the key aspects of convergence in 1998

BELGIUM

Price developments

Over the reference period from February 1997 to January 1998 the average rate of HICP inflation in Belgium was 1.4%, i.e. well below the reference value of 2.7%. This was also the case in 1997 as a whole. In 1996 average HICP inflation was 1.8% (see Table 1). Seen over the past two years, HICP inflation in Belgium has been at levels which are generally considered to be consistent with price stability.

Looking back, consumer price inflation in Belgium, as measured on the basis of the CPI, has followed a downward trend since the beginning of the 1990s (see Chart 1). This experience of declining rates of inflation reflects a number of important policy choices, most notably the orientation of monetary policy towards price stability from the mid-1980s onwards. Since 1990 this policy has been formalised in the objective of seeking to maintain a close link between the Belgian franc and the Deutsche Mark within the framework of the ERM. The general orientation has been supported by, inter alia, the introduction of legislation limiting wage rises to those obtaining in Belgium's most important trading partners as well as by a reduction in employers' social security contributions. In addition, the macroeconomic environment has contributed to containing upward pressure on prices. In particular, a negative output gap emerged in the context of the 1993 recession (see Table 2). The output gap has remained sizable in subsequent years, despite a recovery in GDP growth. Against this background, growth in compensation per employee has gradually decreased, with growth in unit labour costs falling to almost zero in 1994 and remaining low

thereafter. Control over inflation has benefited from falling or broadly stable import prices during most of the 1990s, although growth in import prices accelerated in 1997. Low rates of inflation are also apparent when it is measured in terms of other relevant price indices (see Table 2).

Looking at recent trends and forecasts, current outturns for consumer price inflation (measured as a percentage change over the corresponding month a year earlier) have been decreasing to around ½% and there are no signs of immediate upward pressure on the basis of the measures shown in Table 3a. Most forecasts of inflation suggest rates of around 1½% for 1998 and 1999 (see Table 3b).

Looking further ahead, maintaining an environment conducive to price stability relates in Belgium to, inter alia, the conduct of fiscal policies over the medium to long term; it will be equally important to strengthen national policies aimed at improving the functioning of labour markets against the background of the current high rate of unemployment in Belgium.

Fiscal developments

In the *reference year* 1997 the general government deficit ratio was 2.1%, i.e. below the 3% reference value, and the debt ratio was 122.2%, i.e. far above the 60% reference value. Compared with the previous year, the deficit ratio has been reduced by 1.1 percentage points and the debt ratio by 4.7 percentage points. In 1998 the deficit ratio is forecast to decrease to 1.7% of GDP, while the debt ratio is projected to decline to 118.1%. In 1996 and 1997 the deficit ratio exceeded the ratio of public investment expenditure to GDP by 2.0 percentage points and 0.7 percentage point, respectively (see Table 4).

Looking back over the years 1990 to 1997, the Belgian *debt-to-GDP ratio* declined by 3.5 percentage points; initially the ratio tended to rise, from 125.7% in 1990 to reach 135.2% in 1993, whereas it declined steadily year by year thereafter to reach 122.2% in 1997 (see Chart 2a), i.e. a decline of 13.0 percentage points over four years. As is shown in greater detail in Chart 2b, the declining primary surpluses during the early 1990s were not sufficient to outweigh the sizable debt-increasing effects of a negative growth/interest rate differential. By contrast, after 1993 higher primary balances more than compensated for the adverse influence of the growth/ interest rate differential, with the latter factor having started to recede in 1997. In addition, "stock-flow adjustments" contributed to a reduction in gross debt in 1996, mainly reflecting the impact of financial operations (sales of assets by the government and the central bank). The patterns observed in the early 1990s may be seen as indicative of the risks which can arise for public finances when macroeconomic conditions deteriorate and the buffer in terms of the primary surplus is insufficient to counterbalance such effects. In this context, it may be noted that the share of debt with a short-term residual maturity has been decreasing from the high levels of the early 1990s, and in parallel the average maturity has increased (see Table 5). With regard to 1997, the proportion of debt with a short-term residual maturity is still relatively high, and, taking into account the current level of the debt ratio, fiscal balances are highly sensitive to changes in interest rates. On the other hand, the proportion of foreign currency denominated debt in Belgium is low and fiscal balances are relatively insensitive to changes in exchange rates.

During the 1990s a similar pattern of first deteriorating and subsequently improving outturns can be observed in the *deficit-to-GDP ratio*. Starting from a ratio of 5.5% in 1990, fiscal imbalances reached 7.1% of GDP in 1993; since then, the deficit has declined year by year to stand at 2.1% of GDP in 1997 (see Chart 3a). As is shown in greater detail in Chart 3b, which focuses on *changes* in deficits, cyclical factors played a major role only in 1993, increasing the deficit. However, the non-cyclical improvements could reflect a lasting, "structural" move towards more balanced fiscal policies and/or a variety of measures with temporary effects. Evidence available suggests that such measures with a temporary effect reduced the deficit ratio by 0.3 percentage point in 1997, compared with 0.4 percentage point in 1996. They were mainly of a "one-off" nature. This implies that the compensating measures already included in the 1998 budget will need to yield their expected results in 1998 in order to keep fiscal balances on the planned path.

Moving on to examine trends in other fiscal indicators, it can be seen from Chart 4 that the general government *total expenditure ratio* rose steadily between 1990 and 1993. Against the background of high and rising unemployment, current transfers to households as well as public consumption increased in particular (see Table 6). In subsequent years the ratio of total expenditure to GDP declined, mainly reflecting a reduction in interest payments and to a lesser extent in current transfers relative to GDP. The expenditure ratio in 1997 was lower than at the beginning of the 1990s, due primarily to a reduction in interest payments. While some further reduction in the ratio of interest payments to GDP can be expected as the debt ratio is reduced further, a continuation of the downward trend of total expenditure to GDP would appear to require additional adjustments in expenditure items other than investment, which is already low. *Government revenue* in relation to GDP tended to increase continuously up to

1994, remaining broadly unchanged thereafter, and may have approached a level which is detrimental to growth.

According to the Belgian *medium-term fiscal policy strategy*, as presented in the Convergence Programme for 1997-2000 issued in December 1996, a declining trend in deficit and debt ratios is projected to continue in 1998. The budget for 1998 is well ahead of the programme. It foresees a further reduction in the overall deficit ratio to 1.7% of GDP, which reflects the planned increase in the primary surplus-to-GDP ratio (to 6.0%) and a further fall in interest payments. The total revenue ratio of the federal government and social security system is projected to decrease by 0.5 percentage point, in line with the envisaged reduction in the primary expenditure-to-GDP ratio. Measures with a temporary effect have been further reduced in the 1998 budget to 0.2% of GDP. According to current plans, and if assumptions regarding economic growth are fulfilled, in the year 2000 the overall deficit-to-GDP ratio is expected to stand at 1.0% and the debt ratio at 111.0%, depending on economic developments. Compared with fiscal balances projected in the Convergence Programme for 1999-2000, further substantial fiscal consolidation is needed in order to comply with the medium-term objective of the Stability and Growth Pact, effective from 1999 onwards, of having a budgetary position that is close to balance or in surplus.

With regard to the future horizon for reducing the debt ratio to the 60% reference value in countries with a debt ratio of above 100% of GDP, two different kinds of calculations are presented. On the assumption that fiscal balances and debt ratios as projected by the European Commission for 1998 are achieved, the first exercise, as detailed in Table 7, shows the fiscal balances which would be consistent with convergence of the debt ratio to 60% of GDP over different time

horizons. As an illustration, focusing on the period of ten years, i.e. reducing the debt ratio to 60% by 2007, would imply realising from 1999 onwards an overall surplus of 2.7% of GDP per year (see Table 7a) or realising from 1999 onwards a primary surplus of 8.0% of GDP per year (see Table 7b). This compares with an overall deficit ratio of 1.7% and a primary surplus ratio of 6.0% projected for 1998, i.e. the difference is 4.4 and 2.0 percentage points respectively.

A second exercise, as detailed in Chart 5, shows that maintaining the 1998 overall fiscal balance of -1.7% of GDP over the subsequent years would only reduce the debt ratio to 93.4% in ten years; the 60% reference value would then be reached in 2031. Maintaining the 1998 primary surplus of 6.0% of GDP would reduce the debt-to-GDP ratio to 79.6% in ten years; in this case, the 60% level would be reached in 2012. Finally, realising balanced budgets annually from 1999 onwards would bring the debt ratio down to 80.7% in ten years, and the 60% reference value would be reached in 2015.

Such calculations are based on the normative assumption of a constant nominal rate of interest of 6% (average real cost of public debt outstanding of 4% and 2% inflation) and the assumption of a constant real GDP growth rate of 2.3%, as estimated by the Commission for real trend GDP growth in 1998. Stock-flow adjustments are not taken into account. While these calculations are purely illustrative, and can by no means be seen as forecasts, they do provide an illustration of why consolidation efforts need to be all the more resolute and lasting the higher the initial stock of debt, in order to forcefully reduce the debt-to-GDP ratio to 60% or below within an appropriate period of time.

Stressing the need for sustained consolidation over an extended period of time resulting in the achievement of growing and sizable overall fiscal surpluses is indeed critical in the case of Belgium, since the current high level of debt would otherwise impose a continuous burden on fiscal policy and the economy as a whole. As has been seen in the past, high levels of debt increase the vulnerability of fiscal positions to unexpected shocks, thus heightening the risk of a sudden worsening of public finances. In addition, as is highlighted in Table 8, from around 2010 onwards a marked ageing of the population is expected and, in the context of an unfunded pension system, public pension expenditure is projected to increase in terms of GDP, particularly if policies regarding benefits continue unchanged. Alleviation of the overall burden of population ageing will only be feasible if public finances have created sufficient room for manoeuvre before entering the period during which the demographic situation worsens.

Exchange rate developments

The Belgian franc has been participating in the ERM since its inception on 13 March 1979, i.e. for much longer than two years prior to the examination (see Table 9a). As mentioned above, Belgian monetary policy has focused on the objective of seeking to maintain a close link between the Belgian franc and the Deutsche Mark within the context of the ERM. Focusing on the *reference period* from March 1996 to February 1998, the currency has normally traded close to its central rates against other ERM currencies and very close to those vis-à-vis the Deutsche Mark, the Dutch guilder and the Austrian schilling (see Chart 6 and Table 9a). On occasion the Belgian franc traded outside a range close to its central rates vis-à-vis several partner currencies. The maximum upward and downward deviations from central rates, on the basis of 10 business day moving averages, were 2.5% and -3.0% respectively, abstracting from the autonomous upward trend of the Irish

pound (see Table 9a). The episodes in which such deviations occurred were temporary, the degree of exchange rate volatility vis-à-vis the Deutsche Mark was continuously very low (see Table 9b) and short-term interest rate differentials against those EU countries with the lowest short-term interest rates were insignificant. During the reference period Belgium has not devalued its currency's bilateral central rate against any other Member State's currency.

In a longer-term context, measures of the real effective exchange rate of the Belgian franc vis-à-vis the currencies of ERM participating Member States depicted in Table 10 suggest that current levels are close to historical values. As regards other external developments, Belgium has maintained large current account surpluses, a situation which has been reflected in a steady improvement in the net external asset position (see Table 11). It may also be recalled that Belgium is a small open economy with, according to the most recent data available, a ratio of foreign trade to GDP of 84% for exports and 79% for imports, and with a share of intra-EU trade of 70% for exports and 74% for imports.

Long-term interest rate developments

Over the *reference period* from February 1997 to January 1998 *long-term interest rates* in Belgium were 5.7% on average, and thus stood well below the reference value for the interest rate criterion of 7.8% set on the basis of the three best-performing Member States in terms of price stability. This was also the case for 1997 as a whole, as well as for 1996 (see Table 12).

Long-term interest rates have been on a broadly declining trend since the early 1990s (see Chart 7a). At the same time, a relatively close convergence of Belgian long-term interest rates with those prevailing in the EU countries with the lowest bond yields has been observed since the beginning of the 1990s; over the past two years the differential has declined to almost zero (see Chart 7b). The main factors underlying this trend were favourable developments in rates of inflation, the relative stability of the Belgian franc's exchange rate, the pursuit of a similar monetary policy stance to that followed in the above-mentioned countries, the reduction in fiscal deficits and the improvement in the current account of the balance of payments.

Concluding summary

Over the reference period Belgium has achieved a rate of HICP inflation of 1.4%, which is well below the reference value stipulated by the Treaty. The increase in unit labour costs was subdued and low rates of inflation were also apparent in terms of other relevant price indices. Looking ahead, there are no signs of immediate upward pressure on inflation; forecasts project inflation to be around 1½% in 1998 and 1999. The Belgian franc has been participating in the ERM for much longer than two years. Over the reference period it remained broadly stable, generally close to its unchanged central parities without the need for measures to support the exchange rate. The level of long-term interest rates was 5.7%, i.e. well below the respective reference value.

In 1997 Belgium achieved a fiscal deficit ratio of 2.1% of GDP, i.e. below the reference value, and the outlook is for a further decline to 1.7% in 1998. The debt-to-GDP ratio is far above the 60% reference value. After having reached a peak in 1993, it declined by 13.0 percentage points to stand at 122.2% in 1997; the outlook is for a further decline to 118.1% of GDP in 1998. Notwithstanding the efforts and the substantial progress made towards improving the current fiscal situation, there is an evident ongoing concern as to whether the ratio of government debt to GDP will be "sufficiently diminishing and approaching the reference value at a satisfactory pace" and whether sustainability of the fiscal position has been achieved; addressing this issue will have to remain a key priority for the Belgian authorities. The maintenance of a primary surplus of at least 6% of GDP per year and the achievement of growing and sizable overall fiscal surpluses are needed in order to be able to forcefully reduce the debt ratio to 60% within an appropriate period of time. This compares with a recorded fiscal deficit of 2.1% of GDP in 1997, as well as the forecast deficit of 1.7% in 1998. The Stability and Growth Pact also requires, as a medium-term objective, a budgetary position that is close to balance or in surplus.

With regard to other factors, in 1996 and 1997 the deficit ratio exceeded the ratio of public investment to GDP, while Belgium has maintained large current account surpluses and a strong net external asset position.

List of Tables and Charts*

---

* Chart scales may differ across countries.

I Price developments

Table I

Belgium: HICP inflation
(annual percentage changes)

	1996	1997	Nov 97	Dec 97	Jan 98	**Feb 97- Jan 98**
HICP inflation	1.8	1.5	1.3	0.9	0.5	1.4
Reference value	2.5	2.7	-	-	-	2.7

Source: European Commission.

Chart I

Belgium: Price developments
(annual percentage changes)

Source: National data.

Belgium: Measures of inflation and related indicators
(annual percentage changes unless otherwise stated)

	1990	1991	1992	1993	1994	1995	1996	1997[a]
Measures of inflation								
Consumer price index (CPI)	3.4	3.2	2.4	2.8	2.4	1.5	2.1	1.6
CPI excluding changes in net indirect taxes[b]	3.1	3.1	2.3	2.4	1.6	1.5	1.5	1.4
Private consumption deflator	3.3	3.3	2.3	3.5	2.8	1.7	2.3	1.6
GDP deflator	3.1	3.2	3.6	4.2	2.3	1.7	1.6	1.4
Producer prices	0.0	-1.0	-0.0	-1.5	1.7	2.3	0.7	1.9
Related indicators								
Real GDP growth	3.0	1.6	1.5	-1.5	2.4	2.1	1.5	2.7
Output gap (p.pts)	2.9	2.4	2.0	-1.4	-1.0	-0.9	-1.5	-1.0
Unemployment rate (%)	6.7	6.6	7.3	8.8	10.0	9.9	9.8	9.5
Unit labour costs, whole economy	3.8	6.8	4.0	5.7	0.3	1.2	-0.2	0.5
Compensation per employee, whole economy	6.1	7.9	5.9	5.1	3.6	3.2	1.1	2.8
Labour productivity, whole economy	2.3	1.1	1.8	-0.6	3.4	2.0	1.3	2.3
Import price deflator	-1.5	-0.6	-2.9	-2.6	0.9	1.0	2.0	4.5
Exchange rate appreciation[c]	4.9	-0.2	2.0	1.0	1.6	4.2	-1.9	-4.0
Broad monetary aggregate (M3H)[d]	10.2	5.9	4.4	9.2	7.6	-6.0	6.8	6.4
Stock prices	-8.2	-7.6	-1.5	10.5	11.5	-2.2	20.5	33.9
House prices	9.2	6.6	9.1	6.6	7.7	4.6	4.5	3.5

Source: National data except real GDP growth and the output gap (European Commission, spring 1998 forecasts) and exchange rate (BIS).
(a) Partly estimated.
(b) National estimates.
(c) Nominal effective exchange rate against 25 industrialised countries.
    Note: a positive (negative) sign indicates an appreciation (depreciation).
(d) National harmonised data.

Belgium: Recent inflation trends and forecasts
(annual percentage change unless otherwise stated)

(a) Recent trends in consumer price inflation

	Sep 97	Oct 97	Nov 97	Dec 97	Jan 98
National consumer price index (CPI)					
Annual percentage change	1.6	1.3	1.4	1.2	0.4
Change in the average of latest 3 months from previous					
3 months, annualised rate, seasonally adjusted	2.4	1.6	1.2	1.0	0.6
Change in the average of latest 6 months from previous					
6 months, annualised rate, seasonally adjusted	1.1	1.2	1.4	1.4	1.4

Source: National non-harmonised data.

(b) Inflation forecasts

	1998	1999
European Commission (spring 1998), HICP	1.3	1.5
OECD (December 1997), private consumption deflator	1.6	1.6
IMF (October 1997), CPI	1.9	.

Source: European Commission (spring 1998 forecasts), OECD and IMF.

II Fiscal developments

Table 4

Belgium: General government financial position
(as a percentage of GDP)

	1996	**1997**	1998[a]
General government surplus (+) / deficit (-)	-3.2	-2.1	-1.7
Reference value	-3	-3	-3
Surplus (+) / deficit (-), net of public investment expenditure[b]	-2.0	-0.7	.
General government gross debt	126.9	122.2	118.1
Reference value	60	60	60

Source: European Commission (spring 1998 forecasts) and EMI calculations.
(a) European Commission projections.
(b) A negative sign indicates that the government deficit is higher than investment expenditure.

Chart 2

Belgium: General government gross debt
(as a percentage of GDP)

(a) Levels

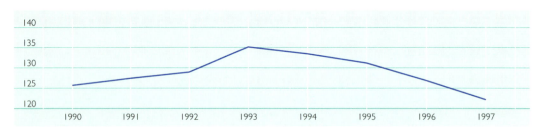

(b) Annual changes and underlying factors

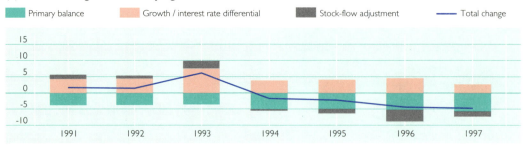

Source: European Commission (spring 1998 forecasts) and EMI calculations.
Note: In Chart 2b negative values indicate a contribution of the respective factor to a decrease in the debt ratio, while positive values indicate a contribution to its increase.

48

Table 5

Belgium: General government gross debt – structural features

	1990	1991	1992	1993	1994	1995	1996	1997
Total debt (as a percentage of GDP)	125.7	127.5	129.0	135.2	133.5	131.3	126.9	122.2
Composition by currency (% of total)								
In domestic currency	86.2	87.3	89.1	84.9	87.0	89.7	93.0	92.7
In foreign currencies	13.8	12.7	10.9	15.1	13.0	10.3	7.0	7.3
Domestic ownership (% of total)	80.3	76.6	77.6	75.7	77.9	77.7	78.2	.
Average maturity[a] (years)	.	3.4	3.9	4.5	4.6	4.8	4.5	4.3
Composition by maturity[a] (% of total)								
Short-term[b] (< 1 year)	39.3	33.6	31.6	34.3	30.7	24.9	23.6	24.6
Medium-term (1-5 years)	31.8	37.1	36.9	30.5	31.0	33.1	37.3	35.7
Long-term (> 5 years)	28.9	29.3	31.5	35.2	38.3	42.0	39.1	39.7

Source: National data except for total debt (European Commission (spring 1998 forecasts)). End-year data. Differences in the totals are due to rounding.
(a)   Residual maturity. Treasury debt only.
(b)   Including short-term debt and debt linked to short-term interest rates.

Chart 3

Belgium: General government surplus (+) / deficit (-)
(as a percentage of GDP)

(a) Levels

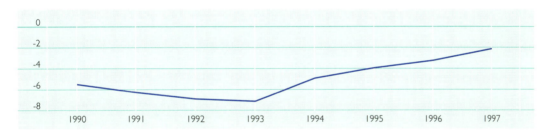

(b) Annual changes and underlying factors

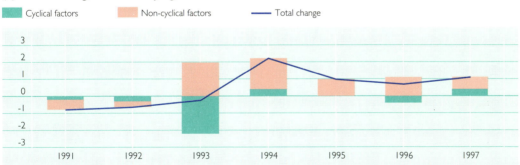

Source: European Commission (spring 1998 forecasts).
Note: In Chart 3b negative values indicate a contribution to an increase in deficits, while positive values indicate a contribution to their reduction.

Chart 4

Belgium: General government expenditure and receipts
(as a percentage of GDP)

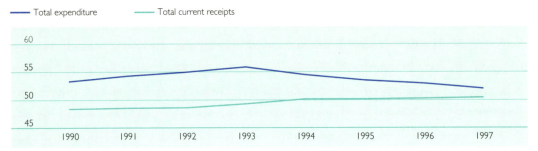

Source: European Commission (spring 1998 forecasts).

Table 6

Belgium: General government budgetary position
(as a percentage of GDP)

	1990	1991	1992	1993	1994	1995	1996	1997
Total current receipts	47.8	48.0	48.0	48.7	49.5	49.6	49.7	49.9
Taxes	28.9	28.5	28.4	28.7	30.3	30.4	30.7	31.3
Social security contributions	17.0	17.6	17.8	18.2	17.7	17.7	17.4	17.2
Other current receipts	1.8	1.9	1.8	1.8	1.5	1.5	1.6	1.4
Total expenditure	53.2	54.2	54.9	55.8	54.4	53.5	52.9	52.0
Current transfers	27.0	28.0	28.0	28.4	28.0	27.9	28.2	27.8
Actual interest payments	10.5	10.1	10.7	10.7	10.0	9.0	8.5	7.9
Public consumption	14.0	14.4	14.2	14.7	14.6	14.7	14.5	14.5
Net capital expenditure	1.8	1.8	2.0	2.1	1.8	1.9	1.7	1.8
Surplus (+) or deficit (-)	-5.5	-6.3	-6.9	-7.1	-4.9	-3.9	-3.2	-2.1
Primary balance	5.0	3.8	3.8	3.6	5.1	5.1	5.3	5.8
Surplus (+) or deficit (-), net of public investment expenditure[a]	.	.	.	-5.6	-3.3	-2.5	-2.0	-0.7

Source: European Commission (spring 1998 forecasts) and EMI calculations. Differences in the totals are due to rounding.
(a) A negative sign indicates that the government deficit is higher than investment expenditure.

Table 7

Belgium: Debt convergence calculations

(a) On the basis of overall fiscal balances
(as a percentage of GDP)

Total gross debt		Overall fiscal balance (deficit: (-); surplus (+))		Overall fiscal balance consistent with reduction of debt level to 60% of GDP in[a]		
1997	1998	1997	1998	2002	2007	2012
122.2	118.1	-2.1	-1.7	10.6	2.7	0.5

Source: European Commission (spring 1998 forecasts) and EMI calculations.
(a) Calculations indicate that the debt ratio would fall to 60% in 2002, 2007 and 2012 respectively, if the overall fiscal balance for 1998 is as forecast and the overall fiscal balances were maintained at 10.6%, 2.7% and 0.5% of GDP respectively, from 1999 onwards. The underlying assumptions are a real trend GDP growth rate of 2.3% in 1998, as estimated by the Commission, and an inflation rate of 2%. Stock-flow adjustments are disregarded.

(b) On the basis of primary fiscal balances
(as a percentage of GDP)

Total gross debt		Primary fiscal balance		Primary fiscal balance consistent with reduction of debt level to 60% of GDP in[a]		
1997	1998	1997	1998	2002	2007	2012
122.2	118.1	5.8	6.0	16.2	8.0	5.7

Source: European Commission (spring 1998 forecasts) and EMI calculations.
(a) Calculations indicate that the debt ratio would fall to 60% in 2002, 2007 and 2012 respectively, if the primary fiscal balance for 1998 is as forecast and the primary fiscal balances were maintained at 16.2%, 8.0% and 5.7% of GDP respectively, from 1999 onwards. The underlying assumptions are a real trend GDP growth rate of 2.3% in 1998, as estimated by the Commission, an inflation rate of 2% and a nominal interest rate of 6%. Stock-flow adjustments are disregarded.

Chart 5

Belgium: Potential future debt ratios under alternative assumptions for fiscal balance ratios
(as a percentage of GDP)

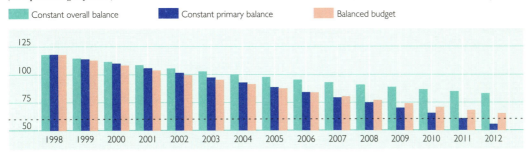

Source: European Commission (spring 1998 forecasts) and EMI calculations.
Note: The three scenarios assume that the debt ratio of 118.1% of GDP for 1998 is as forecast and that the 1998 overall balance of -1.7% of GDP or the primary balance of 6.0% of GDP will be kept constant over the period considered (as a percentage of GDP), or, alternatively, that a balanced budget is maintained from 1999 onwards. The underlying assumptions are a real trend GDP growth rate in 1998 of 2.3% as estimated by the Commission; an inflation rate of 2%; and, in the constant primary balance scenario, a nominal interest rate of 6%. Stock-flow adjustments are disregarded.

Table 8

Belgium: Projections of elderly dependency ratio

	1990	2000	2010	2020	2030
Elderly dependency ratio (population aged 65 and over as a proportion of the population aged 15-64)	22.4	25.1	25.6	31.9	41.1

Source: Bos, E. et al. (1994), World population projections 1994-95, World Bank, Washington DC.

III Exchange rate developments

Table 9

(a) Belgium: Exchange rate stability
(1 March 1996 - 27 February 1998)

Membership of the Exchange Rate Mechanism (ERM)	Yes
Membership since	13 March 1979
Devaluation of bilateral central rate on country's own initiative	No

Maximum upward (+) and downward (-) deviations from central rates
in the ERM grid (%) against[a]

Danish krone	1.6	-0.3
Deutsche Mark	0.4	-0.1
Spanish peseta	0.2	-2.0
French franc	2.5	-0.3
Irish pound	4.2	-10.6
Italian lira	1.1	-1.9
Dutch guilder	0.1	-0.5
Austrian schilling	0.4	-0.1
Portuguese escudo	1.4	-2.7
Finnish markka	-0.2	-3.0

Source: European Commission and EMI calculations.
(a) Daily data at business frequency; 10-day moving average. Deviations against the Finnish markka refer to the period from 14 October 1996 onwards, while deviations against the Italian lira refer to the period from 25 November 1996 onwards.

(b) Key indicators of exchange rate pressure for the Belgian franc

Average of 3 months ending:	May 96	Aug 96	Nov 96	Feb 97	May 97	Aug 97	Nov 97	Feb 98
Exchange rate volatility[a]	0.2	0.2	0.2	0.3	0.1	0.1	0.2	0.1
Short-term interest rate differentials[b]	-0.2	-0.2	-0.2	-0.1	0.0	0.2	0.2	0.0

Source: European Commission, national data and EMI calculations.
(a) Annualised monthly standard deviation of daily percentage changes of the exchange rate against the DEM, in percentages.
(b) Differential of three-month interbank interest rates against a weighted average of interest rates in Belgium, Germany, France, the Netherlands and Austria, in percentage points.

Chart 6

Belgian franc: Deviations from ERM bilateral central rates
(daily data; percentages; 1 March 1996 to 27 February 1998)

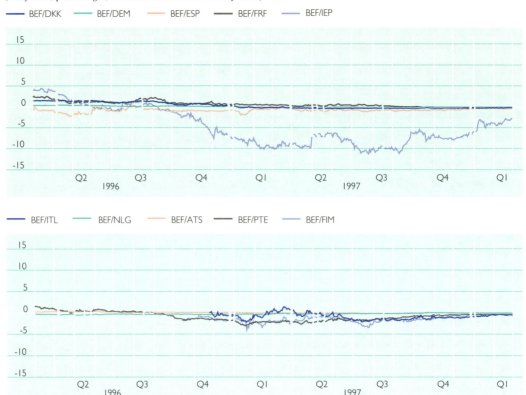

──── BEF/DKK   ──── BEF/DEM   ──── BEF/ESP   ──── BEF/FRF   ──── BEF/IEP

──── BEF/ITL   ──── BEF/NLG   ──── BEF/ATS   ──── BEF/PTE   ──── BEF/FIM

Source: European Commission.
Note: Deviations against the Finnish markka refer to the period from 14 October 1996 onwards, while deviations against the Italian lira refer to the period from 25 November 1996 onwards.

Table 10

Belgian franc: Measures of the real effective exchange rate vis-à-vis ERM Member States
(monthly data; percentage deviations; February 1998 compared with different benchmark periods)

	Average Apr 73-Feb 98	Average Jan 87-Feb 98	Average 1987
Real effective exchange rates:			
CPI-based	-2.9	-0.3	-0.4
PPI/WPI-based	-8.6	0.5	0.9
Memo item:			
Nominal effective exchange rate	3.2	2.3	5.6

Source: BIS and EMI calculations.
Note: A positive (negative) sign indicates an appreciation (depreciation).

Table 11

Belgium: External developments
(as a percentage of GDP)

	1990	1991	1992	1993	1994	1995	1996	1997[a]
Current account plus new capital account [b]	1.8	2.3	2.8	5.0	5.1	4.2	4.2	4.7
Net foreign assets (+) or liabilities (-)[c]	4.2	7.8	10.4	15.1	15.5	16.2	17.9	21.9
Exports (goods and services)[d]	68.2	69.2	70.6	71.2	76.1	79.6	81.0	83.6
Imports (goods and services)[e]	65.9	66.7	68.5	69.0	72.9	75.8	76.8	78.9

Source: National data except exports and imports (European Commission, spring 1998 forecasts).

(a) Partly estimated.

(b) According to the 5th edition of the IMF Balance of Payments Manual, which is conceptually the equivalent of the current account in previous editions of the Manual. Data up to and including 1994 include Luxembourg.

(c) International investment position (IIP) as defined by the IMF (see Balance of Payments Yearbook, Part 1, 1994), or the closest possible substitute.

(d) In 1996 the share of intra-EU exports of goods in BLEU national exports of goods was 70.4%; Direction of Trade Statistics Yearbook 1997, IMF.

(e) In 1996 the share of intra-EU imports of goods in BLEU national imports of goods was 73.6%; Direction of Trade Statistics Yearbook 1997, IMF.

IV Long-term interest rate developments

Belgium: Long-term interest rates
(percentages)

	1996	1997	Nov 97	Dec 97	Jan 98	**Feb. 97- Jan 98**
Long-term interest rate	6.5	5.8	5.7	5.5	5.2	5.7
Reference value	9.1	8.0	-	-	-	7.8

Source: European Commission.

Chart 7

(a) Belgium: Long-term interest rate
   (monthly averages; in percentages)

(b) Belgium: Long-term interest rate and CPI inflation differentials against EU countries
   with lowest long-term interest rates*
   (monthly averages; in percentage points)

— Long-term interest rate differential   — CPI inflation differential

Source: Interest rates: European Commission (where these are not available the most comparable data have been used); the CPI data used are
non-harmonised national data.
* Weighted average of data for Belgium, Germany, France, the Netherlands and Austria.

DENMARK

Price developments

Over the reference period from February 1997 to January 1998 the average rate of HICP inflation in Denmark was 1.9%, i.e. well below the reference value of 2.7%. This was also the case in 1997 as a whole. In 1996 average HICP inflation was 2.1% (see Table 1). Seen over the past two years, HICP inflation in Denmark has been at levels which are generally considered to be consistent with price stability.

Looking back, consumer price inflation in Denmark, as measured on the basis of the CPI, has remained steady at around 2% since 1992 (see Chart 1). This experience of generally low inflation reflects a number of important policy choices, most notably the orientation of monetary policy towards keeping the exchange rate of the Danish krone stable vis-à-vis the strongest ERM currencies. Moreover, in recent years fiscal policy has contributed to reducing the risks to inflation. The stabilisation of inflation at a low level has also been supported by, inter alia, labour market reforms in both the 1980s and the 1990s. Until 1993 the macroeconomic environment contributed to containing upward pressure on prices, as GDP grew at relatively low, albeit continuously positive rates (see Table 2). Although Denmark was less affected by the 1993 recession than other Member States, the negative output gap widened in 1992-93. However, since 1994 a robust recovery has been under way, accompanied by a closing of the output gap. Control over inflation has benefited from modest growth in unit labour costs and falling or broadly stable import prices during most of the 1990s. However, in 1997 growth in both unit labour costs and import prices accelerated. Low rates of inflation are also apparent when it is measured in terms of other relevant indicators of inflation, although the CPI excluding changes in net indirect taxes has risen steadily since 1993 and exceeded 2% in 1997 (see Table 2).

Looking at recent trends and forecasts, current outturns for consumer price inflation (measured as a percentage change over the corresponding month a year earlier) have been decreasing to below 2% and there are no signs of immediate upward pressure on the basis of the measures shown in Table 3a. Forecasts of inflation suggest a rise over the next two years to somewhat above 2% in 1998 and slightly higher in 1999 (see Table 3b). Risks for price stability over this period are associated with a narrowing of the output gap, tight labour market conditions and trends in asset prices.

Looking further ahead, although Denmark does not intend to participate in the single monetary policy, its close exchange rate and economic links with other EU countries are likely to warrant national monetary and economic policies which are aligned closely with those of the euro area, with the pursuit of price stability via stable exchange rates providing the most appropriate policy objective. The environment of low domestic inflation also needs to be supported by the conduct of appropriate fiscal policies as well as by measures aimed at further enhancing competition in product markets and further reducing rigidities in the labour market.

Fiscal developments

In the *reference year* 1997 the general government budget balance showed a surplus of 0.7% of GDP, hence the 3% reference value for the deficit ratio was comfortably met, while the debt ratio was 65.1%, i.e. above the 60% reference value. Compared with the previous year, the fiscal balance has improved by 1.4

percentage points, moving into surplus, while the debt ratio has fallen by 5.5 percentage points. In 1998 the surplus is forecast to increase to 1.1% of GDP, while the debt ratio is projected to decline to 59.5% i.e. just below the reference value. In 1996 the deficit ratio was below the ratio of public investment expenditure to GDP (see Table 4).

Looking back over the years 1990 to 1997, the Danish *debt-to-GDP ratio* increased by 4.3 percentage points; initially the ratio rose, from 60.8% of GDP in 1990 to 81.6% of GDP in 1993; thereafter it declined steadily year by year to stand at 65.1% in 1997 (see Chart 2a), i.e. a decline of 16.5 percentage points over four years. As is shown in greater detail in Chart 2b, in the early 1990s the primary surplus was close to outweighing the sizable debt-increasing effects of a negative growth/ interest rate differential. However, there was a strong upward effect on the debt ratio as a result of "stock-flow adjustments", most notably in 1993. These upward adjustments reflected, inter alia, the creation of sizable deposits at the central bank to boost foreign exchange reserves. After 1993 a growth rate of above 3%, and later an improvement in the budget, contributed to reducing the debt ratio. Furthermore, stock-flow adjustments, (redemption of foreign debt and portfolio shifts of government funds) have also caused a decline in the debt ratio. The patterns observed in the early 1990s may be seen as indicative of the risks which can arise from an unforeseen deterioration in the economic environment, including pressure on the currency, when such effects are not counterbalanced by a sufficiently high primary surplus. In this context, it may be noted that the share of debt with a short-term residual maturity has been low over the 1990s, and the average maturity has tended to increase (see Table 5). Accordingly, also taking into account the current level of the debt ratio, fiscal balances are relatively insensitive to changes in

interest rates. In addition, the proportion of foreign currency debt in Denmark has declined to levels which make fiscal balances relatively insensitive to changes in exchange rates.

During the 1990s a pattern of first deteriorating and subsequently improving results can be observed in the *deficit-to-GDP ratio*, whereby the ratio remained consistently below the 3% reference value. Starting from a ratio of 1.5% in 1990, the deficit reached 2.8% in 1993; since then, the deficit has declined year by year and became a surplus of 0.7% in 1997 (see Chart 3a). As is shown in greater detail in Chart 3b, which focuses on *changes* in deficits, cyclical factors contributed considerably to the increase in the deficit until 1993, as well as to its reduction in 1994, but played a minor role thereafter. The non-cyclical improvements could reflect a lasting, "structural" move towards more balanced fiscal policies and/or a variety of measures with temporary effects. However, evidence available suggests that measures with a temporary effect did not improve fiscal balances in 1997 by more than 0.1% of GDP.

Moving on to examine trends in other fiscal indicators, it can be seen from Chart 4 that the general government *total expenditure ratio* rose between 1990 and 1994. Against the background of high and rising unemployment, current transfers to households increased, accounting for most of the increase in total expenditure, while the interest payments ratio diminished slightly (see Table 6). After 1994 the ratio of total expenditure to GDP declined, reflecting a reduction in transfers to households, interest payments and public consumption relative to GDP. On balance, the expenditure ratio in 1997 was lower than at the beginning of the 1990s, while transfer payments have increased. A continuation of the downward trend would seem to require the main emphasis to be placed on both current transfers and public consumption. *Government revenue* in relation to GDP was 1.6 percentage points higher in 1997 than in 1990 and it may be at a level which is detrimental to economic growth.

Looking at the Danish *medium-term fiscal policy strategy,* as presented in the Convergence Programme updated in May 1997, a broadly stable general government surplus of somewhat less than 1% of GDP is expected in 1998, and the debt ratio is projected to decline to 64% of GDP. The budget plan for 1998 shows a larger surplus in the financial balance than envisaged in the programme. It foresees both a reduced expenditure ratio (as a result of cuts in all spending categories in relation to GDP and the postponement of investments) and a decreased revenue ratio (mostly due to income and wealth tax reductions, while social security contributions in particular are projected to increase). Currently, there is no evidence of significant measures with a temporary effect in the 1998 budget. By the year 2000 a further increase in the budget surplus is planned. These projections show a slower improvement in the general government budget balance position than envisaged in the previous programme, although the new target for the budget balance in 1998 is somewhat more ambitious and a more favourable development of the debt ratio is now expected. If fiscal balances turn out as projected in the Convergence Programme for 1999-2000, Denmark would comply with the medium-term objective of the Stability and Growth Pact, effective from 1999 onwards, of having a budgetary position that is close to balance or in surplus.

With regard to the potential future course of the debt ratio, the EMI's Report does not consider this issue in detail for countries forecast to have a debt ratio of below 60% of GDP in 1998. Projected developments underline the benefits of the surplus position achieved in 1997, and forecast to increase

in 1998, for rapidly reducing the debt ratio. Stressing the benefits of a surplus position in public finances and of a substantial further reduction in the debt ratio is indeed appropriate in the case of Denmark. As has been seen in the past, unexpected shocks can substantially increase the debt ratio. Moreover, the Danish Social Pension Fund (which does not have pension liabilities and is run by the government) invests most of its assets in government paper, thereby reducing the consolidated general government gross debt. The unlikely event of a change in this investment policy would affect the debt ratio (but not, however, the interest burden). In addition, as is highlighted in Table 8, from around 2010 onwards a marked ageing of the population is expected. While Denmark benefits from a rapidly expanding private pension sector, unfunded social security pensions remain substantial and public sector pension expenditure is projected to increase in terms of GDP, particularly if policies regarding benefits continue unchanged. Alleviation of the overall burden of population ageing will be facilitated if public finances have created sufficient room for manoeuvre before entering the period during which the demographic situation worsens.

Exchange rate developments

The Danish krone has been participating in the ERM since its inception on 13 March 1979, i.e. for much longer than two years prior to the examination (see Table 8a). As mentioned above, the orientation of monetary policy has been to keep the Danish krone stable vis-à-vis the strongest ERM currencies. Focusing on the *reference period* from March 1996 to February 1998, the currency has normally traded close to its central rates against other ERM currencies (see Chart 5 and Table 8a). On occasion the Danish krone traded outside a range close to its central rates vis-à-vis several partner currencies. The maximum upward and downward deviations from central rates, on the basis of 10 business day moving averages, were 1.2% and -3.4% respectively, abstracting from the autonomous upward trend of the Irish pound (see Table 8a). The episodes in which such deviations occurred were temporary, the degree of exchange rate volatility vis-à-vis the Deutsche Mark was continuously very low and decreasing (see Table 8b) and short-term interest rate differentials against those EU countries with the lowest short-term interest rates were small. During the reference period Denmark has not devalued its currency's bilateral central rate against any other Member State's currency.

In a longer-term context, measures of the real effective exchange rate of the Danish krone vis-à-vis the currencies of ERM participating Member States depicted in Table 9 suggest that current levels are close to historical values. As regards other external developments, Denmark has maintained current account surpluses over the 1990s, a situation which has been reflected in a reduction in the net external liability position (see Table 10). It may also be recalled that Denmark is a small open economy with, according to the most recent data available, a ratio of foreign trade to GDP of 39% for exports and 35% for imports, and a share of intra-EU trade of 64% for exports and 69% for imports.

Long-term interest rate developments

Over the *reference period* from February 1997 to January 1998 *long-term interest rates* in Denmark were 6.2% on average, and thus stood below the reference value for the interest rate criterion of 7.8% set on the basis of the three best-performing Member States in terms of price stability. This was also the case for 1997 as a whole, as well as for 1996 (see Table 11).

Long-term interest rates have been on a broadly declining trend since the early 1990s (see Chart 6a). At the same time, a comparatively close convergence of Danish long-term interest rates with those prevailing in the EU countries with the lowest bond yields has been observed since the early 1990s, although long-term interest rates have not converged completely towards the lowest levels observed in the Union (see Chart 6b). The main factors underlying this trend were the comparatively low rates of inflation, the relative stability of the Danish krone's exchange rate and the improvement in the fiscal position.

Concluding summary

Denmark, in accordance with the terms of Protocol No. 12 of the Treaty, has given notification to the EU Council that it will not participate in Stage Three of EMU. Nevertheless, its progress towards convergence is examined in detail.

Over the reference period Denmark has achieved a rate of HICP inflation of 1.9%, which is well below the reference value stipulated by the Treaty. The increase in unit labour costs has picked up recently and some other relevant indicators of inflation exceeded 2% in 1997. Looking ahead, there are no signs of immediate upward pressure on inflation; forecasts project inflation will rise to somewhat above 2% in 1998 and slightly higher in 1999. The Danish krone has been participating in the ERM for much longer than two years. Over the reference period it remained broadly stable, generally close to its unchanged central parities, without the need for measures to support the exchange rate. The level of long-term interest rates was 6.2%, i.e. below the respective reference value.

In 1997 Denmark achieved a general government surplus of 0.7% of GDP, thus comfortably meeting the reference value, and the outlook is for a surplus of 1.1% in 1998. The debt-to-GDP ratio is above the 60% reference value. After having reached a peak in 1993, the ratio declined by 16.5 percentage points to stand at 65.1% in 1997. Regarding the sustainability of fiscal developments, the outlook is for a decrease in the debt ratio to 59.5% of GDP in 1998, i.e. just below the reference value. Looking further ahead, if current fiscal surpluses are maintained, Denmark should comply with the medium-term objective of the Stability and Growth Pact, effective from 1999 onwards, of having a budgetary position that is close to balance or in surplus, and the debt ratio would fall further below 60%.

With regard to other factors, in 1996 the deficit ratio was below the ratio of public investment to GDP. Moreover, Denmark has recorded current account surpluses, while continuing to have a net external liability position. In the context of the ageing of the population, Denmark benefits from a rapidly expanding private pension sector.

List of Tables and Charts*

DENMARK

---

* Chart scales may differ across countries.

I Price developments

Table I

Denmark: HICP inflation
(annual percentage changes)

	1996	1997	Nov 97	Dec 97	Jan 98	**Feb 97- Jan 98**
HICP inflation	2.1	1.9	1.6	1.6	1.7	1.9
Reference value	2.5	2.7	-	-	-	2.7

Source: European Commission.

Chart I

Denmark: Price developments
(annual percentage changes)

Source: National data.

63

Denmark: Measures of inflation and related indicators
(annual percentage changes unless otherwise stated)

	1990	1991	1992	1993	1994	1995	1996	1997[a]
Measures of inflation								
Consumer price index (CPI)	2.6	2.4	2.1	1.2	2.0	2.1	2.1	2.2
CPI excluding changes in net indirect taxes[b]	3.1	2.6	2.1	1.4	1.6	1.9	2.0	2.2
Private consumption deflator	2.7	2.7	1.2	0.4	2.6	2.1	2.5	2.1
GDP deflator	3.4	2.5	2.2	0.8	2.4	2.1	1.9	1.9
Producer prices	3.8	2.4	0.2	1.2	1.3	3.4	1.4	1.3
Related indicators								
Real GDP growth	1.4	1.3	0.2	1.5	4.2	2.6	2.7	2.9
Output gap (p.pts)	-0.1	-0.6	-2.2	-2.7	-0.7	-0.4	-0.2	0.1
Unemployment rate (%)	9.6	10.5	11.2	12.3	12.2	10.3	8.7	7.8
Unit labour costs, whole economy	2.0	1.9	1.9	-0.7	0.0	2.0	0.9	3.0
Compensation per employee, whole economy	4.1	3.9	4.2	1.9	3.8	3.5	3.1	4.0
Labour productivity, whole economy	2.0	2.0	2.2	2.7	3.8	1.5	2.1	1.0
Import price deflator	-0.9	1.9	-1.3	-3.0	-0.5	-1.1	-0.5	3.0
Exchange rate appreciation[c]	6.6	-1.5	2.5	2.8	-0.0	4.3	-1.0	-3.0
Broad monetary aggregate (M3H)[d]	6.0	8.3	1.8	4.3	4.1	-2.0	7.2	4.8
Stock prices	12.1	-1.6	-12.8	0.8	18.7	-3.7	16.2	42.3
House prices	-7.5	1.3	-1.6	-0.9	12.1	7.6	10.8	9.0

Source: National data except real GDP growth and the output gap (European Commission, spring 1998 forecasts) and exchange rate (BIS).
(a) Partly estimated.
(b) National estimates.
(c) Nominal effective exchange rate against 25 industrialised countries.
    Note: A positive (negative) sign indicates an appreciation (depreciation).
(d) National harmonised data.

Denmark: Recent inflation trends and forecasts
(annual percentage change unless otherwise stated)

(a) Recent trends in consumer price inflation

	Sep 97	Oct 97	Nov 97	Dec 97	Jan 98
National consumer price index (CPI)					
Annual percentage change	2.3	2.2	2.1	2.1	1.7
Change in the average of latest 3 months from previous					
3 months, annualised rate, seasonally adjusted	3.5	2.7	1.8	1.4	1.1
Change in the average of latest 6 months from previous					
6 months, annualised rate, seasonally adjusted	2.2	2.5	2.6	2.6	2.5

Source: National non-harmonised data.

(b) Inflation forecasts

	1998	1999
European Commission (spring 1998), HICP	2.1	2.2
OECD (December 1997), private consumption deflator	2.6	2.9
IMF (October 1997), CPI	2.6	.

Source: European Commission (spring 1998 forecasts), OECD and IMF.

II Fiscal developments

Table 4

Denmark: General government financial position
(as a percentage of GDP)

	1996	**1997**	1998[a]
General government surplus (+) / deficit (-)	-0.7	0.7	1.1
Reference value	-3	-3	-3
Surplus (+) / deficit (-), net of public investment expenditure[b]	1.4	2.5	.
General government gross debt[c]	70.6	65.1	59.5
Reference value	60	60	60

Source: European Commission (spring 1998 forecasts) and EMI calculations.

(a) European Commission projections.

(b) A negative sign indicates that the government deficit is higher than investment expenditure.

(c) General government gross debt figures are not adjusted for the assets held by the Danish Social Pension Fund against sectors outside general government, nor for government deposits at the central bank for the management of foreign exchange reserves. According to statements 5 and 6 relating to Council Regulation (EC) No. 3605/93 of 22 November 1993, the Council and the Commission agree that, for Denmark, these items shall be specified in the presentation of general government gross debt. They totalled 9.6% of GDP in 1996 and 8.0% of GDP in 1997. In addition, the data are not adjusted for the amounts outstanding in the government debt from the financing of public undertakings, which, according to statement 3 relating to the aforementioned Regulation, will be subject to a separate presentation for the Member States. In Denmark this item amounted to 5.2% of GDP in 1996 and 4.9% of GDP in 1997.

Chart 2

Denmark: General government gross debt
(as a percentage of GDP)

(a) Levels

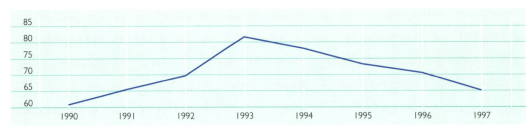

Note: See footnote (c) in Table 4.

(b) Annual changes and underlying factors

■ Primary balance   ■ Growth / interest rate differential   ■ Stock-flow adjustment   — Total change

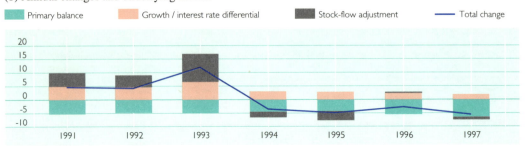

Source: European Commission (spring 1998 forecasts) and EMI calculations.
Note: In Chart 2b negative values indicate a contribution of the respective factor to a decrease in the debt ratio, while positive values indicate a contribution to its increase.

Table 5

Denmark: General government gross debt – structural features

	1990	1991	1992	1993	1994	1995	1996	1997
Total debt[a] (as a percentage of GDP)	60.8	65.5	69.7	81.6	78.1	73.3	70.6	65.1
Composition by currency (% of total)								
In domestic currency	77.5	83.6	83.2	77.4	82.6	86.2	87.0	87.0
In foreign currencies	22.5	16.4	16.8	22.6	17.4	13.8	13.0	13.0
Domestic ownership[b] (% of total)	.	.	67.0	55.0	72.0	68.0	65.0	59.3
Average maturity[c] (years)	4.4	3.6	4.2	4.2	4.4	5.0	5.3	5.3
Composition by maturity[d] (% of total)								
Short-term[e] (< 1 year)	9.2	9.3	12.0	11.2	7.6	7.8	8.1	8.1
Medium and long-term (≥ 1 year)	90.8	90.7	88.0	88.8	92.4	92.2	91.9	91.9

Source: National data except for total debt (European Commission (spring 1998 forecasts)). End-year data. Differences in the totals are due to rounding.
(a) See footnote (c) in Table 4.
(b) Central government domestic debt only (market value), including debt held by the Social Pension Fund. For 1992 data refer to the third quarter only.
(c) Residual maturity. Central government domestic debt only.
(d) Residual maturity.
(e) Including short-term debt and debt linked to short-term interest rates.

Chart 3

Denmark: General government surplus (+) / deficit (-)
(as a percentage of GDP)

(a) Levels

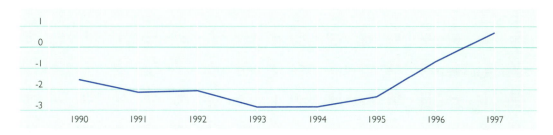

(b) Annual changes and underlying factors

Source: European Commission (spring 1998 forecasts).
Note: In Chart 3b negative values indicate a contribution to an increase in deficits, while positive values indicate a contribution to their reduction.

Chart 4

Denmark: General government expenditure and receipts
(as a percentage of GDP)

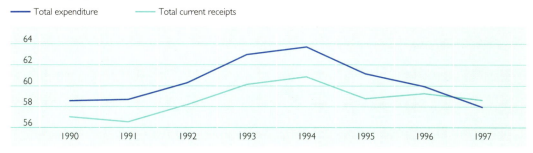

Source: European Commission (spring 1998 forecasts).

Table 6

Denmark: General government budgetary position
(as a percentage of GDP)

	1990	1991	1992	1993	1994	1995	1996	1997
Total current receipts	57.0	56.6	58.2	60.1	60.9	58.8	59.3	58.6
Taxes	47.9	47.7	47.9	49.3	51.1	50.3	50.5	50.5
Social security contributions	2.6	2.6	2.7	2.9	3.0	2.8	2.8	2.8
Other current receipts	6.5	6.2	7.6	8.0	6.8	5.7	6.0	5.4
Total expenditure	58.6	58.7	60.3	63.0	63.7	61.1	59.9	57.9
Current transfers	23.4	24.0	25.2	26.0	27.8	26.9	26.3	25.0
Actual interest payments	7.5	7.5	6.9	7.9	7.3	6.7	6.2	5.8
Public consumption	25.9	25.9	25.9	26.8	26.3	25.5	25.4	25.4
Net capital expenditure	1.9	1.3	2.3	2.4	2.3	2.0	2.1	1.8
Surplus (+) or deficit (-)	-1.5	-2.1	-2.1	-2.8	-2.8	-2.4	-0.7	0.7
Primary balance	5.9	5.3	4.9	5.0	4.5	4.3	5.5	6.5
Surplus (+) or deficit (-), net of public investment expenditure[a]	.	.	.	-0.9	-0.9	-0.4	1.4	2.5

Source: European Commission (spring 1998 forecasts) and EMI calculations. Differences in the totals are due to rounding.
(a) A negative sign indicates that the government deficit is higher than investment expenditure.

Table 7

Denmark: Projections of elderly dependency ratio

	1990	2000	2010	2020	2030
Elderly dependency ratio (population aged 65 and over as a proportion of the population aged 15-64)	22.7	21.6	24.9	31.7	37.7

Source: Bos, E. et al. (1994), World population projections 1994-95, World Bank, Washington DC.

III Exchange rate developments

Table 8

(a) Denmark: Exchange rate stability
(1 March 1996 - 27 February 1998)

Membership of the Exchange Rate Mechanism (ERM)	Yes	
Membership since	13 March 1979	
Devaluation of bilateral central rate on country's own initiative	No	
Maximum upward (+) and downward (-) deviations from central rates in the ERM grid (%) against[a]		
Belgian franc	0.3	-1.6
Deutsche Mark	0.2	-1.4
Spanish peseta	-0.2	-3.4
French franc	0.9	-0.4
Irish pound	2.6	-10.4
Italian lira	1.2	-1.7
Dutch guilder	0.3	-2.0
Austrian schilling	0.3	-1.4
Portuguese escudo	-0.0	-2.7
Finnish markka	-0.1	-2.7

Source: European Commission and EMI calculations.

(a) Daily data at business frequency; 10-day moving average. Deviations against the Finnish markka refer to the period from 14 October 1996 onwards, while deviations against the Italian lira refer to the period from 25 November 1996 onwards.

(b) Key indicators of exchange rate pressure for the Danish krone

Average of 3 months ending:	May 96	Aug 96	Nov 96	Feb 97	May 97	Aug 97	Nov 97	Feb 98
Exchange rate volatility[a]	0.5	0.6	0.8	0.9	0.5	0.4	0.2	0.2
Short-term interest rate differentials[b]	0.4	0.3	0.4	0.3	0.3	0.3	0.2	0.3

Source: European Commission, national data and EMI calculations.

(a) Annualised monthly standard deviation of daily percentage changes of the exchange rate against the DEM, in percentages.

(b) Differential of three-month interbank interest rates against a weighted average of interest rates in Belgium, Germany, France, the Netherlands and Austria, in percentage points.

Chart 5

Danish krone: Deviations from ERM bilateral central rates
(daily data; percentages; 1 March 1996 to 27 February 1998)

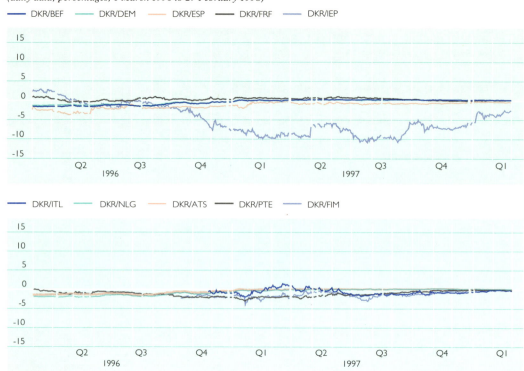

Source: European Commission.
Note: Deviations against the Finnish markka refer to the period from 14 October 1996 onwards, while deviations against the Italian lira refer to the period from 25 November 1996 onwards.

Table 9

Danish krone: Measures of the real effective exchange rate vis-à-vis ERM Member States

(monthly data; percentage deviations; February 1998 compared with different benchmark periods)

	Average Apr 73-Feb 98	Average Jan 87-Feb 98	Average 1987
Real effective exchange rates:			
CPI-based	3.3	1.0	1.2
PPI/WPI-based	3.5	4.5	7.9
Memo item:			
Nominal effective exchange rate	0.3	3.9	5.8

Source: BIS and EMI calculations.
Note: A positive (negative) sign indicates an appreciation (depreciation).

Table 10

Denmark: External developments

(as a percentage of GDP)

	1990	1991	1992	1993	1994	1995	1996	1997[a]
Current account plus new capital account[b]	1.0	1.5	2.8	3.4	1.8	1.1	1.7	0.6
Net foreign assets (+) or liabilities (-)[c]	-41.9	-38.7	-35.1	-32.1	-26.9	-26.3	-23.7	-23.9
Exports (goods and services)[d]	35.5	37.7	38.1	37.3	38.7	38.9	38.8	39.4
Imports (goods and services)[e]	30.1	30.9	31.1	29.7	32.2	33.7	33.5	35.2

Source: National data except exports and imports (European Commission, spring 1998 forecasts).

(a) Partly estimated.

(b) According to the 5th edition of the IMF Balance of Payments Manual, which is conceptually the equivalent of the current account in previous editions of the Manual.

(c) International investment position (IIP) as defined by the IMF (see Balance of Payments Yearbook, Part 1, 1994), or the closest possible substitute.

(d) In 1996 the share of intra-EU exports of goods in total national exports of goods was 64.4%; Direction of Trade Statistics Yearbook 1997, IMF.

(e) In 1996 the share of intra-EU imports of goods in total national imports of goods was 68.9%; Direction of Trade Statistics Yearbook 1997, IMF.

IV Long-term interest rate developments

Table 11

Denmark: Long-term interest rates
(percentages)

	1996	1997	Nov 97	Dec 97	Jan 98	**Feb 97- Jan 98**
Long-term interest rate	7.2	6.3	6.1	5.7	5.4	6.2
Reference value	9.1	8.0	-	-	-	7.8

Source: European Commission.

Chart 6

(a) Denmark: Long-term interest rate
(monthly averages; in percentages)

(b) Denmark: Long-term interest rate and CPI inflation differentials against EU countries with lowest long-term interest rates*
(monthly averages; in percentage points)

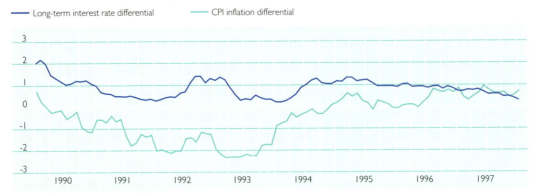

Source: Interest rates: European Commission (where these are not available the most comparable data have been used); the CPI data used are non-harmonised national data.
* Weighted average of data for Belgium, Germany, France, the Netherlands and Austria.

GERMANY

Price developments

Over the reference period from February 1997 to January 1998 the average rate of HICP inflation in Germany was 1.4%, i.e. well below the reference value of 2.7%. This was also the case in 1997 as a whole. In 1996 average HICP inflation was 1.2% (see Table 1). Seen over the past two years, HICP inflation in Germany has been at levels which are generally considered to be consistent with price stability.

Looking back, consumer price developments in Germany, as measured on the basis of the CPI, were adversely affected by the economic consequences of unification in the early 1990s. Consumer price inflation reached a peak of 5.1% in 1992 (the first year for which CPI statistics for unified Germany are available). In subsequent years inflation in Germany has followed a downward trend, falling to just below 2% in 1995 and thereafter (see Chart 1). This experience of successful stabilisation following an inflationary shock to the economy reflects the continued pursuit of stability-oriented policies. Notably, monetary policy has been consistently geared towards price stability through the pursuit of an intermediate target for monetary growth. Some attempts have also been made to increase the flexibility of the economy, including the labour markets. In addition, the macroeconomic environment has contributed to containing upward pressure on prices. Following the slowdown in the economy in 1993, when output declined by over 1%, economic growth recovered, but not sufficiently to prevent the emergence of a negative output gap (see Table 2). Against this background, since the mid-1990s wage moderation and consistent productivity growth have helped to contain the rise in unit labour costs, which had increased sharply in the early

1990s. Until 1996 control over inflation also benefited from broadly stable import prices, whereas a marked acceleration was seen in 1997. Low rates of inflation are also apparent when it is measured in terms of other relevant price indices (see Table 2).

Looking at recent trends and forecasts, current outturns for consumer price inflation (measured as a percentage change over the corresponding month a year earlier) have been decreasing to around 1% and there are no signs of immediate upward pressure on the basis of the measures shown in Table 3a. Forecasts of inflation suggest a rate of around 2% for 1998 and 1999 (see Table 3b). Risks for price stability over this period are associated with higher administered prices and an increase in value added taxes.

Looking further ahead, maintaining an environment conducive to price stability relates in Germany to, inter alia, the conduct of fiscal policies over the medium to long term; it will be equally important to strengthen national policies aimed at enhancing competition in product markets and improving the functioning of labour markets against the background of the current high rate of unemployment in Germany.

Fiscal developments

In the *reference year* 1997 the general government deficit ratio was 2.7%, i.e. below the 3% reference value, and the debt ratio was 61.3%, i.e. just above the 60% reference value. Compared with the previous year, the deficit ratio has been reduced by 0.7 percentage point and the debt ratio increased by 0.9 percentage point. In 1998 the deficit ratio is forecast to decrease to 2.5% of GDP, while the debt ratio is projected to decline marginally to 61.2%. In 1996 and 1997 the deficit ratio exceeded the ratio of public investment expenditure to GDP (see Table 4).

Looking back over the years 1991 (the first year for which fiscal data for unified Germany are available) to 1997, the German *debt-to-GDP ratio* increased by 19.8 percentage points. During the first years considered the ratio increased steadily, from 41.5% of GDP in 1991 to 50.2% in 1994, while in 1995 it jumped to 58.0%. In 1996 the ratio exceeded the 60% reference value for the first time and in 1997 it increased further to reach 61.3% of GDP (see Chart 2a). As is shown in greater detail in Chart 2b, primary surpluses were generally small and thus not sufficient to outweigh the debt-increasing effects of a negative growth/interest rate differential. However, until 1995, the most important underlying factors were "stock-flow adjustment items", including in particular unification-related debt assumptions by the Federal Government. The strongest impact was recorded in 1995, mainly reflecting the assumption by general government of the debt of the Treuhand agency, which will be a lasting burden on fiscal policy. The patterns observed during the 1990s, which continue to be affected by the additional strain placed on public finances by German unification, may be seen as indicative of the need to adopt early corrective measures to deal with the budgetary consequences of adverse shocks, even when initial budgetary imbalances are not excessive. They also reflect the need to provide a buffer of a primary surplus as a precaution against deteriorating macroeconomic conditions, even when the structure of the general government debt is relatively favourable. In this context, it may be noted that the share of debt with a short-term residual maturity has been increasing during the 1990s, while the average maturity has remained broadly stable (see Table 5). With regard to 1996, the proportion of debt with a short-term residual maturity is

noticeable, and, taking into account the current level of the debt ratio, fiscal balances are relatively sensitive to changes in interest rates. However, given the fact that the debt is refinanced at long maturities, this sensitivity relates particularly to long-term interest rates. On the other hand, the proportion of foreign currency debt is negligible and fiscal balances are insensitive to changes in exchange rates.

During the 1990s a relatively trendless pattern can be observed in the *deficit-to-GDP ratio*, with outturns of around 3% of GDP (see Chart 3a). Compared with the period immediately prior to unification, this represented a deterioration in fiscal balances, which had been slightly in surplus in 1989. As is shown in greater detail in Chart 3b, which focuses on *changes* in deficits, cyclical factors made a large negative contribution in 1993 following a strong boom mainly triggered by excessive demand in the wake of unification; a smaller negative contribution was seen in 1996. In general, such cyclical factors were mostly offset by other measures, thereby limiting their impact on the overall deficit. However, the non-cyclical improvements could reflect a lasting, "structural" move towards more balanced fiscal policies and/or a variety of measures with temporary effects. Evidence available suggests that measures with a temporary effect played a role in improving the fiscal balance in 1996 and 1997, but that the impact did not exceed 0.2% of GDP per annum. As these measures were mainly of a "one-off" nature, compensating measures already introduced in 1998 budgets will need to yield their expected results in 1998 in order to keep fiscal balances on the planned path.

Moving on to examine trends in other fiscal indicators, it can be seen from Chart 4 that between 1991 and 1995 the *total expenditure ratio* rose, with all expenditure items increasing, except for net capital expenditure (see Table 6). After 1995 expenditures declined, due to lower ratios of all major expenditure items. On balance, the expenditure ratio in 1997, at 48%, had been brought back very close to the level seen in 1991 but it remains markedly higher than just before unification, when it had been close to 45%. As the burden of interest payments has increased in line with a rising debt ratio, and capital expenditure has been cut back, bringing down expenditure ratios would appear to require the fiscal authorities to focus mainly on transfer payments and public consumption. *Government revenue* in relation to GDP reached a peak in 1994 before returning close to the level of 1991. The current level of around 45% of GDP is also very close to that observed before unification, but this is partly due to the erosion of the tax base. Additionally, from 1996 onwards, this ratio as well as the expenditure ratio was reduced by an amount equivalent to ½% of GDP owing to the new treatment of child benefits.

According to the German *medium-term fiscal policy strategy*, as presented in the Convergence Programme for 1997-2000 dated December 1996, a reduction in the deficit ratio to 2½% of GDP and a broad stabilisation of the debt ratio is to be achieved in 1998. The budget plan for 1998 forecasts the general government deficit to stand at 2¾% of GDP and the debt ratio to stabilise at around 62% of GDP while Commission forecasts are slightly more favourable. The 1998 budget shows a combination of expenditure restraint and only moderate revenue increases. The increase in tax revenue is expected to be lower than nominal GDP growth. Value added tax will be increased from April 1998, with the proceeds to be transferred to the pension system, but the "solidarity tax surcharge" has been reduced and the structural "decoupling" of tax revenue from economic growth may continue. Furthermore, the tax on business capital has been abolished, but the loss of receipts is to be compensated by the reduction of enterprise tax privileges.

Currently, there is no evidence of significant measures with a temporary effect in the 1998 budget. For the year 2000, the Convergence Programme targets a deficit of 1½% of GDP but the debt ratio is projected to remain above 60% of GDP for the rest of the decade. The intention is to reduce the share of government expenditure in GDP to the pre-unification level by the end of the decade. The intentions regarding deficit and debt reductions are somewhat less ambitious than those contained in previous programmes. Compared with fiscal balances projected in the Convergence Programme for 1999-2000, further substantial fiscal consolidation is required in order to both compensate for the tax shortfalls not yet reflected in the Convergence Programme and to comply with the medium-term objective of the Stability and Growth Pact, effective from 1999 onwards, of having a budgetary position that is close to balance or in surplus.

With regard to the reduction of the debt ratio to the 60% reference value for those countries in which this ratio is currently exceeded only marginally, the EMI emphasises that debt can be brought down in relation to GDP within a short period of time. As may be seen from Chart 5, in the case of Germany, achieving overall fiscal positions and debt ratios forecast by the European Commission for 1998 and realising a balanced budget in 1999 would reduce the debt ratio to below 60% of GDP in the same year, while maintaining fiscal balances over subsequent years at the levels forecast for 1998 would not be sufficient to bring the debt ratio down to 60% of GDP within an appropriate period of time. Such calculations are based on the normative assumption of a constant nominal rate of interest of 6% (average real cost of public debt outstanding of 4% and 2% inflation) and the assumption of a constant real GDP growth rate of 2.3%, as estimated by the Commission for real trend GDP growth in 1998. Stock-flow adjustments are not taken into account. While they are purely illustrative, and can by no means be regarded as forecasts, these calculations provide an illustration of the need for further substantial progress in consolidation in order to reduce the debt ratio to 60% of GDP or below within an appropriate period of time.

Stressing the need for considerable improvement in the deficit ratio and to sustain consolidation over time is indeed warranted in the case of Germany, since additional room for manoeuvre is necessary in order to be able to address *future budgetary challenges*. As is highlighted in Table 8, from around 2010 onwards a marked ageing of the population is expected and, in the context of an unfunded pension system, public pension expenditure is projected to increase in terms of GDP, particularly if policies regarding benefits are not tightened further. The overall burden of population ageing will become more manageable the better the state of public finances when the demographic situation worsens. There must, however, be further retrenchment efforts in pension payments, which is underlined by the fact that the burden of levies in Germany has reached a relatively high level.

Exchange rate developments

The Deutsche Mark has been participating in the ERM since its inception on 13 March 1979, i.e. for much longer than two years prior to the examination (see Table 8a). Focusing on the *reference period* from March 1996 to February 1998, the currency has normally traded close to its central rates against other ERM currencies and very close to those vis-à-vis the Belgian franc, the Dutch guilder and the Austrian schilling (see Chart 6 and Table 8a). On occasion the Deutsche Mark traded outside a range close to its central rates vis-à-vis several partner currencies. The maximum upward and downward deviations from

central rates, on the basis of 10 business day moving averages, were 2.2% and -2.9% respectively, abstracting from the autonomous upward trend of the Irish pound (see Table 8a). The episodes in which such deviations occurred were temporary and short-term interest rate differentials against those EU countries with the lowest short-term interest rates were insignificant. During the reference period Germany has not devalued its currency's bilateral central rate against any other Member State's currency.

In a longer-term context, measures of the real effective exchange rate of the Deutsche Mark vis-à-vis the currencies of ERM participating Member States depicted in Table 9 suggest that current levels are close to historical values. Current account deficits emerged as a consequence of unification; these have narrowed more recently, thus slowing the rate of deterioration in the net external asset position (see Table 10). It may also be recalled that Germany has, according to the most recent data available, a ratio of foreign trade to GDP of 30% for exports and 29% for imports, and a share of intra-EU trade of 56% for exports and 55% for imports.

Long-term interest rate developments

Over the *reference period* from February 1997 to January 1998 *long-term interest rates* in Germany were 5.6% on average, and thus stood well below the reference value for the interest rate criterion of 7.8% set on the basis of the three best-performing Member States in terms of price stability. This was also the case for 1997 as a whole, as well as for 1996 (see Table 11).

Long-term interest rates have been on a broadly declining trend since the early 1990s (see Chart 7a). For most of the period since the beginning of the 1990s, a relatively narrow and typically negative gap between German long-term interest rates and those prevailing in the EU countries with the lowest bond yields has been observed (see Chart 7b). The main factors underlying this trend of relatively low long-term interest rates were that the inflationary impulse following German unification was contained and that inflation returned to a comparatively low rate.

Concluding summary

Over the reference period Germany has achieved a rate of HICP inflation of 1.4%, which is well below the reference value stipulated by the Treaty. Unit labour costs fell and low rates of inflation were also apparent in terms of other relevant price indices. Looking ahead, there are no signs of immediate upward pressure on inflation; forecasts project inflation will stand at around 2% in 1998 and 1999. The Deutsche Mark has been participating in the ERM for much longer than two years. Over the reference period it remained broadly stable, generally close to its unchanged central parities, without the need for measures to support the exchange rate. The level of long-term interest rates was 5.6%, i.e. well below the respective reference value.

In 1997 Germany achieved a fiscal deficit ratio of 2.7% of GDP, i.e. below the reference value, and the outlook is for a further decline to 2.5% in 1998. The debt-to-GDP ratio is just above the 60% reference value. As of 1991, the first year after German unification, the ratio increased by 19.8 percentage points to stand at 61.3% in 1997, reflecting to a large extent the fiscal burden relating to unification. Regarding the sustainability of fiscal developments, the outlook is for a marginal decline in the debt ratio to 61.2% of GDP in 1998. Keeping the deficit ratio at current levels would not be sufficient to bring the debt ratio down to 60% of GDP within an appropriate period of time, thus pointing to the need for further substantial progress in consolidation. The Stability and Growth Pact also requires as a medium-term objective a budgetary position that is close to balance or in surplus. Given the current debt ratio of just above 60% of GDP, achieving the fiscal position forecast for 1998 and realising a balanced budget thereafter would reduce the debt ratio to below 60% as early as 1999.

With regard to other factors, in 1996 and 1997 the deficit ratio exceeded the ratio of public investment to GDP, and Germany recorded current account deficits as a consequence of unification, while maintaining a net external asset position.

List of Tables and Charts*

---

* Chart scales may differ across countries.

I Price developments

Table I

Germany: HICP inflation
(annual percentage changes)

	1996	1997	Nov 97	Dec 97	Jan 98	**Feb 97- Jan 98**
HICP inflation	1.2	1.5	1.4	1.4	0.8	1.4
Reference value	2.5	2.7	-	-	-	2.7

Source: European Commission.

Chart I

Germany: Price developments
(annual percentage changes)

Source: National data.

Germany*: Measures of inflation and related indicators
(annual percentage changes unless otherwise stated)

	1990	1991	1992	1993	1994	1995	1996	1997
Measures of inflation								
Consumer price index (CPI)	2.7	3.6	5.1	4.5	2.7	1.8	1.5	1.8
CPI excluding changes in net indirect taxes[a]	2.7	3.3	3.6	3.6	2.3	1.8	1.5	1.8
Private consumption deflator	2.7	3.7	4.7	4.1	3.0	1.7	2.0	1.9
GDP deflator	3.2	3.9	5.6	4.0	2.4	2.1	1.0	0.6
Producer prices	1.5	2.1	1.6	0.1	0.7	2.2	0.1	0.8
Related indicators								
Real GDP growth	5.7	5.0	2.2	-1.2	2.7	1.8	1.4	2.2
Output gap (p.pts)	2.4	4.9	3.9	0.1	0.4	-0.1	-1.0	-1.1
Unemployment rate (%)	6.4	5.7	7.7	8.9	9.6	9.4	10.4	11.4
Unit labour costs, whole economy	2.0	3.3	6.2	3.7	0.2	1.6	-0.2	-1.8
Compensation per employee, whole economy	4.7	5.9	10.6	4.3	3.6	3.9	2.5	1.8
Labour productivity, whole economy	2.7	2.5	4.1	0.6	3.4	2.2	2.7	3.7
Import price deflator	-0.7	2.2	-1.5	-1.4	0.5	0.6	0.7	3.0
Exchange rate appreciation[b]	5.5	-1.1	3.1	2.8	0.2	5.6	-2.3	-4.6
Broad monetary aggregate (M3H)[c]	5.0	20.0	8.6	8.2	8.3	-0.1	7.1	5.8
Stock prices	17.1	-8.1	3.6	10.3	17.5	0.8	20.2	44.5
House prices[d]	.	.	.	.	.	.	-0.1	.

Source: National data except real GDP growth and the output gap (European Commission, spring 1998 forecasts) and exchange rate (BIS).
* Refers to unified Germany from 1992 onwards.
(a) National estimates, 1990-94 western Germany.
(b) Nominal effective exchange rate against 25 industrialised countries.
    Note: a positive (negative) sign indicates an appreciation (depreciation).
(c) National harmonised data.
(d) Prices for new houses.

Germany: Recent inflation trends and forecasts
(annual percentage change unless otherwise stated)

(a) Recent trends in consumer price inflation

	Sep 97	Oct 97	Nov 97	Dec 97	Jan 98
National consumer price index (CPI)					
Annual percentage change	1.9	1.8	1.9	1.8	1.3
Change in the average of latest 3 months from previous 3 months, annualised rate, seasonally adjusted	2.9	2.2	1.6	1.2	0.9
Change in the average of latest 6 months from previous 6 months, annualised rate, seasonally adjusted	1.9	2.1	2.0	2.0	1.9

Source: National non-harmonised data.

(b) Inflation forecasts

	1998	1999
European Commission (spring 1998), HICP	1.7	1.9
OECD (December 1997), private consumption deflator	1.9	1.9
IMF (October 1997), CPI	2.3	.

Source: European Commission (spring 1998 forecasts), OECD and IMF.

II Fiscal developments

Table 4

Germany: General government financial position
(as a percentage of GDP)

	1996	**1997**	1998[a]
General government surplus (+) / deficit (-)	-3.4	-2.7	-2.5
Reference value	-3	-3	-3
Surplus (+) / deficit (-), net of public investment expenditure[b]	-1.4	-0.8	.
General government gross debt	60.4	61.3	61.2
Reference value	60	60	60

Source: European Commission (spring 1998 forecasts) and EMI calculations.
(a) European Commission projections.
(b) A negative sign indicates that the government deficit is higher than investment expenditure.

Chart 2

Germany: General government gross debt
(as a percentage of GDP)

(a) Levels

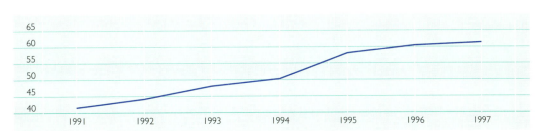

(b) Annual changes and underlying factors

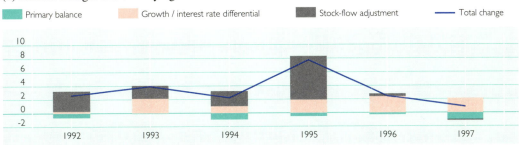

Source: European Commission (spring 1998 forecasts) and EMI calculations.
Note: In Chart 2b negative values indicate a contribution of the respective factor to a decrease in the debt ratio, while positive values indicate a contribution to its increase.

Table 5

Germany: General government gross debt – structural features

	1991	1992	1993	1994	1995	1996	1997
Total debt (as a percentage of GDP)	41.5	44.1	48.0	50.2	58.0	60.4	61.3
Composition by currency (% of total)							
In domestic currency	100.0	100.0	100.0	100.0	100.0	100.0	100.0
In foreign currencies	0.0	0.0	0.0	0.0	0.0	0.0	0.0
Domestic ownership (% of total)	77.0	75.6	71.0	74.3	71.9	71.1	.
Average maturity[a] (years)	4.4	4.4	4.8	4.8	5.3	4.7	.
Composition by maturity[b] (% of total)							
Short-term[c] (≤ 1 year)	13.2	16.1	16.3	18.5	16.8	18.5	.
Medium and long-term (> 1 year)	86.8	83.9	83.7	81.5	83.2	81.5	.

Source: National data except for total debt (European Commission (spring 1998 forecasts)). End-year data. Differences in the totals are due to rounding.
(a) Residual maturity. Federal government and its special funds debt only (which represent almost 2/3 of the general government gross debt).
(b) Residual maturity. Where data on floating rate debt are not available these items are classified according to their residual maturity.
(c) Including short-term debt and debt linked to short-term interest rates.

Chart 3

Germany: General government surplus (+) / deficit (-)
(as a percentage of GDP)

(a) Levels

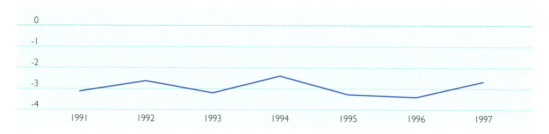

(b) Annual changes and underlying factors

Source: European Commission (spring 1998 forecasts).
Note: In Chart 3b negative values indicate a contribution to an increase in deficits, while positive values indicate a contribution to their reduction.

Chart 4

Germany: General government expenditure and receipts
(as a percentage of GDP)

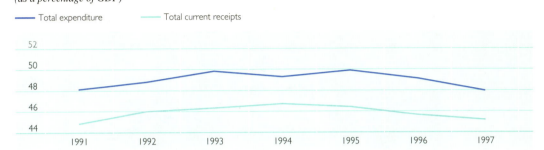

— Total expenditure   — Total current receipts

Source: European Commission (spring 1998 forecasts).

Table 6

Germany: General government budgetary position
(as a percentage of GDP)

	1991	1992	1993	1994	1995	1996	1997
Total current receipts	44.8	46.0	46.3	46.7	46.4	45.6	45.2
Taxes	24.2	24.5	24.4	24.4	24.2	23.2	22.6
Social security contributions	18.0	18.3	18.8	19.3	19.5	19.9	20.1
Other current receipts	2.7	3.2	3.1	3.1	2.7	2.6	2.5
Total expenditure	48.1	48.8	49.9	49.3	49.9	49.1	48.0
Current transfers	21.4	21.2	22.4	22.6	22.8	22.6	22.1
Actual interest payments	2.7	3.3	3.3	3.3	3.8	3.7	3.7
Public consumption	19.5	20.0	20.1	19.8	19.8	19.8	19.4
Net capital expenditure	4.6	4.3	4.1	3.6	3.5	3.0	2.7
Surplus (+) or deficit (-)	-3.1	-2.6	-3.2	-2.4	-3.3	-3.4	-2.7
Primary balance	-0.4	0.6	0.1	1.0	0.5	0.3	1.1
Surplus (+) or deficit (-), net of public investment expenditure[a]	.	.	-0.7	0.0	-1.1	-1.4	-0.8

Source: European Commission (spring 1998 forecasts) and EMI calculations. Differences in the totals are due to rounding.
(a) A negative sign indicates that the government deficit is higher than investment expenditure.

Chart 5

Germany: Potential future debt ratios under alternative assumptions for fiscal balance ratios
(as a percentage of GDP)

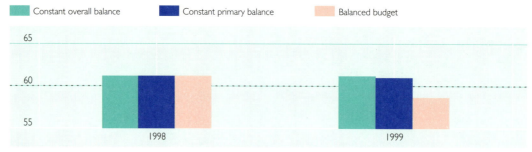

Source: European Commission (spring 1998 forecasts) and EMI calculations.
Note: The three scenarios assume that the debt ratio of 61.2% of GDP for 1998 is as forecast and that the 1998 overall balance of -2.5% of GDP or the primary balance of 1.2% of GDP will be kept constant over the period considered (as a percentage of GDP), or, alternatively, that a balanced budget is maintained from 1999 onwards. The underlying assumptions are a real trend GDP growth rate in 1998 of 2.3% as estimated by the Commission; an inflation rate of 2%; and, in the constant primary balance scenario, a nominal interest rate of 6%. Stock-flow adjustments are disregarded.

Table 7

Germany: Projections of elderly dependency ratio

	1990[a]	2000	2010	2020	2030
Elderly dependency ratio (population aged 65 and over as a proportion of the population aged 15-64)	21.7	23.8	30.3	35.4	49.2

Source: Bos, E. et al. (1994), World population projections 1994-95, World Bank, Washington DC.
(a) Western Germany.

III Exchange rate developments

(a) Germany: Exchange rate stability
(1 March 1996 - 27 February 1998)

Membership of the Exchange Rate Mechanism (ERM)	Yes	
Membership since	13 March 1979	
Devaluation of bilateral central rate on country's own initiative	No	
Maximum upward (+) and downward (-) deviations from central rates in the ERM grid (%) against[a]		
Belgian franc	0.1	-0.4
Danish krone	1.4	-0.2
Spanish peseta	0.1	-2.4
French franc	2.2	-0.2
Irish pound	3.9	-10.6
Italian lira	1.2	-1.8
Dutch guilder	0.0	-0.8
Austrian schilling	0.0	-0.1
Portuguese escudo	1.1	-2.8
Finnish markka	-0.2	-2.9

Source: European Commission and EMI calculations.

(a) Daily data at business frequency; 10-day moving average. Deviations against the Finnish markka refer to the period from 14 October 1996 onwards, while deviations against the Italian lira refer to the period from 25 November 1996 onwards.

(b) Key indicators of exchange rate pressure for the Deutsche Mark

Average of 3 months ending:	May 96	Aug 96	Nov 96	Feb 97	May 97	Aug 97	Nov 97	Feb 98
Exchange rate volatility[a]	-	-	-	-	-	-	-	-
Short-term interest rate differentials[b]	-0.2	-0.2	-0.1	-0.1	-0.1	-0.1	-0.0	-0.0

Source: European Commission, national data and EMI calculations.

(a) Not applicable.

(b) Differential of three-month interbank interest rates against a weighted average of interest rates in Belgium, Germany, France, the Netherlands and Austria, in percentage points.

Chart 6

Deutsche Mark: Deviations from ERM bilateral central rates
(daily data; percentages; 1 March 1996 to 27 February 1998)

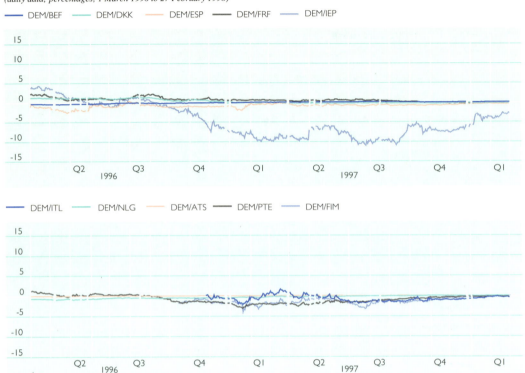

Source: European Commission.
Note: Deviations against the Finnish markka refer to the period from 14 October 1996 onwards, while deviations against the Italian lira refer to the period from 25 November 1996 onwards.

Table 9

Deutsche Mark: Measures of the real effective exchange rate vis-à-vis ERM Member States
(monthly data; percentage deviations; February 1998 compared with different benchmark periods)

	Average Apr 73-Feb 98	Average Jan 87-Feb 98	Average 1987
Real effective exchange rates:			
CPI-based	1.8	3.2	5.7
PPI/WPI-based	4.2	1.2	4.1
Memo item:			
Nominal effective exchange rate	24.1	4.1	9.8

Source: BIS and EMI calculations.
Note: A positive (negative) sign indicates an appreciation (depreciation).

Table 10

Germany: External developments
(as a percentage of GDP)

	1990	1991	1992	1993	1994	1995	1996	1997[a]
Current account plus new capital account[b]	3.2	-1.1	-1.0	-0.7	-1.0	-1.0	-0.6	-0.1
Net foreign assets (+) or liabilities (-)[c]	20.7	16.6	13.8	11.2	9.1	4.7	4.1	.
Exports (goods and services)[d]	32.1	26.1	25.5	24.5	25.7	26.9	27.7	30.0
Imports (goods and services)[e]	26.3	26.0	25.9	24.7	25.9	27.2	27.4	28.7

Source: National data except exports and imports (European Commission, spring 1998 forecasts).
Western Germany up to 1990, unified Germany thereafter.

(a) Partly estimated.
(b) According to the 5th edition of the IMF Balance of Payments Manual, which is conceptually the equivalent of the current account in previous editions of the Manual.
(c) International investment position (IIP) as defined by the IMF (see Balance of Payments Yearbook, Part 1, 1994), or the closest possible substitute.
(d) In 1996 the share of intra-EU exports of goods in total national exports of goods was 56.4%; Direction of Trade Statistics Yearbook 1997, IMF.
(e) In 1996 the share of intra-EU imports of goods in total national imports of goods was 55.1%; Direction of Trade Statistics Yearbook 1997, IMF.

IV Long-term interest rate developments

Table II

Germany: Long-term interest rates
(percentages)

	1996	1997	Nov 97	Dec 97	Jan 98	**Feb 97- Jan 98**
Long-term interest rate	6.2	5.6	5.6	5.3	5.1	5.6
Reference value	9.1	8.0	-	-	-	7.8

Source: European Commission.

Chart 7

(a) Germany: Long-term interest rate
(monthly averages; in percentages)

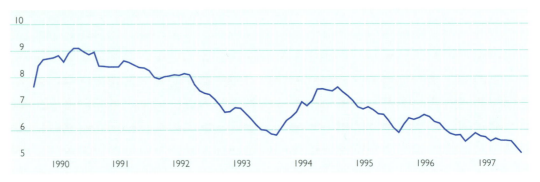

(b) Germany: Long-term interest rate and CPI inflation differentials against EU countries with lowest long-term interest rates*
(monthly averages; in percentage points)

Source: Interest rates: European Commission (where these are not available the most comparable data have been used); the CPI data used are non-harmonised national data.
* Weighted average of data for Belgium, Germany, France, the Netherlands and Austria.

GREECE

Price developments

Over the reference period from February 1997 to January 1998 the average rate of HICP inflation in Greece was 5.2%, i.e. considerably above the reference value of 2.7%. This was also the case in 1997 as a whole. In 1996 average HICP inflation was 7.9% (see Table 1). Seen over the past two years, HICP inflation in Greece has been significantly reduced without, as yet, having reached a level generally considered to be consistent with price stability.

Looking back, a clear trend towards lower rates of inflation in Greece has been discernible since the early 1990s. Consumer price inflation, as measured on the basis of the CPI, decreased steadily from above 20% in 1990 to 5½% in 1997 (see Chart 1). This experience of disinflation reflects a number of important policy choices, most notably the progressive tightening of monetary policy since the turn of the decade with a view to reducing rates of inflation. Initially, policy-makers sought to achieve the inflation target via an exchange rate policy which did not fully accommodate inflation differentials relative to Greece's main trading partners; since 1995 the authorities have linked the Greek drachma closely to the ECU. The reduction in inflation has been supported both by adjustments in fiscal policy which aim, inter alia, at broadening the tax base and combating tax evasion, as well as by structural changes in the labour market and the liberalisation of financial markets. In addition, the macroeconomic environment has contributed to containing upward pressure on prices. In particular, in the context of the recession in 1993, a negative output gap emerged (see Table 2). Since 1996 economic growth has recovered and the output gap has narrowed. Against this background, both growth in compensation per employee and

growth in unit labour costs decelerated but still grew at over 10% per annum on average until 1995; in 1997 growth in unit labour costs was reduced to 7½%. Increases in import prices have been curbed from above 13% in 1990 to below 3% in 1997. A reduction in inflationary tendencies is also indicated by other relevant measures of inflation (see Table 2).

Looking at recent trends and forecasts, current outturns for consumer price inflation (measured as a percentage change over the corresponding month a year earlier) have been decreasing to 4.4% (see Table 3a). Most forecasts of inflation suggest a rate of around 4½% for 1998 and 3½% for 1999 (see Table 3b). Upside risks over this period are associated with wage growth.[7]

Looking further ahead, creating an environment conducive to price stability relates in Greece to, inter alia, the conduct of fiscal policies over the medium to long term; it will be equally important to strengthen national policies aimed at enhancing competition in product markets and improving the functioning of labour markets against the background of the current high rate of unemployment in Greece.

Fiscal developments

In the *reference year* 1997 the general government deficit ratio was 4.0%, i.e. above the 3% reference value, and the debt ratio was 108.7%, i.e. far above the 60% reference value. Compared with the previous year, the deficit ratio has been reduced by 3.5 percentage points and the

---

[7] An adjustment plan which accompanies the entry of the drachma to the ERM effective from 16 March 1998 seeks to limit any associated inflationary risks.

debt ratio by 2.9 percentage points. In 1998 the deficit ratio is forecast to decrease to 2.2% of GDP, while the debt ratio is projected to decline to 107.7%. In 1996 and 1997 the deficit ratio exceeded the ratio of public investment expenditure to GDP by 4.5 percentage points and 0.7 percentage point respectively (see Table 4).

Looking back over the years 1990 to 1997, the Greek *debt-to-GDP ratio* increased by 18.6 percentage points; initially the ratio tended to rise continuously, from 90.1% in 1990 to 111.6% in 1993, to broadly stabilise thereafter, decreasing to 108.7% in 1997 (see Chart 2a), i.e. a decline of 2.9 percentage points since the latest peak in 1996. As is shown in greater detail in Chart 2b, in the early 1990s the strongest factor underlying the increase in the ratio, notably in 1993, came from the so-called "stock-flow adjustment item" of public debt, reflecting the adverse effects of the depreciation of the Greek drachma and of consolidation operations. By contrast, since 1994 the primary balance has recorded a surplus, thus outweighing the sizable impact of further stock-flow adjustments. The patterns observed in the early 1990s may be seen as indicative of the risks to public finances which can arise when special factors exert upward pressures on the debt which are only partly compensated by equivalent primary surpluses. In this context, it may be noted that the share of debt with a short-term maturity has been decreasing from the high levels of the early 1990s, which is a development in the right direction. With respect to 1997, the proportion of debt with a short-term maturity is still noticeable, and, taking into account the current level of the debt ratio, fiscal balances are relatively sensitive to changes in interest rates. In addition, the proportion of foreign currency debt in Greece is relatively high and fiscal balances are sensitive to changes in exchange rates.

During the 1990s a pattern of first adverse and subsequently improving outturns can be observed in the *deficit-to-GDP ratio*. Starting from a ratio of 16.1% of GDP in 1990, the deficit declined to 11.5% in 1991, but increased again in the following two years to stand at 13.8% in 1993. Since then, the deficit has declined year by year to stand at 4.0% in 1997 As is shown in Chart 3a, it has been reduced over four consecutive years by a total of 9.8 percentage points. Although the deficit ratio has declined substantially and continuously, it has not reached a level close to the reference value of 3% of GDP in 1997. As is shown in greater detail in Chart 3b, which focuses on *changes* in deficits, cyclical factors played a major role only in 1993. However, the non-cyclical improvements could reflect a lasting, "structural" move towards more balanced fiscal policies and/or a variety of measures with temporary effects. Evidence available suggests that such measures with a temporary effect reduced the deficit ratio by 0.2 percentage point in 1997, compared with 0.3 percentage point in 1996. As they were mainly of a "one-off" nature, the compensating measures already introduced in the 1998 budget will need to yield their expected results in 1998 in order to keep fiscal balances on the planned path.

Moving on to examine trends in other fiscal indicators, it can be seen from Chart 4 that the general government *total expenditure ratio*, after declining in 1991, showed an upward movement until 1993, mainly reflecting a steep increase in interest payments (see Table 6) as a result of a surge in debt. Since 1995 a downward trend in the total expenditure ratio has been discernible, mainly reflecting lower interest payments and a reduction in net capital expenditure. Overall the expenditure ratio in 1997 was more than 6 percentage points lower than at the beginning of the 1990s, reflecting in particular a sharp reduction in net capital expenditure and also some reductions in all other main expenditure categories in relation to GDP. Given this pattern, a balanced continuation of the downward trend of total expenditure to GDP would appear to require greater adjustments in expenditure items other than capital expenditure. *Government revenue* has tended to increase in relation to GDP continuously over the period considered, and was nearly 6 percentage points higher in 1997 than in 1990.

According to the Greek *medium-term fiscal policy strategy*, as presented in the Convergence Programme for 1994-99 updated in July 1997, the deficit ratio is expected to decline to 2.4% of GDP in 1998, and the debt ratio to 107% of GDP. The budget plan for 1998 is broadly in line with the programme. The reduction in the deficit ratio projected for 1998 will mainly be achieved by reducing the share of current expenditure in GDP and by increasing the share of government revenue in GDP. Currently, there is no evidence of significant measures with a temporary effect in the 1998 budget. Further improvement is projected in 1999, when the deficit ratio is planned to reach 2.1% and the debt ratio to stand at 101% of GDP. The planned development of Greece's public deficit is broadly in line with previous programmes - except for 1999, when a less favourable outcome is expected. The path of the debt ratio is projected to be more favourable than previously foreseen. Compared with fiscal balances projected in the Convergence Programme for 1999, further substantial consolidation is required in order to comply with the medium-term objective of the Stability and Growth Pact, effective from 1999 onwards, of having a budgetary position that is close to balance or in surplus. However, fiscal deficits as projected in the Convergence Programme for 1998 and 1999 are below the reference value of the Treaty.

With regard to the future horizon for reducing the debt ratio to the 60% reference value in countries with a debt ratio of above 100% of GDP, two different kinds of calculations are presented. On the assumption that fiscal balances and debt ratios as projected by the European Commission for 1998 are achieved, the first exercise, as detailed in Table 7, shows the fiscal balances which would be consistent with convergence of the debt ratio to 60% of GDP over different time horizons. As an illustration, focusing on the period of ten years, i.e. reducing the debt ratio to 60% by 2007, would imply realising from 1999 onwards an overall surplus of 1.4% of GDP per year (see Table 7a) or realising from 1999 onwards a primary surplus of 6.4% of GDP per year (see Table 7b). This compares with an overall deficit ratio of 2.2% and a primary surplus ratio of 6.8% projected for 1998, i.e. the difference is 3.6 and -0.4 percentage points respectively.

A second exercise, as detailed in Chart 5, shows that maintaining the 1998 overall fiscal balance of -2.2% of GDP over the subsequent years would only reduce the debt ratio to 87.5% in ten years; the 60% reference value would be reached in 2034. Maintaining the 1998 primary surplus of 6.8% of GDP would reduce the debt-to-GDP ratio to below 60% in ten years. Finally, realising balanced budgets annually from 1999 onwards would bring the debt ratio down to 70.6% in ten years, and the 60% reference level would be reached in 2011.

Such calculations are based on the normative assumption of a constant nominal rate of interest of 6% (average real cost of public debt outstanding of 4% and 2% inflation), and the assumption of a constant real GDP growth rate of 2.7%, as estimated by the Commission for real trend GDP growth in 1998. Stock-flow adjustments are not taken into account. While these calculations are purely illustrative, and can by no means be seen as forecasts, they do provide an illustration of why consolidation efforts need to be all the more resolute and lasting the higher the initial stock of debt, in order to forcefully reduce the debt-to-GDP ratio to 60% or below within an appropriate period of time.

Stressing the need for sustained consolidation over an extended period of time resulting in persistent, sizable overall fiscal surpluses is indeed critical in the case of Greece, since the current high level of debt would otherwise impose a continuous burden on fiscal policy and the economy as a whole. As has been seen in the past, high levels of debt increase the vulnerability of fiscal positions to unexpected shocks, thus heightening the risk of a sudden worsening of public finances. In addition, as is highlighted in Table 8, there are *future budgetary challenges* to meet. From around 2010 onwards a marked ageing of the population is expected and public pension expenditure is projected to increase in relation to GDP, particularly if policies regarding benefits continue unchanged. Greece benefits, however, from a partly funded pension system. One aspect of particular relevance in Greece is that the partly funded pension system currently invests a large part of its surpluses in government paper, thereby reducing the consolidated general government gross debt. As a result, any change in this investment policy would pose a risk to the gross debt ratio (but not, however, to the interest burden). Moreover, the demographic trend over the next few decades will have an adverse effect on the current surpluses in the pension system, thereby making improvements in the general government fiscal balance essential. Alleviation of the overall burden of population ageing will only be feasible if public finances have created sufficient room for manoeuvre before entering the period during which the demographic situation worsens.

Exchange rate developments

During the *reference period* from March 1996 to February 1998 the Greek drachma has not participated in the ERM[8] (see Table 9a). Monetary policy has been guided by an exchange rate target linking the drachma closely to the ECU with a view to reducing rates of inflation. Focusing on the reference period, the currency has normally traded above its March 1996 average bilateral exchange rates against most other EU currencies, which are used as a benchmark for illustrative purposes in the absence of central rates (see Chart 6 and Table 9a). The main exceptions were the development against the Irish pound, the pound sterling and, to a lesser extent, the Italian lira. In parallel with these developments the degree of volatility of the drachma's exchange rate against the Deutsche Mark fluctuated within a range of 2-4% (see Table 9b) and short-term interest rate differentials against those EU countries with the lowest short-term interest rates remained high, having narrowed until mid-1997 and widened significantly since November 1997.

In a longer-term context, the real effective exchange rates of the Greek drachma against other EU currencies depicted in Table 10 are above historical average values. This reflects an ongoing and not yet completed process of reducing inflation, based on a policy of not accommodating inflation differentials by nominal depreciation. With regard to other external developments, during the 1990s Greece has recorded current account deficits and a net external liability position (see Table 11). It may also be recalled that, according to the most recent data available, Greece has a ratio of foreign trade to GDP of 19% for exports and 31% for imports, and a share of intra-EU trade of 56% for exports and 70% for imports.

Long-term interest rate developments

Over the *reference period* from February 1997 to January 1998 *long-term interest rates* in Greece were 9.8% on average, and

---

[8] *The Greek drachma was incorporated in the exchange rate mechanism of the EMS, effective from 16 March 1998.*

thus stood well above the reference value for the interest rate criterion of 7.8% set on the basis of the three best-performing Member States in terms of price stability. This was also the case for 1997 as a whole, while in 1996 the rate was considerably above the reference value (see Table 12).

Long-term interest rates have been on a broadly declining trend during the 1990s, with the exception of 1997 (see Chart 7a). At the same time, a tendency towards a closer convergence of Greek long-term interest rates with those prevailing in the EU countries with the lowest bond yields has been observed since the mid-1990s, although the differential still remains significantly positive (see Chart 7b). The main factor underlying this trend was the significant decline in the inflation differential. In addition, the relative stability of the Greek drachma's exchange rate in recent years against the currencies of the above-mentioned countries and the recent improvement in the country's fiscal position have played a role in the narrowing of the differential during most of the period considered, while more recently the differential has increased.

Concluding summary

A clear trend towards lower inflation has been discernible in Greece, with the CPI rate falling from above 20% in 1990 to 5½% in 1997. HICP inflation was 5.2% over the reference period. At the same time, the increase in unit labour costs decelerated to 7½% in 1997, and the reduction in inflationary tendencies is also indicated by other relevant measures of inflation. Looking ahead, forecasts suggest a fall in inflation to 4½% in 1998 and to 3½% in 1999. Long-term interest rates have been on a broadly declining trend during the 1990s, with the exception of 1997; they averaged 9.8% over the reference period. Overall, notwithstanding the progress made, Greece has not achieved a rate of HICP inflation or a level of long-term interest

rates which are below the respective reference values stipulated by the Treaty.

Greece did not participate in the ERM during the reference period referred to in this Report.[9] Over the reference period, the Greek drachma traded above its March 1996 average bilateral exchange rates against most other EU currencies, which are used as a benchmark for illustrative purposes in the absence of central rates.

Since 1993 the fiscal deficit ratio has been reduced by a total of 9.8 percentage points to stand at 4.0% of GDP in 1997, above the reference value stipulated in the Treaty; the outlook for 1998 is for a decline in the deficit ratio to 2.2%, i.e. a level below the reference value. The debt-to-GDP ratio is far above the 60% reference value. After having reached a peak in 1993, the ratio broadly stabilised, before decreasing by 2.9 percentage points to 108.7% in 1997; the outlook for 1998 is for a decline in the debt ratio to 107.7% of GDP. Notwithstanding the efforts and the substantial progress made towards improving the current fiscal situation, there must be an ongoing concern as to whether the ratio of government debt to GDP will be "sufficiently diminishing and approaching the reference value at a satisfactory pace" and whether sustainability of the fiscal position has been achieved; addressing this issue will have to remain a key priority for the Greek authorities. Substantial primary surpluses and persistent, sizable overall fiscal surpluses will be needed to be able to reduce the debt ratio to 60% within an appropriate period of time. This compares with a recorded fiscal deficit of 4.0% of GDP in 1997, as well as the deficit forecast of 2.2% in 1998. The Stability and Growth Pact also requires, as a medium-term objective, a budgetary position that is close to balance or in surplus.

---

[9]   As noted above, the Greek drachma was incorporated in the exchange rate mechanism of the EMS, effective from 16 March 1998.

With regard to other factors, in 1996 and 1997 the deficit ratio exceeded the ratio of public investment to GDP, Greece recorded current account deficits and had a net external liability position. In the context of the ageing of the population, Greece benefits from a partly funded pension system.

List of Tables and Charts*

GREECE

---

* Chart scales may differ across countries.

I Price developments

Table I

Greece: HICP inflation
(annual percentage changes)

	1996	1997	Nov 97	Dec 97	Jan 98	**Feb 97- Jan 98**
HICP inflation	7.9	5.4	5.0	4.5	4.3	5.2
Reference value	2.5	2.7	-	-	-	2.7

Source: European Commission.

Chart I

Greece: Price developments
(annual percentage changes)

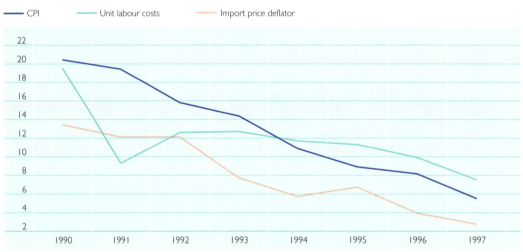

Source: National data.

Table 2

Greece: Measures of inflation and related indicators
(annual percentage changes unless otherwise stated)

	1990	1991	1992	1993	1994	1995	1996	1997[a]
Measures of inflation								
Consumer price index (CPI)	20.4	19.4	15.9	14.4	10.9	8.9	8.2	5.5
CPI excluding changes in net indirect taxes[b]	18.5	17.9	14.9	15.6	10.8	8.9	8.4	4.9
Private consumption deflator	19.9	19.7	15.6	14.2	11.0	8.6	8.5	5.5
GDP deflator	20.6	19.8	14.8	14.5	11.3	9.1	8.5	6.8
Producer prices	13.9	17.0	12.1	11.7	7.4	9.8	8.1	6.9
Related indicators								
Real GDP growth	0.0	3.1	0.7	-1.6	1.7	1.8	2.6	3.5
Output gap (p.pts)	0.8	2.3	1.3	-2.1	-2.2	-2.5	-2.3	-1.3
Unemployment rate (%)	6.4	7.3	7.6	7.1	7.2	7.1	7.5	7.9
Unit labour costs, whole economy	19.5	9.3	12.6	12.7	11.7	11.3	9.9	7.5
Compensation per employee, whole economy	17.9	15.4	11.8	9.8	11.9	12.6	11.5	10.7
Labour productivity, whole economy	-1.3	5.5	-0.7	-2.5	0.1	1.2	1.4	3.0
Import price deflator	13.4	12.1	12.1	7.7	5.7	6.7	3.9	2.7
Exchange rate appreciation[c]	-8.5	-11.4	-8.0	-8.6	-6.9	-2.8	-1.3	-1.9
Broad monetary aggregate (M3H)[d]	19.2	10.6	17.3	13.5	11.9	6.4	9.8	14.5
Stock prices	188.8	-2.1	-21.2	2.8	14.7	-3.7	5.4	58.0
House prices	-	-	-	-	-	-	-	-

Source: National data except real GDP growth and the output gap (European Commission, spring 1998 forecasts) and exchange rate (BIS).
(a) Partly estimated.
(b) National estimates.
(c) Nominal effective exchange rate against 25 industrialised countries.
  Note: A positive (negative) sign indicates an appreciation (depreciation).
(d) National harmonised data.

Table 3

Greece: Recent inflation trends and forecasts
(annual percentage change unless otherwise stated)

(a) Recent trends in consumer price inflation

	Sep 97	Oct 97	Nov 97	Dec 97	Jan 98
National consumer price index (CPI)					
Annual percentage change	4.9	4.7	5.1	4.7	4.4
Change in the average of latest 3 months from previous					
3 months, annualised rate, seasonally adjusted	4.6	4.4	3.8	4.2	4.3
Change in the average of latest 6 months from previous					
6 months, annualised rate, seasonally adjusted	5.1	4.9	4.7	4.6	4.4

Source: National non-harmonised data.

(b) Inflation forecasts

	1998	1999
European Commission (spring 1998), HICP	4.5	3.6
OECD (December 1997), private consumption deflator	4.5	3.5
IMF (October 1997), CPI	4.7	

Source: European Commission (spring 1998 forecasts), OECD and IMF.

II Fiscal developments

Table 4

Greece: General government financial position
(as a percentage of GDP)

	1996	**1997**	1998[a]
General government surplus (+) / deficit (-)	-7.5	-4.0	-2.2
Reference value	-3	-3	-3
Surplus (+) / deficit (-), net of public investment expenditure[b]	-4.5	-0.7	.
General government gross debt	111.6	108.7	107.7
Reference value	60	60	60

Source: European Commission (spring 1998 forecasts) and EMI calculations.
(a) European Commission projections.
(b) A negative sign indicates that the government deficit is higher than investment expenditure.

Chart 2

Greece: General government gross debt
(as a percentage of GDP)

(a) Levels

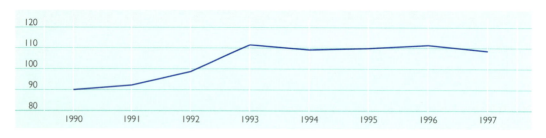

(b) Annual changes and underlying factors

Source: European Commission (spring 1998 forecasts) and EMI calculations.
Note: In Chart 2b negative values indicate a contribution of the respective factor to a decrease in the debt ratio, while positive values indicate a contribution to its increase.

98

Table 5

Greece: General government gross debt – structural features

	1990	1991	1992	1993	1994	1995	1996	1997
Total debt (as a percentage of GDP)	90.1	92.3	98.8	111.6	109.3	110.1	111.6	108.7
Composition by currency (% of total)								
In domestic currency	76.8	76.3	76.4	77.8	76.2	77.7	78.3	78.4
In foreign currencies	23.2	23.7	23.6	22.2	23.8	22.3	21.7	21.6
Domestic ownership (% of total)	74.9	75.2	75.5	76.1	74.5	76.6	77.9	76.3
Average maturity (years)	.	.	.	.	.	.	.	
Composition by maturity[a] (% of total)								
Short-term (≤ 1 year)	52.2	41.1	37.9	25.5	26.6	24.2	21.8	13.3
Medium and long-term (> 1 year)	47.8	58.9	62.1	74.5	73.4	75.8	78.2	86.7

Source: National data except for total debt (European Commission (spring 1998 forecasts)). End-year data. Differences in the totals are due to rounding.

(a) Original maturity.

Chart 3

Greece: General government surplus (+) / deficit (-)
(as a percentage of GDP)

(a) Levels

(b) Annual changes and underlying factors

Source: European Commission (spring 1998 forecasts).
Note: In Chart 3b negative values indicate a contribution to an increase in deficits, while positive values indicate a contribution to their reduction.

99

Chart 4

Greece: General government expenditure and receipts
(as a percentage of GDP)

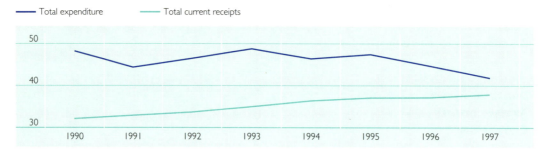

Source: European Commission (spring 1998 forecasts).

Table 6

Greece: General government budgetary position
(as a percentage of GDP)

	1990	1991	1992	1993	1994	1995	1996	1997
Total current receipts	32.1	32.9	33.7	35.0	36.4	37.2	37.2	37.9
Taxes	18.7	19.4	20.1	19.8	20.6	20.8	21.0	21.9
Social security contributions	11.7	11.2	11.1	12.1	12.0	12.0	11.9	11.6
Other current receipts	1.7	2.2	2.5	3.1	3.8	4.4	4.3	4.3
Total expenditure	48.2	44.4	46.5	48.8	46.4	47.5	44.7	41.9
Current transfers	16.2	15.6	15.2	15.8	15.4	16.0	15.9	15.5
Actual interest payments	10.2	9.4	11.7	12.8	14.1	12.9	11.9	9.6
Public consumption	15.3	14.4	13.9	14.5	13.9	15.4	14.7	14.8
Net capital expenditure	6.6	5.0	5.7	5.7	2.9	3.2	2.2	2.0
Surplus (+) or deficit (-)	-16.1	-11.5	-12.8	-13.8	-10.0	-10.3	-7.5	-4.0
Primary balance	-6.0	-2.1	-1.1	-1.0	4.1	2.6	4.4	5.6
Surplus (+) or deficit (-),								
net of public investment expenditure[a]	.	.	.	-10.6	-7.0	-7.1	-4.5	-0.7

Source: European Commission (spring 1998 forecasts) and EMI calculations. Differences in the totals are due to rounding.
(a)   A negative sign indicates that the government deficit is higher than investment expenditure.

Table 7

Greece: Debt convergence calculations

(a) On the basis of overall fiscal balances
(as a percentage of GDP)

Total gross debt		Overall fiscal balance (deficit: (-); surplus (+))		Overall fiscal balance consistent with reduction of debt level to 60% of GDP in[a]		
1997	1998	1997	1998	2002	2007	2012
108.7	107.7	-4.0	-2.2	7.8	1.4	-0.4

Source: European Commission (spring 1998 forecasts) and EMI calculations.
(a) Calculations indicate that the debt ratio would fall to 60% in 2002, 2007 and 2012 respectively, if the overall fiscal balance for 1998 is as forecast and the overall fiscal balances were maintained at 7.8%, 1.4% and -0.4% of GDP respectively, from 1999 onwards. The underlying assumptions are a real trend GDP growth rate of 2.7% in 1998, as estimated by the Commission, and an inflation rate of 2%. Stock-flow adjustments are disregarded.

(b) On the basis of primary fiscal balances
(as a percentage of GDP)

Total gross debt		Primary fiscal balance		Primary fiscal balance consistent with reduction of debt level to 60% of GDP in[a]		
1997	1998	1997	1998	2002	2007	2012
108.7	107.7	5.6	6.8	13.0	6.4	4.5

Source: European Commission (spring 1998 forecasts) and EMI calculations.
(a) Calculations indicate that the debt ratio would fall to 60% in 2002, 2007 and 2012 respectively, if the primary fiscal balance for 1998 is as forecast and the primary fiscal balances were maintained at 13.0%, 6.4% and 4.5% of GDP, respectively from 1999 onwards. The underlying assumptions are a real trend GDP growth rate of 2.7% in 1998, as estimated by the Commission, an inflation rate of 2% and a nominal interest rate of 6%. Stock-flow adjustments are disregarded.

Chart 5

Greece: Potential future debt ratios under alternative assumptions for fiscal balance ratios
(as a percentage of GDP)

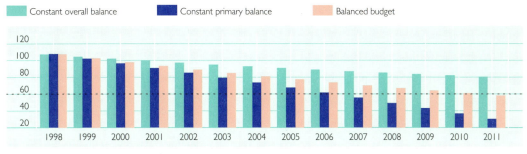

Source: European Commission (spring 1998 forecasts) and EMI calculations.
Note: The three scenarios assume that the debt ratio of 107.7% of GDP for 1998 is as forecast and that the 1998 overall balance of -2.2% of GDP or the primary balance of 6.8% of GDP will be kept constant over the period considered (as a percentage of GDP), or, alternatively, that a balanced budget is maintained from 1999 onwards. The underlying assumptions are a real trend GDP growth rate in 1998 of 2.7% as estimated by the Commission; an inflation rate of 2%; and, in the constant primary balance scenario, a nominal interest rate of 6%. Stock-flow adjustments are disregarded.

Table 8

Greece: Projections of elderly dependency ratio

	1990	2000	2010	2020	2030
Elderly dependency ratio (population aged 65 and over as a proportion of the population aged 15-64)	21.2	25.5	28.8	33.3	40.9

Source: Bos, E. et al. (1994), World population projections 1994-95, World Bank, Washington DC.

III Exchange rate developments

(a) Greece: Exchange rate stability
(1 March 1996 - 27 February 1998)

Membership of the Exchange Rate Mechanism (ERM)		No
Membership since		-
Devaluation of bilateral central rate on country's own initiative		-
Maximum upward (+) and downward (-) deviations from March 1996 average bilateral rates (%) against[a]		
ERM currencies:		
Belgian franc	5.1	-0.1
Danish krone	3.8	-0.1
Deutsche Mark	4.7	-0.1
Spanish peseta	5.2	-0.2
French franc	3.2	-0.1
Irish pound	0.4	-10.2
Italian lira	0.5	-4.6
Dutch guilder	5.3	-0.1
Austrian schilling	4.8	-0.1
Portuguese escudo	3.3	-0.3
Finnish markka	4.2	-1.5
Non-ERM currencies:		
Swedish krona	3.5	-3.0
Pound sterling	0.8	-22.3

Source: European Commission and EMI calculations.
(a)   Daily data at business frequency; 10-day moving average.

(b) Key indicators of exchange rate pressure for the Greek drachma

Average of 3 months ending:	May 96	Aug 96	Nov 96	Feb 97	May 97	Aug 97	Nov 97	Feb 98
Exchange rate volatility[a]	2.7	2.6	2.1	4.4	3.1	2.5	3.1	1.6
Short-term interest rate differentials[b]	10.6	10.5	9.9	9.1	7.7	8.2	12.4	13.4

Source: European Commission, national data and EMI calculations.
(a)   Annualised monthly standard deviation of daily percentage changes of the exchange rate against the DEM, in percentages.
(b)   Differential of three-month interbank interest rates against a weighted average of interest rates in Belgium, Germany, France, the Netherlands and Austria, in percentage points.

Greek drachma: Bilateral exchange rates
(daily data; average of March 1996=100; 1 March 1996 to 27 February 1998)

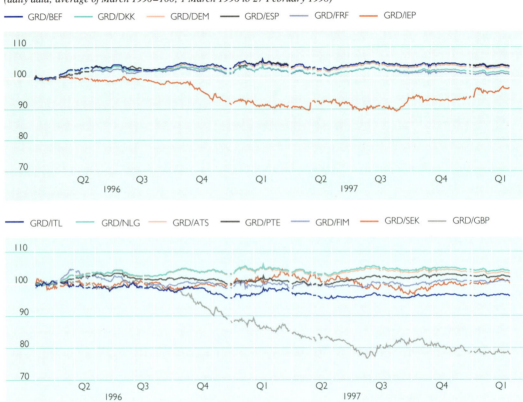

Source: European Commission.

Greek drachma: Measures of the real effective exchange rate vis-à-vis EU Member States
(monthly data; percentage deviations; February 1998 compared with different benchmark periods)

	Average Apr 73-Feb 98	Average Jan 87-Feb 98	Average 1987
Real effective exchange rates:			
CPI-based	12.1	12.3	26.7
PPI/WPI-based	10.9	13.8	26.0
Memo item:			
Nominal effective exchange rate	-71.2	-25.1	-47.8

Source: BIS and EMI calculations.
Note: A positive (negative) sign indicates an appreciation (depreciation).

Table 11

Greece: External developments
(as a percentage of GDP)

	1990	1991	1992	1993	1994	1995	1996	1997[a]
Current account plus new capital account[b]	-4.3	-1.7	-2.1	-0.8	-0.1	-2.5	-3.7	-3.8
Net foreign assets (+) or liabilities (-)[c]	-24.3	-23.2	-21.4	-22.7	-21.5	-19.8	-15.5	-19.5
Exports (goods and services)[d]	16.8	16.9	18.6	18.2	19.0	18.9	18.5	18.7
Imports (goods and services)[e]	28.1	28.9	27.9	28.4	28.4	29.6	30.0	30.6

Source: National data except exports and imports (European Commission, spring 1998 forecasts).

(a) Partly estimated.

(b) According to the 5th edition of the IMF Balance of Payments Manual, which is conceptually the equivalent of the current account in previous editions of the Manual.

(c) International investment position (IIP) as defined by the IMF (see Balance of Payments Yearbook, Part 1, 1994), or the closest possible substitute.

(d) In 1996 the share of intra-EU exports of goods in total national exports of goods was 56.4%; Direction of Trade Statistics Yearbook 1997, IMF.

(e) In 1996 the share of intra-EU imports of goods in total national imports of goods was 69.5%; Direction of Trade Statistics Yearbook 1997, IMF.

IV Long-term interest rate developments

Table 12

Greece: Long-term interest rates
(percentages)

	1996	1997	Nov 97	Dec 97	Jan 98	**Feb 97- Jan 98**
Long-term interest rate	14.4	9.9	10.8	10.5	11.0	9.8
Reference value	9.1	8.0	-	-	-	7.8

Source: European Commission.
Note: The harmonised series for Greece starts in mid-1997. Before this, data were based on available best proxies: for the period from March to June 1997, yield data for long-term bonds with shorter maturities than the harmonised series were used; before that period, yields at issue for long-term bonds with shorter maturities than the harmonised series were used.

Chart 7

(a) Greece: Long-term interest rate
(monthly averages; in percentages)

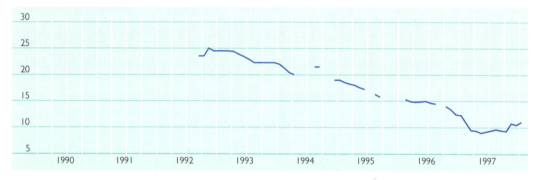

(b) Greece: Long-term interest rate and CPI inflation differentials against EU countries with lowest long-term interest rates*
(monthly averages; in percentage points)

Long-term interest rate differential   CPI inflation differential

Source: Interest rates: European Commission (where these are not available the most comparable data have been used); for further explanation of the data used, see footnote on Table 12; the CPI data used are non-harmonised national data.
* Weighted average of data for Belgium, Germany, France, the Netherlands and Austria.

SPAIN

Price developments

Over the reference period from February 1997 to January 1998 the average rate of HICP inflation in Spain was 1.8%, i.e. well below the reference value of 2.7%. This was also the case in 1997 as a whole. In 1996 average HICP inflation was 3.6% (see Table 1). Seen over the past two years, Spain has reduced the rate of HICP inflation to a level which is generally considered to be consistent with price stability.

Looking back, consumer price inflation in Spain, as measured on the basis of the CPI, has followed a downward trend since the early 1990s, when inflation stood at 6.7% (see Chart 1). This experience of disinflation reflects a number of important policy choices, most notably the shift in the orientation of monetary policy towards the achievement of price stability in the medium term within the framework of the ERM. Since 1995 this objective has been enshrined in explicit inflation targets, which currently seek to maintain inflation at 2%. The stabilisation of price developments has been supported by recent adjustments in fiscal policy, labour market reforms and reforms designed to enhance product market competition. In addition, the macroeconomic environment has contributed to containing upward pressure on prices. In particular, real GDP growth decelerated markedly in the early 1990s and the economy entered a recession in 1993, with output declining by over 1% (see Table 2). As a result, a negative output gap emerged. Since 1994 economic activity has recovered significantly, but the output gap has remained sizable. Against this background, growth in compensation per employee has been restrained and growth in unit labour costs has come down markedly since the early 1990s. Import price increases varied considerably in the 1990s, partly as a result of exchange rate movements. Since 1993 growth rates of import prices have declined gradually before picking up again in 1997. Low rates of inflation are also apparent when it is measured in terms of other relevant price indices (see Table 2).

Looking at recent trends and forecasts, current outturns for consumer price inflation (measured as a percentage change over the corresponding month a year earlier) have been stable at 2% and there is little sign of immediate upward pressure on the basis of the measures shown in Table 3a. Forecasts of inflation suggest rates of somewhat above 2% for 1998 and 1999 (see Table 3b). Risks for price stability over this period are associated with the development of wages in the light of a strengthening of economic activity.

Looking further ahead, maintaining an environment conducive to price stability relates in Spain to, inter alia, the conduct of fiscal policies over the medium to long term; it will be equally important to strengthen national policies aimed at enhancing competition in product markets and improving the functioning of labour markets against the background of the current very high, albeit declining, rate of unemployment in Spain.

Fiscal developments

In the *reference year* 1997 the general government deficit ratio was 2.6%, i.e. below the 3% reference value, and the debt ratio was 68.8%, i.e. above the 60% reference value. Compared with the previous year, the deficit ratio has been reduced by 2.0 percentage points and the debt ratio by 1.3 percentage points. In 1998 the deficit ratio is forecast to decrease to 2.2% of GDP, while the debt ratio is projected to decline to 67.4%. In 1996 the deficit ratio exceeded the ratio of public investment but it fell below it in 1997 (see Table 4).

Looking back over the years 1990 to 1997, the Spanish *debt-to-GDP ratio* increased by 24.0 percentage points; initially the ratio tended to rise gradually, from 44.8% in 1990 to 48.0% in 1992, whereas there was a steep increase in 1993 to 60.0% of GDP. In subsequent years the ratio climbed to 70.1% in 1996, before declining to 68.8% in 1997 (see Chart 2a), i.e. a decline of 1.3 percentage points in one year. As is shown in greater detail in Chart 2b, until 1995 primary deficits in general contributed to debt growth, adding to a negative growth/interest rate differential which also had a debt-increasing effect. In addition, an important factor underlying the steep rise in the debt ratio has been the impact of "stock-flow adjustments". In particular, in 1993 a sizable overfunding of the deficit took place in order to build up a deposit of the Treasury at the Banco de España as a buffer stock to cover unforeseen liquidity needs, and in the same year the depreciation of the Spanish peseta, which increased the peseta value of debt denominated in foreign currency, had a minor impact. The patterns observed thus far during the 1990s may be seen as indicative of the risks to public finances which can arise when macroeconomic conditions deteriorate while special factors drive up the debt ratio, particularly in an environment where the primary surplus is insufficient to counterbalance these effects. In this context, it may be noted that the share of debt with a short-term residual maturity has been decreasing from the high levels of the early 1990s, and in parallel the average maturity has increased (see Table 5). With regard to 1997, the proportion of debt with a short-term residual maturity is still high, and, taking into account the current level of the debt ratio, fiscal balances are sensitive to changes in interest rates. On the other hand, the proportion of foreign currency debt is low and fiscal balances are relatively

insensitive to changes in exchange rates.

During the 1990s diverse patterns can be observed in the *deficit-to-GDP ratio*. Starting from a ratio of around 4% of GDP in 1990-92, fiscal imbalances reached 6.9% of GDP in 1993 and peaked at 7.3% in 1995; since then, the deficit ratio has been declining, to stand at 2.6% in 1997 (see Chart 3a). As is shown in greater detail in Chart 3b, which focuses on *changes* in deficits, cyclical factors contributed substantially to the increase in the deficit ratio in 1993, but did not play a major role thereafter. The non-cyclical improvements could reflect a lasting, "structural" move towards more balanced fiscal policies and/or a variety of measures with temporary effects. However, evidence available suggests that measures with a temporary effect did not improve the fiscal balance in 1997 by more than 0.1% of GDP.

Moving on to examine trends in other fiscal indicators, it can be seen from Chart 4 that the general government *total expenditure ratio* rose steeply between 1990 and 1993. Against the background of high and rising unemployment, current transfers to households increased sharply, while the surge in debt led to higher interest payments. Meanwhile, public consumption also increased relative to GDP (see Table 6). In the years following 1993 the ratio of total expenditure to GDP was on a declining path, mainly reflecting a reduction in transfers to households and cuts in public consumption and investment. On balance, the expenditure ratio has returned to the level observed in 1990, whereby categories like current transfers, interest payments and public consumption are now higher as a percentage of GDP (although interest payments have eased in recent years), and public investment and other capital expenditures are lower. Given the successive reduction in public investment and other capital expenditure as a percentage of GDP during the 1990s, a continuation of the downward trend of total expenditure to GDP would appear to require greater adjustments in other expenditure items. In contrast to the swings in expenditure, *government revenue* in relation to GDP has tended to fluctuate around 40% over most of the period considered.

According to the Spanish *medium-term fiscal policy strategy*, as presented in the Convergence Programme for 1997-2000 updated in April 1997, a declining trend in deficit and debt ratios is targeted for 1998. The budget for 1998 foresees a reduction in the general government deficit to 2.4% of GDP, which is slightly more ambitious than the figure specified in the programme, and Commission forecasts suggest a deficit ratio of 2.2%. The improvement in the budget is planned to result from a decline in the share of public expenditure in GDP as a result, in particular, of restraint in personnel spending, a moderate reduction in unemployment benefits and a drop in interest payments. Currently, there is no evidence of significant measures with a temporary effect in the 1998 budget. In the year 2000 deficits are projected to decline to 1.6% of GDP and the debt ratio to stand at 65.3%. The 1997 deficit is better than expected, but the improvement in the debt ratio was somewhat less favourable than envisaged earlier. Compared with fiscal balances projected in the Convergence Programme for 1999-2000, further substantial fiscal consolidation is required in order to comply with the medium-term objective of the Stability and Growth Pact, effective from 1999 onwards, of having a budgetary position that is close to balance or in surplus.

With regard to the future horizon for reducing the debt ratio to the 60% reference value for countries with a debt ratio clearly above 60% but below 80% of GDP, the EMI presents calculations as detailed in Chart 5. On the assumption that overall fiscal positions and debt ratios

as projected by the European Commission for 1998 are achieved, realising a balanced budget from 1999 onwards would reduce the debt ratio to below 60% of GDP as early as 2001. Instead, maintaining the 1998 overall and primary balance ratios of -2.2% and 2.1% constant in subsequent years would imply a slower path of debt reduction and would generate a debt ratio of below 60% of GDP in 2007 and 2004 respectively. Such calculations are based on the normative assumption of a constant nominal rate of interest of 6% (average real cost of public debt outstanding of 4% and 2% inflation) and the assumption of a constant real GDP growth rate of 2.9%, as estimated by the Commission for real trend GDP growth in 1998. Stock-flow adjustments are not taken into account. While they are purely illustrative, and can by no means be regarded as forecasts, the calculations, which indicate that maintaining 1998 levels for overall deficits would imply attainment of the 60% reference value not before 2007, provide an illustration of the need for further substantial progress in consolidation.

Stressing the need for considerable improvement in the deficit ratio and to sustain consolidation over time is indeed warranted in the case of Spain, since additional room for manoeuvre is necessary in order to be able to address *future budgetary challenges*. As is highlighted in Table 7, from around 2010 onwards a marked ageing of the population is expected, and, in the context of an unfunded pension system, public pension expenditure is projected to increase in relation to GDP, particularly if policies regarding benefits continue unchanged. The overall burden of population ageing will become more manageable the better the state of public finances when the demographic situation worsens.

Exchange rate developments

The Spanish peseta has been participating in the ERM since 19 June 1989, i.e. for considerably longer than two years prior to the examination (see Table 8a). As mentioned above, Spanish monetary policy has focused on the achievement of price stability over the medium term within the context of the ERM. Focusing on the *reference period* from March 1996 to February 1998, the currency, benefiting from sizable short-term interest rate differentials vis-à-vis most partner currencies, has normally traded close to its central rates against other ERM currencies (see Chart 6 and Table 8a). On occasion the Spanish peseta traded outside a range close to its central rates vis-à-vis various partner currencies. The maximum upward and downward deviations from central rates, on the basis of 10 business day moving averages, were 3.5% and -2.1% respectively, abstracting from the autonomous upward trend of the Irish pound (see Table 8a). The episodes in which such deviations occurred were temporary, the degree of exchange rate volatility vis-à-vis the Deutsche Mark decreased steadily to a low level (see Table 8b) and short-term interest rate differentials against those EU countries with the lowest short-term interest rates narrowed significantly over the reference period. During the reference period Spain has not devalued its currency's bilateral central rate against any other Member State's currency.

In a longer-term context, measures of the real effective exchange rate of the Spanish peseta vis-à-vis the currencies of ERM participating Member States depicted in Table 9 suggest that current levels are close to historical values. As regards other external developments, over the 1990s, current account deficits turned into surpluses. This turnaround in the balance of payments has been reflected in a tendency towards reductions in the net external liability position (see Table 10). It may also be recalled that, according to the most recent data available, Spain has a ratio of foreign trade to GDP of 30% for exports and 28% for imports, and a share of intra-EU trade of 71% for exports and 66% for imports.

Long-term interest rate developments

Over the *reference period* from February 1997 to January 1998 *long-term interest rates* in Spain were 6.3% on average, and thus stood below the reference value for the interest rate criterion of 7.8% set on the basis of the three best-performing Member States in terms of price stability. This was also the case for 1997 as a whole, as well as for 1996 (see Table 11). Twelve-month average long-term interest rates have been below the reference value since November 1996.

Long-term interest rates have been on a broadly declining trend during the 1990s (see Chart 7a). A broad trend towards the convergence of Spanish long-term interest rates with those prevailing in the EU countries with the lowest bond yields has also been observed for most of the period since the early 1990s. Since mid-1995 the process of convergence towards these levels has accelerated, and the differential has now been virtually eliminated (see Chart 7b). The main factor underlying this trend was the significant decline in the inflation differential vis-à-vis those countries with the lowest long-term bond yields, which has recently approached zero. The relative stability of the Spanish peseta's exchange rate against the currencies of the above-mentioned countries and an improvement in the country's fiscal position also helped to account for the narrowing of the differential. These underlying developments were seen by markets as improving the prospects for participation in Stage Three of EMU - an element which may in turn have played an independent role in accelerating the narrowing of yield differentials, both directly and by further improving the prospects for price and exchange rate stability.

Concluding summary

Over the reference period Spain has achieved a rate of HICP inflation of 1.8%, which is well below the reference value stipulated by the Treaty. The increase in unit labour costs was subdued and a general trend towards low rates of inflation was also apparent in terms of other relevant price indices. Looking ahead, there is little sign of immediate upward pressure on inflation; forecasts project inflation will rise to somewhat above 2% in 1998 and 1999. The Spanish peseta has been participating in the ERM for considerably longer than two years. Over the reference period it remained broadly stable, generally close to its unchanged central parities, without the need for measures to support the exchange rate. The level of long-term interest rates was 6.3%, i.e. below the respective reference value.

In 1997 Spain achieved a fiscal deficit ratio of 2.6%, i.e. below the reference value, and the outlook is for a further decline to 2.2% in 1998. The debt-to-GDP ratio is above the 60% reference value. After having reached a peak in 1996, the ratio declined by 1.3 percentage points to stand at 68.8% in 1997. Regarding the sustainability of fiscal developments, the outlook is for a decrease in the debt ratio to 67.4% of GDP in 1998. Given the current debt ratio of somewhat below 70% of GDP, achieving the fiscal balance forecast for 1998 and a balanced budget thereafter would reduce the debt ratio to below 60% in 2001. Instead, keeping the 1998 overall or primary balances constant in the following years would bring the debt ratio down to 60% of GDP not before 2007 and 2004 respectively, thus pointing to the need for further substantial progress in consolidation. The Stability and Growth Pact also requires as a medium-term objective a budgetary position that is close to balance or in surplus.

With regard to other factors, in 1996 the fiscal deficit ratio exceeded the ratio of public investment to GDP, but it fell below that level in 1997. Furthermore, Spain has recorded current account surpluses, while continuing to have a net external liability position.

List of Tables and Charts*

SPAIN

I Price developments

II Fiscal developments

III Exchange rate developments

IV Long-term interest rate developments

---

* Chart scales may differ across countries.

1 Price developments

Table 1

Spain: HICP inflation
(annual percentage changes)

	1996	1997	Nov 97	Dec 97	Jan 98	**Feb 97- Jan 98**
HICP inflation	3.6	1.9	1.9	1.9	1.9	1.8
Reference value	2.5	2.7	-	-	-	2.7

Source: European Commission.

Chart 1

Spain: Price developments
(annual percentage changes)

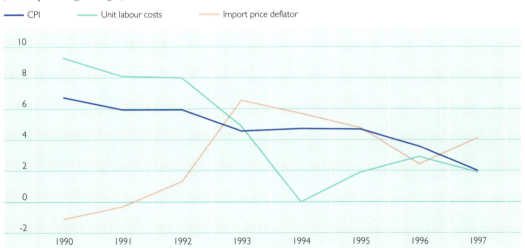

Source: National data.

Table 2

Spain: Measures of inflation and related indicators

(annual percentage changes unless otherwise stated)

	1990	1991	1992	1993	1994	1995	1996	1997[a]
Measures of inflation								
Consumer price index (CPI)	6.7	5.9	5.9	4.6	4.7	4.7	3.6	2.0
CPI excluding changes in net indirect taxes[b]	.	.	.	.	4.4	3.7	3.4	1.7
Private consumption deflator	6.5	6.4	6.4	5.6	4.8	4.7	3.4	2.5
GDP deflator	7.3	7.1	6.9	4.3	4.0	4.8	3.1	2.2
Producer prices	2.0	1.3	1.2	2.4	4.5	6.9	1.7	1.3
Related indicators								
Real GDP growth	3.7	2.3	0.7	-1.2	2.1	2.8	2.3	3.4
Output gap (p.pts)	4.5	4.1	2.2	-1.5	-1.9	-1.7	-2.1	-1.5
Unemployment rate (%)	16.3	16.3	18.4	22.7	24.2	22.9	22.2	20.8
Unit labour costs, whole economy	9.3	8.1	8.0	4.9	0.0	1.9	2.9	1.9
Compensation per employee, whole economy	9.5	9.5	10.4	6.8	2.8	2.9	3.8	2.7
Labour productivity, whole economy	0.1	1.3	2.3	1.8	2.7	1.1	0.8	0.8
Import price deflator	-1.2	-0.3	1.3	6.5	5.7	4.7	2.4	4.1
Exchange rate appreciation[c]	4.4	-0.1	-2.1	-12.2	-6.7	-0.0	0.9	-4.5
Broad monetary aggregate (M3H)[d]	13.7	12.4	6.4	7.1	7.5	9.6	7.8	3.0
Stock prices	-12.5	0.4	-12.0	14.7	18.5	-6.2	22.1	52.7
House prices	15.6	14.3	-1.3	-0.4	0.7	3.5	1.9	1.3

Source: National data except real GDP growth and the output gap (European Commission, spring 1998 forecasts) and exchange rate (BIS).
(a) Partly estimated.
(b) National estimates.
(c) Nominal effective exchange rate against 25 industrialised countries.
      Note: a positive (negative) sign indicates an appreciation (depreciation).
(d) National harmonised data.

Table 3

Spain: Recent inflation trends and forecasts

(annual percentage change unless otherwise stated)

(a) Recent trends in consumer price inflation

	Sep 97	Oct 97	Nov 97	Dec 97	Jan 98
National consumer price index (CPI)					
Annual percentage change	2.0	1.9	2.0	2.0	2.0
Change in the average of latest 3 months from previous					
3 months, annualised rate, seasonally adjusted	2.8	2.9	2.8	2.4	2.2
Change in the average of latest 6 months from previous					
6 months, annualised rate, seasonally adjusted	1.6	1.8	2.1	2.3	2.4

Source: National non-harmonised data.

(b) Inflation forecasts

	1998	1999
European Commission (spring 1998), HICP	2.1	2.1
OECD (December 1997), private consumption deflator	2.4	2.4
IMF (October 1997), CPI	2.2	.

Source: European Commission (spring 1998 forecasts), OECD and IMF.

II Fiscal developments

Spain: General government financial position
(as a percentage of GDP)

	1996	**1997**	1998[a]
General government surplus (+) / deficit (-)	-4.6	-2.6	-2.2
Reference value	-3	-3	-3
Surplus (+) / deficit (-), net of public investment expenditure[b]	-1.7	0.3	.
General government gross debt	70.1	68.8	67.4
Reference value	60	60	60

Source: European Commission (spring 1998 forecasts) and EMI calculations.
(a) European Commission projections.
(b) A negative sign indicates that the government deficit is higher than investment expenditure.

Spain: General government gross debt
(as a percentage of GDP)

(a) Levels

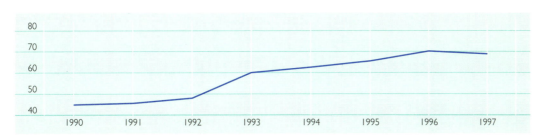

(b) Annual changes and underlying factors

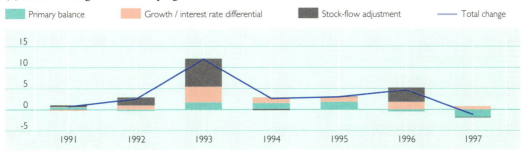

Source: European Commission (spring 1998 forecasts) and EMI calculations.
Note: In Chart 2b negative values indicate a contribution of the respective factor to a decrease in the debt ratio, while positive values indicate a contribution to its increase.

Table 5

Spain: General government gross debt – structural features

	1990	1991	1992	1993	1994	1995	1996	1997
Total debt (as a percentage of GDP)	44.8	45.5	48.0	60.0	62.6	65.5	70.1	68.8
Composition by currency (% of total)								
In domestic currency	96.6	96.0	93.3	91.5	90.8	90.7	91.1	90.4
In foreign currencies	3.4	4.0	6.7	8.5	9.2	9.3	8.9	9.6
Domestic ownership (% of total)	94.1	87.6	86.5	72.0	80.7	78.4	80.0	78.5
Average maturity[a] (years)	1.0	1.4	1.8	3.0	3.0	3.1	3.1	3.7
Composition by maturity[b] (% of total)								
Short-term[c] (< 1 year)	65.7	62.8	60.5	43.7	41.7	42.1	41.0	30.6
Medium-term (1-5 years)	32.4	31.6	26.4	34.9	33.6	29.6	29.7	37.2
Long-term (> 5 years)	1.9	5.6	13.0	21.5	24.7	28.3	29.3	32.1

Source: National data except for total debt (European Commission (spring 1998 forecasts)). End-year data. Differences in the totals are due to rounding.

(a) Residual maturity. Only those domestic currency securities that are recorded in the centralised book-entry system.

(b) Residual maturity. Domestic currency securities that are recorded in the centralised book-entry system, foreign currency securities and assumed debt; overall, these represent between 70% (1992) and 81% (1997) of the total debt.

(c) Including short-term debt and debt linked to short-term interest rates.

Chart 3

Spain: General government surplus (+) / deficit (-)
(as a percentage of GDP)

(a) Levels

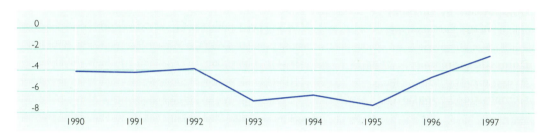

(b) Annual changes and underlying factors

Source: European Commission (spring 1998 forecasts).
Note: In Chart 3b negative values indicate a contribution to an increase in deficits, while positive values indicate a contribution to their reduction.

Chart 4

Spain: General government expenditure and receipts
(as a percentage of GDP)

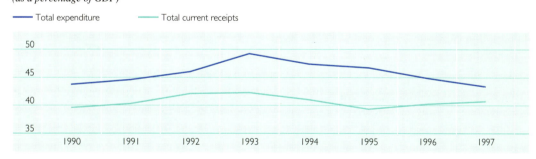

Source: European Commission (spring 1998 forecasts).

Table 6

Spain: General government budgetary position
(as a percentage of GDP)

	1990	1991	1992	1993	1994	1995	1996	1997
Total current receipts	39.6	40.3	42.1	42.3	41.0	39.4	40.2	40.8
Taxes	22.6	22.6	23.5	22.3	22.2	22.1	22.4	22.9
Social security contributions	13.3	13.6	14.5	14.8	14.5	13.5	13.8	13.9
Other current receipts	3.8	4.2	4.1	5.2	4.3	3.8	4.0	4.0
Total expenditure	43.7	44.6	46.0	49.2	47.4	46.7	44.9	43.4
Current transfers	18.3	19.2	20.0	21.4	20.9	19.7	19.7	19.4
Actual interest payments	3.9	3.7	4.1	5.2	4.8	5.5	5.1	4.5
Public consumption	15.5	16.1	17.0	17.4	16.8	16.6	16.4	16.0
Net capital expenditure	6.0	5.6	4.8	5.2	4.8	4.9	3.7	3.5
Surplus (+) or deficit (-)	-4.1	-4.2	-3.8	-6.9	-6.3	-7.3	-4.6	-2.6
Primary balance	-0.2	-0.5	0.3	-1.7	-1.5	-1.8	0.5	1.9
Surplus (+) or deficit (-), net of public investment expenditure[a]	.	.	.	-2.9	-2.5	-3.6	-1.7	0.3

Source: European Commission (spring 1998 forecasts) and EMI calculations. Differences in the totals are due to rounding.
(a)   A negative sign indicates that the government deficit is higher than investment expenditure.

Chart 5

Spain: Potential future debt ratios under alternative assumptions for fiscal balance ratios
(as a percentage of GDP)

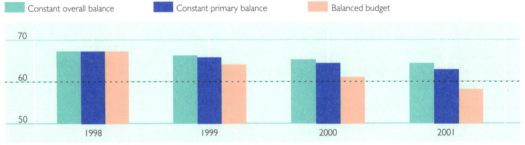

Source: European Commission (spring 1998 forecasts) and EMI calculations.
Note: The three scenarios assume that the debt ratio of 67.4% of GDP for 1998 is as forecast and that the 1998 overall balance of -2.2% of GDP or the primary balance of 2.1% of GDP will be kept constant over the period considered (as a percentage of GDP), or, alternatively, that a balanced budget is maintained from 1999 onwards. The underlying assumptions are a real trend GDP growth rate in 1998 of 2.9% as estimated by the Commission; an inflation rate of 2%; and, in the constant primary balance scenario, a nominal interest rate of 6%. Stock-flow adjustments are disregarded.

Table 7

Spain: Projections of elderly dependency ratio

	1990	2000	2010	2020	2030
Elderly dependency ratio (population aged 65 and over as a proportion of the population aged 15-64)	19.8	23.5	25.9	30.7	41.0

Source: Bos, E. et al. (1994), World population projections 1994-95, World Bank, Washington DC.

III Exchange rate developments

Table 8

(a) Spain: Exchange rate stability
(1 March 1996 - 27 February 1998)

Membership of the Exchange Rate Mechanism (ERM)	Yes	
Membership since	19 June 1989	
Devaluation of bilateral central rate on country's own initiative	No	
Maximum upward (+) and downward (-) deviations from central rates in the ERM grid (%) against[a]		
Belgian franc	2.0	-0.2
Danish krone	3.5	0.2
Deutsche Mark	2.4	-0.1
French franc	3.3	0.2
Irish pound	5.1	-9.7
Italian lira	1.4	-0.9
Dutch guilder	1.7	-0.5
Austrian schilling	2.4	-0.1
Portuguese escudo	2.4	-1.7
Finnish markka	0.2	-2.1

Source: European Commission and EMI calculations.

(a) Daily data at business frequency; 10-day moving average. Deviations against the Finnish markka refer to the period from 14 October 1996 onwards, while deviations against the Italian lira refer to the period from 25 November 1996 onwards.

(b) Key indicators of exchange rate pressure for the Spanish peseta

Average of 3 months ending:	May 96	Aug 96	Nov 96	Feb 97	May 97	Aug 97	Nov 97	Feb 98
Exchange rate volatility[a]	3.7	2.9	1.3	2.2	1.6	1.4	0.8	0.5
Short-term interest rate differentials[b]	4.4	3.8	3.6	2.9	2.3	2.0	1.6	1.1

Source: European Commission, national data and EMI calculations.

(a) Annualised monthly standard deviation of daily percentage changes of the exchange rate against the DEM, in percentages.

(b) Differential of three-month interbank interest rates against a weighted average of interest rates in Belgium, Germany, France, the Netherlands and Austria, in percentage points.

Chart 6

Spanish peseta: Deviations from ERM bilateral central rates
(daily data; percentages; 1 March 1996 to 27 February 1998)

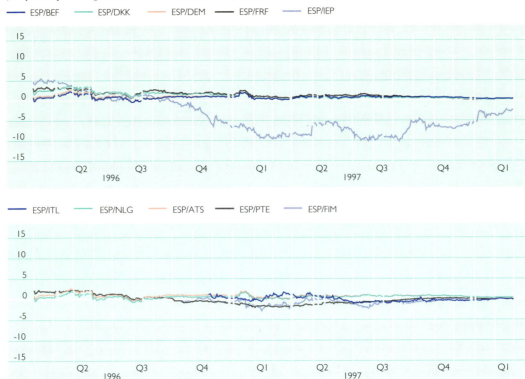

Source: European Commission.
Note: Deviations against the Finnish markka refer to the period from 14 October 1996 onwards, while deviations against the Italian lira refer to the period from 25 November 1996 onwards.

Table 9

Spanish peseta: Measures of the real effective exchange rate vis-à-vis ERM Member States

(monthly data; percentage deviations; February 1998 compared with different benchmark periods)

	Average Apr 73-Feb 98	Average Jan 87-Feb 98	Average 1987
Real effective exchange rates:			
CPI-based	0.3	-5.1	3.5
PPI/WPI-based	-1.6	-3.8	2.2
Memo item:			
Nominal effective exchange rate	-27.8	-12.1	-12.4

Source: BIS and EMI calculations.
Note: A positive (negative) sign indicates an appreciation (depreciation).

Table 10

Spain: External developments
(as a percentage of GDP)

	1990	1991	1992	1993	1994	1995	1996	1997[a]
Current account plus new capital account[b]	-3.4	-3.0	-3.0	-0.4	-0.8	1.2	1.3	1.4
Net foreign assets (+) or liabilities (-)[c]	-11.6	-14.4	-17.3	-19.7	-19.8	-18.6	-18.0	.
Exports (goods and services)[d]	17.1	18.0	19.2	21.1	24.1	25.4	27.2	29.7
Imports (goods and services)[e]	20.4	21.8	23.1	22.2	24.2	25.6	26.6	28.3

Source: National data except exports and imports (European Commission, spring 1998 forecasts).

(a) Partly estimated.

(b) According to the 5th edition of the IMF Balance of Payments Manual, which is conceptually the equivalent of the current account in previous editions of the Manual.

(c) International investment position (IIP) as defined by the IMF (see Balance of Payments Yearbook, Part 1, 1994), or the closest possible substitute.

(d) In 1996 the share of intra-EU exports of goods in national exports of goods was 71.0%; Direction of Trade Statistics Yearbook 1997, IMF.

(e) In 1996 the share of intra-EU imports of goods in national imports of goods was 66.3%; Direction of Trade Statistics Yearbook 1997, IMF.

IV Long-term interest rate developments

Table 11

Spain: Long-term interest rates
(percentages)

	1996	1997	Nov 97	Dec 97	Jan 98	**Feb 97- Jan 98**
Long-term interest rate	8.7	6.4	6.0	5.6	5.4	6.3
Reference value	9.1	8.0	-	-	-	7.8

Source: European Commission.

Chart 7

(a) Spain: Long-term interest rate
(monthly averages; in percentages)

(b) Spain: Long-term interest rate and CPI inflation differentials against EU countries
with lowest long-term interest rates*
(monthly averages; in percentage points)

Source: Interest rates: European Commission (where these are not available the most comparable data have been used); the CPI data used are non-harmonised national data.
* Weighted average of data for Belgium, Germany, France, the Netherlands and Austria.

FRANCE

Price developments

Over the reference period from February 1997 to January 1998 the average rate of HICP inflation in France was 1.2%, i.e. well below the reference value of 2.7%. This was also the case in 1997 as a whole. In 1996 average HICP inflation was 2.1% (see Table 1). Seen over the past two years, HICP inflation in France has been low and has fallen to a level which is generally considered to be consistent with price stability.

Looking back, consumer price inflation in France, as measured on the basis of the CPI, has followed a downward trend since the early 1990s. Since 1993 inflation has been close to or below 2% (see Chart 1). This experience of low inflation reflects a number of important policy choices, in particular the continued orientation of monetary policy towards exchange rate and price stability within the framework of the ERM. Recent adjustments in fiscal policy, together with some structural measures aimed at increasing product market competition, especially in formerly sheltered sectors, have reinforced the low inflation climate. In addition, the macroeconomic environment has contributed to containing upward pressure on prices. Notably, a negative output gap emerged in the context of the 1993 recession (see Table 2). Since 1994 economic growth has recovered, but this has not been sufficient to eliminate the output gap. Against this background, growth in unit labour costs has been moderate since 1994. Moreover, the broadly stable effective exchange rate during the 1990s has helped to keep growth in import prices subdued. Low rates of inflation are also apparent when it is measured in terms of other relevant price indices (see Table 2).

Looking at recent trends and forecasts, current outturns for consumer price inflation (measured as a percentage change over the corresponding month a year earlier) have been decreasing to ½% and there are no signs of immediate upward pressure on the basis of the measures shown in Table 3a. Forecasts of inflation suggest rates of generally well below 2% for 1998 and 1999 (see Table 3b). Risks for price stability over this period are associated with a narrowing of the output gap.

Looking further ahead, maintaining an environment conducive to price stability relates in France to, inter alia, the conduct of fiscal policies over the medium to long term; it will be equally important to strengthen national policies aimed at enhancing competition in product markets and improving the functioning of labour markets against the background of the current high rate of unemployment in France.

Fiscal developments

In the *reference year* 1997 the deficit ratio was 3.0%, i.e. at the level of the 3% reference value, and the debt ratio was 58.0%, i.e. just below the 60% reference value. Compared with the previous year, the deficit ratio has been reduced by 1.1 percentage points and the debt ratio has increased by 2.3 percentage points. In 1998 the deficit ratio is forecast to decrease to 2.9% of GDP, while the debt ratio is projected to increase marginally to 58.1%. In 1996 and 1997 the deficit ratio exceeded the ratio of public investment expenditure to GDP by 1.5 percentage points and 0.2 percentage points respectively (see Table 4).

Looking back over the years 1990 to 1997, the French *debt-to-GDP ratio* increased by 22.5 percentage points (see Chart 2a). As is shown in greater detail in Chart 2b, the main factors underlying the evolution of the debt ratio were, on the one hand, primary deficits recorded in the years 1992-96 and, on the other, the debt-increasing effects of a negative growth/ interest rate differential over the whole period. "Stock-flow adjustments" played a relatively minor role, albeit increasing debt in most years. Only in 1997 did the primary balance again show a small surplus, thereby marginally curbing the growth of the debt ratio. The patterns observed thus far during the 1990s may be seen as indicative of the risks to the debt ratio which can arise when the lasting effects of an unfavourable growth/interest rate differential are not counteracted by primary surpluses. In this context, it may be noted that the share of debt with a short-term residual maturity has remained at relatively high levels since the early 1990s (though decreasing), while the average maturity has remained broadly stable (see Table 5). With regard to 1997, the proportion of debt with a short-term residual maturity is still relatively high, and, taking into account the current level of the debt ratio, fiscal balances are relatively sensitive to changes in interest rates. On the other hand, the proportion of foreign currency debt in France is low and most is in ECU and may eventually be redenominated in euro; hence, fiscal balances are relatively insensitive to changes in exchange rates.

During the 1990s a pattern of first deteriorating and subsequently improving outturns was observed in the *deficit-to-GDP ratio*. Starting from a ratio of 1.6% in 1990, the deficit increased sharply to reach a peak of 5.8% in 1994; since then, the deficit has declined year by year to stand at 3.0% in 1997 (see Chart 3a). As is shown in greater detail in Chart 3b, which focuses on *changes* in deficits, cyclical factors played a dominant role in increasing the deficit ratio in 1991 and 1993, and in checking its increase in 1994. Thereafter, mainly "non-cyclical" factors contributed to the reduction in deficits. However, these non-cyclical

improvements could reflect a lasting, "structural" move towards more balanced fiscal policies and/or a variety of measures with temporary effects. Evidence available suggests that measures with a temporary effect played a deficit-reducing role in 1997, amounting to 0.6% of GDP. As they were mainly of a "self-reversing" nature, compensating measures already included in the 1998 budget will need to yield their expected results and, in addition, compensating measures will need to be taken in later years when the self-reversing effects unwind.

Moving on to examine trends in other fiscal indicators, it can be seen from Chart 4 that the general government *total expenditure ratio* rose sharply between 1990 and 1993. In particular, current transfers increased substantially, reflecting a marked increase in social spending, particularly on pensions, health care and unemployment benefits; but public consumption and interest payments as a percentage of GDP also increased (see Table 6). More recently, the total expenditure ratio has been declining, mainly reflecting a reduction in net capital expenditure in relation to GDP, as well as lower ratios of current transfers and public consumption to GDP. On balance, the expenditure ratio in 1997 was nearly 3½ percentage points higher than at the beginning of the 1990s, reflecting higher ratios to GDP for all major items with the exception of public investment and other net capital expenditure. Given this pattern, a continuation of the downward trend of total expenditure to GDP would appear to require greater adjustments in items other than public investment. *Government revenue* in relation to GDP has tended to increase since 1994; it was nearly 2 percentage points higher in 1997 than in 1990, and it may have approached a level which is detrimental to economic growth.

According to the French *medium-term fiscal policy strategy*, as presented in the

Convergence Programme for 1997-2001 dated February 1997, the general government deficit is expected to decline to 2.7-2.8% of GDP and the debt ratio to increase to 58.5-59.0% of GDP in 1998, depending on economic developments. The budget plan for 1998 foresees a somewhat lower debt ratio and a deficit of 3% of GDP, which is somewhat higher than envisaged in the updated programme. A marginal reduction in the central government deficit ratio is foreseen through a stabilisation of expenditure in real terms. In particular, there are plans to reduce public consumption and social security spending. Currently, there is no evidence of significant measures with a temporary effect in the 1998 budget. The deficit ratio is projected to be cut gradually to less than 1.5% by 2001 and the ratio of government debt to GDP is expected to remain at just under 60% before declining. Compared with fiscal balances projected in the Convergence Programme for 1999-2000, further substantial progress in fiscal consolidation is required in order to comply with the medium-term objective of the Stability and Growth Pact, effective from 1999 onwards, of having a budgetary position that is close to balance or in surplus.

With regard to the *potential future course of the debt ratio,* the EMI's Report does not consider this issue in detail for those countries with a debt ratio of below 60% of GDP. It is, however, important to highlight the fact that current fiscal positions, in terms of both overall and primary balances, would not appear to be sufficient to stabilise the debt ratio at below 60%, while over time a balanced budget would allow it to be brought further below the reference value. In order to allow for a stabilisation of the debt ratio at just below 60% of GDP, a deficit ratio of just below 2.5% would be required. As noted above, a further reduction in the deficit ratio is necessary in the context of the Stability and Growth Pact. Such considerations are also important in the case of France since additional room for manoeuvre will be necessary in order to be able to address *future budgetary*

challenges. As is highlighted in Table 7, from around 2010 onwards a marked ageing of the population is expected and, in the context of an unfunded pension system, public pension expenditure is forecast to increase in terms of GDP, particularly if policies regarding benefits continue unchanged. The overall burden of population ageing will become the more manageable the better the state of public finances when the demographic situation worsens.

Exchange rate developments

The French franc has been participating in the ERM since its inception on 13 March 1979, i.e. for much longer than two years prior to the examination (see Table 8a). As mentioned above, French monetary policy has focused on exchange rate and price stability within the framework of the ERM. Focusing on the *reference period* from March 1996 to February 1998, the currency has normally traded close to its central rates against other ERM currencies (see Chart 5 and Table 8a). On occasion the French franc traded outside a range close to its central rates vis-à-vis various partner currencies. The maximum upward and downward deviations from central rates, on the basis of 10 business day moving averages, were 0.6% and -3.5% respectively, abstracting from the autonomous upward trend of the Irish pound (see Table 8a). The episodes in which such deviations occurred were temporary, the degree of exchange rate volatility vis-à-vis the Deutsche Mark was low and declining (see Table 8b) and short-term interest rate differentials against those EU countries with the lowest short-term interest rates were small and narrowing. During the reference period France has not devalued its currency's bilateral central rate against any other Member State's currency.

In a longer-term context, measures of the real effective exchange rate of the French franc vis-à-vis the currencies of ERM participating Member States depicted in Table 9 suggest that current levels are close to historical values. As regards other external developments, France has maintained current account surpluses in recent years, a situation which has been reflected in an improvement in the net external liability position (see Table 10). It may also be recalled that, according to the most recent data available, France has a ratio of foreign trade to GDP of 29% for exports and 25% for imports, and a share of intra-EU trade of 63% for exports as well as for imports.

Long-term interest rate developments

Over the *reference period* from February 1997 to January 1998 *long-term interest rates* in France were 5.5% on average, and thus stood well below the reference value for the interest rate criterion of 7.8% set on the basis of the three best-performing Member States in terms of price stability. This was also the case for 1997 as a whole, as well as for 1996 (see Table 11).

Long-term interest rates have been on a broadly declining trend since the early 1990s (see Chart 6a). A close convergence of French long-term interest rates with those prevailing in the EU countries with the lowest bond yields has been observed throughout most of the 1990s (see Chart 6b). The main factors underlying this trend were the comparatively low rate of inflation, the relative stability of the French franc's exchange rate, the pursuit of a similar monetary policy stance to that followed in the above-mentioned countries and, more recently, an improvement in the fiscal position.

Concluding summary

Over the reference period France has achieved a rate of HICP inflation of 1.2%,

which is well below the reference value stipulated by the Treaty and one of the three lowest inflation rates in the Union. The increase in unit labour costs was subdued and low rates of inflation were also apparent in terms of other relevant price indices. Looking ahead, there are no signs of immediate upward pressure on inflation; forecasts project inflation will stand at well below 2% in 1998 and 1999. The French franc has been participating in the ERM for much longer than two years. Over the reference period it remained broadly stable, generally close to its unchanged central parities, without the need for measures to support the exchange rate. The level of long-term interest rates was 5.5%, i.e. well below the respective reference value.

In 1997 France achieved a fiscal deficit ratio of 3.0% of GDP, i.e. a level equal to the reference value, and the outlook is for virtually no further improvement in 1998 (a decrease to 2.9%) in spite of the favourable conjunctural situation. In addition, the fiscal debt ratio, though increasing to 58.0% of GDP in 1997, remained just below the 60% reference value; the outlook is for a marginal increase to 58.1% in 1998. Regarding the sustainability of fiscal developments, keeping the deficit ratio at current levels would not be sufficient to keep the debt ratio below 60% of GDP, thus pointing to a need for further substantial progress in consolidation. The Stability and Growth Pact also requires as a medium-term objective a budgetary position that is close to balance or in surplus. This would also imply a reduction in the debt ratio to further below 60% of GDP.

With regard to other factors, in 1996 and 1997 the deficit ratio exceeded the ratio of public investment expenditure to GDP. Furthermore, France has recorded current account surpluses and a net external liability position.

List of Tables and Charts*

FRANCE

I   Price developments

II   Fiscal developments

III   Exchange rate developments

IV   Long-term interest rate developments

---

* Chart scales may differ across countries.

1 Price developments

France: HICP inflation
(annual percentage changes)

	1996	1997	Nov 97	Dec 97	Jan 98	**Feb 97- Jan 98**
HICP inflation	2.1	1.3	1.4	1.2	0.6	1.2
Reference value	2.5	2.7	-	-	-	2.7

Source: European Commission.

France: Price developments
(annual percentage changes)

— CPI　　— Unit labour costs　　— Import price deflator

Source: National data.

Table 2

France: Measures of inflation and related indicators
(annual percentage changes unless otherwise stated)

	1990	1991	1992	1993	1994	1995	1996	1997[a]
Measures of inflation								
Consumer price index (CPI)	3.4	3.2	2.4	2.1	1.7	1.8	2.0	1.2
CPI excluding changes in net indirect taxes[b]	.	3.9	3.6	2.6	1.5	1.1	1.1	0.8
Private consumption deflator	2.8	3.1	2.4	2.2	2.1	1.5	1.8	1.4
GDP deflator	3.1	3.3	2.1	2.5	1.6	1.6	1.2	1.2
Producer prices[c]	1.4	0.8	-0.3	-0.5	0.8	1.7	-1.1	-0.4
Related indicators								
Real GDP growth	2.5	0.8	1.2	-1.3	2.8	2.1	1.5	2.4
Output gap (p.pts)	3.2	2.0	1.2	-2.0	-1.1	-1.0	-1.5	-1.2
Unemployment rate (%)	8.9	9.5	10.4	11.7	12.3	11.6	12.3	12.6
Unit labour costs, whole economy	4.1	3.6	2.7	3.1	-0.3	1.8	1.4	1.3
Compensation per employee, whole economy	4.9	4.4	4.3	2.7	2.2	2.7	2.7	3.2
Labour productivity, whole economy	0.8	0.8	1.6	-0.4	2.5	0.9	1.3	1.9
Import price deflator	-1.3	0.0	-2.6	-2.5	1.7	1.3	1.1	0.9
Exchange rate appreciation[d]	5.8	-2.1	3.3	2.3	0.7	3.6	0.2	-3.5
Broad monetary aggregate (M3H)[e]	9.1	6.3	4.4	1.5	-2.7	4.1	0.8	-0.7
Stock prices	4.2	-3.9	4.9	8.8	2.1	-9.1	11.2	31.9
House prices	16.7	-0.4	-5.7	1.7	2.8	-4.3	-7.0	-2.0

Source: National data except real GDP growth and the output gap (European Commission, spring 1998 forecasts) and exchange rate (BIS).
(a) Partly estimated.
(b) National estimates.
(c) Manufacturing sector.
(d) Nominal effective exchange rate against 25 industrialised countries.
Note: A positive (negative) sign indicates an appreciation (depreciation).
(e) National harmonised data.

Table 3

France: Recent inflation trends and forecasts
(annual percentage change unless otherwise stated)

(a) Recent trends in consumer price inflation

	Sep 97	Oct 97	Nov 97	Dec 97	Jan 98
National consumer price index (CPI)					
Annual percentage change	1.3	1.0	1.3	1.1	0.5
Change in the average of latest 3 months from previous 3 months, annualised rate, seasonally adjusted	1.7	1.7	1.3	0.9	0.5
Change in the average of latest 6 months from previous 6 months, annualised rate, seasonally adjusted	0.8	0.8	1.0	1.1	1.2

Source: National non-harmonised data.

(b) Inflation forecasts

	1998	1999
European Commission (spring 1998), HICP	1.0	1.6
OECD (December 1997), private consumption deflator	1.4	1.5
IMF (October 1997), CPI	1.3	.

Source: European Commission (spring 1998 forecasts), OECD and IMF.

II Fiscal developments

Table 4

France: General government financial position
(as a percentage of GDP)

	1996	**1997**	1998[a]
General government surplus (+) / deficit (-)	-4.1	-3.0	-2.9
Reference value	-3	-3	-3
Surplus (+) / deficit (-), net of public investment expenditure[b]	-1.5	-0.2	.
General government gross debt	55.7	58.0	58.1
Reference value	60	60	60

Source: European Commission (spring 1998 forecasts) and EMI calculations.
(a) European Commission projections.
(b) A negative sign indicates that the government deficit is higher than investment expenditure.

Chart 2

France: General government gross debt
(as a percentage of GDP)

(a) Levels

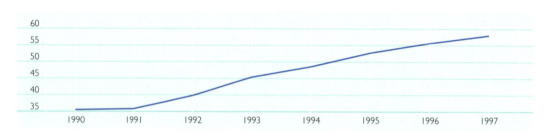

(b) Annual changes and underlying factors

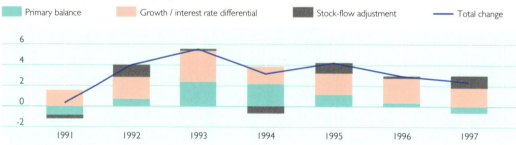

Source: European Commission (spring 1998 forecasts) and EMI calculations.
Note: In Chart 2b negative values indicate a contribution of the respective factor to a decrease in the debt ratio, while positive values indicate a contribution to its increase.

130

Table 5

France: General government gross debt – structural features

	1990	1991	1992	1993	1994	1995	1996	1997
Total debt (as a percentage of GDP)	35.5	35.8	39.8	45.3	48.5	52.7	55.7	58.0
Composition by currency (% of total)								
In domestic currency	97.7	97.2	97.2	96.9	96.5	96.3	94.2	93.0
In foreign currencies	2.3	2.8	2.8	3.1	3.5	3.7	5.8	7.0
Domestic ownership (% of total)	83.0	81.0	78.6	76.8	83.9	85.0	87.3	86.7
Average maturity[a] (years)	4.6	4.8	5.2	5.3	5.4	5.3	5.3	5.3
Composition by maturity[b] (% of total)								
Short-term[c] (< 1 year)	33.5	32.6	32.5	31.2	27.1	28.7	30.0	29.4
Medium-term (1-5 years)	34.8	35.4	33.3	32.9	32.5	30.7	28.1	29.5
Long-term (> 5 years)	31.7	32.0	34.2	35.9	40.4	40.6	41.9	41.1

Source: National data except for total debt (European Commission (spring 1998 forecasts)). End-year data. Differences in the totals are due to rounding.
(a) Residual maturity.
(b) Residual maturity. Where residual maturity is less than 5 years, floating rate notes are classified as short-term notes.
(c) Including short-term debt and debt linked to short-term interest rates.

Chart 3

France: General government surplus (+) / deficit (-)
(as a percentage of GDP)

(a) Levels

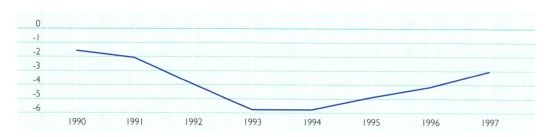

(b) Annual changes and underlying factors

Source: European Commission (spring 1998 forecasts).
Note: In Chart 3b negative values indicate a contribution to an increase in deficits, while positive values indicate a contribution to their reduction.

Chart 4

France: General government expenditure and receipts
(as a percentage of GDP)

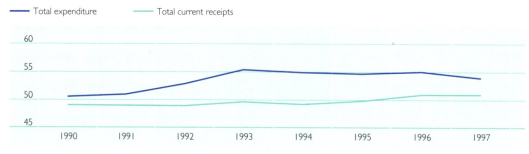

Source: European Commission (spring 1998 forecasts).

Table 6

France: General government budgetary position

(as a percentage of GDP)

	1990	1991	1992	1993	1994	1995	1996	1997
Total current receipts	49.0	49.0	48.9	49.6	49.2	49.8	50.9	50.9
Taxes	24.0	24.0	23.5	23.9	24.4	24.7	25.6	26.3
Social security contributions	21.0	21.0	21.3	21.6	21.1	21.3	21.6	21.0
Other current receipts	4.0	4.0	4.1	4.2	3.7	3.8	3.7	3.6
Total expenditure	50.6	51.0	52.9	55.4	55.0	54.7	55.0	54.0
Current transfers	25.6	26.3	27.3	28.7	28.2	28.2	28.5	28.4
Actual interest payments	2.9	2.9	3.2	3.4	3.6	3.7	3.8	3.6
Public consumption	18.0	18.2	18.9	19.9	19.5	19.3	19.5	19.4
Net capital expenditure	4.0	3.5	3.5	3.5	3.7	3.4	3.3	2.6
Surplus (+) or deficit (-)	-1.6	-2.1	-3.9	-5.8	-5.8	-4.9	-4.1	-3.0
Primary balance	1.4	0.9	-0.7	-2.4	-2.2	-1.1	-0.3	0.6
Surplus (+) or deficit (-), net of public investment expenditure[a]	.	.	.	-2.5	-2.6	-1.8	-1.5	-0.2

Source: European Commission (spring 1998 forecasts) and EMI calculations. Differences in the totals are due to rounding.
(a) A negative sign indicates that the government deficit is higher than investment expenditure.

Table 7

France: Projections of elderly dependency ratio

	1990	2000	2010	2020	2030
Elderly dependency ratio (population aged 65 and over as a proportion of the population aged 15-64)	20.8	23.6	24.6	32.3	39.1

Source: Bos, E. et al. (1994), World population projections 1994-95, World Bank, Washington DC.

III Exchange rate developments

Table 8

(a) France: Exchange rate stability
(1 March 1996 – 27 February 1998)

Membership of the Exchange Rate Mechanism (ERM)	Yes
Membership since	13 March 1979
Devaluation of bilateral central rate on country's own initiative	No

Maximum upward (+) and downward (-) deviations from central rates
in the ERM grid (%) against[a]

Belgian franc	0.3	-2.4
Danish krone	0.4	-0.9
Deutsche Mark	0.2	-2.1
Spanish peseta	-0.2	-3.2
Irish pound	1.9	-11.1
Italian lira	0.6	-2.4
Dutch guilder	0.3	-2.7
Austrian schilling	0.2	-2.2
Portuguese escudo	0.0	-3.4
Finnish markka	-0.1	-3.5

Source: European Commission and EMI calculations.
(a) Daily data at business frequency; 10-day moving average. Deviations against the Finnish markka refer to the period from 14 October 1996 onwards, while deviations against the Italian lira refer to the period from 25 November 1996 onwards.

(b) Key indicators of exchange rate pressure for the French franc

Average of 3 months ending:	May 96	Aug 96	Nov 96	Feb 97	May 97	Aug 97	Nov 97	Feb 98
Exchange rate volatility[a]	1.8	1.5	1.9	1.2	0.9	1.1	0.5	0.3
Short-term interest rate differentials[b]	0.5	0.4	0.3	0.2	0.1	0.1	0.0	0.0

Source: European Commission, national data and EMI calculations.
(a) Annualised monthly standard deviation of daily percentage changes of the exchange rate against the DEM, in percentages.
(b) Differential of three-month interbank interest rates against a weighted average of interest rates in Belgium, Germany, France, the Netherlands and Austria, in percentage points.

Chart 5

French franc: Deviations from ERM bilateral central rates
(daily data; percentages; 1 March 1996 to 27 February 1998)

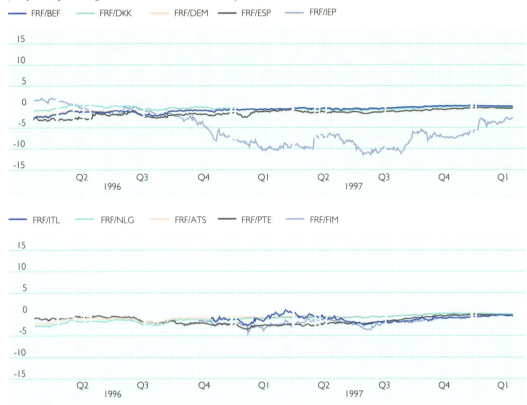

— FRF/BEF   — FRF/DKK   — FRF/DEM   ▬▬ FRF/ESP   — FRF/IEP

— FRF/ITL   — FRF/NLG   — FRF/ATS   — FRF/PTE   — FRF/FIM

Source: European Commission.
Note: Deviations against the Finnish markka refer to the period from 14 October 1996 onwards, while deviations against the Italian lira refer to the period from 25 November 1996 onwards.

Table 9

French franc: Measures of the real effective exchange rate vis-à-vis ERM Member States
(monthly data; percentage deviations; February 1998 compared with different benchmark periods)

	Average Apr 73-Feb 98	Average Jan 87-Feb 98	Average 1987
Real effective exchange rates:			
CPI-based	-2.2	0.2	-1.5
PPI/WPI-based	-0.8	-0.5	-1.6
Memo item:			
Nominal effective exchange rate	1.5	6.3	10.1

Source: BIS and EMI calculations.
Note: A positive (negative) sign indicates an appreciation (depreciation).

135

Table 10

France: External developments
(as a percentage of GDP)

	1990	1991	1992	1993	1994	1995	1996	1997[a]
Current account plus new capital account[b]	-0.8	-0.5	0.4	0.9	0.6	0.7	1.3	2.9
Net foreign assets (+) or liabilities (-)[c]	.	-8.3	-7.4	-9.1	-4.4	-1.9	-0.4	.
Exports (goods and services)[d]	22.6	23.3	24.2	24.4	25.1	26.2	27.0	29.3
Imports (goods and services)[e]	22.6	23.1	23.1	22.6	23.4	24.1	24.4	25.3

Source: National data except exports and imports (European Commission, spring 1998 forecasts).

(a) Partly estimated.

(b) According to the 5th edition of the IMF Balance of Payments Manual, which is conceptually the equivalent of the current account in previous editions of the Manual.

(c) International investment position (IIP) as defined by the IMF (see Balance of Payments Yearbook, Part 1, 1994), or the closest possible substitute.

(d) In 1996 the share of intra-EU exports of goods in total national exports of goods was 62.6%; Direction of Trade Statistics Yearbook 1997, IMF.

(e) In 1996 the share of intra-EU imports of goods in total national imports of goods was 63.3%; Direction of Trade Statistics Yearbook 1997, IMF.

IV Long-term interest rate developments

Table 11

France: Long-term interest rates
(percentages)

	1996	1997	Nov 97	Dec 97	Jan 98	**Feb 97- Jan 98**
Long-term interest rate	6.3	5.6	5.6	5.3	5.1	5.5
Reference value	9.1	8.0	-	-	-	7.8

Source: European Commission.

Chart 6

(a) France: Long-term interest rate
(monthly averages; in percentags)

(b) France: Long-term interest rate and CPI inflation differentials against EU countries with lowest long-term interest rates*
(monthly averages; in percentage points)

— Long-term interest rate differential   — CPI inflation differential

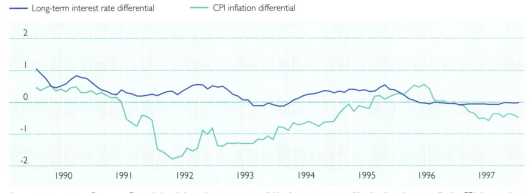

Source: Interest rates: European Commission (where these are not available the most comparable data have been used); the CPI data used are non-harmonised national data.
* Weighted average of data for Belgium, Germany, France, the Netherlands and Austria.

137

IRELAND

Price developments

Over the reference period from February 1997 to January 1998 the average rate of HICP inflation in Ireland was 1.2%, i.e. well below the reference value of 2.7%. This was also the case in 1997 as a whole. In 1996 average HICP inflation was 2.2%. Seen over the past two years, HICP inflation in Ireland has been low and has fallen to a level which is generally considered to be consistent with price stability.

Looking back, consumer price inflation in Ireland, as measured on the basis of the CPI, has followed a broad downward trend since the early 1990s (see Chart 1). Inflation fell from 3.4% in 1990 to 1.5% in 1993. Thereafter, it rose to around 2.5% in 1994-95, before declining again to around 1.5% in 1996-97. This experience of a general decline in rates of inflation reflects a number of important policy choices, notably a monetary policy stance geared towards the primary objective of price stability within the framework of the ERM. The reduction in inflation has also been supported by other policies, in particular wage moderation. With regard to the macroeconomic environment, it is notable that lower inflation has been achieved against the background of buoyant real GDP growth, which stood at over 7% on average in the eight years to 1997 (see Table 2). Notwithstanding a tightening of labour market conditions, growth in compensation per employee was moderate in 1994-96. In 1997 wage increases picked up while remaining moderate in manufacturing industry. In combination with strong growth in labour productivity, unit labour costs have declined from 1994 onwards. Import price increases have varied in recent years, partly as a result of effective exchange rate movements, but were subdued in 1996-97. Low rates of inflation are also apparent when it is measured in terms of other relevant price indices (see Table 2).

Looking at recent trends and forecasts, the latest available outturns for consumer price inflation (measured as a percentage change over the corresponding month a year earlier) show a rate of inflation of 1.6% but there are some signs of immediate upward pressure on the basis of the measures shown in Table 3a. Forecasts of inflation suggest it may rise towards 3% over the next two years (see Table 3b). Risks for price stability over this period are mainly associated with the domestic environment, in particular strong money and credit growth, the procyclical fiscal policy, the development of asset prices, tight labour market conditions and strong GDP growth. These risks to inflation are being exacerbated in the run-up to EMU by the expected further decline in short-term interest rates and, should this materialise, by a resulting decline in the effective exchange rate.

Looking further ahead, maintaining an environment conducive to price stability relates in Ireland to, inter alia, the conduct of fiscal policies over the medium to long term; it will be equally important to maintain policies aimed at enhancing competition in product markets and improving the functioning of labour markets against the background of the current high, albeit declining, rate of unemployment in Ireland.

Fiscal developments

In the *reference year* 1997 Ireland recorded a general government surplus of 0.9% of GDP, thereby comfortably meeting the 3% reference value, and the debt ratio was 66.3%, i.e. above the 60% reference value. Compared with the previous year, the fiscal balance has improved by 1.3

percentage points and the debt ratio has decreased by 6.4 percentage points. In 1998 the fiscal surplus is forecast to increase to 1.1% of GDP, while the debt ratio is projected to decline to 59.5%, i.e. just below the reference value. In 1996 the deficit ratio did not exceed the ratio of public investment expenditure to GDP.

Looking back over the years 1990 to 1997, the Irish *debt-to-GDP ratio* declined by 29.7 percentage points. Initially the ratio fluctuated around its 1990 level of 96.0%, but since 1994 a strong downward trend has been apparent, with a continuous reduction in the debt from 96.3% in 1993 to 66.3% in 1997 (see Chart 2a), i.e. a decline of 30.0 percentage points over four years. As is shown in greater detail in Chart 2b, the main forces underlying this reduction were sizable primary surpluses, combined with a very favourable growth and interest rate environment since 1994. Only in 1993 did significant "stock-flow adjustments" increase the debt ratio, owing to a valuation effect on foreign currency debt of the depreciation of the Irish pound. The patterns observed thus far during the 1990s may be seen as indicative of the debt-reducing effect of continuous primary surpluses, while, on the other hand, these effects were reinforced by strong growth. In this context, it may be noted that the share of debt with a short-term residual maturity has been low over the 1990s, while the average maturity has decreased (see Table 5). With regard to 1997, taking into account the current level of the debt ratio, fiscal balances are relatively insensitive to changes in interest rates. On the other hand, the proportion of foreign currency debt is relatively high and fiscal balances are relatively sensitive to changes in exchange rates.

During the 1990s a pattern of initially stable and subsequently improving outturns can be observed in the *deficit-to-GDP ratio*, whereby the ratio remained consistently below the 3% reference value. Starting from a ratio of 2.3% in 1990, the deficit remained broadly at that level for several years. Thereafter, there was a sharp improvement, beginning in 1996, leading to a small deficit in that year and to a surplus of 0.9% in 1997 (see Chart 3a). As is shown in greater detail in Chart 3b, which focuses on *changes* in deficits, cyclical factors complicated the stabilisation of the deficit ratio in the early 1990s and played an important role in reducing the deficit ratio later on. In the last two years "non-cyclical" factors also contributed to reducing the deficit. These non-cyclical improvements could reflect a lasting, "structural" move towards more balanced fiscal policies and/ or a variety of measures with temporary effects. However, evidence available suggests that measures with a temporary effect did not play a role in reducing deficits in 1996 or 1997.

Moving on to examine trends in other fiscal indicators, it can be seen from Chart 4 that the general government *total expenditure ratio* was broadly stable between 1990 and 1994. Increased transfer payments and public consumption were compensated for by reduced interest payments (see Table 6). After 1994, however, the expenditure-to-GDP ratio declined and, by 1997, had dropped by 4½ percentage points, reflecting reductions across all major categories of spending relative to GDP. On balance, the expenditure ratio in 1997 was considerably lower than at the beginning of the 1990s, particularly on account of the sharp reduction in interest payments as a consequence of lower interest rates and the reduction in the debt ratio. *Government revenue* in relation to GDP also fell during the 1990s, but this was largely the result of a single drop in 1995 (of 2.5 percentage points) and thereafter the ratio tended to increase slightly. Overall, reductions in expenditure and revenue ratios in Ireland have been dominated by very strong GDP growth.

According to the Irish *medium-term fiscal policy strategy*, as stated in the Convergence Programme for 1997-99 updated in December 1997, a somewhat declining budget surplus and a declining debt ratio are expected in 1998. The budget for 1998 foresees the maintenance of a surplus in the general government financial balance, and a debt ratio which nearly attains the reference value, while Commission forecasts indicate more favourable developments. The 1998 budget contains reductions in income tax rates and increased spending, but owing to the high economic growth rate both revenue and expenditure ratios are expected to decline. Currently, there is no evidence of significant measures with a temporary effect in the 1998 budget. For 1999 the Convergence Programme foresees an increase in the budget surplus to 0.7% of GDP and a debt ratio of 56%. In general, Ireland has outperformed the targets of previous programmes. If fiscal balances turn out as projected in the Convergence Programme for 1999-2000, or are more favourable, Ireland should comply with the medium-term objective of the Stability and Growth Pact, effective from 1999 onwards, of having a budgetary position that is close to balance or in surplus. However, the fiscal position benefits from a strong economy, with the structural balance probably being in a slight deficit position. Therefore, risks may arise if economic growth slows down.

With regard to the *potential future course of the debt ratio,* the EMI's Report does not consider this issue in detail for those countries forecast to have a debt ratio of below 60% of GDP in 1998. Projected developments underline the benefits of the surplus position achieved in 1997, and forecast to increase in 1998, for rapidly reducing the debt ratio. However, stressing the need for sound fiscal balances over time is also evident in the case of Ireland. While the issue of public pension cost is not a major concern in Ireland, given the relatively favourable demographic situation (see Table 7), the pension system's reliance on funded private pensions and the relatively minor role of unfunded social security pensions, challenges remain. As a small open economy Ireland may need to have sufficient room for manoeuvre to react to country-specific circumstances, and it needs to reduce its vulnerability to unexpected shocks which could potentially reverse debt trends. As mentioned above, a decline in growth rates could pose a further challenge to consolidation.

Exchange rate developments

The Irish pound has been participating in the ERM since its inception on 13 March 1979, i.e. for much longer than two years prior to the examination (see Table 8a). As mentioned above, Irish monetary policy has been geared towards the objective of price stability within the context of the ERM. Focusing on the *reference period* from March 1996 to February 1998, the currency, benefiting from sizable interest rate differentials vis-à-vis most partner currencies, has normally traded significantly above its central rates and above a range close to its central rates vis-à-vis partner currencies (see Chart 5 and Table 8a). The maximum upward and downward deviations from central rates, on the basis of 10 business day moving averages, were 12.5% and -4.8% respectively (see Table 8a); at the end of the reference period the Irish pound stood just over 3% above its central rates vis-à-vis other ERM currencies. In parallel with the strength of the Irish pound, the degree of exchange rate volatility vis-à-vis the Deutsche Mark increased until mid-1997 (see Table 8b) and short-term interest rate differentials against those EU countries with the lowest short-term interest rates widened over the same period. The former has decreased and the latter narrowed somewhat in more recent months, while remaining relatively high. During the reference period Ireland has not devalued its currency's bilateral central rate against any other Member State's currency.[10]

In a longer-term context, measures of the real effective exchange rate of the Irish pound vis-à-vis the currencies of ERM participating Member States depicted in Table 9 suggest that current levels are close to historical values. As regards other external developments, Ireland has maintained large current account surpluses in recent years (see Table 10). It may also be recalled that Ireland is a small open economy with, according to the most recent data available, a ratio of foreign trade to GDP of 84% for exports and 63% for imports, and a share of intra-EU trade of 66% for exports and 54% for imports.

Long-term interest rate developments

Over the *reference period* from February 1997 to January 1998 *long-term interest rates* in Ireland were 6.2% on average, and thus stood below the reference value for the interest rate criterion of 7.8% set on the basis of the three best-performing Member States in terms of price stability. This was also the case for 1997 as a whole, as well as for 1996 (see Table 11).

Long-term interest rates have been on a broadly declining trend since the early 1990s (see Chart 6a). A comparatively close convergence of Irish long-term interest rates with those prevailing in the EU countries with the lowest bond yields has been observed over most of the period since the beginning of the 1990s, with the exception of late 1992 and early 1993, the period marked by the ERM crisis (see Chart 6b). The main factors underlying this trend were the comparatively low rates of inflation and the improvement in the country's fiscal position.

Concluding summary

Over the reference period Ireland has achieved a rate of HICP inflation of 1.2%, which is well below the reference value stipulated by the Treaty and one of the three lowest inflation rates in the Union. Unit labour costs declined, and low rates of inflation were also apparent in terms of other relevant price indices. Looking ahead, there are some signs of immediate upward pressure on inflation, which may rise towards 3% over the next two years. The level of long-term interest rates was 6.2%, i.e. below the respective reference value.

The Irish pound has been participating in the ERM for much longer than two years. During the reference period it has normally traded significantly above its unchanged central rates against other ERM currencies, reflecting an autonomous upward trend of the currency in the light of buoyant domestic economic conditions. This is also mirrored in relatively high exchange rate volatility and short-term interest rate differentials, both of which have declined more recently as the Irish pound has moved closer to its bilateral central rates against other ERM currencies.[11]

In 1997 Ireland achieved a general government surplus of 0.9% of GDP, thereby comfortably meeting the 3% reference value, and the outlook is for a surplus of 1.1% of GDP in 1998. The debt-to-GDP ratio is above the 60% reference value. After having reached a peak in 1993, the ratio declined by 30.0 percentage points to stand at 66.3% in 1997, reflecting inter alia very strong real GDP growth. Regarding the sustainability of fiscal developments, the outlook is for a decline

---

[10] With effect from 16 March 1998, i.e. after the reference period applied in this Report, the bilateral central rates of the Irish pound against other currencies of the ERM were revalued by 3%.

[11] With effect from 16 March 1998, i.e. after the reference period referred to in this Report, the bilateral central rates of the Irish pound against other currencies of the ERM were revalued by 3%.

in the debt ratio to 59.5% of GDP in 1998, i.e. just below the reference value. Looking further ahead, if current fiscal surpluses are maintained, Ireland should comply with the medium-term objective of the Stability and Growth Pact, effective from 1999 onwards, of having a budgetary position that is close to balance or in surplus, and the debt ratio would fall further below 60%.

With regard to other factors, in 1996 the deficit position did not exceed the ratio of public investment to GDP. Moreover, Ireland has maintained current account surpluses. In the context of a relatively favourable demographic situation, the pension system relies on funded private pensions and unfunded social security pensions play a relatively minor role.

List of Tables and Charts*

---

* Chart scales may differ across countries.

143

I Price developments

Table I

Ireland: HICP inflation
(annual percentage changes)

	1996	1997	Nov 97	Dec 97	Jan 98	**Feb 97- Jan 98**
HICP inflation	2.2	1.2	1.1	1.0	1.2	1.2
Reference value	2.5	2.7	-	-	-	2.7

Source: European Commission.

Chart I

Ireland: Price developments
(annual percentage changes)

Source: National data.

Table 2

Ireland: Measures of inflation and related indicators
(annual percentage changes unless otherwise stated)

	1990	1991	1992	1993	1994	1995	1996	1997[a]
Measures of inflation								
Consumer price index (CPI)	3.4	3.2	3.0	1.5	2.4	2.5	1.6	1.5
CPI excluding changes in net indirect taxes[b]	4.1	3.3	2.7	1.1	2.1	2.4	1.5	1.2
Private consumption deflator	2.0	3.0	2.5	1.9	2.8	2.0	1.2	1.2
GDP deflator	-0.8	1.8	2.3	4.2	1.1	0.5	1.1	1.6
Producer prices	-1.6	0.8	1.7	4.6	1.1	2.5	0.7	-0.8
Related indicators								
Real GDP growth	8.5	2.4	4.6	3.6	7.8	11.1	8.6	10.0
Output gap (p.pts)	2.2	-0.8	-2.1	-4.7	-4.0	-0.7	0.1	1.9
Unemployment rate (%)	13.3	14.7	15.5	15.6	14.1	12.2	11.8	10.8
Unit labour costs. whole economy	0.0	2.2	3.1	3.8	-1.7	-4.1	-2.6	-1.3
Compensation per employee, whole economy	5.4	4.6	6.8	5.6	2.3	1.9	2.4	4.0
Labour productivity, whole economy	5.4	2.4	3.6	1.8	4.1	6.3	5.1	5.3
Import price deflator	-3.7	2.3	-1.3	4.4	2.7	4.0	-0.7	1.1
Exchange rate appreciation[c]	7.1	-1.6	3.3	-5.9	0.2	1.0	2.3	-0.1
Broad monetary aggregate (M3H)[d]	.	.	.	.	9.3	10.7	14.4	21.3
Stock prices	-4.4	-11.5	-5.2	20.2	17.6	7.5	25.2	33.7
House prices[e]	12.7	2.1	3.5	0.9	4.1	7.2	11.8	15.1

Source: National data except real GDP growth and the output gap (European Commission, spring 1998 forecasts) and exchange rate (BIS).
(a) Partly estimated.
(b) National estimates.
(c) Nominal effective exchange rate against 25 industrialised countries.
     Note: a positive (negative) sign indicates an appreciation (depreciation).
(d) National harmonised data.
(e) Prices for new houses.

Table 3

Ireland: Recent inflation trends and forecasts
(annual percentage change unless otherwise stated)

(a) Recent trends in consumer price inflation

	Sep 97	Oct 97	Nov 97	Dec 97	Jan 98
National consumer price index (CPI)					
Annual percentage change	-	-	1.6	-	-
Change in the average of latest 3 months from previous 3 months, annualised rate, seasonally adjusted	-	-	3.7	-	-
Change in the average of latest 6 months from previous 6 months, annualised rate, seasonally adjusted	-	-	1.6	-	-

Source: National non-harmonised data.

(b) Inflation forecasts

	1998	1999
European Commission (spring 1998), HICP	2.8	3.1
OECD (December 1997), private consumption deflator	2.2	2.4
IMF (October 1997), CPI	2.1	.

Source: European Commission (spring 1998 forecasts), OECD and IMF.

II   Fiscal developments

Table 4

Ireland: General government financial position
(as a percentage of GDP)

	1996	**1997**	1998[a]
General government surplus (+) / deficit (-)	-0.4	0.9	1.1
Reference value	-3	-3	-3
Surplus (+) / deficit (-), net of public investment expenditure[b]	1.8	3.2	.
General government gross debt	72.7	66.3	59.5
Reference value	60	60	60

Source: European Commission (spring 1998 forecasts) and EMI calculations.
(a)   European Commission projections.
(b)   A negative sign indicates that the government deficit is higher than investment expenditure.

Chart 2

Ireland: General government gross debt
(as a percentage of GDP)

(a) Levels

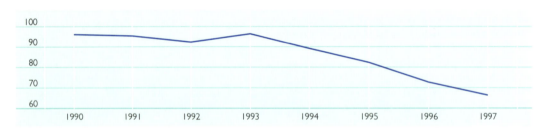

(b) Annual changes and underlying factors

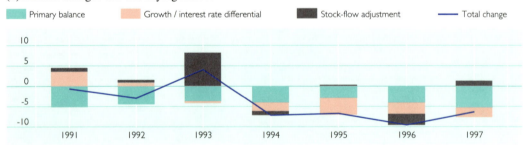

Source: European Commission (spring 1998 forecasts) and EMI calculations.
Note: In Chart 2b negative values indicate a contribution of the respective factor to a decrease in the debt ratio, while positive values indicate a contribution to its increase.

Table 5

Ireland: General government gross debt – structural features

	1990	1991	1992	1993	1994	1995	1996	1997
Total debt (as a percentage of GDP)	96.0	95.3	92.3	96.3	89.1	82.3	72.7	66.3
Composition by currency (% of total)								
In domestic currency	65.9	65.9	60.0	59.0	61.7	65.0	71.6	73.8
In foreign currencies	34.1	34.1	40.0	41.0	38.3	35.0	28.4	26.2
Domestic ownership (% of total)	51.0	50.4	51.4	45.6	49.4	51.1	64.1	.
Average maturity[a] (years)	.	6.7	6.5	6.7	6.0	5.7	5.3	5.0
Composition by maturity[a] (% of total)								
Short-term[b] (≤ 1 year)	.	9.0	9.7	8.7	10.5	9.1	9.2	8.9
Medium-term (2-5 years)	.	41.8	40.0	37.0	38.9	40.4	43.2	44.8
Long-term (> 5 years)	.	49.2	50.3	54.2	50.6	50.5	47.6	46.3

Source: National data except for total debt (European Commission (spring 1998 forecasts)). End-year data. Differences in the totals are due to rounding.
(a) Residual maturity. Government bonds and foreign loans only, which represent between 82.4% (1997) and 90.4% (1993) of the total debt.
(b) Including short-term debt and debt linked to short-term interest rates.

Chart 3

Ireland: General government surplus (+) / deficit (-)
(as a percentage of GDP)

(a) Levels

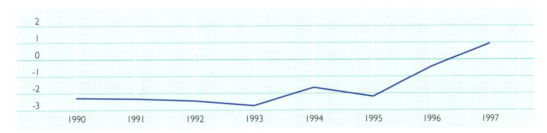

(b) Annual changes and underlying factors

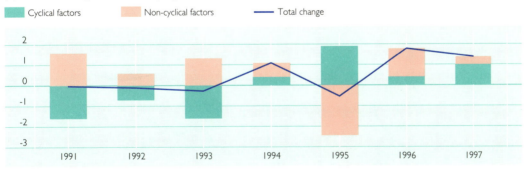

Source: European Commission (spring 1998 forecasts).
Note: In Chart 3b negative values indicate a contribution to an increase in deficits, while positive values indicate a contribution to their reduction.

Chart 4

Ireland: General government expenditure and receipts
(as a percentage of GDP)

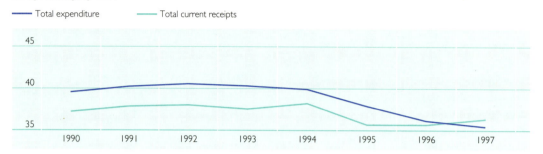

Source: European Commission (spring 1998 forecasts).

Table 6

Ireland: General government budgetary position
(as a percentage of GDP)

	1990	1991	1992	1993	1994	1995	1996	1997
Total current receipts	37.3	37.9	38.1	37.6	38.2	35.7	35.7	36.3
Taxes	29.8	29.9	30.1	29.7	30.9	28.9	29.3	30.2
Social security contributions	5.2	5.3	5.4	5.4	5.2	4.9	4.5	4.5
Other current receipts	2.3	2.6	2.6	2.5	2.1	1.9	1.8	1.7
Total expenditure	39.6	40.2	40.5	40.3	39.9	37.9	36.1	35.4
Current transfers	15.6	16.0	16.6	16.8	16.4	16.1	15.7	15.2
Actual interest payments	7.7	7.5	6.9	6.4	5.6	5.1	4.5	4.3
Public consumption	14.8	15.6	15.8	15.8	15.5	14.8	14.2	14.3
Net capital expenditure	1.4	1.1	1.2	1.2	2.3	1.9	1.8	1.6
Surplus (+) or deficit (-)	-2.3	-2.3	-2.5	-2.7	-1.7	-2.2	-0.4	0.9
Primary balance	5.4	5.1	4.4	3.7	4.0	2.9	4.0	5.2
Surplus (+) or deficit (-), net of public investment expenditure[a]	.	.	.	-0.6	0.7	-0.0	1.8	3.2

Source: European Commission (spring 1998 forecasts) and EMI calculations. Differences in the totals are due to rounding.
(a)   A negative sign indicates that the government deficit is higher than investment expenditure.

Table 7

Ireland: Projections of elderly dependency ratio

	1990	2000	2010	2020	2030
Elderly dependency ratio (population aged 65 and over as a proportion of the population aged 15-64)	18.4	16.7	18.0	21.7	25.3

Source: Bos, E. et al. (1994), World population projections 1994-95, World Bank, Washington DC.

III Exchange rate developments

Table 8

(a) Ireland: Exchange rate stability
(1 March 1996 – 27 February 1998)

Membership of the Exchange Rate Mechanism (ERM)	Yes	
Membership since	13 March 1979	
Devaluation of bilateral central rate on country's own initiative	No	

Maximum upward (+) and downward (-) deviations from central rates
in the ERM grid (%) against[a]

Belgian franc	11.9	-4.1
Danish krone	11.6	-2.5
Deutsche Mark	11.8	-3.7
Spanish peseta	10.7	-4.8
French franc	12.5	-1.8
Italian lira	11.3	2.3
Dutch guilder	11.7	-4.4
Austrian schilling	11.8	-3.8
Portuguese escudo	10.3	-2.9
Finnish markka	10.0	0.6

Source: European Commission and EMI calculations.
(a) Daily data at business frequency; 10-day moving average. Deviations against the Finnish markka refer to the period from 14 October 1996 onwards, while deviations against the Italian lira refer to the period from 25 November 1996 onwards.

(b) Key indicators of exchange rate pressure for the Irish pound

Average of 3 months ending:	May 96	Aug 96	Nov 96	Feb 97	May 97	Aug 97	Nov 97	Feb 98
Exchange rate volatility[a]	3.4	4.8	4.7	7.5	8.2	7.3	6.8	6.1
Short-term interest rate differentials[b]	1.6	2.0	2.4	2.6	2.6	2.9	2.6	2.4

Source: European Commission, national data and EMI calculations.
(a) Annualised monthly standard deviation of daily percentage changes of the exchange rate against the DEM, in percentages.
(b) Differential of three-month interbank interest rates against a weighted average of interest rates in Belgium, Germany, France, the Netherlands and Austria, in percentage points.

Chart 5

Irish pound: Deviations from ERM bilateral central rates
(daily data; percentages; 1 March 1996 to 27 February 1998)

Source: European Commission.

Note: Deviations against the Finnish markka refer to the period from 14 October 1996 onwards, while deviations against the Italian lira refer to the period from 25 November 1996 onwards.

Table 9

Irish pound: Measures of the real effective exchange rate vis-à-vis ERM Member States
(monthly data; percentage deviations; February 1998 compared with different benchmark periods)

	Average Apr 73-Feb 98	Average Jan 87-Feb 98	Average 1987
Real effective exchange rates:			
CPI-based	0.7	-2.1	-5.4
PPI/WPI-based	0.1	0.7	0.4
Memo item:			
Nominal effective exchange rate	-10.4	0.1	-0.8

Source: BIS and EMI calculations.

Note: A positive (negative) sign indicates an appreciation (depreciation).

Table 10

Ireland: External developments
(as a percentage of GDP)

	1990	1991	1992	1993	1994	1995	1996	1997[a]
Current account plus new capital account[b]	0.0	2.1	2.6	5.5	3.6	4.1	3.2	2.8
Net foreign assets (+) or liabilities (-)[c]	.	.	.	.	.	.	.	.
Exports (goods and services)[d]	58.7	60.3	65.5	69.3	73.4	78.9	80.0	83.7
Imports (goods and services)[e]	52.8	52.2	53.4	54.7	57.7	59.6	60.5	62.8

Source: National data except exports and imports (European Commission, spring 1998 forecasts).

(a) Partly estimated.

(b) According to the 5th edition of the IMF Balance of Payments Manual, which is conceptually the equivalent of the current account in previous editions of the Manual.

(c) International investment position (IIP) as defined by the IMF (see Balance of Payments Yearbook, Part 1, 1994), or the closest possible substitute.

(d) In 1996 the share of intra-EU exports of goods in total national exports of goods was 66.0%; Direction of Trade Statistics Yearbook 1997, IMF.

(e) In 1996 the share of intra-EU imports of goods in total national imports of goods was 53.6%; Direction of Trade Statistics Yearbook 1997, IMF.

IV Long-term interest rate developments

Ireland: Long-term interest rates
(percentages)

	1996	1997	Nov 97	Dec 97	Jan 98	**Feb 97- Jan 98**
Long-term interest rate	7.3	6.3	6.0	5.6	5.4	6.2
Reference value	9.1	8.0	-	-	-	7.8

Source: European Commission.

Chart 6

(a) Ireland: Long-term interest rate
   (monthly averages; in percentages)

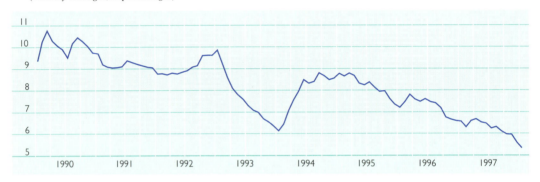

(b) Ireland: Long-term interest rate and CPI inflation differentials against EU countries
   with lowest long-term interest rates*
   (monthly averages; in percentage points)

Source: Interest rates: European Commission (where these are not available the most comparable data have been used); the CPI data used are non-harmonised national data.
* Weighted average of data for Belgium, Germany, France, the Netherlands and Austria

ITALY

Price developments

Over the reference period from February 1997 to January 1998 the average rate of HICP inflation in Italy was 1.8%, i.e. well below the reference value of 2.7%. This was also the case in 1997 as a whole. In 1996 average HICP inflation was 4.0% (see Table 1). Seen over the past two years, Italy has reduced the rate of HICP inflation to a level which is generally considered to be consistent with price stability.

Looking back, consumer price inflation in Italy, as measured on the basis of the CPI, has followed a broad downward trend since the early 1990s (see Chart 1). Inflation gradually declined from 6.4% in 1991 to 3.9% in 1994. Following an interruption in the downward movement in 1995, which was partly due to the impact of increased VAT rates, it has continued to fall at an accelerated pace. This experience of disinflation reflects a number of important policy choices. Most notably, monetary policy has been geared towards the achievement of price stability in the medium term, recently again within the framework of the ERM. The reduction in inflation has been supported by, inter alia, adjustments in fiscal policy, enhanced product market competition and labour market reforms such as the abolition of wage indexation. In addition, the macroeconomic environment has contributed to containing upward pressure on prices. Notably, in the context of the recession in 1993, a negative output gap emerged (see Table 2). The output gap persisted into 1997 as the recovery in economic activity in 1994-95 proved to be short-lived. Against this background, growth in compensation per employee declined in the mid-1990s, which helped to subdue increases in unit labour costs. Wage increases were 5.0% over 1995-97 while over the same period, unit labour costs rose by 3.3% per annum. Meanwhile, import price changes have varied considerably, partly as a result of large effective exchange rate movements, which have complicated the task of controlling inflation in some years. More recently, falling import prices have improved the price climate. The general trend towards low rates of inflation is also apparent when it is measured in terms of other relevant price indices, while some measures exceeded HICP inflation in 1997 (see Table 2).

Looking at recent trends and forecasts, current outturns for consumer price inflation (measured as a percentage change over the corresponding month a year earlier) have been broadly stable at around 1½% and there is little sign of immediate upward pressure on the basis of the measures shown in Table 3a. The most recent forecast of inflation suggests a rate of slightly below 2% for 1998 and of around 2% for 1999 (see Table 3b). Risks for price stability over this period may be associated with higher administered prices and increases in indirect taxes.

Looking further ahead, maintaining an environment conducive to price stability relates in Italy to, inter alia the conduct of fiscal policies over the medium to long term; it will be equally important to strengthen national policies aimed at enhancing competition in product markets and improving the functioning of labour markets against the background of the current high rate of unemployment in Italy.

Fiscal developments

In the *reference year* 1997 the general government deficit ratio was 2.7%, i.e. below the 3% reference value, and the debt ratio was 121.6%, i.e. far above the 60% reference value. Compared with the previous year, the deficit ratio has been reduced by 4.0 percentage points and the debt ratio by 2.4 percentage points. In 1998 the deficit ratio is forecast to decrease to 2.5% of GDP, while the debt ratio is projected to decline to 118.1%. In 1996 and 1997 the deficit ratio exceeded the ratio of public investment expenditure to GDP by 4.4 percentage points and 0.3 percentage point respectively (see Table 4).

Looking back over the years 1990 to 1997, the Italian *debt-to-GDP ratio* increased by 23.6 percentage points; initially the ratio tended to rise steeply, from 98% in 1990 to reach 124.9% in 1994, whereas it declined year by year thereafter, initially by around 0.5% per annum and by 2.4% in 1997 to reach 121.6% that year (see Chart 2a), i.e. a decline of 3.3 percentage points over three years. As is shown in greater detail in Chart 2b, for most of the time up to 1994 growing primary surpluses were not sufficient to outweigh the sizable debt-increasing effects of a negative growth/interest rate differential. In addition, a number of "stock-flow adjustments" contributed to debt growth in these years, related to, inter alia, the depreciation of the Italian lira in 1992 and the issuance of Treasury bonds in 1993, as a result of a sizable overfunding aimed at building up a deposit of the Treasury at the Banca d'Italia as a liquidity reserve in the context of the abolition of the Treasury's overdraft facility at the central bank, effective in 1994. After 1994 the primary surplus increased further, and it outweighed the debt-increasing effects of the macroeconomic environment. Moreover, privatisation resulted in a positive stock-flow adjustment. The patterns observed during the early 1990s may be seen as indicative of the risks to public finances which can arise when macroeconomic conditions deteriorate and the primary surplus is insufficient to counterbalance such effects. In this context, it may be noted that the share of debt with a short-term residual maturity has been decreasing

from the high levels of the early 1990s, and in parallel the average maturity has increased (see Table 5). This is a development in the right direction. With regard to 1997, the proportion of debt with a short-term residual maturity is still high, and, taking into account the current level of the debt ratio, fiscal balances are highly sensitive to changes in interest rates. On the other hand, the proportion of foreign currency debt in Italy is low and fiscal balances are relatively insensitive to changes in exchange rates.

During the 1990s a pattern of continuously improving outturns can be observed in the *deficit-to-GDP ratio,* with a particularly strong deficit reduction in 1997. Starting from a ratio of 11.1% in 1990, the fiscal imbalance was reduced to 9.2% of GDP in 1994; since then, the deficit has declined faster to stand at 2.7% of GDP in 1997 (see Chart 3a). As is shown in greater detail in Chart 3b, which focuses on *changes* in deficits, cyclical factors tended to hinder the reduction in deficits in the first years of the decade and in particular during 1993. Thereafter they have played a limited role. However, the non-cyclical improvements could reflect a lasting, "structural" move towards more balanced fiscal policies and/or a variety of measures with temporary effects. Evidence available suggests that measures with a temporary effect reduced the deficit ratio in 1997, with an impact of around 1% of GDP, and that they were mostly of a "one-off" nature. Compensating measures have already been included in the 1998 budget. Additional compensating measures will be required when the effects of "self-reversing" measures (amounting to 0.3% of GDP in 1997) unwind in the future.

Moving on to examine trends in other fiscal indicators, it can be seen from Chart 4 that the general government *total expenditure ratio* rose by 3.3 percentage points between 1990 and 1993, in particular on account of increased interest payments

(+2.6 percentage points) and current transfers (see Table 6). After 1993 the ratio of total expenditure to GDP declined by 6.3 percentage points, mainly reflecting a decline in interest payments (-2.6 percentage points) and capital expenditure but also due to reductions in current transfers and public consumption. The expenditure ratio in 1997 was 3 percentage points lower than at the beginning of the 1990s, primarily due to a reduction in net capital expenditure and public consumption. Given this pattern, also when allowing for a further substantial reduction in interest payments on the basis of unchanged interest rates, a continuation of the downward trend of primary expenditure to GDP would appear to require further adjustments in expenditure items such as current transfers. *Government revenue* in relation to GDP has tended to increase over the 1990s and is now 5½ percentage points higher than in 1990; it may thereby have approached a level which is detrimental to economic growth.

According to the Italian *medium-term fiscal policy strategy*, as presented in the Convergence Programme for 1998-2000 issued in June 1997, the declining trend in deficit and debt ratios is projected to continue in 1998. The budget for 1998 foresees somewhat more favourable outcomes than the Convergence Programme. The reduction in the budget deficit will mainly be achieved by expenditure restraint. Tax revenue as a percentage of GDP is projected to decline, as the Government has decided not to fully compensate the expiring one-off revenue measures. Tax-increasing measures enacted with the budget include an increase in the rates of value added tax and a widening of the bases for income taxes and social security contributions. Currently, there is evidence of measures with a temporary effect in the 1998 budget amounting to 0.3% of GDP. According to the Convergence Programme, in the year 2000 the deficit ratio is projected to stand

at 1.8% of GDP and the debt ratio to decrease to 116.3%. The programme is based on the previous medium-term financial plans of the Government dated May 1997, which accelerated the consolidation plans previously envisaged. Compared with fiscal balances projected in the Convergence Programme for 1998-2000, further substantial consolidation measures are required in order to comply with the medium-term objective of the Stability and Growth Pact, effective from 1999 onwards, of having a budgetary position that is close to balance or in surplus.

With regard to the future horizon for reducing the debt ratio to the 60% reference value in countries with a debt ratio of above 100% of GDP, two different kinds of calculations are presented. On the assumption that fiscal balances and debt ratios as projected by the European Commission for 1998 are achieved, the first exercise, as detailed in Table 7, shows the fiscal balances which would be consistent with convergence of the debt ratio to 60% of GDP over different time horizons. As an illustration, focusing on the period of ten years, i.e. reducing the debt ratio to 60% by 2007, would imply realising from 1999 onwards an overall surplus of 3.1% of GDP per year (see Table 7a) or realising from 1999 onwards a primary surplus of 8.4% of GDP per year (see Table 7b). This compares with an overall deficit ratio of 2.5% and a primary surplus ratio of 5.5% projected for 1998, i.e. the difference is 5.6 and 2.9 percentage points respectively.

A second exercise, as detailed in Chart 5, shows that maintaining the 1998 overall fiscal balance of -2.5% of GDP over the subsequent years would only reduce the debt ratio to 103.4% in ten years; the 60% reference value would never be reached as the debt ratio would cease to decline in the long term, to remain at around 67%. Maintaining the 1998 primary surplus of

5.5% of GDP would reduce the debt-to-GDP ratio to 88.8% in ten years; in this case, the 60% level would be reached in 2015. Finally, realising balanced budgets annually from 1999 onwards would bring the debt ratio down to 84.0% in ten years; the 60% reference value would be reached in 2016.

Such calculations are based on the normative assumption of a constant nominal rate of interest of 6% (average real cost of public debt outstanding of 4% and 2% inflation) and the assumption of a constant real GDP growth rate of 1.8%, as estimated by the Commission for real trend GDP growth in 1998. Stock-flow adjustments are not taken into account.

On the alternative assumption of a 2.5% yearly rate of real GDP growth, a growth assumption more in line with that applied to most other EU countries, the overall surplus ratio and the primary surplus ratio required to reach the 60% level in ten years would be 2.5% and 7.8% respectively. This means, respectively, a difference in the overall balance ratio projected for 1998 of 5.0 and to the primary surplus projected for 1998 of 2.3 percentage points.

While these calculations are purely illustrative, and can by no means be seen as forecasts, they do provide an illustration of why consolidation efforts need to be all the more resolute and lasting the higher the initial stock of debt, in order to forcefully reduce the debt-to-GDP ratio to 60% or below within an appropriate period of time.

Stressing the need for sustained consolidation efforts over an extended period of time resulting in significant and persistent overall fiscal surpluses is indeed critical in the case of Italy, since the current high level of debt would otherwise impose a continuous burden on fiscal policy and the economy as a whole. As has been seen in the past, high levels of debt increase the vulnerability of fiscal positions in unfavourable circumstances, thus heightening the risk of a serious worsening of public finances. In addition, there are *future budgetary challenges* to meet concerning budgetary procedures and the implications of demographic changes.

As regards the first issue, new legislation and changes in procedures have been introduced since December 1996 in order to control cash payments and reduce the deposits with the Treasury ("conti di tesoreria") of local authorities and other public bodies. These deposits, which represent readily available cash balances, declined from 7.1% of GDP at the end of 1996 to 4.1% at the end of 1997, thus reducing risks for expenditure control. This induced an increase in budget expenditure carryovers ("residui passivi") from 7.0 to 8.7% of GDP. These amounts do not represent resources which are freely available for expenditure, as state budget expenditure on a cash basis cannot exceed the limit set by Parliament to be consistent with fiscal targets (for 1998 cash authorisations amount to 32.3% of GDP). Tight control of expenditure nevertheless requires further action.

Regarding demographic changes, as is highlighted in Table 8, from around 2010 onwards a marked ageing of the population is expected and, in the context of an unfunded public pension system, public pension expenditure is projected to increase in terms of GDP, on the assumption that policies regarding benefits continue unchanged. Alleviation of the overall burden of population ageing will only be feasible if public finances have created sufficient room for manoeuvre before entering the period during which the demographic situation worsens.

Exchange rate developments

The Italian lira, which had participated in the ERM from its inception on 13 March 1979 until 17 September 1992, returned to the ERM on 25 November 1996, i.e. it has participated in the ERM for around 15 months of the two-year *reference period* (from March 1996 to February 1998) prior to the examination by the EMI (see Table 9a). As mentioned above, Italian monetary policy has been geared towards the primary objective of price stability, most recently again within the ERM.

At the beginning of the reference period, before it rejoined the ERM, the lira initially experienced a small and temporary setback in its strengthening trend, reaching a maximum downward deviation of 7.6% below its future central rate against one ERM currency in March 1996. Thereafter, it resumed its appreciation and tended towards its later central parities, moving for most of the time within a narrow range (see Chart 6).

Since joining the ERM in November 1996 the lira, benefiting from sizable short-term interest rate differentials vis-à-vis most partner currencies, has normally traded close to its central rates against other ERM currencies (see Chart 6 and Table 9a). On occasion the Italian lira traded outside a range close to its central rates vis-à-vis several partner currencies. The maximum upward and downward deviations from central rates, on the basis of 10 business day moving averages, were 2.5% and -3.0% respectively, abstracting from the autonomous upward trend of the Irish pound (see Table 9a). The episodes in which such deviations occurred were temporary, the relatively high degree of exchange rate volatility vis-à-vis the Deutsche Mark recorded initially declined to low levels during the reference period (see Table 9b) and short-term interest rate differentials against those EU countries with the lowest short-term interest rates

narrowed steadily. Since rejoining the ERM Italy has not devalued its currency's bilateral central rate against any other Member State's currency.

In a longer-term context, when measured in terms of real effective exchange rates, current exchange rates of the Italian lira against other ERM participating currencies suggest that current levels are somewhat below the average of the year 1987 but generally close to historical average values (see Table 10). As regards other external developments, Italy has recorded sizable and growing current account surpluses since 1993, which have brought the country's net external liability position near to balance (see Table 11). It may also be recalled that, according to the most recent data available, Italy has a ratio of foreign trade to GDP of 28% for exports and 24% for imports, and a share of intra-EU trade of 55% for exports and 61% for imports.

Long-term interest rate developments

Over the *reference period* from February 1997 to January 1998 *long-term interest rates* in Italy were 6.7% on average, and thus stood below the reference value for the interest rate criterion of 7.8% set on the basis of the three best-performing Member States in terms of price stability. While this was also the case for 1997 as a whole, twelve-month average long-term interest rates were above the reference value in 1996 (see Table 12); they have been below the reference value since February 1997.

Long-term interest rates were broadly stable in the early 1990s, underwent a phase of volatility in 1993-94, and from mid-1995 onwards have been on a steeply declining trend (see Chart 7a). In the early 1990s Italian long-term interest rates did not converge systematically with those prevailing in the EU countries with the lowest bond yields (see Chart 7b).

However, since early 1995 the process of convergence has accelerated, and the differential has now been virtually eliminated. The main factors underlying this trend were the significant decline and ultimate elimination of the inflation differential against the EU countries with the lowest long-term interest rates and the recent improvement in the country's fiscal position. In addition, the recovery of the exchange rate of the Italian lira in late 1995 and in the first half of 1996 as well as its relative stability more recently in the context of the ERM also account for the narrowing of the differential. These underlying developments were seen by markets as improving the prospects for participation in Stage Three of EMU - an element which may in turn have played an independent role in accelerating the narrowing of yield differentials, both directly and by further improving the prospects for price and exchange rate stability.

Concluding summary

Over the reference period Italy has achieved a rate of HICP inflation of 1.8%, which is well below the reference value stipulated by the Treaty. The growth of unit labour costs picked up in 1996, before slowing to 3.1% in 1997, and a general trend towards low rates of inflation was also apparent in terms of other relevant price indices. Looking ahead, there is little sign of immediate upward pressure on inflation; the most recent forecast projects inflation to stand slightly below 2% in 1998 and around 2% in 1999. The level of long-term interest rates was 6.7%, i.e. below the respective reference value.

The Italian lira has been participating in the ERM for around 15 months, i.e. for less than two years prior to the examination by the EMI. On the basis of the evidence reviewed in the Report, in an ex post assessment, the lira has been broadly stable over the reference period as a whole. Within the ERM it has remained generally close to its unchanged central parities, without the need for measures to support the exchange rate.

In 1997 Italy achieved a fiscal deficit ratio of 2.7% of GDP, i.e. below the reference value, and the outlook is for a further decrease to 2.5% in 1998. The debt-to-GDP ratio is far above the 60% reference value. After having reached a peak in 1994, the ratio declined by 3.3 percentage points to stand at 121.6% in 1997. The outlook is for a decline in the debt ratio to 118.1% of GDP in 1998. Notwithstanding the efforts and the substantial progress made towards improving the current fiscal situation, there must be an ongoing concern as to whether the ratio of government debt to GDP will be "sufficiently diminishing and approaching the reference value at a satisfactory pace" and whether sustainability of the fiscal position has been achieved; addressing this issue will have to remain a key priority for the Italian authorities. Significant and persistent overall fiscal surpluses are rapidly needed to be able to forcefully reduce the debt ratio to 60% of GDP within an appropriate period of time. This compares with a recorded fiscal deficit of 2.7% of GDP in 1997 as well as the deficit forecast for 1998 of 2.5%. The Stability and Growth Pact also requires, as a medium-term objective, a budgetary position that is close to balance or in surplus.

With regard to other factors, in 1996 and 1997 the deficit ratio exceeded the ratio of public investment to GDP, while Italy has recorded sizable and increasing current account surpluses which brought the net external liability position near to balance.

List of Tables and Charts*

ITALY

I Price developments

II Fiscal developments

III Exchange rate developments

IV Long-term interest rate developments

---

* Chart scales may differ across countries.

I Price developments

Table I

Italy: HICP inflation
(annual percentage changes)

	1996	1997	Nov 97	Dec 97	Jan 98	**Feb 97- Jan 98**
HICP inflation	4.0	1.9	1.8	1.8	1.9	1.8
Reference value	2.5	2.7	-	-	-	2.7

Source: European Commission.

Chart I

Italy: Price developments
(annual percentage changes)

Source: National data.

Table 2

Italy: Measures of inflation and related indicators
(annual percentage changes unless otherwise stated)

	1990	1991	1992	1993	1994	1995	1996	1997[a]
Measures of inflation								
Consumer price index (CPI)	6.1	6.4	5.4	4.2	3.9	5.4	3.9	1.7
CPI excluding changes in net indirect taxes[b]	5.7	6.0	5.2	4.2	3.6	4.7	3.8	1.7
Private consumption deflator	6.3	6.9	5.6	5.1	4.6	5.7	4.4	2.2
GDP deflator	7.6	7.7	4.7	4.4	3.5	5.1	5.0	2.6
Producer prices	4.1	3.3	1.9	3.8	3.7	7.9	1.9	1.3
Related indicators								
Real GDP growth	2.2	1.1	0.6	-1.2	2.2	2.9	0.7	1.5
Output gap (p.pts)	2.5	1.9	0.7	-2.0	-1.5	-0.2	-1.2	-1.4
Unemployment rate (%)[c]	9.1	8.6	8.8	10.2	11.3	12.0	12.1	12.3
Unit labour costs, whole economy	9.3	8.5	3.7	1.4	-0.4	1.8	4.9	3.1
Compensation per employee, whole economy	10.7	8.7	5.8	3.7	2.9	4.8	5.5	4.6
Labour productivity, whole economy	1.3	0.2	2.0	2.3	3.4	2.9	0.6	1.5
Import price deflator	-0.5	-0.3	1.1	11.6	5.1	12.2	-1.8	-0.1
Exchange rate appreciation[d]	2.6	-1.7	-3.1	-16.4	-4.6	-9.5	9.5	0.7
Broad monetary aggregate (M3H)[e]	6.9	5.7	2.8	3.0	3.5	-2.3	-0.7	9.9
Stock prices	0.7	-15.3	-16.8	18.5	24.7	-8.4	0.6	36.9
House prices	-	-	-	-	-	-	-	-

Source: National data except real GDP growth and the output gap (European Commission, spring 1998 forecasts) and exchange rate (BIS).
(a) Partly estimated.
(b) National estimates.
(c) Data prior to 1993 have been adjusted for breaks.
(d) Nominal effective exchange rate against 25 industrialised countries.
    Note: A positive (negative) sign indicates an appreciation (depreciation).
(e) National harmonised data.

Table 3

Italy: Recent inflation trends and forecasts
(annual percentage change unless otherwise stated)

(a) Recent trends in consumer price inflation

	Sep 97	Oct 97	Nov 97	Dec 97	Jan 98
National consumer price index (CPI)					
Annual percentage change	1.4	1.6	1.6	1.5	1.6
Change in the average of latest 3 months from previous					
3 months, annualised rate, seasonally adjusted	1.3	1.4	1.7	1.9	2.1
Change in the average of latest 6 months from previous					
6 months, annualised rate, seasonally adjusted	1.4	1.4	1.4	1.5	1.6

Source: National non-harmonised data.

(b) Inflation forecasts

	1998	1999
European Commission (spring 1998), HICP	1.9	2.0
OECD (December 1997), private consumption deflator	2.4	2.2
IMF (October 1997), CPI	2.1	.

Source: European Commission (spring 1998 forecasts), OECD and IMF.

II Fiscal developments

Table 4

Italy: General government financial position
(as a percentage of GDP)

	1996	**1997**	1998[a]
General government surplus (+) / deficit (-)	-6.7	-2.7	-2.5
Reference value	-3	-3	-3
Surplus (+) / deficit (-), net of public investment expenditure[b]	-4.4	-0.3	.
General government gross debt	124.0	121.6	118.1
Reference value	60	60	60

Source: European Commission (spring 1998 forecasts) and EMI calculations.
(a) European Commission projections.
(b) A negative sign indicates that the government deficit is higher than investment expenditure.

Chart 2

Italy: General government gross debt
(as a percentage of GDP)

(a) Levels

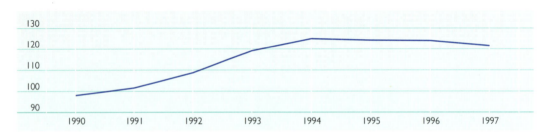

(b) Annual changes and underlying factors

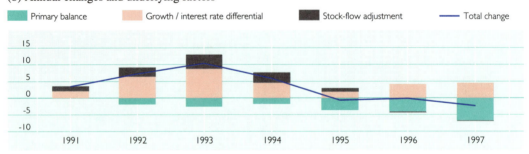

Source: European Commission (spring 1998 forecasts) and EMI calculations.
Note: In Chart 2b negative values indicate a contribution of the respective factor to a decrease in the debt ratio, while positive values indicate a contribution to its increase.

Table 5

Italy: General government gross debt – structural features

	1990	1991	1992	1993	1994	1995	1996	1997
Total debt (as a percentage of GDP)	98.0	101.5	108.7	119.1	124.9	124.2	124.0	121.6
Composition by currency (% of total)								
In domestic currency	94.0	94.3	93.9	93.0	93.0	92.7	93.4	93.1
In foreign currencies	6.0	5.7	6.1	7.0	7.0	7.3	6.6	6.9
Domestic ownership (% of total)	94.5	93.8	92.8	88.8	86.8	85.4	82.8	79.0
Average maturity[a] (years)	2.4	2.8	2.8	3.0	4.5	4.3	4.3	4.5
Composition by maturity[b] (% of total)								
Short-term (< 1 year)	67.3	66.9	65.0	60.6	51.7	51.0	51.5	49.4
Medium-term (1-5 years)	21.1	18.2	19.4	23.0	26.8	26.6	25.6	25.8
Long-term (> 5 years)	11.6	15.0	15.6	16.4	21.5	22.4	22.9	24.8

Source: National data except for total debt (European Commission (spring 1998 forecasts)). End-year data. Differences in the totals are due to rounding.
(a) Residual maturity. Domestic debt only.
(b) Residual maturity. The short-term component includes all floating rate securities, irrespective of their residual maturities.

Chart 3

Italy: General government surplus (+) / deficit (-)
(as a percentage of GDP)

(a) Levels

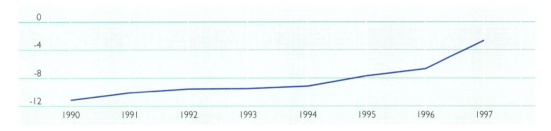

(b) Annual changes and underlying factors

Source: European Commission (spring 1998 forecasts).
Note: In Chart 3b negative values indicate a contribution to an increase in deficits, while positive values indicate a contribution to their reduction.

163

Chart 4

Italy: General government expenditure and receipts
(as a percentage of GDP)

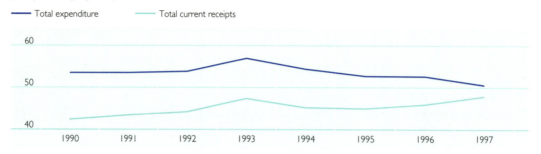

Source: European Commission (spring 1998 forecasts).

Table 6

Italy: General government budgetary position
(as a percentage of GDP)

	1990	1991	1992	1993	1994	1995	1996	1997
Total current receipts	42.4	43.4	44.3	47.4	45.2	45.0	46.0	47.9
Taxes	25.1	25.6	25.9	28.2	26.7	26.5	27.0	28.1
Social security contributions	14.4	14.7	15.1	15.5	14.9	14.8	15.1	15.5
Other current receipts	2.9	3.1	3.3	3.7	3.7	3.8	3.9	4.3
Total expenditure	53.6	53.5	53.8	56.9	54.4	52.7	52.7	50.6
Current transfers	21.2	21.4	22.3	23.1	22.6	21.5	22.0	22.2
Actual interest payments	9.5	10.2	11.5	12.1	11.0	11.3	10.8	9.5
Public consumption	17.6	17.6	17.7	17.6	17.1	16.1	16.3	16.3
Net capital expenditure	5.3	4.4	2.4	4.1	3.7	3.8	3.5	2.5
Surplus (+) or deficit (-)	-11.1	-10.1	-9.6	-9.5	-9.2	-7.7	-6.7	-2.7
Primary balance	-1.7	0.1	1.9	2.6	1.8	3.7	4.1	6.8
Surplus (+) or deficit (-),								
net of public investment expenditure[a]	.	.	.	-6.8	-6.9	-5.5	-4.4	-0.3

Source: European Commission (spring 1998 forecasts) and EMI calculations. Differences in the totals are due to rounding.
(a) A negative sign indicates that the government deficit is higher than investment expenditure.

Table 7

Italy: Debt convergence calculations

(a) On the basis of overall fiscal balances
(as a percentage of GDP)

Total gross debt		Overall fiscal balance (deficit: (-); surplus (+))		Overall fiscal balance consistent with reduction of debt level to 60% of GDP in		
1997	1998	1997	1998	2002	2007	2012
121.6	118.1	-2.7	-2.5	11.0*	3.1*	0.9*
				10.4**	2.5**	0.3**

Source: European Commission (spring 1998 forecasts) and EMI calculations.

(*) Calculations indicate that the debt ratio would fall to 60% in 2002, 2007 and 2012 respectively, if the overall fiscal balance for 1998 is as forecast and the overall fiscal balances were maintained at 11.0%, 3.1% and 0.9% of GDP respectively, from 1999 onwards. The underlying assumptions are a real trend GDP growth rate of 1.8% in 1998, as estimated by the Commission, and an inflation rate of 2%. Stock-flow adjustments are disregarded.

(**) Calculations indicate that the debt ratio would fall to 60% in 2002, 2007 and 2012 respectively, if the overall fiscal balance for 1998 is as forecast and the overall fiscal balances were maintained at 10.4%, 2.5% and 0.3% of GDP respectively, from 1999 onwards. The underlying assumptions are a real GDP growth rate of 2.5% and an inflation rate of 2%. Stock-flow adjustments are disregarded.

(b) On the basis of primary fiscal balances
(as a percentage of GDP)

Total gross debt		Primary fiscal balance		Primary fiscal balance consistent with reduction of debt level to 60% of GDP in		
1997	1998	1997	1998	2002	2007	2012
121.6	118.1	6.8	5.5	16.6*	8.4*	6.1*
				15.9**	7.8**	5.5**

Source: European Commission (spring 1998 forecasts) and EMI calculations.

(*) Calculations indicate that the debt ratio would fall to 60% in 2002, 2007 and 2012 respectively, if the primary fiscal balance for 1998 is as forecast and the primary fiscal balances were maintained at 16.6%, 8.4% and 6.1% of GDP respectively, from 1999 onwards. The underlying assumptions are a real trend GDP growth rate of 1.8% in 1998, as estimated by the Commission, an inflation rate of 2% and a nominal interest rate of 6%. Stock-flow adjustments are disregarded.

(**) Calculations indicate that the debt ratio would fall to 60% in 2002, 2007 and 2012 respectively, if the primary fiscal balance for 1998 is as forecast and the primary fiscal balances were maintained at 15.9%, 7.8% and 5.5% of GDP respectively, from 1999 onwards. The underlying assumptions are a real GDP growth rate of 2.5%, an inflation rate of 2% and a nominal interest rate of 6%. Stock-flow adjustments are disregarded.

Chart 5

Italy: Potential future debt ratios under alternative assumptions for fiscal balance ratios
(as a percentage of GDP)

(a) Real GDP growth rate: 1.8%

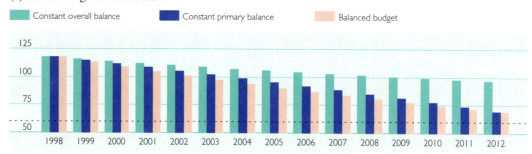

Source: European Commission (spring 1998 forecasts) and EMI calculations.
Note: The three scenarios assume that the debt ratio of 118.1% of GDP for 1998 is as forecast and that the 1998 overall balance of -2.5% of GDP or the primary balance of 5.5% of GDP will be kept constant over the period considered (as a percentage of GDP), or, alternatively, that a balanced budget is maintained from 1999 onwards. The underlying assumptions are a real trend GDP growth rate in 1998 of 1.8% as estimated by the Commission; an inflation rate of 2%; and, in the constant primary balance scenario, a nominal interest rate of 6%. Stock-flow adjustments are disregarded.

(b) Real GDP growth rate: 2.5%

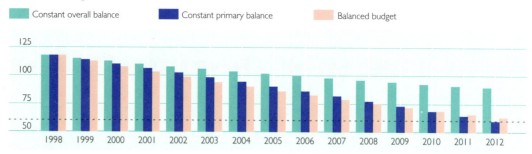

Source: European Commission (spring 1998 forecasts) and EMI calculations.
Note: The three scenarios assume that the debt ratio of 118.1% of GDP for 1998 is as forecast and that the 1998 overall balance of -2.5% of GDP or the primary balance of 5.5% of GDP will be kept constant over the period considered (as a percentage of GDP), or, alternatively, that a balanced budget is maintained from 1999 onwards. The underlying assumptions are a real GDP growth rate of 2.5%; an inflation rate of 2%; and, in the constant primary balance scenario, a nominal interest rate of 6%. Stock-flow adjustments are disregarded.

Table 8

Italy: Projections of elderly dependency ratio

	1990	2000	2010	2020	2030
Elderly dependency ratio (population aged 65 and over as a proportion of the population aged 15-64)	21.6	26.5	31.2	37.5	48.3

Source: Bos, E. et al. (1994), World population projections 1994-95, World Bank, Washington DC.

III Exchange rate developments

(a) Italy: Exchange rate stability
(25 November 1996 - 27 February 1998)

Membership of the Exchange Rate Mechanism (ERM)	Yes	
Membership since	25 November 1996	
Devaluation of bilateral central rate on country's own initiative	No	
Maximum upward (+) and downward (-) deviations from central rates in the ERM grid (%) against[a]		
Belgian franc	1.9	-1.1
Danish krone	1.7	-1.2
Deutsche Mark	1.8	-1.1
Spanish peseta	0.9	-1.3
French franc	2.5	-0.6
Irish pound	-2.3	-10.1
Dutch guilder	1.7	-1.3
Austrian schilling	1.8	-1.1
Portuguese escudo	0.7	-3.0
Finnish markka	0.4	-2.9

Source: European Commission and EMI calculations.

(a) Daily data at business frequency; 10-day moving average.

(b) Key indicators of exchange rate pressure for the Italian lira

Average of 3 months ending:	May 96	Aug 96	Nov 96	Feb 97	May 97	Aug 97	Nov 97	Feb 98
Exchange rate volatility[a]	6.4	5.5	4.5	4.5	4.1	3.0	2.5	1.1
Short-term interest rate differentials[b]	6.0	5.3	4.7	4.1	3.8	3.6	3.1	2.5

Source: European Commission, national data and EMI calculations.

(a) Annualised monthly standard deviation of daily percentage changes of the exchange rate against the DEM, in percentages.

(b) Differential of three-month interbank interest rates against a weighted average of interest rates in Belgium, Germany, France, the Netherlands and Austria, in percentage points.

Chart 6

Italian lira: Deviations from ERM bilateral central rates
(daily data; percentages; 1 March 1996 to 27 February 1998)

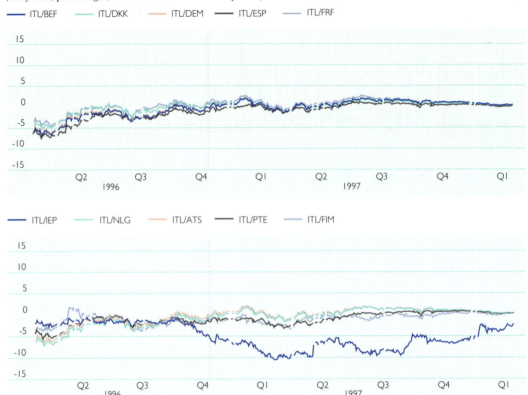

Source: European Commission.
Note: The vertical line indicates when Italy rejoined the ERM (25 November 1996).
Deviations prior to 25 November 1996 refer to the Italian lira's bilateral central rates as established upon ERM re-entry.

Table 10

Italian lira: Measures of the real effective exchange rate vis-à-vis ERM Member States
(monthly data; percentage deviations; February 1998 compared with different benchmark periods)

	Average Apr 73-Feb 98	Average Jan 87-Feb 98	Average 1987
Real effective exchange rates:			
CPI-based	-0.2	-4.5	-8.6
PPI/WPI-based	-4.4	-3.2	-9.9
Memo item:			
Nominal effective exchange rate	-36.1	-13.0	-25.2

Source: BIS and EMI calculations.
Note: A positive (negative) sign indicates an appreciation (depreciation).

Table 11

Italy: External developments
(as a percentage of GDP)

	1990	1991	1992	1993	1994	1995	1996	1997[a]
Current account plus new capital account[b]	-1.5	-2.1	-2.4	1.0	1.4	2.5	3.4	3.1
Net foreign assets (+) or liabilities (-)[c]	-7.4	-8.6	-10.9	-9.4	-7.2	-4.8	-3.2	-0.5
Exports (goods and services)[d]	20.0	19.8	21.1	23.4	25.2	27.4	27.0	28.0
Imports (goods and services)[e]	20.0	20.4	21.8	20.1	21.1	22.3	21.6	23.6

Source: National data except exports and imports (European Commission, spring 1998 forecasts).

(a) Partly estimated.

(b) According to the 5th edition of the IMF Balance of Payments Manual, which is conceptually the equivalent of the current account in previous editions of the Manual.

(c) International investment position (IIP) as defined by the IMF (see Balance of Payments Yearbook, Part I, 1994), or the closest possible substitute.

(d) In 1996 the share of intra-EU exports of goods in total national exports of goods was 55.4%; Direction of Trade Statistics Yearbook 1997, IMF.

(e) In 1996 the share of intra-EU imports of goods in total national imports of goods was 60.8%; Direction of Trade Statistics Yearbook 1997, IMF.

IV Long-term interest rate developments

Italy: Long-term interest rates
(percentages)

	1996	1997	Nov 97	Dec 97	Jan 98	**Feb 97- Jan 98**
Long-term interest rate	9.4	6.9	6.1	5.7	5.4	6.7
Reference value	9.1	8.0	-	-	-	7.8

Source: European Commission.

(a) Italy: Long-term interest rate
(monthly averages; in percentages)

(b) Italy: Long-term interest rate and CPI inflation differentials against EU countries with lowest long-term interest rates*
(monthly averages; in percentage points)

—— Long-term interest rate differential   —— CPI inflation differential

Source: Interest rates: European Commission (where these are not available the most comparable data have been used); the CPI data used are non-harmonised national data.
* Weighted average of data for Belgium, Germany, France, the Netherlands and Austria.

LUXEMBOURG

Price developments

Over the reference period from February 1997 to January 1998 the average rate of HICP inflation in Luxembourg was 1.4%, i.e. well below the reference value of 2.7%. This was also the case in 1997 as a whole. In 1996 average HICP inflation was 1.2% (see Table 1). Seen over the past two years, HICP inflation in Luxembourg has been at a level which is generally considered to be consistent with price stability.

Looking back, consumer price inflation in Luxembourg, as measured on the basis of the CPI, has followed a broad downward trend since the early 1990s (see Chart 1). This experience of declining rates of inflation reflects a number of important policy choices, most notably an exchange rate policy which links the Luxembourg franc to the Belgian franc in a monetary association. The general orientation has also been supported by prudent fiscal policies. The reduction in inflation during the 1990s has been achieved within the context of a relatively buoyant macroeconomic environment, although growth decelerated between 1993 and 1996 from around 9% to 3% (see Table 2). Against this background, growth in compensation per employee has been restrained in recent years. In 1997 an acceleration took place. Reflecting the absence of significant effective exchange rate movements, import price increases in the 1990s have been subdued or negative, thus contributing to the curbing of inflationary pressures. Low rates of inflation are also apparent when it is measured in terms of other relevant price indices (see Table 2).

Looking at recent trends and forecasts, current outturns for consumer price inflation (measured as a percentage change over the corresponding month a year earlier) have been decreasing to 1½% and there is little sign of immediate upward pressure on the basis of the measures shown in Table 3a. Forecasts of inflation suggest rates of between 1½ and 2% for 1998 and 1999 (see Table 3b). Risks for price stability over this period are associated with capacity constraints and somewhat accelerating unit labour costs.

Looking further ahead, a continuation of the long-standing economic and fiscal policies can be seen as being conducive to maintaining price stability. It will also be important to sustain wage moderation, ensuring that the rate of unemployment in Luxembourg remains low.

Fiscal developments

In the *reference year* 1997 the general government budget balance showed a surplus of 1.7% of GDP, hence the 3% reference value for the deficit ratio was comfortably met. The debt ratio was 6.7%, i.e. far below the 60% reference value. Compared with the previous year, the fiscal surplus has decreased by 0.8 percentage point, while the debt ratio has increased marginally. In 1998 the surplus is forecast to decrease to 1.0% of GDP, while the debt ratio is projected to increase to 7.1% (see Table 4).

Looking back over the years 1990 to 1997, Luxembourg's *debt-to-GDP ratio* gradually increased by 2.0 percentage points (see Chart 2a). As is shown in greater detail in Chart 2b, the typical pattern is that primary surpluses partly compensated for the debt-increasing effects resulting from the "stock-flow adjustment item". In Luxembourg these adjustments are due to the fact that the government sector is building up reserves for the pension scheme accumulated in special funds, annual transfer payments to which are not recorded in the general government surplus. Owing to the low level of debt, practically no effect on the debt ratio during the 1990s is attributable to the growth and interest rate environment. In this context it may be noted that Luxembourg's general government gross debt is almost entirely denominated in domestic currency and the share of debt with a short-term residual maturity is negligible (see Table 5).

During the 1990s a similarly sound pattern has been observed in annual fiscal balances, which have always been in surplus (see Chart 3 and Table 6). However, the overall fiscal surplus decreased rapidly during the early 1990s, dropping from 5.0% in 1990 to 0.8% in 1992. It broadly stabilised at around 2% thereafter, to reach a level of 1.7% in 1997. Against this background, a closer examination of Luxembourg's performance in terms of the deficit ratio is not considered necessary.

Luxembourg's *medium-term fiscal policy strategy* aims at balancing government finances, thereby complying with the respective provision of the Stability and Growth Pact, and linking expenditure to GDP growth, thus preventing an increase in the public sector's expenditure ratio.

With regard to the *potential future course of the debt ratio*, the EMI's Report does not consider this issue in detail for those countries with a debt ratio of below 60% of GDP. As regards longer-term challenges to public finances, Luxembourg appears to be in a favourable position, notably by having maintained low debt ratios. However, the longer-term fiscal position might be challenged by developments in the pension system stemming from the marked ageing of the population, which is expected to accelerate from around 2010 onwards (see Table 7).

Exchange rate developments

As Luxembourg is in a monetary association with Belgium, the development of the Luxembourg franc is largely identical to that of the Belgian franc. Therefore, the following paragraph virtually restates the text on exchange rate developments in the chapter on Belgium.

The Luxembourg franc has been participating in the ERM since its inception on 13 March 1979, i.e. for much longer than two years prior to the examination (see Table 8a). Focusing on the *reference period* from March 1996 to February 1998, the currency has normally traded close to its central rates against other ERM currencies and very close to those vis-à-vis the Deutsche Mark, the Dutch guilder and the Austrian schilling (see Chart 4 and Table 8a). On occasion the Luxembourg franc traded outside a range close to its central rates vis-à-vis several partner currencies. The maximum upward and downward deviations from central rates, on the basis of 10 business day moving averages, were 2.5% and -3.0% respectively, abstracting from the autonomous upward trend of the Irish pound (see Table 8a). The episodes in which such deviations occurred were temporary, the degree of exchange rate volatility vis-à-vis the Deutsche Mark was continuously very low (see Table 8b) and short-term interest rate differentials against those EU countries with the lowest short-term interest rates were insignificant. During the reference period Luxembourg has not devalued its currency's bilateral central rate against any other Member State's currency.

Luxembourg has traditionally maintained large current account surpluses (see Table 9). As regards other external developments, it may be recalled that Luxembourg is a small open economy with, according to the most recent data available, a ratio of foreign trade to GDP of 95% for exports and 86% for imports, and a share of intra-EU trade of 70% for exports and 74% for imports.

Long-term interest rate developments

Over the *reference period* from February 1997 to January 1998 *long-term interest rates* in Luxembourg were 5.6% on average, and thus stood well below the reference value for the interest rate criterion of 7.8% set on the basis of the three best-performing Member States in terms of price stability. This was also the case for 1997 as a whole, as well as for 1996 (see Table 10).

Long-term interest rates have been on a broadly declining trend since the early 1990s (see Chart 5a). A close convergence of Luxembourg's long-term interest rates with those prevailing in the EU countries with the lowest bond yields has been observed for most of the period since the early 1990s (see Chart 5b). The main factors underlying this trend were the comparatively low rate of inflation and sound fiscal policies.

Concluding summary

Over the reference period Luxembourg has achieved a rate of HICP inflation of 1.4%, which is well below the reference value stipulated by the Treaty. The increase in unit labour costs was subdued and low rates of inflation were also apparent in terms of other relevant price indices. Looking ahead, there is little sign of immediate upward pressure on inflation; forecasts project inflation will stand at 1½-2% in 1998 and 1999. The Luxembourg franc, which is in a monetary association with the Belgian franc, has been participating in the ERM for much longer than two years. Over the reference period it remained broadly stable, generally close to its unchanged central parities without the need for measures to support the exchange rate. The level of long-term interest rates was 5.6%, i.e. well below the respective reference value.

Luxembourg achieved a general government surplus of 1.7% of GDP in 1997, thereby comfortably meeting the 3% reference value, and the outlook is for a surplus of 1.0% in 1998. In addition, the fiscal debt ratio was virtually stable at 6.7% of GDP in 1997, i.e. remaining far below the 60% reference value, and the outlook is for an increase to 7.1% in 1998. With regard to the sustainability of fiscal developments, looking ahead, if current fiscal surpluses are maintained for 1998, Luxembourg should comply with the medium-term objective of the Stability and Growth Pact, effective from 1999 onwards, of having a budgetary position that is close to balance or in surplus.

With regard to other factors, Luxembourg has maintained large current account surpluses.

List of Tables and Charts*

LUXEMBOURG

I Price developments

II Fiscal developments

III Exchange rate developments

IV Long-term interest rate developments

---

* Chart scales may differ across countries.

I Price developments

Table I

Luxembourg: HICP inflation
(annual percentage changes)

	1996	1997	Nov 97	Dec 97	Jan 98	**Feb 97- Jan 98**
HICP inflation	1.2	1.4	1.5	1.5	1.5	1.4
Reference value	2.5	2.7	-	-	-	2.7

Source: European Commission.

Chart I

Luxembourg: Price developments
(annual percentage changes)

— CPI — Unit labour costs — Import price deflator

Source: National data.

Table 2

Luxembourg: Measures of inflation and related indicators

(annual percentage changes unless otherwise stated)

	1990	1991	1992	1993	1994	1995	1996	1997[a]
Measures of inflation								
Consumer price index (CPI)	3.7	3.1	3.2	3.6	2.2	1.9	1.4	1.4
CPI excluding changes in net indirect taxes[b]	3.7	3.1	3.1	2.9	2.1	1.8	1.4	1.4
Private consumption deflator	4.0	2.9	3.9	3.8	2.1	1.8	1.4	1.2
GDP deflator	3.4	1.3	5.1	0.5	4.9	1.8	1.1	1.7
Producer prices	-2.0	-2.5	-2.1	-1.7	0.5	3.7	-3.1	1.2
Related indicators								
Real GDP growth	2.2	6.1	4.5	8.7	4.2	3.8	3.0	4.1
Output gap (p.pts)	1.0	1.5	0.4	3.6	2.7	1.7	0.1	-0.2
Unemployment rate (%)	1.3	1.4	1.6	2.1	2.7	3.0	3.3	3.6
Unit labour costs, whole economy	6.6	3.5	4.0	-2.2	1.4	2.2	0.7	1.1
Compensation per employee, whole economy	5.5	6.4	5.3	5.1	4.0	2.2	1.8	2.7
Labour productivity, whole economy	-1.0	2.7	1.2	7.4	2.6	0.1	1.1	1.6
Import price deflator	2.5	1.9	0.0	-0.5	1.4	0.1	-0.9	0.9
Exchange rate appreciation[c]	1.7	0.3	0.6	-0.5	1.0	1.2	-0.7	-2.0
Broad monetary aggregate (M3H)[d]	25.1	2.1	10.5	13.6	-7.8	-1.3	1.3	4.9
Stock prices	-15.7	3.3	-10.0	121.1	-9.1	0.6	30.0	24.7
House prices[e]	5.2	4.8	6.9	1.4	1.2	1.8	0.9	1.5

Source: National data except real GDP growth and the output gap (European Commission, spring 1998 forecasts).
(a) Partly estimated.
(b) National estimates.
(c) Nominal effective exchange rate against 11 industrialised countries.
    Note: a positive (negative) sign indicates an appreciation (depreciation).
(d) National harmonised data.
(e) Construction prices for residential and semi-residential buildings.

Table 3

Luxembourg: Recent inflation trends and forecasts

(annual percentage change unless otherwise stated)

(a) Recent trends in consumer price inflation

	Sep 97	Oct 97	Nov 97	Dec 97	Jan 98
National consumer price index (CPI=HICP)					
Annual percentage change	1.7	1.7	1.5	1.5	1.5
Change in the average of latest 3 months from previous					
3 months, annualised rate[a]	1.4	1.6	1.9	2.0	1.7
Change in the average of latest 6 months from previous					
6 months, annualised rate[a]	1.3	1.4	1.5	1.5	1.6

Source: European Commission.
(a) HICP excluding seasonal items.

(b) Inflation forecasts

	1998	1999
European Commission (spring 1998), HICP	1.6	1.7
OECD (December 1997), private consumption deflator	1.5	1.5
IMF (October 1997), CPI	2.0	.

Source: European Commission (spring 1998 forecasts), OECD and IMF.

II Fiscal developments

Table 4

Luxembourg: General government financial position
(as a percentage of GDP)

	1996	**1997**	1998[a]
General government surplus (+) / deficit (-)	2.5	1.7	1.0
Reference value	-3	-3	-3
Surplus (+) / deficit (-), net of public investment expenditure[b]	7.2	6.6	.
General government gross debt	6.6	6.7	7.1
Reference value	60	60	60

Source: European Commission (spring 1998 forecasts) and EMI calculations.
(a) European Commission projections.
(b) A negative sign indicates that the government deficit is higher than investment expenditure.

Chart 2

Luxembourg: General government gross debt
(as a percentage of GDP)

(a) Levels

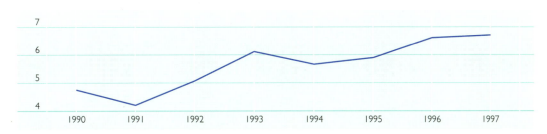

(b) Annual changes and underlying factors

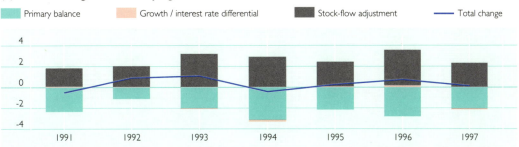

Source: European Commission (spring 1998 forecasts) and EMI calculations.
Note: In Chart 2b negative values indicate a contribution of the respective factor to a decrease in the debt ratio, while positive values indicate a contribution to its increase.

Table 5

Luxembourg: General government gross debt - structural features

	1990	1991	1992	1993	1994	1995	1996	1997
Total debt (as a percentage of GDP)	4.7	4.2	5.1	6.1	5.7	5.9	6.6	6.7
Composition by currency (% of total)								
In domestic currency	96.6	97.7	98.8	99.3	99.4	99.6	99.7	99.8
In foreign currencies	3.4	2.3	1.2	0.7	0.6	0.5	0.3	0.2
Domestic ownership (% of total)	92.0	93.2	95.6	85.2	84.9	84.5	85.4	85.1
Average maturity[a] (years)	.	.	.	.	.	7.8	7.5	7.2
Composition by maturity[a] (% of total)								
Short-term[b] (< 1 year)	5.5	6.9	5.8	3.3	6.4	0.8	3.6	0.1
Medium-term (1-5 years)	63.0	66.6	53.8	30.7	15.0	8.3	1.4	10.1
Long-term (> 5 years)	31.4	26.5	40.5	66.1	78.7	90.9	95.0	89.9

Source: National data except for total debt (European Commission (spring 1998 forecasts)). End-year data. Differences in the totals are due to rounding.
(a) Residual maturity. Central government debt only.
(b) Including short-term debt and debt linked to short-term interest rates.

Chart 3

Luxembourg: General government surplus (+) / deficit (-)
(as a percentage of GDP)

(a) Levels

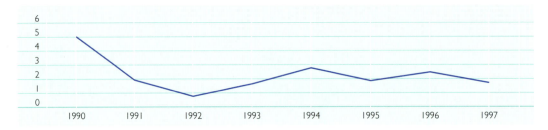

(b) Annual changes and underlying factors

Source: European Commission (spring 1998 forecasts).
Note: In Chart 3b negative values indicate a contribution to an increase in deficits, while positive values indicate a contribution to their reduction.

Luxembourg: General government budgetary position

(as a percentage of GDP)

	1990	1991	1992	1993	1994	1995	1996	1997
Total current receipts	.	.	.	.	.	.	49.0	47.6
Taxes	.	.	.	.	.	.	32.7	31.7
Social security contributions	.	.	.	.	.	.	11.9	11.6
Other current receipts	.	.	.	.	.	.	4.4	4.3
Total expenditure	.	.	.	.	.	.	46.5	45.9
Current transfers	.	.	.	.	.	.	27.3	26.7
Actual interest payments	0.5	0.4	0.4	0.4	0.3	0.3	0.3	0.3
Public consumption	13.4	13.3	13.1	12.9	12.5	13.2	13.6	13.3
Net capital expenditure	.	.	.	.	.	.	5.3	5.5
Surplus (+) or deficit (-)	5.0	1.9	0.8	1.7	2.8	1.9	2.5	1.7
Primary balance	5.5	2.3	1.1	2.0	3.1	2.2	2.8	2.1
Surplus (+) or deficit (-), net of public investment expenditure[a]	.	.	.	7.0	7.2	6.5	7.2	6.6

Source: European Commission (spring 1998 forecasts) and EMI calculations. Differences in the totals are due to rounding.
(a) A negative sign indicates that the government deficit is higher than investment expenditure.

Luxembourg: Projections of elderly dependency ratio

	1990	2000	2010	2020	2030
Elderly dependency ratio (population aged 65 and over as a proportion of the population aged 15-64)	19.9	21.9	25.9	33.2	44.2

Source: Bos, E. et al. (1994), World population projections 1994-95, World Bank, Washington DC.

III Exchange rate developments

Table 8

(a) Luxembourg: Exchange rate stability
(1 March 1996 - 27 February 1998)

Membership of the Exchange Rate Mechanism (ERM)		Yes
Membership since		13 March 1979
Devaluation of bilateral central rate on country's own initiative		No
Maximum upward (+) and downward (-) deviations from central rates in the ERM grid (%) against[a]		
Danish krone	1.6	-0.3
Deutsche Mark	0.4	-0.1
Spanish peseta	0.2	-2.0
French franc	2.5	-0.3
Irish pound	4.2	-10.6
Italian lira	1.1	-1.9
Dutch guilder	0.1	-0.5
Austrian schilling	0.4	-0.1
Portuguese escudo	1.4	-2.7
Finnish markka	-0.2	-3.0

Source: European Commission and EMI calculations.

(a) Daily data at business frequency; 10-day moving average. Deviations against the Finnish markka refer to the period from 14 October 1996 onwards, while deviations against the Italian lira refer to the period from 25 November 1996 onwards.

(b) Key indicators of exchange rate pressure for the Luxembourg franc

Average of 3 months ending:	May 96	Aug 96	Nov 96	Feb 97	May 97	Aug 97	Nov 97	Feb 98
Exchange rate volatility[a]	0.2	0.2	0.2	0.3	0.1	0.1	0.2	0.1
Short-term interest rate differentials[b]	-0.2	-0.2	-0.2	-0.1	0.0	0.2	0.2	0.0

Source: European Commission, national data and EMI calculations.

(a) Annualised monthly standard deviation of daily percentage changes of the exchange rate against the DEM, in percentages.

(b) Differential of three-month interbank interest rates against a weighted average of interest rates in Belgium, Germany, France, the Netherlands and Austria, in percentage points.

Chart 4

Luxembourg franc: Deviations from ERM bilateral central rates
(daily data; percentages; 1 March 1996 to 27 February 1998)

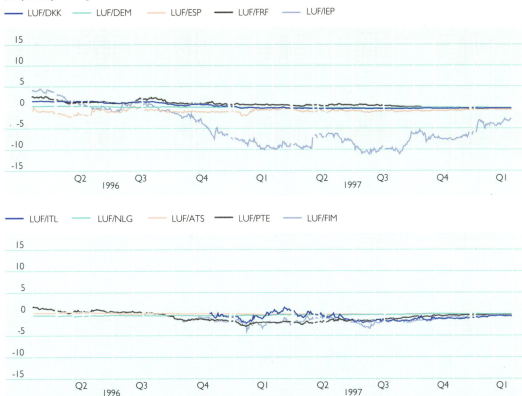

Source: European Commission.
Note: Deviations against the Finnish markka refer to the period from 14 October 1996 onwards, while deviations against the Italian lira refer to the period from 25 November 1996 onwards.

Table 9

Luxembourg: External developments
(as a percentage of GDP)

	1990	1991	1992	1993	1994	1995	1996	1997[a]
Current account plus new capital account[b]	17.0	13.5	15.4	13.7	14.0	18.1	15.9	15.9
Net foreign assets (+) or liabilities (-)[c]	.	.	.	.	.	.	.	.
Exports (goods and services)[d]	97.9	98.4	98.7	93.3	93.4	94.0	93.3	95.3
Imports (goods and services)[e]	96.4	99.0	94.0	88.9	85.2	85.2	83.5	85.5

Source: National data except exports and imports (European Commission, spring 1998 forecasts).
(a) Partly estimated.
(b) According to the 5th edition of the IMF Balance of Payments Manual, which is conceptually the equivalent of the current account in previous editions of the Manual.
(c) International investment position (IIP) as defined by the IMF (see Balance of Payments Yearbook, Part I, 1994), or the closest possible substitute.
(d) In 1996 the share of intra-EU exports of goods in BLEU national exports of goods was 70.4%; Direction of Trade Statistics Yearbook 1997, IMF.
(e) In 1996 the share of intra-EU imports of goods in BLEU national imports of goods was 73.6%; Direction of Trade Statistics Yearbook 1997, IMF.

IV Long-term interest rate developments

Table 10

Luxembourg: Long-term interest rates
(percentages)

	1996	1997	Nov 97	Dec 97	Jan 98	**Feb 97- Jan 98**
Long-term interest rate	6.3	5.6	5.6	5.4	5.2	5.6
Reference value	9.1	8.0	-	-	-	7.8

Source: European Commission.

Chart 5

(a) Luxembourg: Long-term interest rate
(monthly averages; in percentages)

(b) Luxembourg: Long-term interest rate and CPI inflation differentialsagainst EU countries with lowest long-term interest rates*
(monthly averages; in percentage points)

Source: Interest rates: European Commission (where these are not available the most comparable data have been used); the CPI data used are non-harmonised national data.
* Weighted average of data for Belgium, Germany, France, the Netherlands and Austria.

NETHERLANDS

Price developments

Over the reference period from February 1997 to January 1998 the average rate of HICP inflation in the Netherlands was 1.8%, i.e. well below the reference value of 2.7%. This was also the case in 1997 as a whole. In 1996 average HICP inflation was 1.4% (see Table 1). Seen over the past two years, HICP inflation in the Netherlands has tended to increase while remaining at levels which are generally considered to be consistent with price stability.

Looking back, consumer price inflation in the Netherlands, as measured on the basis of the CPI, peaked at 3.2% in 1992 before declining to 1.9% in 1995. Since then, inflation has tended to increase slightly (see Chart 1). The environment of generally moderate rates of inflation reflects the ongoing pursuit of stability-oriented policies. In particular, monetary policy has continued to be geared towards price stability, underpinned by the objective of maintaining a stable exchange rate of the Dutch guilder vis-à-vis the Deutsche Mark within the framework of the ERM. This has been supported by, inter alia, policies seeking to encourage wage moderation and fiscal consolidation. In addition, the macroeconomic environment has contributed to containing upward pressure on prices, with a negative output gap emerging in 1993 (see Table 2). More recently, real GDP growth has accelerated and the output gap has narrowed. However, despite a tightening of labour market conditions, wage growth has remained moderate, notwithstanding a slight acceleration in 1997, and increases in unit labour costs have been low. Import price rises have been subdued throughout most of the 1990s, thereby facilitating control over inflation. In 1997 upward pressure on consumer prices increased, not least as a result of a rise in import prices. This pattern of generally low rates of inflation is also apparent when it is measured in terms of other relevant price indices (see Table 2).

Looking at recent trends and forecasts, current outturns for consumer price inflation (measured as a percentage change over the corresponding month a year earlier) have been decreasing to below 2% but there are some signs of immediate upward pressure on the basis of the measures shown in Table 3a. Forecasts of inflation suggest rates of around 2½% for 1998 and 1999 (see Table 3b). The risks for price stability over this period are associated with tight labour market conditions and a narrowing of the output gap.

Looking further ahead, maintaining an environment conducive to price stability relates in the Netherlands to, inter alia, the conduct of fiscal policies over the medium to long term; it will be equally important to maintain national policies aimed at enhancing competition in product markets and improving the functioning of labour markets.

Fiscal developments

In the *reference year* 1997 the general government deficit ratio was 1.4%, i.e. well below the 3% reference value, and the debt ratio was 72.1%, i.e. above the 60% reference value. Compared with the previous year, the deficit ratio has been reduced by 0.9 percentage point and the debt ratio has decreased by 5.1 percentage points. In 1998 the deficit ratio is forecast to increase to 1.6% of GDP, while the debt ratio is projected to decline to 70.0%. In 1996 and 1997 the deficit ratio did not exceed the ratio of public investment expenditure to GDP (see Table 4).

Looking back over the years 1990 to 1997, the Dutch *debt-to-GDP ratio* declined by 7.1 percentage points. Whereas the debt ratio increased from 79.2% in 1990 to 81.2% in 1993, a downward movement was discernible thereafter, and in 1997 the debt ratio stood at 72.1% (see Chart 2a), i.e. a decline of 9.1 percentage points over four years. As is shown in greater detail in Chart 2b, the primary surplus was not sufficiently high for most of the period up to 1995 to outweigh the debt-increasing effects of a negative growth/interest rate differential. Various financial operations, summarised under the heading of "stock-flow adjustments", occasionally affected the debt dynamics. These exceptional factors were mostly rather small, but two exceptional items exerted a major downward influence. The first, in 1994, related to a financial reform in the social housing sector, and the second, in 1997, occurred when the Treasury moved to a nearly balanced position at De Nederlandsche Bank and used the earlier surplus to pay off debt. In 1996 and 1997 the macroeconomic environment became more favourable: GDP growth strengthened, average interest rates declined marginally, and primary surpluses increased, thereby contributing to a falling debt ratio. The patterns observed in the early 1990s may be seen as indicative of the upward pressure on the debt ratio which can arise when the primary surplus is not sufficiently high to offset the effects of adverse economic conditions. In this context, it may be noted that the share of debt with a short-term residual maturity has been low (though increasing) during the 1990s, and the average maturity has remained broadly stable in the period considered (see Table 5). Also taking into account the current level of the debt ratio, fiscal balances are relatively insensitive to changes in interest rates. In addition, the proportion of foreign currency debt is negligible, rendering fiscal balances insensitive to changes in exchange rates.

During the 1990s a broadly flat trend up to 1995 and subsequently improving outturns can be observed in the *deficit-to-GDP ratio*. Starting from a ratio of 5.1% in 1990, the deficit fluctuated between 2.9% and 4.0% during the period up to 1995; thereafter the deficit fell to 2.3% in 1996 and 1.4% in 1997 (see Chart 3a). The improvement in the deficit ratio has been modest taking into account the favourable macroeconomic environment. As is shown in greater detail in Chart 3b, which focuses on *changes* in deficits, cyclical factors did not play a large role (with the exception of 1993). However, the non-cyclical improvements could reflect a lasting, "structural" move towards more balanced fiscal policies and/or a variety of measures with temporary effects. Evidence available suggests that measures with a temporary effect played a deficit-reducing role in 1996, amounting to 0.6% of GDP, but did not play a role in 1997.

Moving on to examine trends in other fiscal indicators, it can be seen from Chart 4 that the general government *total expenditure ratio* rose steadily between 1990 and 1993, mainly reflecting an increase in current transfers (see Table 6) in the context of the slowdown in the economy and higher unemployment. After 1993 the ratio declined. Against the background of the economic recovery and falling unemployment, current transfers declined substantially as a percentage of GDP, as did all other categories of expenditure. On balance, the expenditure ratio in 1997 was nearly 5 percentage points lower than in 1990, reflecting a downward movement in all major items of government spending. The continuation of such a downward trend would seem to require the main emphasis to be placed on current transfers and public consumption. *Government revenue* in relation to GDP also tended to increase sharply until 1993, but thereafter declined to levels below those observed at the beginning of the 1990s before experiencing a small increase in 1997. It may be at a level which is detrimental to economic growth.

According to the Dutch *medium-term fiscal policy strategy*, as presented in the Convergence Programme for 1995-98 updated in December 1996, a declining or stabilising trend in the deficit ratio and a declining trend in the debt ratio are projected for 1998. The outcome for the debt ratio in 1997 reflects a better performance than was envisaged in the original programme for 1998. Against the background of stronger economic growth than foreseen, the budget for 1998 shows a larger reduction in the deficit ratio than planned in the programme. Currently, there is no evidence of significant measures with a temporary effect in the 1998 budget. While the current programme does not contain projections beyond 1998, the Dutch authorities have committed themselves to complying with the medium-term objective of the Stability and Growth Pact, effective from 1999 onwards, of having a budgetary position that is close to balance or in surplus, which entails a need for further substantial fiscal consolidation compared with projections for 1998.

With regard to the future horizon for reducing the debt ratio to the 60% reference value for countries with a debt ratio of clearly above 60% but below 80% of GDP, the EMI presents calculations, as detailed in Chart 5. On the assumption that overall fiscal positions and debt ratios as projected by the European Commission for 1998 are achieved, realising a balanced budget from 1999 onwards would reduce the debt ratio to below 60% of GDP in 2002. This would also be achieved by maintaining the 1998 primary surplus of 3.3% of GDP but debt reduction would be slower. Instead, maintaining the 1998 overall deficit of 1.6% of GDP would prolong the process to 2005. Such calculations are based on the normative assumption of a constant nominal rate of interest of 6% (average real cost of public debt outstanding of 4% and 2% inflation) and the assumption of a constant real GDP growth rate of 3.1%, as estimated by the Commission for

real trend GDP growth in 1998. Stock-flow adjustments are not taken into account. While such calculations are purely illustrative, and can by no means be regarded as forecasts, they provide an illustration of the need for further substantial progress in consolidation in order to bring the debt ratio in the Netherlands down to 60% of GDP or below within an appropriate period of time.

Stressing the need for considerable improvement in the deficit ratio and to sustain consolidation over time is indeed appropriate in the case of the Netherlands. As has been seen in the past, less favourable economic conditions than those currently prevailing tend to imply an increase in the debt ratio. In addition, as is highlighted in Table 7, from around 2010 onwards a marked ageing of the population is expected. While the Netherlands benefits from a sizable funded occupational pension system covering most private and public sector employees, unfunded social security pensions remain substantial and public pension expenditure is projected to increase in terms of GDP if policies regarding benefits continue unchanged. In this respect, current efforts to build up a reserve fund over time should further strengthen the system. Alleviation of the overall burden of population ageing will be facilitated if public finances have created sufficient room for manoeuvre before entering the period during which the demographic situation worsens.

Exchange rate developments

The Dutch guilder has been participating in the ERM since its inception on 13 March 1979, i.e. for much longer than two years prior to the examination (see Table 8a). As mentioned above, Dutch monetary policy has been geared towards price stability, underpinned by the objective of maintaining a stable exchange rate of the guilder to the Deutsche Mark within the framework of the ERM. The Netherlands and Germany have an agreement whereby the fluctuation margin between the guilder and the Deutsche Mark is set at ±2.25%. Focusing on the *reference period* from March 1996 to February 1998, the currency has normally traded close to its central rates against other ERM currencies and very close to those vis-à-vis the Belgian franc, the Deutsche Mark and the Austrian schilling (see Chart 6 and Table 8a). On occasion the Dutch guilder traded outside a range close to its central rates vis-à-vis several partner currencies. The maximum upward and downward deviations from central rates, on the basis of 10 business day moving averages, were 2.8% and -2.8% respectively, abstracting from the autonomous upward trend of the Irish pound (see Table 8a). The episodes in which such deviations occurred were temporary, the degree of exchange rate volatility vis-à-vis the Deutsche Mark was continuously very low (see Table 8b) and short-term interest rate differentials against those EU countries with the lowest short-term interest rates were insignificant. During the reference period the Netherlands has not devalued its currency's bilateral central rate against any other Member State's currency.

In a longer-term context, measures of the real effective exchange rate of the Dutch guilder vis-à-vis the currencies of ERM participating Member States depicted in Table 9 suggest that current levels are close to historical values. As regards other external developments, the Netherlands has maintained large current account surpluses and a sizable net external asset position (see Table 10). It may also be recalled that the Netherlands is a small open economy with, according to the most recent data available, a ratio of foreign trade to GDP of 63% for exports and 56% for imports, and a share of intra-EU trade of 78% for exports and 60% for imports.

Long-term interest rate developments

Over the *reference period* from February 1997 to January 1998 *long-term interest rates* in the Netherlands were 5.5% on average, and thus stood well below the reference value for the interest rate criterion of 7.8% set on the basis of the three best-performing Member States in terms of price stability. This was also the case for 1997 as a whole, as well as for 1996 (see Table 11).

Long-term interest rates have been on a broadly declining trend since the early 1990s (see Chart 7a). A close convergence of Dutch long-term interest rates with those prevailing in the EU countries with the lowest bond yields has been observed for most of the period since the beginning of the 1990s; in the more recent period the (typically negative) differential has been close to zero (see Chart 7b). The main factors underlying this trend were the comparatively low rate of inflation, the stability of the Dutch guilder's exchange rate, the pursuit of a similar monetary policy stance to that followed in the above-mentioned countries and the improvement in the fiscal position. The more recent moderate increase in inflationary pressures has apparently not had a significant influence on the financial market's general outlook on the Netherlands.

Concluding summary

Over the reference period the Netherlands has achieved a rate of HICP inflation of 1.8% which is well below the reference value stipulated by the Treaty. The increase in unit labour costs was subdued and generally low rates of inflation were also apparent in terms of other relevant price indices. Looking ahead, there are some signs of immediate upward pressure on inflation; forecasts project inflation will rise to around 2½% in 1998 and 1999. The Dutch guilder has been participating in the

ERM for much longer than two years. Over the reference period it remained broadly stable, generally close to its unchanged central parities, without the need for measures to support the exchange rate. The level of long-term interest rates was 5.5%, i.e. well below the respective reference value.

In 1997 the Netherlands achieved a fiscal deficit ratio of 1.4% of GDP, i.e. well below the reference value, and the outlook is for an increase to 1.6% in 1998. The debt-to-GDP ratio is above the 60% reference value. After having reached a peak in 1993, the ratio declined by 9.1 percentage points to stand at 72.1% in 1997. Regarding the sustainability of fiscal developments, the outlook is for a decrease in the debt ratio to 70.0% of GDP in 1998. Looking further ahead, keeping the deficit ratio at current levels would not be sufficient to bring the debt ratio down to 60% of GDP within an appropriate period of time, thus pointing to the need for further substantial progress in consolidation. The Stability and Growth Pact also requires as a medium-term objective a budgetary position that is close to balance or in surplus. Given the current debt ratio of above 70% of GDP, achieving the fiscal position forecast for 1998 and realising a balanced budget thereafter would reduce the debt ratio to below 60% in 2002.

With regard to other factors, in 1996 and 1997 the deficit ratio did not exceed the ratio of public investment to GDP, and the Netherlands maintained large current account surpluses as well as a net external asset position. In the context of the ageing of the population, the Netherlands benefits from a sizable funded occupational pension system.

List of Tables and Charts*

---

* Chart scales may differ across countries.

I   Price developments

Table I

Netherlands: HICP inflation
(annual percentage changes)

	1996	1997	Nov 97	Dec 97	Jan 98	**Feb 97- Jan 98**
HICP inflation	1.4	1.9	2.5	2.2	1.6	1.8
Reference value	2.5	2.7	-	-	-	2.7

Source: European Commission.

Chart I

Netherlands: Price developments
(annual percentage changes)

Source: National data.

Table 2

Netherlands: Measures of inflation and related indicators
(annual percentage changes unless otherwise stated)

	1990	1991	1992	1993	1994	1995	1996	1997[a]
Measures of inflation								
Consumer price index (CPI)	2.4	3.1	3.2	2.6	2.8	1.9	2.0	2.2
CPI excluding changes in net indirect taxes[b]	2.1	2.6	2.6	2.4	2.4	1.8	1.5	2.2
Private consumption deflator	2.2	3.2	3.1	2.1	2.8	1.5	1.3	1.8
GDP deflator	2.4	2.7	2.2	2.0	2.2	1.7	1.3	1.7
Producer prices	-0.6	1.5	0.4	-1.0	0.7	2.6	1.7	1.9
Related indicators								
Real GDP growth	4.1	2.3	2.0	0.8	3.2	2.3	3.3	3.3
Output gap (p.pts)	2.2	1.8	1.1	-0.8	-0.4	-1.0	-0.7	-0.4
Unemployment rate (%)	6.0	5.4	5.3	6.4	7.5	7.0	6.6	5.9
Unit labour costs, whole economy	1.7	3.9	3.1	2.2	-1.3	1.2	0.2	0.1
Compensation per employee, whole economy	2.8	3.8	4.0	3.0	1.5	1.6	1.3	2.5
Labour productivity, whole economy	1.0	-0.1	0.9	0.8	2.8	0.4	1.1	2.4
Import price deflator	-1.3	0.4	-1.4	-2.3	0.1	0.9	0.7	3.2
Exchange rate appreciation[c]	4.0	-0.8	2.3	2.8	0.3	4.2	-1.9	-4.5
Broad monetary aggregate (M3H)[d]	9.9	6.0	6.4	6.7	4.4	0.7	6.1	7.0
Stock prices	-10.0	2.3	8.4	14.3	22.3	6.7	26.8	49.4
House prices	2.0	2.6	8.3	8.3	8.7	3.6	10.3	6.8

Source: National data except real GDP growth and the output gap (European Commission, spring 1998 forecasts) and exchange rate (BIS).
(a) Partly estimated. Unit labour costs, compensation per employee and labour productivity: market economy.
(b) National estimates.
(c) Nominal effective exchange rate against 25 industrialised countries.
    Note: a positive (negative) sign indicates an appreciation (depreciation).
(d) National harmonised data.

Table 3

Netherlands: Recent inflation trends and forecasts
(annual percentage change unless otherwise stated)

(a) Recent trends in consumer price inflation

	Sep 97	Oct 97	Nov 97	Dec 97	Jan 98
National consumer price index (CPI)					
Annual percentage change	2.4	2.3	2.5	2.3	1.8
Change in the average of latest 3 months from previous 3 months, annualised rate, seasonally adjusted	2.3	2.3	3.2	3.3	2.0
Change in the average of latest 6 months from previous 6 months, annualised rate, seasonally adjusted	2.1	2.2	2.2	2.5	2.5

Source: National non-harmonised data.

(b) Inflation forecasts

	1998	1999
European Commission (spring 1998), HICP	2.3	2.5
OECD (December 1997), private consumption deflator	2.3	2.4
IMF (October 1997), CPI	2.3	.

Source: European Commission (spring 1998 forecasts), OECD and IMF.

II   Fiscal developments

Table 4

Netherlands: General government financial position
(as a percentage of GDP)

	1996	**1997**	1998[a]
General government surplus (+) / deficit (-)	-2.3	-1.4	-1.6
Reference value	-3	-3	-3
Surplus (+) / deficit (-), net of public investment expenditure[b]	0.4	1.4	.
General government gross debt	77.2	72.1	70.0
Reference value	60	60	60

Source: European Commission (spring 1998 forecasts) and EMI calculations.
(a)   European Commission projections.
(b)   A negative sign indicates that the government deficit is higher than investment expenditure.

Chart 2

Netherlands: General government gross debt
(as a percentage of GDP)

(a) Levels

(b) Annual changes and underlying factors

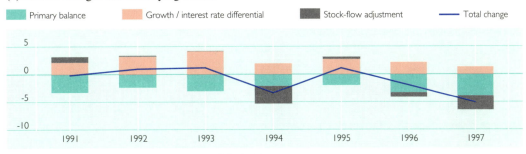

Source: European Commission (spring 1998 forecasts) and EMI calculations.
Note: In Chart 2b negative values indicate a contribution of the respective factor to a decrease in the debt ratio, while positive values indicate a contribution to its increase.

Table 5

Netherlands: General government gross debt – structural features

	1990	1991	1992	1993	1994	1995	1996	1997
Total debt (as a percentage of GDP)	79.2	79.0	80.0	81.2	77.9	79.1	77.2	72.1
Composition by currency (% of total)								
In domestic currency	100.0	100.0	100.0	100.0	100.0	100.0	100.0	100.0
In foreign currencies	0.0	0.0	0.0	0.0	0.0	0.0	0.0	0.0
Domestic ownership (% of total)	86.0	83.8	80.3	77.8	83.1	80.0	82.3	.
Average maturity[a] (years)	.	5.6	6.3	6.8	6.9	6.9	6.4	5.5
Composition by maturity[a] (% of total)								
Short-term[b] (< 1 year)	.	.	3.7	8.5	7.3	3.7	1.3	6.7
Medium-term (1-5 years)	.	.	32.1	23.6	27.9	31.7	30.6	30.3
Long-term (> 5 years)	.	.	64.1	67.9	64.9	64.6	68.1	63.0

Source: National data except for total debt (European Commission (spring 1998 forecasts)). End-year data. Differences in the totals are due to rounding.
(a) Residual maturity. Central government debt only.
(b) Including short-term debt and debt linked to short-term interest rates.

Chart 3

Netherlands: General government surplus (+) / deficit (-)
(as a percentage of GDP)

(a) Levels

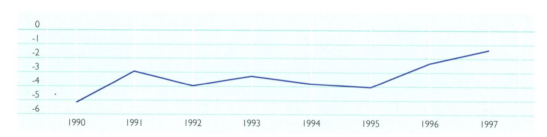

(b) Annual changes and underlying factors

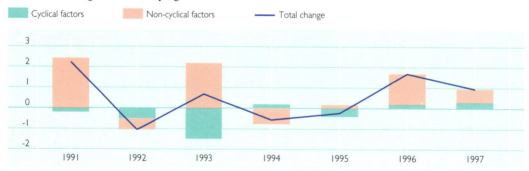

Source: European Commission (spring 1998 forecasts).
Note: In Chart 3b negative values indicate a contribution to an increase in deficits, while positive values indicate a contribution to their reduction.

Chart 4

Netherlands: General government expenditure and receipts
(as a percentage of GDP)

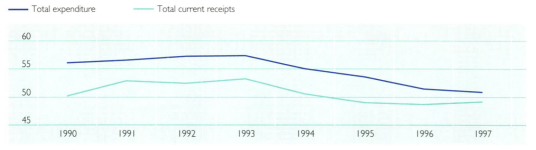

Source: European Commission (spring 1998 forecasts).

Table 6

Netherlands: General government budgetary position
(as a percentage of GDP)

	1990	1991	1992	1993	1994	1995	1996	1997
Total current receipts	50.2	52.8	52.5	53.3	50.6	49.0	48.7	49.2
Taxes	28.0	29.4	28.8	29.8	27.1	26.0	26.8	26.8
Social security contributions	17.1	18.0	18.6	18.6	19.2	19.1	18.1	18.9
Other current receipts	5.1	5.4	5.0	4.8	4.2	3.9	3.8	3.5
Total expenditure	55.3	55.7	56.4	56.5	54.4	53.0	51.0	50.5
Current transfers	31.2	31.8	32.3	32.4	31.2	29.7	28.9	28.7
Actual interest payments	6.0	6.2	6.3	6.3	5.9	6.0	5.6	5.3
Public consumption	14.6	14.5	14.7	14.9	14.5	14.4	14.1	14.1
Net capital expenditure	3.5	3.2	3.0	2.9	2.8	2.9	2.3	2.4
Surplus (+) or deficit (-)	-5.1	-2.9	-3.9	-3.2	-3.8	-4.0	-2.3	-1.4
Primary balance	0.9	3.3	2.4	3.0	2.1	2.0	3.3	3.9
Surplus (+) or deficit (-), net of public investment expenditure[a]	.	.	.	-0.5	-1.1	-1.3	0.4	1.4

Source: European Commission (spring 1998 forecasts) and EMI calculations. Differences in the totals are due to rounding.
(a) A negative sign indicates that the government deficit is higher than investment expenditure.

Chart 5

Netherlands: Potential future debt ratios under alternative assumptions for fiscal balance ratios
(as a percentage of GDP)

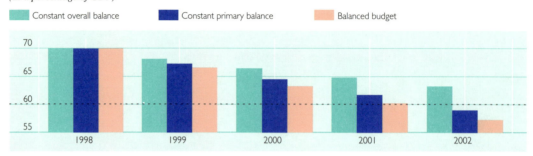

Source: European Commission (spring 1998 forecasts) and EMI calculations.
Note: The three scenarios assume that the debt ratio of 70.0% of GDP for 1998 is as forecast and that the 1998 overall balance of -1.6% of GDP or the primary balance of 3.3% of GDP will be kept constant over the period considered (as a percentage of GDP), or, alternatively, that a balanced budget is maintained from 1999 onwards. The underlying assumptions are a real trend GDP growth rate in 1998 of 3.1% as estimated by the Commission; an inflation rate of 2%; and, in the constant primary balance scenario, a nominal interest rate of 6%. Stock-flow adjustments are disregarded.

Table 7

Netherlands: Projections of elderly dependency ratio

	1990	2000	2010	2020	2030
Elderly dependency ratio (population aged 65 and over as a proportion of the population aged 15-64)	19.1	20.8	24.2	33.9	45.1

Source: Bos, E. et al. (1994), World population projections 1994-95, World Bank, Washington DC.

III Exchange rate developments

(a) Netherlands: Exchange rate stability
(1 March 1996 - 27 February 1998)

Membership of the Exchange Rate Mechanism (ERM)	Yes	
Membership since	13 March 1979	
Devaluation of bilateral central rate on country's own initiative	No	
Maximum upward (+) and downward (-) deviations from central rates in the ERM grid (%) against[a]		
Belgian franc	0.5	-0.1
Danish krone	2.0	-0.3
Deutsche Mark	0.8	-0.0
Spanish peseta	0.5	-1.7
French franc	2.8	-0.3
Irish pound	4.6	-10.5
Italian lira	1.3	-1.7
Austrian schilling	0.8	-0.0
Portuguese escudo	1.8	-2.5
Finnish markka	-0.2	-2.8

Source: European Commission and EMI calculations.
(a) Daily data at business frequency; 10-day moving average. Deviations against the Finnish markka refer to the period from 14 October 1996 onwards, while deviations against the Italian lira refer to the period from 25 November 1996 onwards.

(b) Key indicators of exchange rate pressure for the Dutch guilder

Average of 3 months ending:	May 96	Aug 96	Nov 96	Feb 97	May 97	Aug 97	Nov 97	Feb 98
Exchange rate volatility[a]	0.5	0.5	0.3	0.3	0.4	0.3	0.2	0.1
Short-term interest rate differentials[b]	-0.6	-0.5	-0.4	-0.2	-0.1	0.0	0.0	-0.1

Source: European Commission, national data and EMI calculations.
(a) Annualised monthly standard deviation of daily percentage changes of the exchange rate against the DEM, in percentages.
(b) Differential of three-month interbank interest rates against a weighted average of interest rates in Belgium, Germany, France, the Netherlands and Austria, in percentage points.

Chart 6

Dutch guilder: Deviations from ERM bilateral central rates
(daily data; percentages; 1 March 1996 to 27 February 1998)

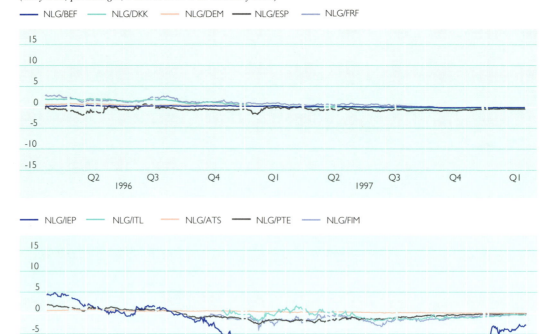

Source: European Commission.
Note: Deviations against the Finnish markka refer to the period from 14 October 1996 onwards, while deviations against the Italian lira refer to the period from 25 November 1996 onwards.

Table 9

Dutch guilder: Measures of the real effective exchange rate vis-à-vis ERM Member States
(monthly data; percentage deviations; February 1998 compared with different benchmark periods)

	Average Apr 73-Feb 98	Average Jan 87-Feb 98	Average 1987
Real effective exchange rates:			
CPI-based	-3.1	-0.3	-3.2
PPI/WPI-based	3.9	2.5	3.2
Memo item:			
Nominal effective exchange rate	11.9	1.8	4.8

Source: BIS and EMI calculations.
Note: A positive (negative) sign indicates an appreciation (depreciation).

196

Table 10

Netherlands: External developments
(as a percentage of GDP)

	1990	1991	1992	1993	1994	1995	1996	1997[a]
Current account plus new capital account[b]	3.2	2.6	2.3	4.4	5.3	5.9	5.2	7.3
Net foreign assets (+) or liabilities (-)[c]	20.9	20.9	17.7	19.8	16.9	13.4	.	.
Exports (goods and services)[d]	54.2	55.4	55.9	56.3	58.2	60.9	61.7	63.2
Imports (goods and services)[e]	49.5	50.4	50.4	49.0	50.7	53.1	54.2	55.7

Source: National data except exports and imports (European Commission, spring 1998 forecasts).

(a) Partly estimated.

(b) According to the 5th edition of the IMF Balance of Payments Manual, which is conceptually the equivalent of the current account in previous editions of the Manual.

(c) International investment position (IIP) as defined by the IMF (see Balance of Payments Yearbook, Part I, 1994), or the closest possible substitute.

(d) In 1996 the share of intra-EU exports of goods in total national exports of goods was 78.1%; Direction of Trade Statistics Yearbook 1997, IMF.

(e) In 1996 the share of intra-EU imports of goods in total national imports of goods was 60.0%; Direction of Trade Statistics Yearbook 1997, IMF.

IV Long-term interest rate developments

Table 11

Netherlands: Long-term interest rates
(percentages)

	1996	1997	Nov 97	Dec 97	Jan 98	**Feb 97- Jan 98**
Long-term interest rate	6.2	5.6	5.5	5.3	5.1	5.5
Reference value	9.1	8.0	-	-	-	7.8

Source: European Commission.

Chart 7

(a) Netherlands: Long-term interest rate
(monthly averages; in percentage)

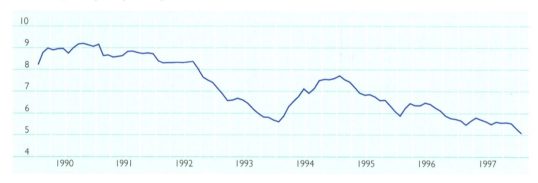

(b) Netherlands: Long-term interest rate and CPI inflation differentials against EU countries with lowest long-term interest rates*
(monthly averages; in percentage points)

Source: Interest rates: European Commission (where these are not available the most comparable data have been used); the CPI data used are non-harmonised national data.
* Weighted average of data for Belgium, Germany, France, the Netherlands and Austria.

AUSTRIA

Price developments

Over the reference period from February 1997 to January 1998 the average rate of HICP inflation in Austria was 1.1%, i.e. well below the reference value of 2.7%. This was also the case in 1997 as a whole. In 1996 average HICP inflation was 1.8% (see Table 1). Seen over the past two years, HICP inflation in Austria has been at levels which are generally considered to be consistent with price stability.

Looking back, consumer price inflation in Austria, as measured on the basis of the CPI, has followed a downward trend after 1992 (see Chart 1). Inflation peaked at 4.1% in 1992 before declining in subsequent years. This experience of declining rates of inflation reflects the pursuit of policies geared towards price stability. Monetary policy has continued to be determined by the objective of closely linking the Austrian schilling to the Deutsche Mark, since January 1995 within the framework of the ERM. This general orientation has also been supported by policies seeking to encourage wage moderation, increased foreign price competition following Austria's accession to the EU in 1995 and consolidation efforts of fiscal policy. In addition, the macroeconomic environment has contributed to containing upward pressure on prices. In particular, in the context of the slowdown in economic activity in 1992-93 and only modest GDP growth since then, a negative output gap has gradually emerged (see Table 2). Against this background, growth in compensation per employee has been restrained, and the increase in nominal unit labour costs has been subdued since 1994. Broadly stable import price rises have helped to contain inflationary pressures. Low rates of inflation are also apparent when it is measured in terms of other relevant price indices (see Table 2).

Looking at recent trends and forecasts, current outturns for consumer price inflation (measured as a percentage change over the corresponding month a year earlier) indicate that monthly rates of inflation have been stable at around 1% but there are some signs of upward pressure on the basis of the measures shown in Table 3a. Forecasts of inflation suggest rates of around 1½% for 1998 and 1999 (see Table 3b).

Looking further ahead, maintaining an environment conducive to price stability relates in Austria to, inter alia, the conduct of fiscal policies over the medium to long term; it will be equally important to strengthen policies aimed at enhancing competition in product markets and improving the functioning of labour markets.

Fiscal developments

In the *reference year* 1997 the general government deficit ratio was 2.5%, i.e. below the 3% reference value, and the debt ratio was 66.1%, i.e. above the 60% reference value. Compared with the previous year, the deficit ratio has been reduced by 1.5 percentage points and the debt ratio has decreased by 3.4 percentage points. In 1998 the deficit ratio is forecast to decline to 2.3% of GDP, while the debt ratio is projected to decrease to 64.7%. In 1996 the deficit ratio exceeded the ratio of public investment expenditure to GDP, while in 1997 the deficit ratio is expected to be virtually identical to the investment ratio (see Table 4).

Looking back over the years 1990 to 1997, the Austrian *debt-to-GDP ratio* increased by 8.2 percentage points. Until 1992 the debt ratio had remained stable at around 58%, while the ratio increased year by year thereafter to reach 69.5% in 1996 before declining to 66.1% in 1997 (see Chart 2a), i.e. a decline of 3.4 percentage points in one year. As shown in greater detail in Chart 2b, in 1991-92 primary surpluses were sufficiently high to compensate for the upward pressure exerted on the debt ratio by other factors. However, in subsequent years the primary surplus disappeared, and a negative growth/interest rate differential, as well as several "stock-flow adjustment items", caused the debt ratio to increase. Only in 1997 could this trend be reversed, largely as a result of privatisation receipts, sales of financial claims and the reclassification of certain public companies to the private sector (see the stock-flow adjustment items). The patterns observed thus far during the 1990s may be seen as indicative of the risks to the debt ratio which can arise when there is an unfavourable growth/interest rate differential and the primary surplus is not sufficiently high to compensate for the effects on debt resulting from the macroeconomic environment. In this context, it may be noted that the share of debt with a short-term residual maturity is noticeable and that the average maturity has tended to decrease (see Table 5). With regard to 1997, taking into account the current level of the debt ratio, fiscal balances are relatively insensitive to changes in interest rates. On the other hand, the proportion of foreign currency debt is relatively high and fiscal balances are in principle relatively sensitive to changes in exchange rates, although the bulk of this debt may eventually be redenominated in euro.

During the 1990s a pattern of first stable, then deteriorating and subsequently improving outturns can be observed in the deficit-to-GDP ratio. Starting from a ratio of 2.4% in 1990, the deficit first improved to 2.0% in 1992; it deteriorated thereafter, reaching a peak of 5.2% of GDP in 1995. Finally, an improvement took place in the

past two years, with the ratio being reduced to 2.5% in 1997 (see Chart 3a). As is shown in greater detail in Chart 3b, which focuses on changes in deficits, cyclical factors contributed to the sharp increase in deficit in 1993, reflecting the fading of the boom of the preceding years, but played less of a role thereafter. Instead, pronounced changes in overall deficits were mainly attributable to the remaining "non-cyclical" factors, both as deficits increased and, more recently, in the context of deficit reduction. However, these non-cyclical improvements could reflect a lasting, "structural" move towards more balanced fiscal policies and/or a variety of measures with temporary effects. Evidence available suggests that measures with a temporary effect reduced the deficit by 0.5% of GDP in 1997, compared with 0.2% of GDP in 1996. As the measures in 1997 were partly "self-reversing", compensating measures already included in the 1998 budget will need to yield their expected results in 1998 in order to keep fiscal balances on the planned path and, in addition, compensating measures will be required when the "self-reversing" effects unwind in the future.

Moving on to examine trends in other fiscal indicators, it can be seen from Chart 4 that the general government total expenditure ratio rose sharply between 1990 and 1995. The increase was mainly caused by a surge in current transfers and public consumption as a percentage of GDP (see Table 6). Thereafter, the expenditure ratio declined as a result of reductions in all expenditure items relative to GDP. On balance, the expenditure ratio in 1997 was 3.0 percentage points higher than in 1990 on account of higher current transfers and public consumption. Given this pattern, a continuation of the recent downward movement in the expenditure ratio and the achievement of levels similar to or below those of the early 1990s would appear to require additional adjustments in terms of both public transfers and consumption. After 1994 *government revenue* in relation to GDP increased and the revenue ratio in 1997 was 3.0 percentage points higher than in 1990; it may thus have approached a level which is detrimental to economic growth.

According to the Austrian *medium-term fiscal policy strategy*, as presented in the Convergence Programme for 1997-2000 updated in October 1997, the general government financial deficit and debt ratios are expected to decline in 1998. The budget for 1998 is in line with the programme and Commission forecasts are slightly more favourable. The budget includes plans for fiscal measures promoting employment without increasing tax rates or non-wage labour costs. Currently, there is no evidence of significant measures with a temporary effect in the 1998 budget. According to current plans, in the year 2000 the overall deficit ratio is planned to stand at just below 2% and the debt ratio to be just below 65% of GDP. This implies a somewhat faster improvement in public sector finances than envisaged in the previous programme. Compared with fiscal balances projected in the Convergence Programme for 1999-2000, further substantial consolidation is needed in order to comply with the medium-term objective of the Stability and Growth Pact, effective from 1999 onwards, of having a budgetary position that is close to balance or in surplus.

With regard to the future horizon for reducing the debt ratio to the 60% reference value for countries with a debt ratio of clearly above 60% but below 80% of GDP, the EMI presents calculations, as detailed in Chart 5. On the assumption that overall fiscal positions and debt ratios as projected by the European Commission for 1998 are achieved, realising a balanced budget from 1999 onwards would reduce the debt ratio to below 60% of GDP as early as the year 2000. Instead, maintaining 1998 overall and primary balances of -2.3%

and 1.7% of GDP constant in subsequent years would imply a slower path of debt reduction and would generate a debt ratio of below 60% in 2010 and 2004 respectively. Such calculations are based on the normative assumption of a constant nominal rate of interest of 6% (average real cost of public debt outstanding of 4% and 2% inflation) and the assumption of a constant real GDP growth rate of 2.5%, as estimated by the Commission for real trend GDP growth in 1998. Stock-flow adjustments are not taken into account. While such calculations are purely illustrative and can by no means be regarded as forecasts, they provide an illustration of the need for further substantial progress in consolidation in order to bring the debt ratio in Austria down to 60% of GDP or below within an appropriate period of time.

Stressing the need for considerable improvement in the deficit ratio and to sustain consolidation over time is indeed warranted in the case of Austria, since additional room for manoeuvre is necessary in order to be able to address *future budgetary challenges*. As is highlighted in Table 7, from around 2010 onwards a marked ageing of the population is expected and, in the context of an unfunded pension system, public pension expenditure is forecast to increase in terms of GDP, particularly if policies regarding benefits continue unchanged. The overall burden of population ageing will become more manageable the better state of public finances when the demographic situation worsens.

Exchange rate developments

The Austrian schilling has been participating in the ERM since 9 January 1995, i.e. for longer than two years prior to the examination (see Table 8a). As mentioned above, Austrian monetary policy has continued to be determined by the objective of closely linking the Austrian schilling to the Deutsche Mark, since January 1995 within the framework of the ERM. Focusing on the *reference period* from March 1996 to February 1998, the currency has normally traded close to its central rates against other ERM currencies and very close to those vis-à-vis the Belgian franc, the Deutsche Mark and the Dutch guilder (see Chart 6 and Table 8a). On occasion the Austrian schilling traded outside a range close to its central rates vis-à-vis several partner currencies. The maximum upward and downward deviations from central rates, on the basis of 10 business day moving averages, were 2.2% and -2.9% respectively, abstracting from the autonomous upward trend of the Irish pound (see Table 8a). The episodes in which such deviations occurred were temporary, the degree of exchange rate volatility vis-à-vis the Deutsche Mark was continuously very low (see Table 8b) and short-term interest rate differentials against those EU countries with the lowest short-term interest rates were insignificant. During the reference period Austria has not devalued its currency's bilateral central rate against any other Member State's currency.

In a longer-term context, measures of the real effective exchange rate of the Austrian schilling vis-à-vis the currencies of ERM participating Member States depicted in Table 9 suggest that current levels are close to historical values. With regard to other external developments, the current account turned negative during the 1990s, which has contributed to an increasing net external liability position (see Table 10). It may also be recalled that Austria is a small open economy with, according to the most recent data available, a ratio of foreign trade to GDP of 49% for exports and 48% for imports, and a share of intra-EU trade of 60% for exports and 75% for imports.

Long-term interest rate developments

Over the *reference period* from February 1997 to January 1998 *long-term interest rates* in Austria were 5.6% on average, and thus stood well below the reference value for the interest rate criterion of 7.8% set on the basis of the three best-performing Member States in terms of price stability. This was also the case for 1997 as a whole, as well as for 1996 (see Table 11).

Long-term interest rates have been on a broadly declining trend since the early 1990s (see Chart 7a). At the same time, a close convergence of Austria's long-term interest rates with those prevailing in the EU countries with the lowest bond yields has been observed since the early 1990s, with the differential typically being around zero (see Chart 7b). The main factors underlying this trend were the comparatively low rate of inflation, the relative stability of the Austrian schilling's exchange rate, the pursuit of a similar monetary policy stance to that followed in the above-mentioned countries and, most recently, the gradual improvement in the state of the country's public finances.

Concluding summary

Over the reference period Austria has achieved a rate of HICP inflation of 1.1%, which is well below the reference value stipulated by the Treaty and one of the three lowest inflation rates in the Union. Unit labour costs were broadly stable over the reference period (having decreased in 1996) and low rates of inflation were also apparent in terms of other relevant price indices. Looking ahead, there are some signs of upward pressure on inflation. The Austrian schilling has been participating in the ERM for longer than two years. Over the reference period it remained broadly stable, generally close to its unchanged central parities, without the need for measures to support the exchange rate.

The level of long-term interest rates was 5.6%, i.e. well below the respective reference value.

In 1997 Austria achieved a fiscal deficit ratio of 2.5%, i.e. below the reference value, and the outlook is for a decrease to 2.3% in 1998. The debt-to-GDP ratio is above the 60% reference value. After having reached a peak in 1996, it declined by 3.4 percentage points to stand at 66.1% in 1997. Regarding the sustainability of fiscal developments, the outlook is for a decrease in the debt ratio to 64.7% of GDP in 1998. Looking further ahead, keeping the deficit ratio at current levels would not be sufficient to bring the debt ratio down to 60% of GDP within an appropriate period of time, thus pointing to the need for further substantial progress in consolidation. The Stability and Growth Pact also requires as a medium-term objective a budgetary position that is close to balance or in surplus. Given the current debt ratio of above 65% of GDP, achieving the fiscal position forecast for 1998 and realising a balanced budget thereafter would reduce the debt ratio to below 60% as early as the year 2000.

With regard to other factors, in 1996 the deficit ratio exceeded the ratio of public investment to GDP, while in 1997 the difference was close to zero. Austria has maintained current account deficits as well as a net external liability position.

List of Tables and Charts*

AUSTRIA

I Price developments

II Fiscal developments

III Exchange rate developments

IV Long-term interest rate developments

---

* Chart scales may differ across countries.

1   Price developments

Table 1

Austria: HICP inflation
(annual percentage changes)

	1996	1997	Nov 97	Dec 97	Jan 98	**Feb 97- Jan 98**
HICP inflation	1.8	1.2	1.1	1.0	1.1	1.1
Reference value	2.5	2.7	-	-	-	2.7

Source: European Commission.

Chart 1

Austria: Price developments
(annual percentage changes)

Source: National data.

Table 2

Austria: Measures of inflation and related indicators
(annual percentage changes unless otherwise stated)

	1990	1991	1992	1993	1994	1995	1996	1997[a]
Measures of inflation								
Consumer price index (CPI)	3.3	3.3	4.1	3.6	3.0	2.2	1.9	1.3
CPI excluding changes in net indirect taxes[b]	3.3	3.3	3.9	3.6	2.8	1.7	1.7	1.2
Private consumption deflator	3.5	3.0	3.9	3.3	3.3	1.5	2.5	1.8
GDP deflator	3.4	3.7	4.3	2.8	2.8	2.1	2.1	1.4
Producer prices[c]	2.9	0.8	-0.2	-0.4	1.3	0.4	0.0	0.4
Related indicators								
Real GDP growth	4.6	3.4	1.3	0.5	2.5	2.1	1.6	2.5
Output gap (p.pts)	2.0	2.9	1.8	-0.1	0.0	-0.3	-1.1	-1.0
Unemployment rate (%)	-	-	-	-	3.8	3.9	4.4	4.4
Unit labour costs, whole economy	2.8	4.5	4.8	3.5	0.8	1.1	-0.5	0.0
Compensation per employee, whole economy	5.5	6.3	5.8	4.6	3.3	3.0	1.6	1.5
Labour productivity, whole economy	2.6	1.8	0.9	1.0	2.5	1.9	2.1	1.6
Import price deflator	0.5	1.0	0.0	0.7	0.8	1.0	1.2	0.7
Exchange rate appreciation[d]	3.4	-0.7	2.0	2.1	0.0	3.5	-1.6	-2.7
Broad monetary aggregate (M3H)[e]	14.3	13.4	9.3	4.0	6.3	6.1	5.7	2.7
Stock prices	64.7	-16.7	-20.6	-2.4	14.7	-13.4	4.8	13.8
House prices	.	.	.	.	.	.	-1.4	-1.7

Source: National data except real GDP growth and the output gap (European Commission, spring 1998 forecasts) and exchange rate (BIS).
(a) Partly estimated.
(b) National estimates.
(c) Wholesale prices.
(d) Nominal effective exchange rate against 25 industrialised countries.
    Note: a positive (negative) sign indicates an appreciation (depreciation).
(e) National harmonised data; annual average.

Table 3

Austria: Recent inflation trends and forecasts
(annual percentage change unless otherwise stated)

(a) Recent trends in consumer price inflation

	Sep 97	Oct 97	Nov 97	Dec 97	Jan 98
National consumer price index (CPI)					
Annual percentage change	1.0	1.1	1.0	1.0	1.2
Change in the average of latest 3 months from previous 3 months, annualised rate, seasonally adjusted	-2.5	0.0	4.1	5.9	4.5
Change in the average of latest 6 months from previous 6 months, annualised rate, seasonally adjusted	0.1	0.2	0.2	0.5	1.2

Source: National non-harmonised data.

(b) Inflation forecasts

	1998	1999
European Commission (spring 1998), HICP	1.3	1.5
OECD (December 1997), private consumption deflator	1.5	1.6
IMF (October 1997), CPI	1.6	.

Source: European Commission (spring 1998 forecasts), OECD and IMF.

II   Fiscal developments

Table 4

Austria: General government financial position
(as a percentage of GDP)

	1996	**1997**	1998[a]
General government surplus (+) / deficit (-)	-4.0	-2.5	-2.3
Reference value	-3	-3	-3
Surplus (+) / deficit (-), net of public investment expenditure[b]	-1.2	0.1	.
General government gross debt	69.5	66.1	64.7
Reference value	60	60	60

Source: European Commission (spring 1998 forecasts) and EMI calculations.
(a) European Commission projections.
(b) A negative sign indicates that the government deficit is higher than investment expenditure.

Chart 2

Austria: General government gross debt
(as a percentage of GDP)

(a) Levels

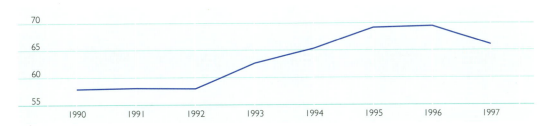

(b) Annual changes and underlying factors

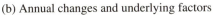

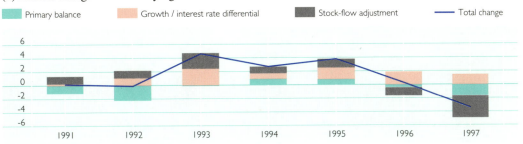

Source: European Commission (spring 1998 forecasts) and EMI calculations.
Note: In Chart 2b negative values indicate a contribution of the respective factor to a decrease in the debt ratio, while positive values indicate a contribution to its increase.

Table 5

Austria: General government gross debt - structural features

	1990	1991	1992	1993	1994	1995	1996	1997
Total debt (as a percentage of GDP)	57.9	58.1	58.0	62.7	65.4	69.2	69.5	66.1
Composition by currency[a] (% of total)								
In domestic currency	84.3	84.2	82.6	80.8	77.5	76.3	76.5	79.7
In foreign currencies	15.7	15.8	17.4	19.2	22.5	23.7	23.5	20.3
Domestic ownership[b] (% of total)	81.5	80.7	77.8	73.1	73.3	69.7	71.3	.
Average maturity[c] (years)	7.7	7.1	6.7	6.2	6.2	6.2	6.1	5.9
Composition by maturity[d] (% of total)								
Short-term (< 1 year)	.	.	.	.	.	.	8.6	10.7
Medium-term (1-5 years)	.	.	.	.	.	.	36.4	40.2
Long-term (> 5 years)	.	.	.	.	.	.	55.0	49.1

Source: National data except for total debt (European Commission (spring 1998 forecasts)). End-year data. Differences in the totals are due to rounding.
(a) 1990-93 Federal government only. 1997 estimated.
(b) 1990-93 Federal government debt; 1994-96 general government debt; all positions are partly estimated.
(c) Residual maturity. Federal government debt only.
(d) Residual maturity. Federal government debt only; debt linked to short-term interest rates according to maturity.

Chart 3

Austria: General government surplus (+) / deficit (-)
(as a percentage of GDP)

(a) Levels

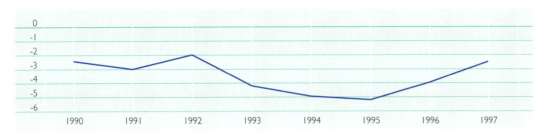

(b) Annual changes and underlying factors

Source: European Commission (spring 1998 forecasts).
Note: In Chart 3b negative values indicate a contribution to an increase in deficits, while positive values indicate a contribution to their reduction.

Chart 4

Austria: General government expenditure and receipts
(as a percentage of GDP)

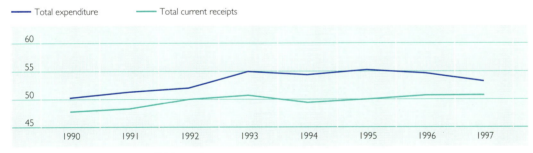

Source: European Commission (spring 1998 forecasts).

Table 6

Austria: General government budgetary position
(as a percentage of GDP)

	1990	1991	1992	1993	1994	1995	1996	1997
Total current receipts	47.8	48.3	50.0	50.7	49.4	50.0	50.7	50.8
Taxes	27.6	28.1	28.7	29.0	27.4	27.9	29.1	29.7
Social security contributions	15.7	15.8	16.4	17.1	17.5	17.6	17.5	17.1
Other current receipts	4.5	4.4	4.9	4.6	4.5	4.6	4.1	4.0
Total expenditure	50.2	51.3	52.0	54.9	54.3	55.2	54.6	53.2
Current transfers	22.9	23.4	23.6	25.4	25.0	26.0	26.1	25.6
Actual interest payments	4.0	4.2	4.3	4.3	4.1	4.4	4.4	4.1
Public consumption	18.6	18.9	19.4	20.2	20.3	20.1	19.8	19.4
Net capital expenditure	4.7	4.8	4.7	5.0	5.0	4.7	4.4	4.2
Surplus (+) or deficit (-)	-2.4	-3.0	-2.0	-4.2	-5.0	-5.2	-4.0	-2.5
Primary balance	1.6	1.2	2.3	0.1	-0.9	-0.8	0.4	1.6
Surplus (+) or deficit (-),								
net of public investment expenditure[a]	.	.	.	-1.0	-1.7	-2.2	-1.2	0.1

Source: European Commission (spring 1998 forecasts) and EMI calculations. Differences in the totals are due to rounding.
(a)   A negative sign indicates that the government deficit is higher than investment expenditure.

Chart 5

Austria: Potential future debt ratios under alternative assumptions for fiscal balance ratios
(as a percentage of GDP)

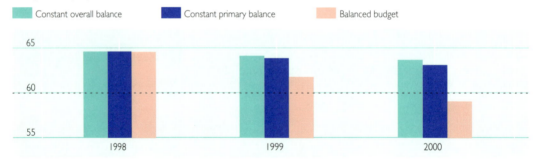

Source: European Commission (spring 1998 forecasts) and EMI calculations.
Note: The three scenarios assume that the debt ratio of 64.7% of GDP for 1998 is as forecast and that the 1998 overall balance of -2.3% of GDP or the primary balance of 1.7% of GDP will be kept constant over the period considered (as a percentage of GDP), or, alternatively, that a balanced budget is maintained from 1999 onwards. The underlying assumptions are a real trend GDP growth rate in 1998 of 2.5% as estimated by the Commission; an inflation rate of 2%; and, in the constant primary balance scenario, a nominal interest rate of 6%. Stock-flow adjustments are disregarded.

Table 7

Austria: Projections of elderly dependency ratio

	1990	2000	2010	2020	2030
Elderly dependency ratio (population aged 65 and over as a proportion of the population aged 15-64)	22.4	23.3	27.7	32.6	44.0

Source: Bos, E. et al. (1994), World population projections 1994-95, World Bank, Washington DC.

III Exchange rate developments

Table 8

(a) Austria: Exchange rate stability
(1 March 1996 - 27 February 1998)

Membership of the Exchange Rate Mechanism (ERM)	Yes
Membership since	9 January 1995
Devaluation of bilateral central rate on country's own initiative	No

Maximum upward (+) and downward (-) deviations from central rates in the ERM grid (%) against[a]

Belgian franc	0.1	-0.4
Danish krone	1.4	-0.3
Deutsche Mark	0.1	-0.0
Spanish peseta	0.1	-2.3
French franc	2.2	-0.2
Irish pound	3.9	-10.6
Italian lira	1.1	-1.8
Dutch guilder	0.0	-0.8
Portuguese escudo	1.1	-2.8
Finnish markka	-0.2	-2.9

Source: European Commission and EMI calculations.

(a)   Daily data at business frequency; 10-day moving average. Deviations against the Finnish markka refer to the period from 14 October 1996 onwards, while deviations against the Italian lira refer to the period from 25 November 1996 onwards.

(b) Key indicators of exchange rate pressure for the Austrian schilling

Average of 3 months ending:	May 96	Aug 96	Nov 96	Feb 97	May 97	Aug 97	Nov 97	Feb 98
Exchange rate volatility[a]	0.1	0.1	0.1	0.2	0.1	0.1	0.1	0.1
Short-term interest rate differentials[b]	-0.2	-0.1	0.1	0.1	0.1	0.1	0.1	0.1

Source: European Commission, national data and EMI calculations.

(a)   Annualised monthly standard deviation of daily percentage changes of the exchange rate against the DEM, in percentages.

(b)   Differential of three-month interbank interest rates against a weighted average of interest rates in Belgium, Germany, France, the Netherlands and Austria, in percentage points.

Austrian schilling: Deviations from ERM bilateral central rates
(daily data; percentages; 1 March 1996 to 27 February 1998)

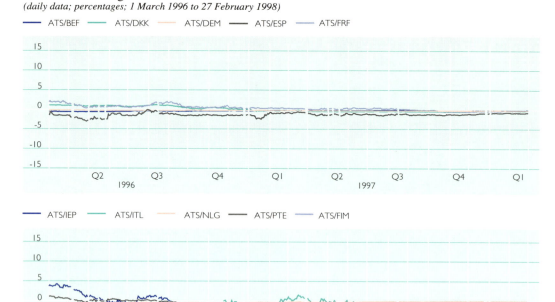

Source: European Commission.
Note: Deviations against the Finnish markka refer to the period from 14 October 1996 onwards, while deviations against the Italian lira refer to the period from 25 November 1996 onwards.

Austrian schilling: Measures of the real effective exchange rate vis-à-vis ERM Member States
(monthly data; percentage deviations; February 1998 compared with different benchmark periods)

	Average Apr 73-Feb 98	Average Jan 87-Feb 98	Average 1987
Real effective exchange rates:			
CPI-based	5.8	1.1	1.9
PPI/WPI-based	1.6	0.1	-0.3
Memo item:			
Nominal effective exchange rate	13.5	2.5	5.9

Source: BIS and EMI calculations.
Note: A positive (negative) sign indicates an appreciation (depreciation).

Table 10

Austria: External developments
(as a percentage of GDP)

	1990	1991	1992	1993	1994	1995	1996	1997[a]
Current account plus new capital account[b]	0.8	0.0	-0.1	-0.4	-0.9	-2.0	-1.8	-1.8
Net foreign assets (+) or liabilities (-)[c]	-4.0	-6.3	-5.8	-6.6	-8.6	-12.7	-12.4	.
Exports (goods and services)[d]	40.2	41.1	41.3	40.5	41.7	43.5	46.8	49.3
Imports (goods and services)[e]	38.9	40.0	40.2	39.7	41.9	44.0	47.0	48.3

Source: National data except exports and imports (European Commission, spring 1998 forecasts).

(a) Partly estimated.

(b) According to the 5th edition of the IMF Balance of Payments Manual, which is conceptually the equivalent of the current account in previous editions of the Manual.

(c) International investment position (IIP) as defined by the IMF (see Balance of Payments Yearbook, Part 1, 1994), or the closest possible substitute.

(d) In 1996 the share of intra-EU exports of goods in total national exports of goods was 59.7%; Direction of Trade Statistics Yearbook 1997, IMF.

(e) In 1996 the share of intra-EU imports of goods in total national imports of goods was 74.8%; Direction of Trade Statistics Yearbook 1997, IMF.

IV Long-term interest rate developments

Austria: Long-term interest rates
(percentages)

	1996	1997	Nov 97	Dec 97	Jan 98	**Feb 97- Jan 98**
Long-term interest rate	6.3	5.7	5.6	5.4	5.2	5.6
Reference value	9.1	8.0	-	-	-	7.8

Source: European Commission.

(a) Austria: Long-term interest rate
(monthly averages; in percentages)

(b) Austria: Long-term interest rate and CPI inflation differentials against EU countries with lowest long-term interest rates*
(monthly averages; in percentage points)

 Long-term interest rate differential    CPI inflation differential

Source: Interest rates: European Commission (where these are not available the most comparable data have been used); the CPI data used are non-harmonised national data.
* Weighted average of data for Belgium, Germany, France, the Netherlands and Austria.

PORTUGAL

Price developments

Over the reference period from February 1997 to January 1998 the average rate of HICP inflation in Portugal was 1.8%, i.e. well below the reference value of 2.7%. This was also the case in 1997 as a whole. In 1996 average HICP inflation was 2.9% (see Table 1). Seen over the past two years, HICP inflation in Portugal has been reduced to a level which is generally considered to be consistent with price stability.

Looking back, consumer price inflation in Portugal, as measured on the basis of the CPI, has followed a downward trend since the early 1990s, with the rate falling steadily from above 13% at the start of the decade (see Chart 1). This experience of disinflation reflects a number of important policy choices. Monetary policy has been geared increasingly towards the reduction of inflation rates, first through a unilateral link to a basket of ERM currencies, and then, from spring 1992 onwards, through membership of the ERM. This general orientation has been supported by adjustments in fiscal policy, reforms designed to enhance product market competition and labour market reforms. In addition, the macroeconomic environment has contributed to containing upward pressure on prices. In particular, in the context of weak GDP growth in 1993-94, a negative output gap emerged. In the subsequent recovery, the output gap has been reduced gradually (see Table 2). Against this background, upward pressures on compensation per employee have been restrained although increases have still been considerable. Growth in unit labour costs has decelerated markedly over the 1990s. Import price developments have underpinned the disinflationary process during most of the period under review. The general trend towards lower rates of inflation is also apparent when it is measured in terms of other relevant price indices, while some measures exceeded HICP inflation in 1997 (see Table 2).

Looking at recent trends and forecasts, current outturns for consumer price inflation (measured as a percentage change over the corresponding month a year earlier) have been around 2% and there are no signs of immediate upward pressure on the basis of the measures shown in Table 3a. Most forecasts of inflation suggest a rate of somewhat above 2% for 1998 and 1999 (see Table 3b). Risks for price stability over this period are associated with a narrowing of the output gap and accelerating unit labour costs.

Looking further ahead, maintaining an environment conducive to price stability relates in Portugal to, inter alia, the conduct of fiscal policies over the medium to long term; it will be equally important to strengthen national policies aimed at enhancing competition in product markets and improving the functioning of labour markets.

Fiscal developments

In the *reference year* 1997 the general government deficit ratio was 2.5%, i.e. below the 3% reference value, and the debt ratio was 62.0%, i.e. just above the 60% reference value. Compared with the previous year, the deficit ratio has been reduced by 0.7 percentage point and the debt ratio has decreased by 3.0 percentage points. In 1998 the deficit ratio is forecast to decrease to 2.2% of GDP, while the debt ratio is projected to decrease to 60.0%, at the level of the reference value. In 1996 and 1997 the deficit ratio did not exceed the ratio of public investment expenditure to GDP (see Table 4).

Looking back over the years 1990 to 1997, the Portuguese *debt-to-GDP ratio* declined by 3.3 percentage points. After falling sharply to 60.1% in 1992 from 67.3% in 1991, the ratio tended to increase continuously until 1995, when it reached 65.9%. Thereafter, it was again on a declining trend, decreasing to 62.0% in 1997 (see Chart 2a), i.e. a decline of 3.9 percentage points over two years. As is shown in greater detail in Chart 2b, the sharp drop in 1992 was the result of both a high primary surplus and a sizable "stock-flow adjustment", reflecting a net disposal of government assets. In the years 1993-95 the primary surplus almost disappeared, while a negative growth/interest rate differential increased the debt ratio. Finally, in the last two years, primary surpluses increased and, together with a less unfavourable growth/interest rate differential, reversed the upward trend in the debt ratio. The patterns observed thus far during the 1990s may be seen as indicative of the risks to the debt ratio which can arise when macroeconomic conditions deteriorate and these effects are not counterbalanced by a sufficiently high primary surplus. In this context, it may be noted that the share of debt with a short-term residual maturity has been decreasing from the high levels of the early 1990s, while the average maturity has remained broadly stable (see Table 5). With respect to 1997, the proportion of debt with a short-term residual maturity is still high, and, taking into account the current level of the debt ratio, fiscal balances are sensitive to changes in interest rates. In addition, the proportion of foreign currency debt has increased to noticeable levels, rendering fiscal balances in principle relatively sensitive to changes in exchange rates, although the bulk of this debt may eventually be redenominated in euro.

During the 1990s a broadly flat trend until 1995 and subsequently improving outturns can be observed in the *deficit-to-GDP ratio*. Starting from a ratio of 5.1% in 1990, the deficit fluctuated around 6% until 1995, with the exception of a lower deficit in 1992; since then, the deficit has fallen to 3.2% in 1996 and 2.5% in 1997 (see Chart 3a). As is shown in greater detail in Chart 3b, which focuses on *changes* in deficits, cyclical factors contributed to an increase in the deficit ratio up to 1995 and to a reduction in 1996-97, but the impact was small with the exception of 1993-94. However, the non-cyclical improvements could reflect a lasting, "structural" move toward more balanced fiscal policies and/ or a variety of measures with temporary effects. Evidence available suggests that measures with a temporary effect played a role in improving the fiscal balance in 1996 and 1997 but that the impact did not exceed 0.2% of GDP. As the measures in 1997 were mainly of a "self-reversing" nature, compensating measures already included in the 1998 budget will need to yield their expected results and, in addition, compensating measures will need to be taken in later years when the self-reversing effects unwind.

Moving on to examine trends in other fiscal indicators, it can be seen from Chart 4 that the general government *total expenditure ratio* rose in the early 1990s. Against the background of rising unemployment, current transfers to households increased, as did public consumption relative to GDP (see Table 6). After 1993 the ratio of total expenditure to GDP was broadly stable, reflecting a sharp reduction in interest payments and upward trends in current transfers and public consumption. On balance, the expenditure ratio in 1997 was more than 3½ percentage points higher than at the beginning of the 1990s, reflecting an increase in current transfers and public consumption, while interest payments are now nearly 4 percentage points lower. Given that interest payments have already come down substantially in recent years and further declines at a similar pace are not expected, controlling public expenditure would seem to require greater emphasis to be placed on the control of other expenditure items. *Government revenue* in relation to GDP has tended to increase since 1994, and it is now more than 6 percentage points higher than in 1990. The national accounts treatment of the State transfers to the civil servants' pension system imply a double counting of these transfers. Over the period 1990-97, State transfers to the civil servants' pension system accounted for increases of 1.3 percentage points in the ratios of both revenue and expenditure to GDP.

According to the Portuguese *medium-term fiscal strategy,* as presented in the new Convergence Programme for 1998-2000 dated March 1997, a declining trend in deficit and debt ratios is projected to continue in 1998. The budget plan for 1998 is in line with the programme and Commission forecasts are slightly more favourable. The budget foresees a reduction in the share of government expenditure in GDP, whereas government revenues are planned to increase in line with GDP. Currently, there is no evidence of significant measures with a temporary effect in the 1998 budget. According to current plans, the deficit ratio is expected to reach 1.5% of GDP in the year 2000. The goals of the previous programmes for 1997 have been more than met. Compared with fiscal balances projected in the Convergence Programme for 1999-2000, further substantial consolidation is required in order to comply with the medium-term objective of the Stability and Growth Pact, effective from 1999 onwards, of having a budgetary position that is close to balance or in surplus.

With regard to the *potential future course of the debt ratio,* the EMI's Report does not consider this issue in detail for those countries forecast to have a debt ratio of 60% of GDP or below in 1998. Projected developments underline the benefits of the reduction in the deficit position achieved in

1997, and forecast to decline further in 1998, for reducing the debt ratio. Stressing the benefits of further improvement in the deficit ratio and of sustaining consolidation over time is indeed appropriate in the case of Portugal. As has been seen in the past, less favourable economic conditions than those currently prevailing tend to imply an increase in the debt ratio. In addition, as is highlighted in Table 7, from around 2010 onwards a marked ageing of the population is expected and in the context of an unfunded pension system, public pension expenditure is projected to increase relative to GDP, particularly if policies regarding benefits continue unchanged. The overall burden of population ageing will become more manageable the better the state of public finances when the demographic situation worsens.

Exchange rate developments

The Portuguese escudo has been participating in the ERM since 6 April 1992, i.e. for considerably longer than two years prior to the examination (see Table 8a). As mentioned above, Portuguese monetary policy has been geared towards the achievement of price stability, from spring 1992 onwards within the context of the ERM. Focusing on the *reference period* from March 1996 to February 1998, the currency, benefiting from sizable short-term interest rate differentials vis-à-vis most partner currencies, has normally traded close to its central rates against other ERM currencies (see Chart 5 and Table 8a). On occasion the Portuguese escudo traded outside a range close to its central rates vis-à-vis various partner currencies. The maximum upward and downward deviations from central rates, on the basis of 10 business day moving averages, were 3.5% and -2.3% respectively, abstracting from the autonomous upward trend of the Irish pound (see Table 8a). The episodes in which such deviations occurred were temporary, the degree of exchange rate volatility vis-à-vis the Deutsche Mark was low (see Table 8b) and short-term interest rate differentials against those EU countries with the lowest short-term interest rates were continuously narrowing. During the reference period Portugal has not devalued its currency's bilateral central rate against any other Member State's currency.

In a longer-term context, the available real effective exchange rate data for the Portuguese escudo against other ERM participating currencies depicted in Table 9 suggest that current levels are above 1987 average values; since 1992 the real exchange rate has been broadly stable. As regards other external developments, after having maintained a virtually balanced position in the period 1990-93, the Portuguese current account shifted into deficit in 1994; the Portuguese economy maintained a net foreign asset position (see Table 10). It may also be recalled that Portugal is a small open economy with, according to the most recent data available, a ratio of foreign trade to GDP of 46% for exports and 59% for imports, and a share of intra-EU trade of 80% for exports and 76% for imports.

Long-term interest rate developments

Over the *reference period* from February 1997 to January 1998 *long-term interest rates* in Portugal were 6.2% on average, and thus stood below the reference value for the interest rate criterion of 7.8% set on the basis of the three best-performing Member States in terms of price stability. This was also the case for 1997 as a whole, as well as for 1996 (see Table 11). Twelve-month average long-term interest rates have been below the reference value since November 1996.

Long-term interest rates have been on a broadly declining trend since the early 1990s (see Chart 6a). A broad trend towards the convergence of Portuguese long-term interest rates with those

prevailing in the EU countries with the lowest bond yields has also been observed for most of the period since the early 1990s. Since mid-1995 this process of convergence has accelerated and the differential has now been virtually eliminated (see Chart 6b). The main factor underlying this trend was the significant narrowing of the inflation differential. In addition, the relative stability of the Portuguese escudo's exchange rate and the improvement in the country's fiscal position also played a role. These underlying developments were seen by markets as improving the prospects for participation in Stage Three of EMU - an element which may in turn have played an independent role in accelerating the narrowing of yield differentials, both directly and by further improving the prospects for price and exchange rate stability.

Concluding summary

Over the reference period Portugal has achieved a rate of HICP inflation of 1.8%, which is well below the reference value stipulated by the Treaty. The increase in unit labour costs has decelerated markedly over the 1990s and the general trend towards low rates of inflation was also apparent in terms of other relevant price indices. Looking ahead, there are no signs of immediate upward pressure on inflation; forecasts project inflation to stand somewhat above 2% in 1998 and 1999. The Portuguese escudo has been participating in the ERM for considerably longer than two years. Over the reference period it remained broadly stable, generally close to its unchanged central parities, without the need for measures to support the exchange rate. The level of long-term interest rates was 6.2%, i.e. below the respective reference value.

In 1997 Portugal achieved a fiscal deficit ratio of 2.5%, i.e. below the reference value, and the outlook is for a decrease to 2.2% in 1998. The debt-to-GDP ratio is just above the 60% reference value. After reaching a peak in 1995 the ratio declined by 3.9 percentage points to stand at 62.0% in 1997. Regarding the sustainability of fiscal developments, the outlook is for a decrease in the debt ratio to 60.0% of GDP in 1998, i.e. a level equal to the reference value. Looking further ahead, current fiscal deficit ratios exceed the medium-term objective of the Stability and Growth Pact, effective from 1999 onwards,

of having a budgetary position that is close to balance or in surplus, thus pointing to a need for further substantial consolidation. This would also imply a reduction in the debt ratio to below 60%.

With regard to other factors, in 1996 and 1997 the deficit ratio did not exceed the ratio of public investment to GDP, and Portugal has recorded current account deficits and a net external asset position.

List of Tables and Charts*

---

* Chart scales may differ across countries.

I   Price developments

Portugal: HICP inflation
(annual percentage changes)

	1996	1997	Nov 97	Dec 97	Jan 98	**Feb 97- Jan 98**
HICP inflation	2.9	1.9	1.9	2.1	1.6	1.8
Reference value	2.5	2.7	-	-	-	2.7

Source: European Commission.

Portugal: Price developments
(annual percentage changes)

Source: National data.

Table 2

Portugal: Measures of inflation and related indicators
(annual percentage changes unless otherwise stated)

	1990	1991	1992	1993	1994	1995	1996	1997[a]
Measures of inflation								
Consumer price index (CPI)	13.4	11.4	8.9	6.5	5.2	4.1	3.1	2.2
CPI excluding changes in net indirect taxes[b]	.	.	6.5	5.3	5.0	3.5	3.3	2.4
Private consumption deflator	13.8	12.1	10.2	6.8	5.4	4.2	3.1	2.2
GDP deflator	13.0	14.8	13.2	6.8	5.0	5.0	2.8	2.9
Producer prices[c]	.	2.2	0.2	2.0	3.2	5.1	4.2	1.9
Related indicators								
Real GDP growth	4.6	2.3	1.8	0.3	0.7	1.9	3.6	3.8
Output gap (p.pts)	4.1	3.5	2.5	0.1	-1.9	-2.7	-2.0	-1.3
Unemployment rate (%)	4.7	4.1	4.1	5.5	6.8	7.2	7.3	6.7
Unit labour costs, whole economy	15.7	15.1	13.3	6.5	4.2	2.0	2.9	2.8
Compensation per employee, whole economy	17.7	14.2	14.1	7.5	4.8	5.0	5.7	4.8
Labour productivity, whole economy	1.7	-0.8	0.7	0.9	0.6	2.9	2.7	1.9
Import price deflator	6.4	0.5	-6.1	3.2	3.4	1.7	0.3	-0.3
Exchange rate appreciation[d]	-2.4	0.7	3.4	-6.0	-4.2	2.0	-0.4	-2.0
Broad monetary aggregate (M3H)[e]	9.4	18.0	21.8	11.2	7.3	10.5	7.5	8.1
Stock prices	-0.5	-16.2	-11.5	14.5	34.1	-3.3	15.6	56.9
House prices	15.0	19.4	12.4	1.3	1.2	1.5	1.6	3.6

Source: National data except real GDP growth and the output gap (European Commission, spring 1998 forecasts) and exchange rate (BIS).
(a) Partly estimated.
(b) National estimates.
(c) Manufacturing sector.
(d) Nominal effective exchange rate against 25 industrialised countries.
    Note: A positive (negative) sign indicates an appreciation (depreciation).
(e) National harmonised data.

Table 3

Portugal: Recent inflation trends and forecasts
(annual percentage change unless otherwise stated)

(a) Recent trends in consumer price inflation

	Sep 97	Oct 97	Nov 97	Dec 97	Jan 98[b]
National consumer price index (CPI)					
Annual percentage change	1.8	1.8	2.1	2.3	1.9
Change in the average of latest 3 months from previous					
3 months, annualised rate, seasonally adjusted[a]	1.5	1.3	1.4	1.6	.
Change in the average of latest 6 months from previous					
6 months, annualised rate, seasonally adjusted[a]	2.4	2.3	1.9	1.9	.

Source: National non-harmonised data.
(a) CPI excluding seasonal items.
(b) New index; no seasonally adjusted data available.

(b) Inflation forecasts

	1998	1999
European Commission (spring 1998), HICP	2.2	2.3
OECD (December 1997), private consumption deflator	2.2	2.1
IMF (October 1997), CPI	2.3	.

Source: European Commission (spring 1998 forecasts), OECD and IMF.

II Fiscal developments

Table 4

Portugal: General government financial position
(as a percentage of GDP)

	1996	**1997**	1998[a]
General government surplus (+) / deficit (-)	-3.2	-2.5	-2.2
Reference value	-3	-3	-3
Surplus (+) / deficit (-), net of public investment expenditure[b]	0.8	1.9	.
General government gross debt	65.0	62.0	60.0
Reference value	60	60	60

Source: European Commission (spring 1998 forecasts) and EMI calculations.
(a) European Commission projections.
(b) A negative sign indicates that the government deficit is higher than investment expenditure.

Chart 2

Portugal: General government gross debt
(as a percentage of GDP)

(a) Levels

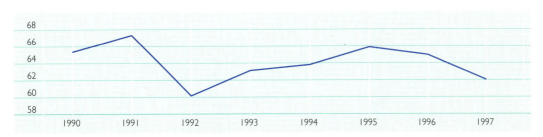

(b) Annual changes and underlying factors

Source: European Commission (spring 1998 forecasts) and EMI calculations.
Note: In Chart 2b negative values indicate a contribution of the respective factor to a decrease in the debt ratio, while positive values indicate a contribution to its increase.

223

Table 5

Portugal: General government gross debt – structural features

	1990	1991	1992	1993	1994	1995	1996	1997
Total debt (as a percentage of GDP)	65.3	67.3	60.1	63.1	63.8	65.9	65.0	62.0
Composition by currency (% of total)								
In domestic currency	90.0	92.9	93.0	88.3	84.7	81.7	81.2	.
In foreign currencies	10.0	7.1	7.0	11.7	15.3	18.3	18.8	.
Domestic ownership (% of total)	86.8	85.3	90.5	83.3	79.3	78.2	75.3	.
Average maturity[a] (years)	3.5	3.6	3.6	3.5	3.0	3.0	3.2	3.4
Composition by maturity[b] (% of total)								
Short-term[c] (< 1 year)	47.7	38.9	35.6	33.5	36.0	38.5	42.1	33.1
Medium-term (1-5 years)	15.3	36.3	58.4	54.5	47.1	39.1	31.5	38.0
Long-term (> 5 years)	37.0	24.8	6.0	12.0	16.9	22.4	26.3	28.9

Source: National data except for total debt (European Commission (spring 1998 forecasts)). End-year data. Differences in the totals are due to rounding.

(a) Residual maturity. Domestic currency debt only. An average maturity of five years is assumed for savings certificates, which represent between 14.3% (1994) and 7.7% (1990) of total debt.

(b) Residual maturity. State debt excluding coins and domestic bank loans, which represents between 87.1% (1991) and 96.3% (1994) of the general government gross debt. Savings certificates are classified as short-term debt. 1990-93 domestic currency debt only.

(c) Including savings certificates.

Chart 3

Portugal: General government surplus (+) / deficit (-)
(as a percentage of GDP)

(a) Levels

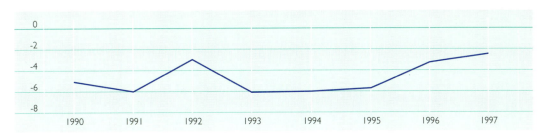

(b) Annual changes and underlying factors

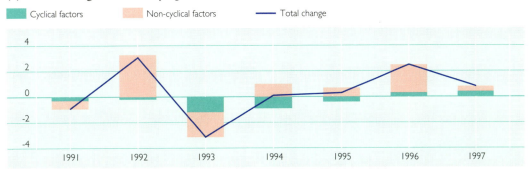

Source: European Commission (spring 1998 forecasts).
Note: In Chart 3b negative values indicate a contribution to an increase in deficits, while positive values indicate a contribution to their reduction.

Chart 4

Portugal: General government expenditure and receipts
(as a percentage of GDP)

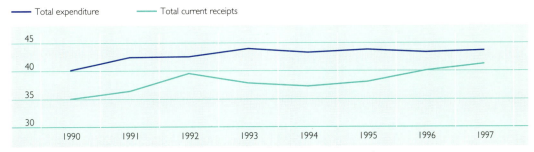

Source: European Commission (spring 1998 forecasts).

Table 6

Portugal: General government budgetary position
(as a percentage of GDP)

	1990	1991	1992	1993	1994	1995	1996	1997
Total current receipts	35.0	36.4	39.6	37.9	37.2	38.0	40.0	41.2
Taxes	21.6	22.4	24.4	22.6	22.8	23.2	24.4	24.8
Social security contributions	10.4	10.9	11.5	12.1	11.8	11.9	11.6	11.9
Other current receipts	3.0	3.2	3.7	3.2	2.7	2.9	4.1	4.5
Total expenditure	40.1	42.4	42.5	44.0	43.3	43.8	43.3	43.7
Current transfers	12.8	13.9	14.1	15.8	16.3	16.4	17.1	17.3
Actual interest payments	8.1	7.9	7.2	6.2	6.2	6.3	4.8	4.3
Public consumption	15.5	17.2	17.4	17.9	17.6	17.7	18.1	18.6
Net capital expenditure	3.6	3.4	3.8	4.0	3.2	3.4	3.2	3.4
Surplus (+) or deficit (-)	-5.1	-6.0	-3.0	-6.1	-6.0	-5.7	-3.2	-2.5
Primary balance	3.0	1.8	4.3	0.1	0.2	0.6	1.6	1.9
Surplus (+) or deficit (-), net of public investment expenditure[a]	.	.	.	-2.1	-2.4	-2.0	0.8	1.9

Source: European Commission (spring 1998 forecasts) and EMI calculations. Differences in the totals are due to rounding.
(a)   A negative sign indicates that the government deficit is higher than investment expenditure.

Table 7

Portugal: Projections of elderly dependency ratio

	1990	2000	2010	2020	2030
Elderly dependency ratio (population aged 65 and over as a proportion of the population aged 15-64)	19.5	20.9	22.0	25.3	33.5

Source: Bos, E. et al. (1994), World population projections 1994-95, World Bank, Washington DC.

III Exchange rate developments

Table 8

(a) Portugal: Exchange rate stability
(1 March 1996 - 27 February 1998)

Membership of the Exchange Rate Mechanism (ERM)	Yes
Membership since	6 April 1992
Devaluation of bilateral central rate on country's own initiative	No

Maximum upward (+) and downward (-) deviations from central rates
in the ERM grid (%) against[a]

Belgian franc	2.8	-1.4
Danish krone	2.8	0.0
Deutsche Mark	2.9	-1.1
Spanish peseta	1.7	-2.3
French franc	3.5	-0.0
Irish pound	3.0	-9.3
Italian lira	3.0	-0.7
Dutch guilder	2.5	-1.7
Austrian schilling	2.9	-1.1
Finnish markka	1.2	-1.4

Source: European Commission and EMI calculations.

(a) Daily data at business frequency; 10-day moving average. Deviations against the Finnish markka refer to the period from 14 October 1996 onwards, while deviations against the Italian lira refer to the period from 25 November 1996 onwards.

(b) Key indicators of exchange rate pressure for the Portuguese escudo

Average of 3 months ending:	May 96	Aug 96	Nov 96	Feb 97	May 97	Aug 97	Nov 97	Feb 98
Exchange rate volatility[a]	2.0	1.3	1.5	1.8	2.0	1.7	1.1	0.4
Short-term interest rate differentials[b]	4.1	3.8	3.8	3.1	2.7	2.5	1.8	1.4

Source: European Commission, national data and EMI calculations.

(a) Annualised monthly standard deviation of daily percentage changes of the exchange rate against the DEM, in percentages.

(b) Differential of three-month interbank interest rates against a weighted average of interest rates in Belgium, Germany, France, the Netherlands and Austria, in percentage points.

Portuguese escudo: Deviations from ERM bilateral central rates

(daily data; percentages; 1 March 1996 to 27 February 1998)

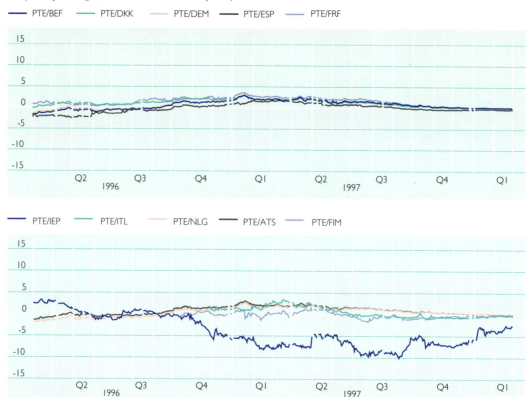

Source: European Commission.
Note: Deviations against the Finnish markka refer to the period from 14 October 1996 onwards, while deviations against the Italian lira refer to the period from 25 November 1996 onwards.

Portuguese escudo: Measures of the real effective exchange rate vis-à-vis ERM Member States

(monthly data; percentage deviations; February 1998 compared with different benchmark periods)

	Average Apr 73-Feb 98	Average Jan 87-Feb 98	Average 1987
Real effective exchange rates:			
CPI-based	11.8	7.7	26.8
PPI/WPI-based	.	.	.
Memo item:			
Nominal effective exchange rate	-55.9	-6.2	-16.3

Source: BIS and EMI calculations.
Note: A positive (negative) sign indicates an appreciation (depreciation).

Table 10

Portugal: External developments

(as a percentage of GDP)

	1990	1991	1992	1993	1994	1995	1996	1997[a]
Current account plus new capital account[b]	-0.3	-0.9	-0.1	0.1	-2.5	-0.2	-1.4	-2.0
Net foreign assets (+) or liabilities (-)[c]	7.7	10.5	13.3	17.4	14.1	7.9	10.6	9.9
Exports (goods and services)[d]	34.3	33.8	34.6	34.5	38.2	42.0	43.9	45.7
Imports (goods and services)[e]	41.9	43.6	47.3	45.7	50.3	53.7	55.7	59.2

Source: National data except exports and imports (European Commission, spring 1998 forecasts).

(a) Partly estimated.

(b) According to the 5th edition of the IMF Balance of Payments Manual, which is conceptually the equivalent of the current account in previous editions of the Manual.

(c) International investment position (IIP) as defined by the IMF (see Balance of Payments Yearbook, Part 1, 1994), or the closest possible substitute.

(d) In 1996 the share of intra-EU exports of goods in total national exports of goods was 80.0%; Direction of Trade Statistics Yearbook 1997, IMF.

(e) In 1996 the share of intra-EU imports of goods in total national imports of goods was 75.7%; Direction of Trade Statistics Yearbook 1997, IMF.

IV Long-term interest rate developments

Table 11

Portugal: Long-term interest rates
(percentages)

	1996	1997	Nov 97	Dec 97	Jan 98	**Feb 97- Jan 98**
Long-term interest rate	8.6	6.4	6.0	5.7	5.4	6.2
Reference value	9.1	8.0	-	-	-	7.8

Source: European Commission.

Chart 6

(a) Portugal: Long-term interest rate
(monthly averages; in percentages)

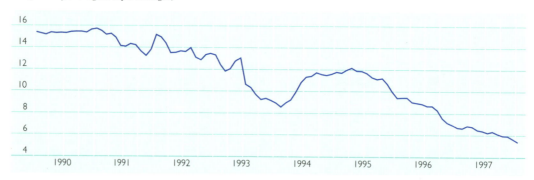

(b) Portugal: Long-term interest rate and CPI inflation differentials against EU
countries with lowest long-term interest rates*
(monthly averages; in percentage points)

Source: Interest rates: European Commission (where these are not available the most comparable data have been used); the CPI data used are non-harmonised national data.
* Weighted average of data for Belgium, Germany, France, the Netherlands and Austria.

FINLAND

Price developments

Over the reference period from February 1997 to January 1998 the average rate of HICP inflation in Finland was 1.3%, i.e. well below the reference value of 2.7%. This was also the case in 1997 as a whole. In 1996 average HICP inflation was 1.1% (see Table 1). Seen over the past two years, HICP inflation in Finland has been at levels which are generally considered to be consistent with price stability.

Looking back, consumer price inflation in Finland, as measured on the basis of the CPI, has followed a downward trend since the early 1990s, with the rate having stood close to, or well below, 2% since 1993 (see Chart 1). This experience of disinflation reflects a number of important policy choices, most notably the shift in monetary policy towards the primary objective of price stability. Since 1993 this objective has been enshrined in a target of around 2% for the underlying rate of consumer price inflation and it has most recently been pursued within the framework of the ERM. This general orientation has been supported by, inter alia, adjustments in fiscal policy and enhanced competition in formerly protected sectors of the economy, linked also to Finland's accession to the EU in 1995. Measures have also been taken to increase the flexibility of the economy, including the labour markets. In addition, the macroeconomic environment has contributed significantly to containing upward pressure on prices. In particular, in the context of the dramatic fall in output between 1990 and 1993, a large negative output gap emerged (see Table 2). Since 1994 a robust recovery has been under way and the output gap has narrowed. Against this background, growth in compensation per employee picked up in 1994-95. Cuts in employers' social security contributions in conjunction with strong growth in labour productivity have contributed to the subdued rise in unit labour costs; import prices have remained broadly stable in recent years, thereby also helping to keep inflationary pressures under control. Low rates of inflation are also apparent when it is measured in terms of other relevant price indices (see Table 2).

Looking at recent trends and forecasts, current outturns for consumer price inflation (measured as a percentage change over the corresponding month a year earlier) have been increasing slightly towards 2% and there are some signs of immediate upward pressure on the basis of the measures shown in Table 3a. Forecasts of inflation suggest a rate of 2-2½% for 1998 and 1999 (see Table 3b). Risks for price stability over this period are associated with capacity constraints and trends in asset prices.

Looking further ahead, maintaining an environment conducive to price stability relates in Finland to, inter alia, the conduct of fiscal policies over the medium to long term; it will be equally important to strengthen national policies aimed at enhancing competition in product markets and improving the functioning of labour markets against the background of the current high rate of unemployment in Finland.

Fiscal developments

In the *reference year* 1997 the general government deficit ratio was 0.9%, i.e. well below the 3% reference value, and the debt ratio was 55.8%, i.e. below the 60% reference value. Compared with the previous year, the deficit ratio has been reduced by 2.4 percentage points and the debt ratio has decreased by 1.8 percentage points. In 1998 a surplus of 0.3% of GDP is expected, while the debt ratio is projected to decrease to 53.6%. Whereas in 1996 the deficit ratio exceeded the ratio of public investment expenditure to GDP, in 1997 it was below it (see Table 4).

Looking back over the years 1990 to 1997, the Finnish *debt-to-GDP ratio* increased by 41.3 percentage points; initially the situation of Finland's government finances deteriorated sharply, and the debt ratio rose from 14.5% of GDP in 1990 to 59.6% in 1994. Thereafter, the debt ratio declined to 55.8% (see Chart 2a). As is shown in greater detail in Chart 2b, in the early 1990s both an unfavourable growth and interest rate environment, reflecting a fall in Finland's GDP of 13% over three years, and a deteriorating primary balance played a role in increasing government debt. However, as is reflected in the so-called "stock-flow adjustment item" of public debt, the financial support granted to the banking sector and the revaluation of foreign currency denominated government debt after the sizable depreciation of the Finnish markka between 1991 and 1993 had the strongest impact. Having reached a balanced position in 1995, the primary surplus started to increase thereafter, thereby compensating for the debt-increasing effects resulting from the macroeconomic environment and further stock-flow adjustments in 1997. The pattern observed thus far during the 1990s is an illustration of the powerful effects which exceptional events combined with a strong deterioration in the macroeconomic environment can have on the debt ratio, particularly if the primary balance does not improve promptly so as to counterbalance such effects. In this context, it may be noted that the share of debt with a short-term residual maturity has tended to increase during the 1990s, while the average maturity has remained broadly stable (see Table 5). With regard to 1997, the proportion of gross debt with a short-term residual maturity is noticeable. However, since short-term debt in Finland is matched by liquid short-term assets, the

sensitivity of the government fiscal balance to changes in interest rates is significantly reduced. On the other hand, the proportion of foreign currency debt is high (although decreasing more recently), rendering fiscal balances in principle sensitive to changes in exchange rates, although part of this debt may eventually be redenominated in euro.

During the 1990s a pattern of first sharply deteriorating and subsequently improving outturns can be observed in the *deficit-to-GDP ratio*. Starting from a surplus of 5.4% of GDP in 1990, a deficit emerged in 1991 and increased quickly to reach a peak of 8.0% in 1993; since then, the deficit has declined year by year to stand at 0.9% in 1997 (see Chart 3a). As is shown in greater detail in Chart 3b, which focuses on *changes* in deficits, cyclical factors dominated the increase in the deficit until 1993 and its decrease thereafter. However, the non-cyclical improvements could reflect a lasting, "structural" move towards more balanced fiscal policies and/or a variety of measures with temporary effects. Evidence available suggests that measures taken in the context of the 1993 tax reform led to a "one-off" increase in revenues in 1997, estimated to amount to 0.6% of GDP.

Moving on to examine trends in other fiscal indicators, it can be seen from Chart 4 that the general government *total expenditure ratio* rose sharply between 1990 and 1993. Against the background of high and rising unemployment current transfers in the form of social security payments increased steeply, and, owing to the rapid increase in the debt ratio, interest payments also surged as a percentage of GDP, while public consumption increased mostly as a result of the decline in GDP (see Table 6). After 1993 the total expenditure ratio declined as a consequence of a reduction in all expenditure categories with the exception of interest payments. The expenditure ratio in 1997 was nearly 8 percentage points higher than at the beginning of the 1990s, reflecting higher ratios for all major items except net capital expenditure and public consumption. Given this pattern and taking into account both that interest payments have increased in line with the higher debt ratio and that current transfers are still well above the level observed in 1990, a continuation of the downward trend of total expenditure to GDP would seem to require greater emphasis to be placed on adjustments in current transfers. *Government revenue* increased in relation to GDP until 1992, since when it has tended to decline. It may be at a level which is detrimental to economic growth.

According to the Finnish *medium-term fiscal policy strategy,* as presented in the Convergence Programme for 1998-2001 dated September 1997, the general government financial position is expected to be close to balance in 1998 and the debt ratio is expected to decline. The budget for 1998 is in line with the programme. On the part of the central government, the budget foresees both reduced expenditure (mostly as a consequence of cuts in transfers and the postponement of investment to prevent the economy overheating) as well as increased income tax revenues. Currently, there is no evidence of significant measures with a temporary effect in the 1998 budget. Surpluses are projected from 1998 onwards and the debt ratio is expected to continue to decline. With regard to the development of fiscal deficits and debt ratios, current projections are more favourable than the 1997 update of the Convergence Programme. If fiscal balances turn out as projected in the Convergence Programme for 1999-2000, Finland should comply with the medium-term objective of the Stability and Growth Pact, effective from 1999 onwards, of having a budgetary position that is close to balance or in surplus. However, the actual fiscal position benefits from a strong economy; risks may arise if economic growth slows down.

With regard to the *potential future course of the debt ratio,* the EMI's Report does not consider this issue in detail for those countries with a debt ratio of below 60% of GDP. In the case of Finland it would appear that a further reduction in the debt ratio to levels of well below 60% can be achieved if current budgetary plans are maintained. Such considerations are also important in the case of Finland since additional room for manoeuvre will be necessary in order to be able to address *future budgetary challenges.* As is highlighted in Table 7, from around 2010 onwards a marked ageing of the population is expected. As a consequence, public pension expenditure is forecast to increase in relation to GDP, particularly if policies regarding benefits continue unchanged. Finland benefits, however, from a partly funded pension system. One aspect of particular relevance in Finland is that the partly funded pension system currently invests a large part of its surpluses in government paper, thereby reducing the consolidated government gross debt. As a result, any change in this investment policy would pose a risk to the gross debt ratio (but not, however, to the interest burden). Moreover, the demographic trend over the next few decades will have an adverse effect on the current surpluses in the pension system, thereby making further improvements in the general government fiscal balance essential. Alleviation of the overall burden of population ageing will be facilitated to a greater degree the better the state of public finances when the demographic situation worsens.

Exchange rate developments

The Finnish markka has been participating in the ERM since 14 October 1996, i.e. for around 16 months of the two-year *reference period* (from March 1996 to February 1998) prior to the examination by the EMI (see Table 8a). As mentioned above, in 1993 Finnish monetary policy adopted price stability as its primary objective, which has most recently been pursued within the context of the ERM.

At the beginning of the reference period, before it joined the ERM, the markka initially continued its weakening movement apparent over the previous few months, which had interrupted the longer-term upward movement since 1993. It reached a maximum downward deviation of 6.5% below its future central rate against one ERM currency in April 1996. Thereafter, it appreciated and generally traded within a narrow range around its later central parities.

Since joining the ERM in October 1996 the markka has normally traded close to its central rates against other ERM currencies (see Chart 5 and Table 8a). On occasion the Finnish markka traded outside a range close to its central rates vis-à-vis various partner currencies. The maximum upward and downward deviations from central rates, on the basis of 10 business day moving averages, were 3.6% and -1.1% respectively, abstracting from the autonomous upward trend of the Irish pound (see Table 8a). The episodes in which such deviations occurred were temporary, the relatively high degree of exchange rate volatility vis-à-vis the Deutsche Mark observed in specific periods declined to low levels over the reference period (see Table 8b) and short-term interest rate differentials against those EU countries with the lowest short-term interest rates were insignificant. Since joining the ERM Finland has not devalued its currency's bilateral central rate against any other Member State's currency.

In a longer-term context, when measured in terms of real effective exchange rates, current exchange rates of the Finnish markka against other ERM participating currencies suggest that the currency is somewhat below historical values based on long-term averages and on the year 1987 (see Table 9). With regard to other external developments, sizable current account surpluses have been recorded since 1994, which have reduced the large net external liability position which occurred as a result of the accumulation of deficit positions over several decades (see Table 10). It may also be recalled that Finland is a small open economy with, according to the most recent data, a ratio of foreign trade to GDP of 37% for exports and 29% for imports, and a share of intra-EU trade of 53% for exports and 59% for imports.

Long-term interest rate developments

Over the *reference period* from February 1997 to January 1998 *long-term interest rates* in Finland were 5.9% on average, and thus stood below the reference value for the interest rate criterion of 7.8% set on the basis of the three best-performing Member States in terms of price stability. For 1997 as a whole, as well as for 1996, they were well below the reference value (see Table 11).

Long-term interest rates have been on a broadly declining trend since the early 1990s (see Chart 6a). A trend towards the convergence of Finnish long-term interest rates with those prevailing in the EU countries with the lowest bond yields has also been observed for most of the period since the early 1990s. This process of convergence has accelerated since late 1994, and the differential has now been virtually eliminated (see Chart 6b). The main factors underlying this trend were the comparatively low rate of inflation, the relative stability of the Finnish markka's exchange rate and an improvement in the country's fiscal position.

Concluding summary

Over the reference period Finland has achieved a rate of HICP inflation of 1.3%, which is well below the reference value stipulated by the Treaty. Unit labour costs declined in 1997 and low rates of inflation were also apparent in terms of other relevant price indices. Looking ahead, there are some signs of immediate upward pressure on inflation; forecasts suggest a rate of 2-2½% in 1998 and 1999. The level of long-term interest rates was 5.9%, i.e. below the respective reference value.

The Finnish markka has been participating in the ERM for around 16 months, i.e. for less than two years prior to the examination by the EMI. On the basis of the evidence reviewed in the Report, in an ex post assessment, the Finnish markka has been broadly stable over the reference period as a whole. Within the ERM, it has remained generally close to its unchanged central parities without the need for measures to support the exchange rate.

In 1997 Finland achieved a fiscal deficit ratio of 0.9% of GDP, i.e. well below the reference value, and the outlook is for a surplus of 0.3% in 1998. In addition, the fiscal debt ratio declined to 55.8% of GDP in 1997, thus remaining below the 60% reference value. Regarding the sustainability of fiscal developments, the outlook is for a further decline to 53.6% in 1998. Against this background, Finland should comply with the medium-term objective of the Stability and Growth Pact, effective from 1999 onwards, of having a budgetary position that is close to balance or in surplus, and the debt ratio would fall further below 60%.

With regard to other factors, Finland has recorded sizable current account surpluses while continuing to have a net foreign liability position. In the context of the ageing of the population, Finland benefits from a partly funded pension system.

List of Tables and Charts*

FINLAND

I Price developments

II Fiscal developments

III Exchange rate developments

IV Long-term interest rate developments

---

* Chart scales may differ across countries.

I Price developments

Table I

Finland: HICP inflation
(annual percentage changes)

	1996	1997	Nov 97	Dec 97	Jan 98	**Feb 97- Jan 98**
HICP inflation	1.1	1.2	1.8	1.6	1.8	1.3
Reference value	2.5	2.7	-	-	-	2.7

Source: European Commission.

Chart I

Finland: Price developments
(annual percentage changes)

Source: National data.

Table 2

Finland: Measures of inflation and related indicators
(annual percentage changes unless otherwise stated)

	1990	1991	1992	1993	1994	1995	1996	1997[a]
Measures of inflation								
Consumer price index (CPI)	6.2	4.3	2.9	2.2	1.1	1.0	0.6	1.2
CPI excluding changes in net indirect taxes[b]	4.6	2.6	1.6	0.8	0.5	-0.1	-0.2	0.8
Private consumption deflator	6.0	5.7	4.1	4.2	1.4	0.3	1.6	1.4
GDP deflator	5.8	2.5	0.7	2.4	1.3	2.4	1.3	1.2
Producer prices	2.1	-0.1	2.5	3.6	1.6	3.4	0.1	0.5
Related indicators								
Real GDP growth	0.0	-7.1	-3.6	-1.2	4.5	5.1	3.6	5.9
Output gap (p.pts)	7.7	-1.1	-5.8	-8.3	-5.9	-3.3	-2.4	0.3
Unemployment rate (%)	3.3	7.4	12.7	17.3	17.8	16.7	15.8	14.5
Unit labour costs, whole economy	8.8	7.7	-1.8	-4.7	-2.2	0.7	0.6	-2.4
Compensation per employee, whole economy	9.4	5.7	1.9	1.0	3.5	4.0	3.2	-0.4
Labour productivity, whole economy	0.6	-2.0	3.7	5.7	5.7	3.3	2.6	2.0
Import price deflator	1.1	0.5	7.2	8.7	-0.3	0.4	1.8	1.6
Exchange rate appreciation[c]	1.8	-4.0	-12.9	-14.0	7.8	10.6	-2.8	-2.4
Broad monetary aggregate (M3H)[d]	5.3	9.9	2.4	4.0	0.0	3.1	-1.2	7.4
Stock prices	-27.3	-27.5	-19.4	59.5	49.4	3.5	6.6	56.9
House prices	-5.5	-13.9	-17.0	-8.8	6.0	-3.6	5.5	17.5

Source: National data except real GDP growth and the output gap (European Commission, spring 1998 forecasts) and exchange rate (BIS).
(a) Partly estimated.
(b) National estimates.
(c) Nominal effective exchange rate against 25 industrialised countries.
   Note: a positive (negative) sign indicates an appreciation (depreciation).
(d) National harmonised data.

Table 3

Finland: Recent inflation trends and forecasts
(annual percentage change unless otherwise stated)

(a) Recent trends in consumer price inflation

	Sep 97	Oct 97	Nov 97	Dec 97	Jan 98
National consumer price index (CPI)					
Annual percentage change	1.6	1.7	1.9	1.9	2.0
Change in the average of latest 3 months from previous					
3 months, annualised rate, seasonally adjusted	2.3	2.6	2.5	2.6	2.5
Change in the average of latest 6 months from previous					
6 months, annualised rate, seasonally adjusted	2.1	2.2	2.3	2.5	2.6

Source: National non-harmonised data.

(b) Inflation forecasts

	1998	1999
European Commission (spring 1998), HICP	2.0	2.0
OECD (December 1997), private consumption deflator	2.2	2.5
IMF (October 1997), CPI	2.3	.

Source: European Commission (spring 1998 forecasts), OECD and IMF.

II   Fiscal developments

Table 4

Finland: General government financial position
(as a percentage of GDP)

	1996	**1997**	1998[a]
General government surplus (+) / deficit (-)	-3.3	-0.9	0.3
Reference value	-3	-3	-3
Surplus (+) / deficit (-), net of public investment expenditure[b]	-0.6	1.7	.
General government gross debt	57.6	55.8	53.6
Reference value	60	60	60

Source: European Commission (spring 1998 forecasts) and EMI calculations.
(a) European Commission projections.
(b) A negative sign indicates that the government deficit is higher than investment expenditure.

Chart 2

Finland: General government gross debt
(as a percentage of GDP)

(a) Levels

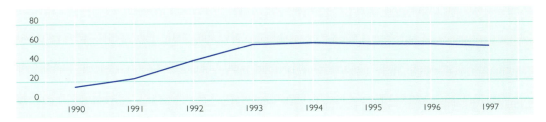

(b) Annual changes and underlying factors

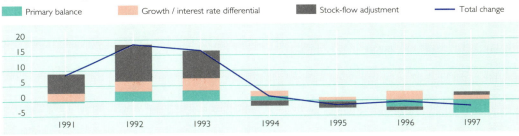

Source: European Commission (spring 1998 forecasts) and EMI calculations.
Note: In Chart 2b negative values indicate a contribution of the respective factor to a decrease in the debt ratio, while positive values indicate a contribution to its increase.

Table 5

Finland: General government gross debt – structural features

	1990	1991	1992	1993	1994	1995	1996	1997
Total debt (as a percentage of GDP)	14.5	23.0	41.5	58.0	59.6	58.1	57.6	55.8
Composition by currency (% of total)								
In domestic currency	66.1	60.8	45.1	43.3	41.0	45.1	46.6	50.4
In foreign currencies	33.9	39.2	54.9	56.7	59.0	54.9	53.4	49.6
Domestic ownership (% of total)	60.2	48.4	38.2	36.2	36.3	40.3	39.3	36.8
Average maturity[a] (years)	4.6	4.9	5.2	4.9	4.7	4.3	4.4	4.7
Composition by maturity[a] (% of total)								
Short-term[b] (< 1 year)	11.3	10.0	12.2	13.8	13.7	20.3	24.1	19.1
Medium-term (1-5 years)	73.8	64.0	59.8	52.8	54.2	52.8	48.2	48.1
Long-term (> 5 years)	14.9	25.9	28.0	33.3	32.1	26.9	27.8	32.8

Source: National data except for total debt (European Commission (spring 1998 forecasts)). End-year data. Differences in the totals are due to rounding.
(a) Residual maturity.
(b) Including short-term debt and debt linked to short-term interest rates.

Chart 3

Finland: General government surplus (+) / deficit (-)
(as a percentage of GDP)

(a) Levels

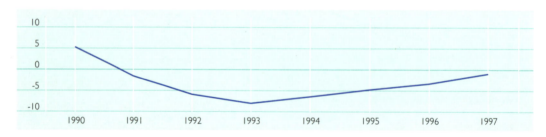

(b) Annual changes and underlying factors

Source: European Commission (spring 1998 forecasts).
Note: In Chart 3b negative values indicate a contribution to an increase in deficits, while positive values indicate a contribution to their reduction.

Chart 4

Finland: General government expenditure and receipts
(as a percentage of GDP)

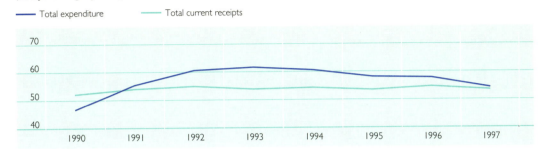

Source: European Commission (spring 1998 forecasts).

Table 6

Finland: General government budgetary position
(as a percentage of GDP)

	1990	1991	1992	1993	1994	1995	1996	1997
Total current receipts	52.1	54.0	54.9	53.8	54.4	53.5	54.6	53.5
Taxes	33.1	33.2	32.3	30.3	31.3	31.2	33.1	33.2
Social security contributions	13.0	13.9	14.9	15.4	16.2	15.2	14.5	13.7
Other current receipts	6.0	6.9	7.7	8.1	6.8	7.1	7.0	6.6
Total expenditure	46.8	55.5	60.7	61.8	60.8	58.3	57.9	54.5
Current transfers	20.4	25.2	29.5	31.0	30.2	28.4	27.4	25.7
Actual interest payments	1.5	1.9	2.6	4.6	5.0	5.2	5.6	5.4
Public consumption	21.1	24.2	24.8	23.3	22.3	21.8	21.9	20.9
Net capital expenditure	3.9	4.1	3.7	3.0	3.3	2.9	3.1	2.4
Surplus (+) or deficit (-)	5.4	-1.5	-5.9	-8.0	-6.4	-4.7	-3.3	-0.9
Primary balance	6.8	0.4	-3.2	-3.4	-1.4	0.4	2.3	4.5
Surplus (+) or deficit (-), net of public investment expenditure(a)	.	.	.	-5.2	-3.6	-2.1	-0.6	1.7

Source: European Commission (spring 1998 forecasts) and EMI calculations. Differences in the totals are due to rounding.
(a) A negative sign indicates that the government deficit is higher than investment expenditure.

Table 7

Finland: Projections of elderly dependency ratio

	1990	2000	2010	2020	2030
Elderly dependency ratio (population aged 65 and over as a proportion of the population aged 15-64)	19.7	21.5	24.3	34.7	41.1

Source: Bos, E. et al. (1994), World population projections 1994-95, World Bank, Washington DC.

III   Exchange rate developments

Table 8

(a) Finland: Exchange rate stability
(14 October 1996 - 27 February 1998)

Membership of the Exchange Rate Mechanism (ERM)	Yes	
Membership since	14 October 1996	
Devaluation of bilateral central rate on country's own initiative	No	
Maximum upward (+) and downward (-) deviations from central rates in the ERM grid (%) against[a]		
Belgian franc	3.1	0.2
Danish krone	2.8	0.1
Deutsche Mark	3.0	0.2
Spanish peseta	2.1	-0.2
French franc	3.6	0.1
Irish pound	-0.3	-9.1
Italian lira	3.0	-0.4
Dutch guilder	2.9	0.2
Austrian schilling	3.0	0.2
Portuguese escudo	1.4	-1.1

Source: European Commission and EMI calculations.
(a)   Daily data at business frequency; 10-day moving average. Deviations against the Italian lira refer to the period from 25 November 1996 onwards.

(b) Key indicators of exchange rate pressure for the Finnish markka

Average of 3 months ending:	May 96	Aug 96	Nov 96	Feb 97	May 97	Aug 97	Nov 97	Feb 98
Exchange rate volatility[a]	4.5	4.0	2.2	5.3	4.4	3.5	2.3	1.1
Short-term interest rate differentials[b]	0.4	0.1	-0.1	-0.1	-0.2	-0.2	-0.0	-0.1

Source: European Commission, national data and EMI calculations.
(a)   Annualised monthly standard deviation of daily percentage changes of the exchange rate against the DEM, in percentages.
(b)   Differential of three-month interbank interest rates against a weighted average of interest rates in Belgium, Germany, France, the Netherlands and Austria, in percentage points.

Chart 5

Finnish markka: Deviations from ERM bilateral central rates
(daily data; percentages; 1 March 1996 to 27 February 1998)

—— FIM/BEF   —— FIM/DKK   —— FIM/DEM   —— FIM/ESP   —— FIM/FRF

—— FIM/IEP   —— FIM/ITL   —— FIM/NLG   —— FIM/ATS   —— FIM/PTE

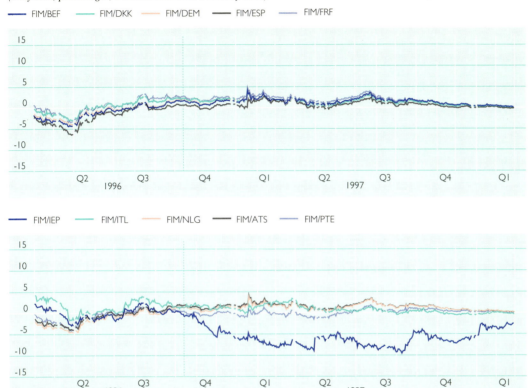

Source: European Commission.
Note: The vertical line indicates when Finland joined the ERM (14 October 1996).
Deviations prior to 14 October 1996 refer to the Finnish markka's bilateral central rates as established upon ERM entry except in the case of the Italian lira. In this case, deviations prior to 25 November 1996 refer to the bilateral central rate established upon the lira's re-entry to the ERM.

Table 9

Finnish markka: Measures of the real effective exchange rate vis-à-vis ERM Member States
(monthly data; percentage deviations; February 1998 compared with different benchmark periods)

	Average Apr 73-Feb 98	Average Jan 87-Feb 98	Average 1987
Real effective exchange rates:			
CPI-based	-11.3	-11.1	-14.8
PPI/WPI-based	-8.8	-5.5	-9.4
Memo item:			
Nominal effective exchange rate	-15.2	-7.7	-14.8

Source: BIS and EMI calculations.
Note: A positive (negative) sign indicates an appreciation (depreciation).

Table 10

Finland: External developments

(as a percentage of GDP)

	1990	1991	1992	1993	1994	1995	1996	1997[a]
Current account plus new capital account[b]	-5.1	-5.5	-4.6	-1.3	1.3	4.1	3.8	5.3
Net foreign assets (+) or liabilities (-)[c]	-27.4	-35.3	-47.8	-54.1	-51.7	-42.2	-42.6	-43.4
Exports (goods and services)[d]	23.1	23.2	26.4	31.2	33.8	34.8	34.9	37.4
Imports (goods and services)[e]	24.6	23.3	24.5	24.9	26.9	27.4	27.6	28.5

Source: National data except exports and imports (European Commission, spring 1998 forecasts).

(a) Partly estimated.

(b) According to the 5th edition of the IMF Balance of Payments Manual, which is conceptually the equivalent of the current account in previous editions of the Manual.

(c) International investment position (IIP) as defined by the IMF (see Balance of Payments Yearbook, Part 1, 1994), or the closest possible substitute.

(d) In 1996 the share of intra-EU exports of goods in total national exports of goods was 53.4%; Direction of Trade Statistics Yearbook 1997, IMF.

(e) In 1996 the share of intra-EU imports of goods in total national imports of goods was 58.5%; Direction of Trade Statistics Yearbook 1997, IMF.

IV Long-term interest rate developments

Table II

Finland: Long-term interest rates
(percentages)

	1996	1997	Nov 97	Dec 97	Jan 98	**Feb 97- Jan 98**
Long-term interest rate	7.1	6.0	5.8	5.6	5.3	5.9
Reference value	9.1	8.0	-	-	-	7.8

Source: European Commission.

Chart 6

(a) Finland: Long-term interest rate
   (monthly averages; in percentages)

(b) Finland: Long-term interest rate and CPI inflation differentials against EU countries
   with lowest long-term interest rates*
   (monthly averages; in percentage points)

 Long-term interest rate differential    CPI inflation differential

Source: Interest rates: European Commission (where these are not available the most comparable data have been used); the CPI data used are
non-harmonised national data.
* Weighted average of data for Belgium, Germany, France, the Netherlands and Austria.

245

SWEDEN

Price developments

Over the reference period from February 1997 to January 1998 the average rate of HICP inflation in Sweden was 1.9%, i.e. well below the reference value of 2.7%. This was also the case in 1997 as a whole. In 1996 average HICP inflation was 0.8% (see Table 1). Seen over the past two years, HICP inflation in Sweden has tended to increase somewhat while remaining at levels which are generally considered to be consistent with price stability.

Looking back, consumer price inflation in Sweden, as measured on the basis of the CPI, has followed a downward trend since the early 1990s, with inflation falling sharply from above 10% at the start of the decade and significantly lower rates being discernible since 1994. In 1996-97 inflation was below 1% and there were generally low inflationary pressures (see Chart 1). This experience of disinflation reflects a number of important policy choices, including, in particular, the shift in the orientation of monetary policy towards the primary objective of price stability. Since 1995 this objective has been expressed as an explicit inflation target of 2% for the consumer price index. This general orientation has been supported by, inter alia, adjustments in fiscal policy and greater product market competition, linked partly to Sweden's accession to the EU in 1995 and fostered by the competition law framework. In addition, the macroeconomic environment has contributed to containing upward pressure on prices. Notably, in the context of the severe recession in the early 1990s a considerable negative output gap emerged (see Table 2). Since 1994 a recovery in economic activity has taken place and the output gap has narrowed appreciably. Against this background, there was an acceleration of growth in compensation per employee in 1996 and

unit labour costs rose to 4.6% in 1996, before declining to 1.2% in 1997. Control over inflationary pressures has been facilitated by declines or only small increases in import prices in 1996-97 and weak domestic demand against the background of fiscal retrenchment. In addition, falling mortgage costs have contributed to lower rates of CPI inflation. Underlying inflation[12] has been close to or below 2% since 1992. Low rates of inflation are also apparent when it is measured in terms of other relevant price indices (see Table 2).

Looking at recent trends and forecasts, current outturns for consumer price inflation (measured as a percentage change over the corresponding month a year earlier) have been decreasing to around 1½% and there is little sign of immediate upward pressure on the basis of the measures shown in Table 3a. Most forecasts of inflation suggest rates of 1½-2% for 1998 and 2% for 1999 (see Table 3b). Risks for price stability over this period are associated with wage developments in the light of the strengthening of economic activity.

Looking further ahead, maintaining an environment conducive to price stability relates in Sweden to, inter alia, the conduct of fiscal policies over the medium to long term; it will be equally important to strengthen national policies aimed at enhancing competition in product markets and improving the functioning of labour markets against the background of the current high rate of unemployment in Sweden.

---

[12] Underlying inflation is defined here as the CPI excluding mortgage interest costs and the effects of indirect taxes and subsidies.

Fiscal developments

In the *reference year* 1997 the general government deficit ratio was 0.8%, i.e. well below the 3% reference value, and the debt ratio was 76.6%, i.e. above the 60% reference value. Compared with the previous year, the deficit ratio has been reduced by 2.7 percentage points and the debt ratio has decreased marginally by 0.1 percentage point. In 1998 a surplus of 0.5% of GDP is expected, while the debt ratio is projected to decrease to 74.1%. In 1996 the deficit ratio exceeded the ratio of public investment expenditure to GDP, whilst in 1997 the deficit ratio was below the investment ratio (see Table 4).

Looking back over the years 1990 to 1997, the Swedish *debt-to-GDP ratio* increased by 33.3 percentage points; initially the situation of Sweden's government finances deteriorated sharply, and the debt ratio rose from 43.3% of GDP in 1990 to 79.0% in 1994. Thereafter, the ratio has decreased to 76.6% in 1997 (see Chart 2a), i.e. a decline of 2.4 percentage points over three years. As is shown in greater detail in Chart 2b, in the early 1990s both a negative growth/interest rate differential, reflecting a 5% fall in Sweden's GDP over three years, and a deteriorating primary balance played a role in increasing government debt. However, as is reflected in the so-called "stock-flow adjustment item" of public debt, the financial support granted to the banking sector and the revaluation of foreign currency denominated government debt after the sizable depreciation of the Swedish krona between 1991 and 1992 had a strong impact. Since 1996 the primary balance has been in surplus and gradually increasing, more than compensating in 1997 for the unfavourable growth/interest rate differential. The pattern observed thus far during the 1990s is an illustration of the powerful effects which a strong deterioration in the macroeconomic environment and exceptional events can have on the debt ratio, particularly in the

absence of a primary surplus to compensate for these factors. In this context, it may be noted that the share of debt with a short-term maturity has been decreasing from the high levels of the early 1990s, while the average maturity has remained broadly stable in recent years (see Table 5). With regard to 1997, the proportion of debt with a short-term residual maturity is still high, and, taking into account the current level of the debt ratio, fiscal balances are sensitive to changes in interest rates. In addition, the proportion of foreign currency debt increased to high levels, rendering fiscal balances in principle sensitive to changes in exchange rates, although part of this debt may eventually be redenominated in euro.

During the 1990s a pattern of first very sharply deteriorating and subsequently improving outturns can be observed in the *deficit-to-GDP ratio*. Starting from a surplus position of 4.2% in 1990, a deficit emerged in 1991, and increased to reach a peak of 12.2% of GDP in 1993; since then, the deficit has declined year by year to stand at 0.8% in 1997 (see Chart 3a). As is shown in greater detail in Chart 3b, which focuses on *changes* in deficits, cyclical factors contributed substantially to the increase in the deficit until 1993, as well as to its decrease in the following two years. In 1996-97 cyclical factors played a minor role. However, the non-cyclical improvements could reflect a lasting, "structural" move towards more balanced fiscal policies and/or a variety of measures with temporary effects. Evidence available suggests that measures with a temporary effect played a deficit-reducing role in 1996, amounting to 0.3% of GDP, but did not play a role in 1997.

Moving on to examine trends in other fiscal indicators, it can be seen from Chart 4 that the general government *total expenditure ratio* rose sharply between 1990 and 1993. In particular, current transfers increased steeply, reflecting a marked increase in payments related to unemployment and other social security items; in addition, all other major expenditure items rose as a percentage of GDP (see Table 6). After 1993 the total expenditure ratio declined rapidly as a consequence of a reduction in all expenditure categories with the exception of interest payments. Nevertheless, the expenditure ratio in 1997 was 3 percentage points higher than at the beginning of the 1990s, reflecting higher ratios in current transfers - notably to the unemployed - and interest payments. Given this pattern and taking into account both that interest payments have increased in line with the higher debt ratio and that capital spending has been reduced substantially since 1993, a continuation of the downward trend of total expenditure to GDP would in particular seem to require emphasis to be placed on current transfers, which are still well above the level observed in 1990. *Government revenue* in relation to GDP tended to decrease until 1994, since when it has been gradually increasing. It may be at a level which is detrimental to economic growth.

According to the Swedish *medium-term fiscal policy strategy*, as presented in the latest review of the Convergence Programme for 1995-2000 dated September 1997, the general government financial position is expected to be in surplus in 1998 and the debt ratio is planned to decrease further. The budget plan for 1998 is in line with the programme. Even though the budget contains some increased expenditure, it does not breach previously set spending ceilings, and both expenditure and revenue ratios are expected to decline. Currently, there is evidence of measures with a temporary effect in the 1998 budget, amounting to 0.8% of GDP. According to current plans, in the year 2000 the overall balance is projected to show a surplus of 1.5% of GDP as a step towards the medium-term

goal of a surplus over the cycle of 2% and the debt ratio is forecast to stand at 67%. The current plans are broadly in line with the previous update of the programme but imply a faster improvement than envisaged in the original 1995 programme. If fiscal balances turn out as projected in the Convergence Programme for 1999-2000, Sweden should comply with the medium-term objective of the Stability and Growth Pact, effective from 1999 onwards, of having a budgetary position that is close to balance or in surplus.

With regard to the future horizon for reducing the debt ratio to the 60% reference value for countries with a debt ratio of clearly above 60% but below 80% of GDP, the EMI presents calculations as detailed in Chart 5. On the assumption that overall fiscal positions and debt ratios as projected by the European Commission for 1998 are achieved, maintaining the projected 1998 primary surplus of 6.8% of GDP constant in subsequent years would be consistent with a reduction in the debt ratio to below 60% in 2001. Maintaining the 1998 overall fiscal surplus of 0.5% of GDP constant in subsequent years would generate a debt ratio of below 60% by 2003. Finally, maintaining a balanced budget would, in the case of Sweden, extend this process to 2004. Such calculations are based on the normative assumption of a constant nominal rate of interest of 6% (average real cost of public debt outstanding of 4% and 2% inflation) and the assumption of a constant real GDP growth rate of 1.9%, as estimated by the Commission for real trend GDP growth in 1998. Stock-flow adjustments are not taken into account. While such calculations are purely illustrative, and can by no means be regarded as forecasts, they provide an illustration of the need to maintain considerable consolidation efforts in order to bring the debt ratio in Sweden down to 60% of GDP or below within an appropriate period of time.

Stressing the need for considerable improvement in the deficit ratio and to sustain consolidation over time is indeed appropriate in the case of Sweden. As has been seen in the past, unexpected shocks can substantially increase the debt ratio. In addition, as is highlighted in Table 7, from around 2010 onwards a marked ageing of the population is expected. Therefore, public pension expenditure would increase in relation to GDP if policies regarding benefits were to continue unchanged. The Swedish pension system is partly funded but is basically of the pay-as-you-go type. It has been decided to gradually supplement the public pension system by a more robust system linked to economic growth and demographic variations, which will reduce the pressure on public finances and diminish the need for a large buffer fund. The buffer fund currently invests a large part of its surpluses in government paper, thereby reducing the consolidated general government gross debt. As a result, any change in this investment policy would introduce a measure of uncertainty for the future course of the gross debt ratio. The demographic trend over the next few decades will have an adverse effect on the current surpluses in the pension system, thereby making improvements in the general government fiscal balance essential. Alleviation of the overall burden of population ageing will be facilitated if public finances have created sufficient room for manoeuvre before entering the period during which the demographic situation worsens.

Exchange rate developments

During the *reference period* from March 1996 to February 1998 the Swedish krona has not participated in the ERM (see Table 8a). Swedish monetary policy has been oriented towards the primary objective of price stability by means of an explicit inflation target of 2% for the CPI. Focusing on the reference period, the currency has normally traded above its March 1996 average bilateral exchange rates against most other EU currencies, which are used as a benchmark for illustrative purposes in the absence of central rates (see Chart 6 and Table 8a). The main exceptions were the development against the Irish pound, the pound sterling and, to a lesser extent, the Italian lira. In parallel with these developments the degree of volatility of the Swedish krona's exchange rate against the Deutsche Mark has tended to decrease recently while remaining relatively high (see Table 8b), while short-term interest rate differentials against those EU countries with the lowest short-term interest rates have narrowed significantly.

In a longer-term context, when measured in terms of real effective exchange rates, current exchange rate levels of the Swedish krona against other EU currencies are somewhat below historical average values and 1987 average values (see Table 9). As regards other external developments, Sweden has maintained an increasing current account surplus since 1994 against the background of a relatively large net external liability position (see Table 10). It may also be recalled that Sweden is a small open economy with, according to the most recent data available, a ratio of foreign trade to GDP of 47% for exports and 38% for imports, and a share of intra-EU trade of 55% for exports and 66% for imports.

Long-term interest rate developments

Over the *reference period* from February 1997 to January 1998 *long-term interest rates* in Sweden were 6.5% on average, and thus stood below the reference value for the interest rate criterion of 7.8% set on the basis of the three best-performing Member States in terms of price stability. This was also the case for 1997 as a whole, as well as for 1996 (see Table 11).

Long-term interest rates have been on a broadly declining trend since the early 1990s (see Chart 7a). At the same time, a trend towards the convergence of Swedish long-term interest rates with those prevailing in the EU countries with the lowest bond yields has been observed since the early 1990s. Since mid-1995 this process of convergence has accelerated and the differential has now been virtually eliminated (see Chart 7b). The main factors underlying this trend were the comparatively low rate of inflation and the improvement in the country's public finances.

Concluding summary

Over the reference period Sweden has achieved a rate of HICP inflation of 1.9%, which is well below the reference value stipulated by the Treaty. The increase in unit labour costs was subdued in 1997 and low rates of inflation were also apparent in terms of other relevant price indices. Looking ahead, there is little sign of immediate upward pressure on inflation; forecasts project inflation will stand at 1½-2% in 1998 and 2% in 1999. The level of long-term interest rates was 6.5%, i.e. below the respective reference value.

Sweden does not participate in the ERM. Over the reference period, the Swedish krona traded above its March 1996 average bilateral exchange rates against most other EU currencies, which are used as a benchmark for illustrative purposes in the absence of central rates.

In 1997 Sweden achieved a fiscal deficit ratio of 0.8% of GDP, i.e. well below the reference value, and the outlook is for a surplus of 0.5% in 1998. The debt-to-GDP ratio is above the 60% reference value. After having reached a peak in 1994, the ratio declined by 2.4 percentage points to stand at 76.6% in 1997. Regarding the sustainability of fiscal developments, the outlook is for a decline in the debt ratio to 74.1% of GDP in 1998. Against the background of recent trends in the deficit ratio, Sweden should comply with the medium-term objective of the Stability and Growth Pact, effective from 1999 onwards, of having a budgetary position that is close to balance or in surplus. Given the current debt ratio of above 75% of GDP, achieving the overall surplus forecast for 1998 and maintaining it in subsequent years would reduce the debt ratio to below 60% of GDP in 2003.

With regard to other factors, the deficit ratio exceeded the ratio of public investment to GDP in 1996, while falling below that level in 1997. In addition, Sweden recorded current account surpluses, while maintaining a net external liability position. In the context of the ageing of the population, Sweden benefits from a partly funded pension system.

List of Tables and Charts*

---

* Chart scales may differ across countries.

I Price developments

Table I

Sweden: HICP inflation
(annual percentage changes)

	1996	1997	Nov 97	Dec 97	Jan 98	**Feb 97- Jan 98**
HICP inflation	0.8	1.8	2.7	2.7	2.1	1.9
Reference value	2.5	2.7	-	-	-	2.7

Source: European Commission.

Chart I

Sweden: Price developments
(annual percentage changes)

Source: National data.

Table 2

Sweden: Measures of inflation and related indicators

(annual percentage changes unless otherwise stated)

	1990	1991	1992	1993	1994	1995	1996	1997[a]
Measures of inflation								
Consumer price index (CPI)	10.4	9.7	2.6	4.7	2.4	2.8	0.8	0.9
CPI excluding changes in net indirect taxes[b]	7.5	5.7	3.4	4.0	2.4	1.9	0.5	0.3
Private consumption deflator	9.9	10.3	2.2	5.7	3.0	2.7	1.2	2.3
GDP deflator	8.9	7.6	1.0	2.6	2.4	3.7	1.1	1.6
Producer prices	4.2	2.4	-0.3	1.1	4.4	8.2	-0.2	1.1
Related indicators								
Real GDP growth	1.4	-1.1	-1.4	-2.2	3.3	3.9	1.3	1.8
Output gap (p.pts)	3.6	1.2	-1.4	-4.7	-2.8	-0.5	-0.9	-0.9
Unemployment rate (%)	1.7	3.0	5.3	8.2	8.0	7.7	8.0	8.3
Unit labour costs, whole economy	10.6	6.4	0.4	1.9	0.5	0.0	4.6	1.2
Compensation per employee, whole economy	11.3	6.8	4.0	4.4	4.8	2.7	6.6	3.9
Labour productivity, whole economy	0.6	0.4	3.5	2.5	4.2	2.7	1.9	2.7
Import price deflator	3.0	0.0	-2.2	14.4	3.5	4.8	-4.9	1.4
Exchange rate appreciation[c]	-1.3	-0.5	1.4	-19.2	-1.3	-0.2	9.8	-3.7
Broad monetary aggregate (M3H)[d]	-	-	-	-	-	-	-	-
Stock prices	-7.5	-4.8	-15.2	31.0	25.7	11.8	23.0	43.9
House prices	11.8	6.9	-9.4	-10.1	3.5	0.5	-0.2	6.2

Source: National data except real GDP growth and the output gap (European Commission, spring 1998 forecasts) and exchange rate (BIS).
(a) Partly estimated.
(b) National estimates.
(c) Nominal effective exchange rate against 25 industrialised countries.
　　Note: a positive (negative) sign indicates an appreciation (depreciation).
(d) National harmonised data.

Table 3

Sweden: Recent inflation trends and forecasts

(annual percentage change unless otherwise stated)

(a) Recent trends in consumer price inflation

	Sep 97	Oct 97	Nov 97	Dec 97	Jan 98
National consumer price index (CPI)					
Annual percentage change	1.7	1.8	1.8	1.9	1.3
Change in the average of latest 3 months from previous 3 months, annualised rate, seasonally adjusted	3.1	3.2	2.6	2.0	0.8
Change in the average of latest 6 months from previous 6 months, annualised rate, seasonally adjusted	1.8	2.1	2.4	2.5	2.5

Source: National non-harmonised data.

(b) Inflation forecasts

	1998	1999
European Commission (spring 1998), HICP	1.5	1.8
OECD (December 1997), private consumption deflator	2.2	2.2
IMF (October 1997), CPI	2.0	.

Source: European Commission (spring 1998 forecasts), OECD and IMF.

II   Fiscal developments

Sweden: General government financial position
(as a percentage of GDP)

	1996	**1997**	1998[a]
General government surplus (+) / deficit (-)	-3.5	-0.8	0.5
Reference value	-3	-3	-3
Surplus (+) / deficit (-), net of public investment expenditure[b]	-1.4	1.6	.
General government gross debt	76.7	76.6	74.1
Reference value	60	60	60

Source: European Commission (spring 1998 forecasts) and EMI calculations.
(a)   European Commission projections.
(b)   A negative sign indicates that the government deficit is higher than investment expenditure.

Sweden: General government gross debt
(as a percentage of GDP)

(a) Levels

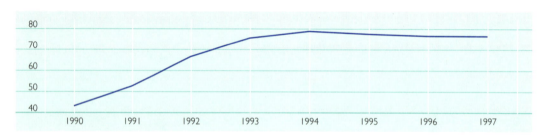

(b) Annual changes and underlying factors

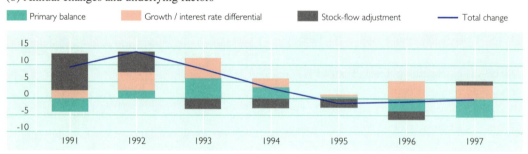

Source: European Commission (spring 1998 forecasts) and EMI calculations.
Note: In Chart 2b negative values indicate a contribution of the respective factor to a decrease in the debt ratio, while positive values indicate a contribution to its increase.

Table 5

Sweden: General government gross debt – structural features

	1990	1991	1992	1993	1994	1995	1996	1997
Total debt (as a percentage of GDP)	43.3	52.8	66.8	75.8	79.0	77.6	76.7	76.6
Composition by currency[a] (% of total)								
In domestic currency	86.1	91.5	73.2	65.4	67.1	66.3	66.6	68.3
In foreign currencies	13.9	8.5	26.8	34.6	32.9	33.7	33.4	31.7
Domestic ownership (% of total)	80.5	78.2	58.3	53.1	57.9	58.7	57.5	54.2
Average maturity[b] (years)	.	.	.	.	2.4	2.8	2.7	2.6
Composition by maturity[c] (% of total)								
Short-term[d] (< 1 year)	54.7	62.5	63.3	43.4	40.6	35.3	35.8	34.0
Medium and long-term (≥ 1 year)	45.3	37.5	36.7	56.6	59.4	64.7	64.2	66.0

Source: National data except for total debt (European Commission (spring 1998 forecasts)). End-year data. Differences in the totals are due to rounding.
(a) Consolidated debt.
(b) Modified duration.
(c) Residual maturity. The decomposition is an approximation based on the composition of the debt instruments of general government.
(d) Including short-term debt and debt linked to short-term interest rates.

Chart 3

Sweden: General government surplus (+) / deficit (-)
(as a percentage of GDP)

(a) Levels

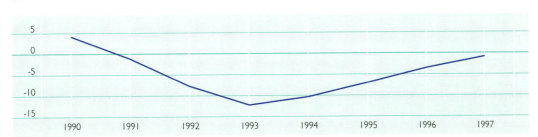

(b) Annual changes and underlying factors

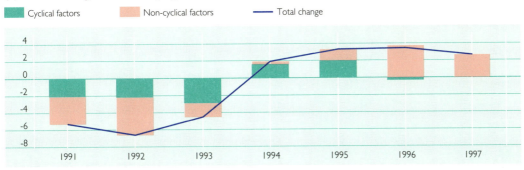

Source: European Commission (spring 1998 forecasts).
Note: In Chart 3b negative values indicate a contribution to an increase in deficits, while positive values indicate a contribution to their reduction.

Chart 4

Sweden: General government expenditure and receipts
(as a percentage of GDP)

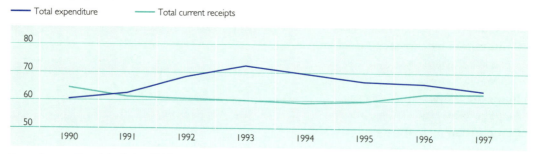

Source: European Commission (spring 1998 forecasts).

Table 6

Sweden: General government budgetary position
(as a percentage of GDP)

	1990	1991	1992	1993	1994	1995	1996	1997
Total current receipts	64.6	61.4	60.6	60.1	59.2	59.8	62.5	62.6
Taxes	40.4	37.5	36.6	36.3	36.0	36.3	37.7	38.9
Social security contributions	15.5	15.4	14.7	14.3	14.4	14.0	15.1	15.2
Other current receipts	8.7	8.5	9.3	9.5	8.9	9.6	9.7	8.6
Total expenditure	60.4	62.5	68.4	72.3	69.5	66.7	66.0	63.4
Current transfers	25.9	27.6	30.8	33.0	32.2	31.5	30.6	29.0
Actual interest payments	5.0	5.1	5.4	6.2	6.8	6.4	7.2	6.2
Public consumption	27.2	27.1	27.8	28.0	27.1	25.7	26.1	25.8
Net capital expenditure	2.3	2.6	4.4	5.2	3.4	3.2	2.1	2.4
Surplus (+) or deficit (-)	4.2	-1.1	-7.7	-12.2	-10.3	-6.9	-3.5	-0.8
Primary balance	9.1	4.0	-2.4	-6.1	-3.5	-0.5	3.7	5.4
Surplus (+) or deficit (-), net of public investment expenditure[a]	.	.	.	-11.2	-7.2	-4.0	-1.4	1.6

Source: European Commission (spring 1998 forecasts) and EMI calculations. Differences in the totals are due to rounding.
(a) A negative sign indicates that the government deficit is higher than investment expenditure.

Chart 5

Sweden: Potential future debt ratios under alternative assumptions for fiscal balance ratios
(as a percentage of GDP)

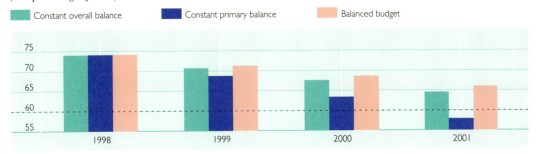

Source: European Commission (spring 1998 forecasts) and EMI calculations.
Note: The three scenarios assume that the debt ratio of 74.1% of GDP for 1998 is as forecast and that the 1998 overall balance of 0.5% of GDP or the primary balance of 6.8% of GDP will be kept constant over the period considered (as a percentage of GDP), or, alternatively, that a balanced budget is maintained from 1999 onwards. The underlying assumptions are a real trend GDP growth rate in 1998 of 1.9% as estimated by the Commission; an inflation rate of 2%; and, in the constant primary balance scenario, a nominal interest rate of 6%. Stock-flow adjustments are disregarded.

Table 7

Sweden: Projections of elderly dependency ratio

	1990	2000	2010	2020	2030
Elderly dependency ratio (population aged 65 and over as a proportion of the population aged 15-64)	27.6	26.9	29.1	35.6	39.4

Source: Bos, E. et al. (1994), World population projections 1994-95, World Bank, Washington DC.

III Exchange rate developments

(a) Sweden: Exchange rate stability
(1 March 1996 - 27 February 1998)

Membership of the Exchange Rate Mechanism (ERM)	No	
Membership since	-	
Devaluation of bilateral central rate on country's own initiative	-	
Maximum upward (+) and downward (-) deviations from March 1996 average bilateral rates (%) against[a]		
ERM currencies:		
Belgian franc	7.0	-1.1
Danish krone	5.1	-1.1
Deutsche Mark	6.6	-1.1
Spanish peseta	6.9	-1.0
French franc	4.6	-1.2
Irish pound	1.3	-11.9
Italian lira	1.6	-5.9
Dutch guilder	7.3	-1.1
Austrian schilling	6.7	-1.1
Portuguese escudo	4.9	-2.5
Finnish markka	4.2	-3.7
Non-ERM currencies:		
Greek drachma	3.1	-3.3
Pound sterling	1.4	-22.5

Source: European Commission and EMI calculations.

(a) Daily data at business frequency; 10-day moving average.

(b) Key indicators of exchange rate pressure for the Swedish krona

Average of 3 months ending:	May 96	Aug 96	Nov 96	Feb 97	May 97	Aug 97	Nov 97	Feb 98
Exchange rate volatility[a]	6.9	6.4	4.3	6.2	7.7	6.6	6.9	4.2
Short-term interest rate differentials[b]	3.0	2.0	1.3	0.6	0.8	0.8	0.7	0.8

Source: European Commission, national data and EMI calculations.

(a) Annualised monthly standard deviation of daily percentage changes of the exchange rate against the DEM, in percentages.

(b) Differential of three-month interbank interest rates against a weighted average of interest rates in Belgium, Germany, France, the Netherlands and Austria, in percentage points.

Chart 6

Swedish krona: Bilateral exchange rates
(daily data; average of March 1996=100; 1 March 1996 to 27 February 1998)

Source: European Commission.

Table 9

Swedish krona: Measures of the real effective exchange rate vis-à-vis EU Member States
(monthly data; percentage deviations; February 1998 compared with different benchmark periods)

	Average Apr 73-Feb 98	Average Jan 87-Feb 98	Average 1987
Real effective exchange rates:			
CPI-based	-13.1	-8.5	-7.5
PPI/WPI-based	-5.2	-2.7	-2.8
Memo item:			
Nominal effective exchange rate	-22.8	-8.4	-15.8

Source: BIS and EMI calculations.
Note: A positive (negative) sign indicates an appreciation (depreciation).

259

Table 10

Sweden: External developments
(as a percentage of GDP)

	1990	1991	1992	1993	1994	1995	1996	1997[a]
Current account plus new capital account[b]	-2.9	-2.0	-3.4	-2.0	0.3	2.2	2.3	2.7
Net foreign assets (+) or liabilities (-)[c]	-37.0	-25.8	-37.4	-46.3	-46.0	-37.2	-43.1	-47.1
Exports (goods and services)[d]	29.9	29.6	30.7	33.8	37.2	40.5	42.4	47.0
Imports (goods and services)[e]	29.5	28.4	29.1	29.1	31.8	33.8	34.6	37.9

Source: National data except exports and imports (European Commission, spring 1998 forecasts).

(a) Partly estimated.

(b) According to the 5th edition of the IMF Balance of Payments Manual, which is conceptually the equivalent of the current account in previous editions of the Manual.

(c) International investment position (IIP) as defined by the IMF (see Balance of Payments Yearbook, Part I, 1994), or the closest possible substitute.

(d) In 1996 the share of intra-EU exports of goods in total national exports of goods was 55.0%; Direction of Trade Statistics Yearbook 1997, IMF.

(e) In 1996 the share of intra-EU imports of goods in total national imports of goods was 66.4%; Direction of Trade Statistics Yearbook 1997, IMF.

IV Long-term interest rate developments

Table 11

Sweden: Long-term interest rates
(percentages)

	1996	1997	Nov 97	Dec 97	Jan 98	**Feb 97- Jan 98**
Long-term interest rate	8.0	6.6	6.3	6.0	5.7	6.5
Reference value	9.1	8.0	-	-	-	7.8

Source: European Commission.

Chart 7

(a) Sweden: Long-term interest rate
(monthly averages; in percentages)

(b) Sweden: Long-term interest rate and CPI inflation differentials against EU countries with lowest long-term interest rates*
(monthly averages; in percentage points)

—— Long-term interest rate differential —— CPI inflation differential

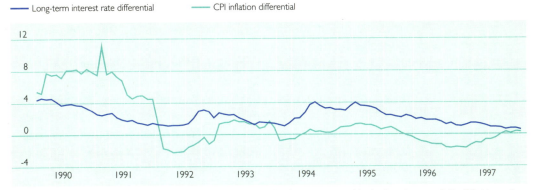

Source: Interest rates: European Commission (where these are not available the most comparable data have been used); the CPI data used are non-harmonised national data.
* Weighted average of data for Belgium, Germany, France, the Netherlands and Austria.

UNITED KINGDOM[13]

Price developments

Over the reference period from February 1997 to January 1998 the average rate of HICP inflation in the United Kingdom was 1.8%, i.e. well below the reference value of 2.7%. This was also the case in 1997 as a whole. In 1996 average HICP inflation was 2.5% (see Table 1). Seen over the past two years, HICP inflation in the United Kingdom has been reduced to a level which is generally considered to be consistent with price stability.

Looking back, consumer price inflation in the United Kingdom, as measured on the basis of the retail price index excluding mortgage interest payments (RPIX), followed a broad downward trend during the early 1990s (see Chart 1). Inflation stood at 8.1% in 1990 and fell to 2.3% in 1994, before edging up to stand at or just under 3% in 1995-97. This experience of disinflation reflects a number of important policy choices, including the shift in monetary policy after the autumn of 1992 towards the pursuit of an explicit inflation target, which is currently specified by the Government to be an objective of 2.5% for the RPIX and, more recently, the granting of operational independence to the Bank of England. The reduction in inflation has been facilitated by, inter alia, the orientation of fiscal policy, enhanced competition in formerly protected sectors of the economy, and labour market reforms. In addition, in the early 1990s the macroeconomic environment contributed to containing upward pressure on prices. Notably, in the context of the recession in 1991-92 a considerable negative output gap emerged (see Table 2). Since then, a robust recovery has been under way and the output gap has gradually been closed. As the labour market has tightened, earnings growth has risen modestly, with unit labour cost growth remaining at around 2% in 1996-97.

Meanwhile, import price rises have varied considerably in recent years, partly as a result of sizable fluctuations in effective exchange rates. In the recent past falling import prices linked to exchange rate appreciation have put downward pressure on prices in an environment of strong domestic demand. A general tendency towards low rates of inflation is also apparent when it is measured in terms of other price indices, although in 1997 consumer prices measured on the basis of the RPIX remained above the target value and well above other measures of inflation before declining to the target value in January 1998[14] (see Table 2).

Looking at recent trends and forecasts, current outturns for consumer price inflation (measured as a percentage change over the corresponding month a year earlier) have been decreasing slightly to 2½% but there are some signs of immediate upward pressure on the basis of the measures shown in Table 3a[15]. Forecasts of inflation suggest a rate of around 2-2½% for 1998 and 1999 (see Table 3b). Risks for price stability over this period are associated with strong money and credit growth as well as pressures in the labour market.

Looking further ahead, although the United Kingdom does not intend to participate in the single monetary policy as from 1999, there will be a need to pursue economic policies which do not overburden monetary policy and which are conducive to exchange rate stability. The environment of low

---

[13] The Convergence Report does not take into account the UK Budget measures which were introduced shortly before the release date.

[14] Inflation as measured on the basis of the RPIX is higher than when measured on the basis of the HICP. A large part of the difference is purely algebraic; RPIX is constructed as an arithmetic mean and HICP as a geometric mean.

[15] These measures may be vulnerable to distortions owing to residual seasonality in the data.

domestic inflation in the United Kingdom also needs to continue to be supported by the conduct of appropriate fiscal policies and the maintenance of national policies aimed at enhancing competition in product markets and improving the functioning of labour markets.

Fiscal developments

In the *reference year* 1997 the deficit ratio was 1.9%, i.e. well below the 3% reference value, and the debt ratio was 53.4%, i.e. below the 60% reference value. Compared with the previous year, the deficit ratio has been reduced by 2.9 percentage points and the debt ratio has decreased by 1.3 percentage points. In 1998 the deficit ratio is forecast to decrease to 0.6% of GDP, while the debt ratio is projected to decline to 52.3%. In 1996 and 1997 the deficit ratio exceeded the ratio of public investment expenditure to GDP (see Table 4).

Looking back over the years 1991 to 1997, the United Kingdom's *debt-to-GDP ratio* increased by 17.8 percentage points. Starting from 35.6% in 1991, the ratio rose continuously to reach 54.7% in 1996, before declining to 53.4% in 1997 (see Chart 2a). As is shown in greater detail in Chart 2b, during the period considered debt growth was mainly driven by at times sizable primary deficits, while some upward pressure resulted from the combination of GDP growth and interest rates. Only in 1997 did a restored primary surplus have a debt-decreasing effect. "Stock-flow adjustments" played a role in checking the rise in the debt ratio in 1994 and 1996. The patterns observed thus far during the 1990s may be seen as indicative of the close link between primary deficits and adverse debt dynamics, irrespective of the starting level of debt - which in the case of the United Kingdom was comparatively low. In this context, it may be noted that the share of debt with a short-term residual

maturity has been decreasing since the early 1990s, while the average maturity has remained stable and is the highest in the Union (see Table 5). With regard to 1997, the proportion of debt with a short-term residual maturity is still indicated to be relatively high but current statistical applications do distort the qualitative picture (see footnote to Table 5). Taking these into account as well as the current level of the debt ratio, fiscal balances may be seen as relatively insensitive to changes in interest rates. In addition, the proportion of foreign currency denominated debt is low, rendering fiscal balances relatively insensitive to changes in exchange rates.

During the 1990s a pattern of rapid deterioration and subsequently improving outturns can be observed in the *deficit-to-GDP ratio*. Starting from a ratio of 0.9% in 1990, fiscal imbalances reached 7.9% in 1993; since then, the deficit has declined year by year to stand at 1.9% of GDP in 1997 (see Chart 3a). As is shown in greater detail in Chart 3b, which focuses on *changes* in deficits, cyclical factors contributed substantially to an increase in the deficit until 1993, as well as to its reduction thereafter. However, the non-cyclical improvements could reflect a lasting, "structural" move towards more balanced fiscal policies and/or a variety of measures with temporary effects. Evidence available suggests that measures with a temporary effect reduced the deficit ratio by 0.5% of GDP in 1997. These were mainly of a "self-reversing" nature. This implies that compensating measures already included in budget plans for 1998 will need to offset the unwinding of these effects in order to maintain the budget on its planned path.

Moving on to examine trends in other fiscal indicators, it can be seen from Chart 4 that the general government *total expenditure ratio* rose between 1990 and 1993. Against the background of rising unemployment both current transfers to households and public consumption increased (see Table 6). After 1993 the ratio of total expenditure to GDP declined, reflecting a reduction in current transfers, public consumption and net capital expenditure relative to GDP; interest payments started to decline only in 1997. The overall expenditure ratio in 1997 has returned broadly to the level observed in 1990, although current transfers are now higher as a percentage of GDP and net capital expenditures are lower. Given the successive reduction in net capital expenditure during the 1990s, a continuation of the downward trend of total expenditure to GDP would require greater adjustments in items such as current transfers and public consumption. Meanwhile, *government revenue* in relation to GDP tended to decline until 1993, and thereafter started to increase, to reach a level in 1997 which was close to that observed in 1990.

According to the United Kingdom's *medium-term fiscal policy strategy*, as presented in the September 1997 Convergence Programme covering the period up to the financial year 2001/02, a declining trend in deficit and debt ratios is projected to continue in 1998, with a position close to balance being reached in the financial year 1998/99. The budget for 1998 is in line with the programme. It foresees a reduction in the expenditure ratio and an increase in the revenue ratio. Currently, there is no evidence of significant measures with a temporary effect in the 1998 budget. For the financial year 2000/01 a surplus of 0.5-1.5% is foreseen, and a further decline in the debt ratio is envisaged. If fiscal balances turn out as projected in the Convergence Programme, the United Kingdom should comply with the medium-term objective of the Stability and Growth Pact, effective from 1999 onwards, of having a budgetary position that is close to balance or in surplus.

With regard to the *potential future course of the debt ratio*, the EMI's Report does not consider this issue in detail for those countries with a debt ratio of below 60% of GDP. Nevertheless, current trends suggest that the debt level can be maintained at below 60%. From around 2010 onwards a marked ageing of the population is expected (see Table 7) but, in contrast to most other EU Member States, the United Kingdom benefits from a pension system which is heavily reliant on funded private pensions, and in which unfunded social security pensions play a lesser role than in other EU countries. Public pension expenditure in terms of GDP is forecast not to increase significantly on present plans. While some comfort may be drawn from such estimates, there are significant uncertainties surrounding them, and developments during the 1990s have indicated the risks to the debt ratio associated with allowing deficit positions to grow rapidly.

Exchange rate developments

During the *reference period* from March 1996 to February 1998 the pound sterling has not participated in the ERM (see Table 8a). The United Kingdom's monetary policy has pursued price stability via an explicit inflation target, which is currently specified by the Government to be an objective of 2.5% for the RPIX. Focusing on the reference period, the currency appreciated against other EU currencies, partly reflecting the differing position in the business cycle and the associated monetary policy stance, as reflected in sizable actual and expected short-term interest rate differentials vis-à-vis ERM countries. Hence, sterling has for the most part traded well above its March 1996 average bilateral exchange rates against other EU currencies, which are used as a benchmark for illustrative purposes in the absence of central rates (see Chart 5 and Table 8a). In parallel with these developments the degree of volatility of the pound's exchange rate against the Deutsche Mark tended to increase from the early 1996 level (see Table 8b) and short-term interest rate differentials against those EU countries with the lowest short-term interest rates widened over the reference period.

In a longer-term context, when measured in terms of real effective exchange rates, current exchange rate levels of the pound sterling against other EU currencies appear to stand well above historical values (see Table 9). As regards other external developments, the current account has been broadly balanced in recent years (with a small surplus in 1997), while net external assets have fallen to between 1% and 2% of GDP (see Table 10). It may also be recalled that, according to the most recent data available, the United Kingdom has a ratio of foreign trade to GDP of 32% for exports and 33% for imports, and a share of intra-EU trade of 53% for exports and 50% for imports.

Long-term interest rate developments

Over the *reference period* from February 1997 to January 1998 *long-term interest rates* in the United Kingdom were 7.0% on average, and thus stood below the reference value for the interest rate criterion of 7.8% set on the basis of the three best-performing Member States in terms of price stability. This was also the case for 1997 as a whole, as well as for 1996 (see Table 11).

Long-term interest rates declined steeply in the early 1990s. Following an interruption in this trend in early 1994 the rate of decline was more gradual (see Chart 6a). Against this background, a broad trend has been observed since the early 1990s of, first, convergence with and, later, divergence from the rates prevailing in the EU countries with the lowest bond yields (see Chart 6b). The main factor underlying the widening of the differential since 1993 was the different position of the United Kingdom in the

cycle vis-à-vis continental European countries (partly in turn reflecting the different pattern of monetary policy and exchange rate developments). More recently, the long-term interest rate differential has shown a tendency to narrow.

Concluding summary

The United Kingdom, in accordance with the terms of Protocol No. 11 of the Treaty, has notified the EU Council that it does not intend to move to the third stage in 1999. As a consequence, it will not participate in the single currency at the start of Stage Three. Nevertheless, its progress towards convergence is examined in detail.

Over the reference period the United Kingdom has achieved a rate of HICP inflation of 1.8%, which is well below the reference value stipulated by the Treaty. The increase in unit labour costs was subdued and a general tendency towards low rates of inflation was also apparent in terms of other relevant price indices. Looking ahead, forecasts project inflation at 2-2½% in 1998 and 1999. The level of long-term interest rates was 7.0%, i.e. below the respective reference value.

The United Kingdom does not participate in the ERM. Over the reference period, the currency appreciated against other EU currencies, partly reflecting the differing position in the cycle and the associated monetary policy stance.

In 1997 the United Kingdom achieved a fiscal deficit ratio of 1.9% of GDP, i.e. a level well below the reference value, and the outlook is for a further decline to 0.6% in 1998. In addition, the fiscal debt ratio decreased to 53.4% of GDP in 1997, thus remaining below the 60% reference value and the outlook is for a further decline to 52.3% in 1998. Regarding the sustainability of fiscal developments, looking ahead, with fiscal balances as projected, the United Kingdom should comply with the medium-term objective of the Stability and Growth Pact, effective from 1999 onwards, of having a budgetary position that is close to balance or in surplus, and the debt ratio would fall further below 60%.

With regard to other factors, the United Kingdom has recorded a small current account surplus in 1997, and has a net foreign asset position. In the context of the ageing of the population, the United Kingdom benefits from a pension system which is heavily reliant on funded private pensions.

List of Tables and Charts*

UNITED KINGDOM

* Chart scales may differ across countries.

I   Price developments

United Kingdom: HICP inflation
(annual percentage changes)

	1996	1997	Nov 97	Dec 97	Jan 98	**Feb 97- Jan 98**
HICP inflation	2.5	1.8	1.9	1.8	1.5	1.8
Reference value	2.5	2.7	-	-	-	2.7

Source: European Commission.

United Kingdom: Price developments
(annual percentage changes)

Source: National data.

268

Table 2

United Kingdom: Measures of inflation and related indicators
(annual percentage changes unless otherwise stated)

	1990	1991	1992	1993	1994	1995	1996	1997[a]
Measures of inflation								
Consumer price index (CPI)[b]	8.1	6.7	4.7	3.0	2.3	2.9	3.0	2.8
CPI excluding changes in net indirect taxes[c]	7.3	6.7	4.3	2.9	1.7	2.3	2.6	2.2
Private consumption deflator	5.5	7.5	5.0	3.5	2.2	2.7	2.4	2.3
GDP deflator	6.4	6.5	4.6	3.2	1.7	2.5	2.9	1.8
Producer prices	6.3	5.4	3.1	3.9	2.6	4.1	2.7	1.1
Related indicators								
Real GDP growth	0.4	-2.0	-0.5	2.1	4.3	2.8	2.3	3.5
Output gap (p.pts)	3.2	-0.8	-3.2	-3.2	-1.1	-0.5	-0.5	0.6
Unemployment rate (%)	5.8	8.0	9.7	10.3	9.3	8.2	7.5	5.8
Unit labour costs, whole economy	10.1	7.1	3.2	0.4	-0.4	1.4	2.1	1.9
Compensation per employee, whole economy	9.6	8.0	6.1	3.4	4.0	3.3	3.9	4.3
Labour productivity, whole economy	0.0	0.8	2.1	3.3	3.7	1.9	1.4	2.2
Import price deflator	3.4	0.3	0.0	8.5	2.9	7.1	0.6	-5.6
Exchange rate appreciation[d]	-1.4	0.6	-3.7	-8.9	0.2	-4.6	2.0	16.3
Broad monetary aggregate (M3H)[e]	17.3	8.6	5.8	4.0	6.1	8.3	13.0	13.4
Stock prices	-1.6	8.7	3.1	19.0	8.0	4.6	15.0	18.0
House prices	0.0	-1.2	-5.6	-2.9	0.5	-1.7	4.5	6.3

Source: National data except real GDP growth and the output gap (European Commission, spring 1998 forecasts) and exchange rate (BIS).
(a) Partly estimated.
(b) RPIX.
(c) RPIY. No CPI excluding net indirect taxes is published.
(d) Nominal effective exchange rate against 25 industrialised countries.
  Note: a positive (negative) sign indicates an appreciation (depreciation).
(e) National harmonised data.

Table 3

United Kingdom: Recent inflation trends and forecasts
(annual percentage change unless otherwise stated)

(a) Recent trends in consumer price inflation

	Sep 97	Oct 97	Nov 97	Dec 97	Jan 98
National consumer price index (CPI)[a]					
Annual percentage change	2.7	2.8	2.8	2.7	2.5
Change in the average of latest 3 months from previous 3 months, annualised rate, seasonally adjusted	3.6	3.0	2.6	2.7	3.0
Change in the average of latest 6 months from previous 6 months, annualised rate, seasonally adjusted	2.5	2.5	2.6	2.9	2.9

Source: National non-harmonised data.
(a) RPIX.

(b) Inflation forecasts

	1998	1999
European Commission (spring 1998), HICP	2.4	1.8
OECD (December 1997), private consumption deflator	2.3	2.6
IMF (October 1997), CPI	2.7	

Source: European Commission (spring 1998 forecasts), OECD and IMF.

II   Fiscal developments

United Kingdom: General government financial position
(as a percentage of GDP)

	1996	**1997**	1998[a]
General government surplus (+) / deficit (-)	-4.8	-1.9	-0.6
Reference value	-3	-3	-3
Surplus (+) / deficit (-), net of public investment expenditure[b]	-3.5	-0.9	.
General government gross debt	54.7	53.4	52.3
Reference value	60	60	60

Source: European Commission (spring 1998 forecasts) and EMI calculations.
(a)   European Commission projections.
(b)   A negative sign indicates that the government deficit is higher than investment expenditure.

United Kingdom: General government gross debt
(as a percentage of GDP)

(a) Levels

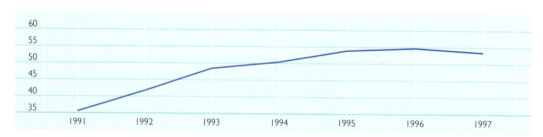

(b) Annual changes and underlying factors

Source: European Commission (spring 1998 forecasts) and EMI calculations.
Note: In Chart 2b negative values indicate a contribution of the respective factor to a decrease in the debt ratio, while positive values indicate a contribution to its increase.

Table 5

United Kingdom: General government gross debt – structural features

	1990	1991	1992	1993	1994	1995	1996	1997
Total debt (as a percentage of GDP)	.	35.6	41.8	48.5	50.5	53.9	54.7	53.4
Composition by currency (% of total)								
In domestic currency	95.9	96.3	91.7	93.8	94.8	95.2	96.3	96.5
In foreign currencies	4.1	3.7	8.3	6.2	5.2	4.8	3.7	3.5
Domestic ownership (% of total)	88.5	83.2	81.0	78.7	81.2	82.3	82.8	82.4
Average maturity[a] (years)	10.2	9.9	10.0	10.8	10.6	10.4	10.1	10.1
Composition by maturity[b] (% of total)								
Short-term[c] (< 1 year)	41.1	40.8	37.1	30.4	29.2	30.6	26.7	26.8
Medium and long-term (≥ 1 year)	58.9	59.2	62.9	69.6	70.8	69.4	73.3	73.2

Source: National data except for total debt (European Commission (spring 1998 forecasts)). End-year data except for 1997: end-March data. Differences in the totals are due to rounding.

(a) Residual maturity. Of dated stocks in market hands as at 31 March.

(b) Residual maturity.

(c) Including short-term debt and debt linked to short-term interest rates. The proportion of short-term debt sensitive to interest rate changes is distorted by the current statistical treatment which includes notes and coins and medium-term National Savings Instruments (i.e. with a maturity exceeding a year) as having a residual maturity of less than one year. In 1997, these items amounted to around 17% of general government gross debt; the implication is that only 9.8% of debt is actually sensitive to interest rate changes. The current statistical treatment is due to change later this year when the United Kingdom adopts ESA95.

United Kingdom: General government surplus (+) / deficit (-)
(as a percentage of GDP)

(a) Levels

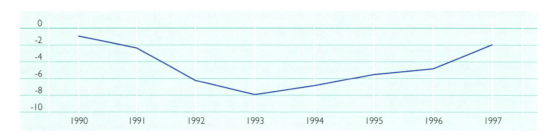

(b) Annual changes and underlying factors

Source: European Commission (spring 1998 forecasts).
Note: In Chart 3b negative values indicate a contribution to an increase in deficits, while positive values indicate a contribution to their reduction.

United Kingdom: General government expenditure and receipts
(as a percentage of GDP)

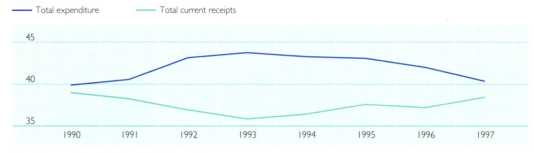

Source: European Commission (spring 1998 forecasts).

Table 6

United Kingdom: General government budgetary position
(as a percentage of GDP)

	1990	1991	1992	1993	1994	1995	1996	1997
Total current receipts	39.0	38.2	36.9	35.8	36.4	37.6	37.2	38.4
Taxes	29.9	29.4	28.3	27.3	27.8	29.0	28.7	30.1
Social security contributions	6.3	6.3	6.2	6.2	6.3	6.3	6.3	6.3
Other current receipts	2.7	2.5	2.4	2.3	2.3	2.2	2.2	2.0
Total expenditure	39.9	40.6	43.1	43.7	43.3	43.1	42.0	40.4
Current transfers	12.7	13.3	15.3	16.0	15.8	15.9	15.3	15.0
Actual interest payments	3.2	2.8	2.7	2.9	3.2	3.5	3.7	3.5
Public consumption	20.6	21.6	22.1	22.0	21.6	21.3	21.0	20.5
Net capital expenditure	3.4	2.9	2.9	2.9	2.6	2.4	2.0	1.4
Surplus (+) or deficit (-)	-0.9	-2.3	-6.2	-7.9	-6.8	-5.5	-4.8	-1.9
Primary balance	2.2	0.4	-3.5	-5.0	-3.6	-2.0	-1.1	1.6
Surplus (+) or deficit (-), net of public investment expenditure[a]	.	.	.	-6.0	-5.0	-3.7	-3.5	-0.9

Source: European Commission (spring 1998 forecasts) and EMI calculations. Differences in the totals are due to rounding.
(a) A negative sign indicates that the government deficit is higher than investment expenditure.

Table 7

United Kingdom: Projections of elderly dependency ratio

	1990	2000	2010	2020	2030
Elderly dependency ratio (population aged 65 and over as a proportion of the population aged 15-64)	24.0	24.4	25.8	31.2	38.7

Source: Bos, E. et al. (1994), World population projections 1994-95, World Bank, Washington DC.

III Exchange rate developments

Table 8

(a) United Kingdom: Exchange rate stability
(1 March 1996 - 27 February 1998)

Membership of the Exchange Rate Mechanism (ERM)	No	
Membership since	-	
Devaluation of bilateral central rate on country's own initiative	-	

Maximum upward (+) and downward (-) deviations from March 1996
average bilateral rates (%) against[a]

ERM currencies:		
Belgian franc	35.2	-0.1
Danish krone	32.7	-0.1
Deutsche Mark	34.6	-0.1
Spanish peseta	34.9	-0.3
French franc	32.6	-0.4
Irish pound	23.5	-1.0
Italian lira	24.1	-1.7
Dutch guilder	35.5	-0.1
Austrian schilling	34.7	-0.1
Portuguese escudo	31.4	-0.3
Finnish markka	28.6	-1.8
Non-ERM currencies:		
Greek drachma	28.8	-0.8
Swedish krona	29.0	-1.4

Source: European Commission and EMI calculations.
(a) Daily data at business frequency; 10-day moving average.

(b) Key indicators of exchange rate pressure for the pound sterling

Average of 3 months ending:	May 96	Aug 96	Nov 96	Feb 97	May 97	Aug 97	Nov 97	Feb 98
Exchange rate volatility[a]	4.2	5.7	6.5	10.1	9.8	10.6	10.5	7.6
Short-term interest rate differentials[b]	2.5	2.3	2.7	3.1	3.1	3.6	3.8	3.9

Source: European Commission, national data and EMI calculations.
(a) Annualised monthly standard deviation of daily percentage changes of the exchange rate against the DEM, in percentages.
(b) Differential of three-month interbank interest rates against a weighted average of interest rates in Belgium, Germany, France, the Netherlands and Austria, in percentage points.

Chart 5

Pound sterling: Bilateral exchange rates
(daily data; average of March 1996=100; 1 March 1996 to 27 February 1998)

Source: European Commission.

Table 9

Pound sterling: Measures of the real effective exchange rate vis-à-vis EU Member States
(monthly data; percentage deviations; February 1998 compared with different benchmark periods)

	Average Apr 73-Feb 98	Average Jan 87-Feb 98	Average 1987
Real effective exchange rates:			
CPI-based	18.3	17.7	24.4
PPI/WPI-based	27.7	21.7	29.9
Memo item:			
Nominal effective exchange rate	1.3	12.4	8.8

Source: BIS and EMI calculations.
Note: A positive (negative) sign indicates an appreciation (depreciation).

Table 10

United Kingdom: External developments
(as a percentage of GDP)

	1990	1991	1992	1993	1994	1995	1996	1997[a]
Current account plus new capital account[b]	-3.4	-1.4	-1.7	-1.6	-0.2	-0.5	-0.3	0.4
Net foreign assets (+) or liabilities (-)[c]	1.3	1.9	3.7	5.9	4.2	3.7	3.2	1.5
Exports (goods and services)[d]	24.4	24.7	25.9	26.3	27.5	28.9	30.2	31.5
Imports (goods and services)[e]	27.1	26.2	28.2	28.5	28.8	29.2	31.0	32.6

Source: National data except exports and imports (European Commission, spring 1998 forecasts).

(a) Partly estimated.

(b) According to the 5th edition of the IMF Balance of Payments Manual, which is conceptually the equivalent of the current account in previous editions of the Manual.

(c) International investment position (IIP) as defined by the IMF (see Balance of Payments Yearbook, Part 1, 1994), or the closest possible substitute.

(d) In 1996 the share of intra-EU exports of goods in total national exports of goods was 52.7%; Direction of Trade Statistics Yearbook 1997, IMF.

(e) In 1996 the share of intra-EU imports of goods in total national imports of goods was 49.7%; Direction of Trade Statistics Yearbook 1997, IMF.

IV Long-term interest rate developments

Table 11

United Kingdom: Long-term interest rates
(percentages)

	1996	1997	Nov 97	Dec 97	Jan 98	**Feb 97- Jan 98**
Long-term interest rate	7.9	7.1	6.7	6.4	6.2	7.0
Reference value	9.1	8.0	-	-	-	7.8

Source: European Commission.

Chart 6

(a) United Kingdom: Long-term interest rate
(monthly averages; in percentages)

(b) United Kingdom: Long-term interest rate and CPI inflation differentials against EU countries with lowest long-term interest rates*
(monthly averages; in percentage points)

Source: Interest rates: European Commission (where these are not available the most comparable data have been used); the CPI data used are non-harmonised national data.
* Weighted average of data for Belgium, Germany, France, the Netherlands and Austria.

Annex I

Developments in the private ECU markets

Developments in the private ECU markets

The overall size of the ECU financial markets declined further in 1997, standing at ECU 146.4 billion at end-September 1997, compared with ECU 154.0 billion at end-September 1996 (see Table). Total outstanding amounts of ECU-denominated international bank assets and liabilities fell by 17% and 13% respectively between end-September 1996 and end-September 1997. Estimated ECU bank lending decreased by 8% during the same period. Meanwhile, the outstanding *total* of international bonds, Euro-CP and Euro-notes at end-September 1997 amounted to ECU 58.0 billion, compared with ECU 60.7 billion at end-September 1996, which represented a decrease of 4.4%. The market share of the ECU in international bond markets continued to decline from 2.8% at end-September 1996 to 1.9% at end-September 1997. Domestic ECU bonds outstanding were flat at ECU 57.8 billion. EU sovereign issuers continued to figure prominently in ECU issuing activity, accounting for over 50% of total announced issues in 1997. The relatively small market for ECU-denominated Euro-CP and short-term Euro-notes remained broadly unchanged, standing at ECU 2.4 billion at end-September 1997, compared with ECU 2.1 billion at end-September 1996.

On 17 June 1997 the Council of Ministers of the European Union approved the Council Regulation (EC) No. 1103/97 "on certain provisions relating to the introduction of the euro". This legislation states that contracts making reference to the Community definition of the ECU (i.e. "basket" ECU) will be converted into euro at the 1:1 rate and establishes a presumption that the same will happen in the case of contracts without such a definition of the ECU, although this presumption will be rebuttable taking into account the intention of the parties, thereby preserving the principle of contractual freedom. Legal counsels and market practitioners generally welcomed the legislation as having struck an appropriate balance between continuity and contractual freedom. The legislation has also prompted other authorities, issuers and private market associations to declare that terms as specified in the Regulation would apply.

The spread between market and basket ECU *exchange rates*, which had been gradually narrowing since early 1996 from a peak of 330 basis points, narrowed further between end-December 1996 and end-December 1997 from around 90 basis points to par, and the market ECU was even at a premium for a short period towards the end of the year (see Chart). The spreads between market and basket ECU *interest rates*, particularly short-term rates, remained within a narrow range during most of 1997. Several factors may be identified to explain the behaviour of exchange rate and interest rate spreads. First, their behaviour reflects the financial market perceptions of improved prospects for EMU combined with the reduction in legal uncertainty. A second factor appears to have been calm overall conditions within the ERM; in the past wide spread divergences were often associated with crises in EU currency markets. Third, technical factors also appear to have played a role, contributing to short-term volatility. Liquidity in the ECU foreign exchange market has diminished, reflecting the reduced number of market-makers, so that large commercial and financial orders may have accentuated temporary fluctuations of the spread.

Table for Annex I

ECU financial markets

(outstanding stocks at end-period: in billions of ECUs)

	1993 Q3	1994 Q3	1995 Q3	1996 Q3	1997 Q1	Q2	Q3	Q4
Bonds, *of which*	124.5	125.4	119.1	110.2	112.1	110.8	113.4	118.1
- *international* [a]	78.2	69.1	62.5	51.8	55.5	55.0	55.6	58.0
- *domestic*	46.3	56.3	56.6	58.4	56.6	55.8	57.8	60.1
(National) Treasury bills	8.3	4.7	3.5	3.5	3.5	3.5	3.5	3.5
Euro-CP and Euro-notes [a]	6.5	6.4	8.2	8.9	2.7	2.3	2.4	2.8
Estimated bank lending [b]	66.6	59.9	57.3	51.4	46.7	45.0	47.1	.
Estimated total market size [c]	185.9	176.4	168.1	154.0	145.0	141.6	146.4	.
Bank assets, *of which:*	196.0	178.4	164.5	142.0	128.1	117.2	118.1	.
- *vis-à-vis non-banks* [d]	61.0	55.6	52.6	46.9	42.2	40.7	42.7	.
Bank liabilities, *of which:*	191.9	174.7	157.7	136.7	129.9	120.6	118.9	.
- *vis-à-vis non-banks* [d]	30.9	27.1	23.1	20.9	21.9	21.7	21.4	.
Memorandum items:								
Central banks' holdings of private ECUs	19.1	24.0	23.3	21.8	22.9	21.4	19.1	19.9
Turnover of ECU securities [e]	333.6	402.0	479.6	392.5	412.1	390.3	337.4	313.6
% of total turnover in all currencies	6.1	6.9	7.4	4.1	3.9	3.6	2.7	2.5

Source: BIS, Euroclear, Cedel and EMI.

(a) From 1997 medium-term notes have been included under international bonds; for earlier years, they are included under Euro-CP and Euro-notes.

(b) Final lending and lending to banks outside the reporting area.

(c) ECU 20 billion are deducted for estimated double counting: there is an overlap between the securities and banking markets owing to the role of banks as issuers and holders of ECU securities. In the absence of comprehensive data, this overlap may only be estimated.

(d) Identified non-banks only.

(e) Primary and secondary market, Euro-bonds and domestic straight bonds, convertibles, floating rate notes, CDs, short and medium-term notes.

Chart for Annex I

Difference between market and theoretical exchange rates of the ECU
(percentages)

Source: National data.

Annex 2

Statistical methodology on convergence indicators

Statistical methodology on convergence indicators

This Annex provides information on the statistical methodology of the convergence indicators and details of the harmonisation achieved in these statistics.

Consumer prices

Protocol No. 6 on the convergence criteria referred to in Article 109j (1) of the Treaty establishing the European Community requires price convergence to be measured by means of the consumer price index on a comparable basis, taking into account differences in national definitions. Although current consumer price statistics in the Member States are largely based on similar principles, there are considerable differences of detail and these affect the comparability of the national results.

The conceptual work on the harmonisation of consumer price indices is carried out by the European Commission (EUROSTAT) in close liaison with the National Statistical Institutes (NSIs). As a key user, the EMI is closely involved in this work. In October 1995 the EU Council adopted a Regulation concerning Harmonised Indices of Consumer Prices (HICPs), which serves as the framework for further detailed harmonisation measures. It sets out a step-by-step approach for harmonising consumer price indices to provide the necessary data for the analysis of convergence.

The first HICPs were released by EUROSTAT for January 1997. Back data are available to 1995. The harmonisation measures introduced for HICPs have so far been based on three comprehensive Regulations of the European Commission. They concern - inter alia - the initial coverage of HICPs, initial standards for the procedures of quality adjustment and common rules for the treatment of new goods and services. Moreover, a detailed harmonised classification for HICP sub-indices has been agreed, which allows for a consistent comparison of price developments in detailed sub-groups of consumer expenditures across the Member States. Finally, a recently adopted Commission Regulation lays down rules for the frequency with which the commodity weights in HICPs are to be revised. The methodological improvements which were introduced for HICPs in 1997 were substantial steps towards the achievement of fully comparable HICPs.

HICPs are used for measuring consumer price convergence in this Report. Furthermore, the HICP covering the euro area as a whole is expected to be the main measure of consumer prices for the single currency area from January 1999 onwards. There is therefore a strong continuing interest in harmonisation in this area.

Public finances

Protocol No. 5 on the excessive deficit procedure annexed to the Treaty together with a Council Regulation of November 1993 define "government", "deficit", "interest expenditure", "investment", "debt" and "gross domestic product (GDP)" by reference to the European System of Integrated Economic Accounts (ESA), second edition. The ESA is a coherent and detailed set of national accounts tables developed in order to facilitate comparative analyses between Member States. According to a Council Regulation of June 1996, the second edition of the ESA will be applied for the excessive deficit procedure up to and including 1999 and will be replaced by the ESA 95 thereafter.

"Government" comprises central government, regional or local government and social security funds. It does not include public enterprises and is therefore to be distinguished from a more broadly defined public sector.

"Government deficit" is mainly the difference between government gross saving and the sum of government investment (defined as gross fixed capital formation) and net capital transfers payable by government. "Government debt" is the sum of the outstanding gross liabilities at nominal value of government as classified in the second edition of the ESA, in the categories currency and deposits, bills and bonds, and other loans. Government debt does not cover trade credits and other liabilities which are not represented by a financial document such as overpaid tax advances, nor does it include contingent liabilities such as government guarantees and pension commitments. The definitions of government deficit and government debt imply that the change in government debt outstanding at the end of two consecutive years may differ substantially from the size of the government deficit for the year under consideration. For example, government debt may be reduced by using the receipts from privatising public enterprises or by selling other financial assets without any immediate impact on the government deficit. Conversely, the government deficit may be reduced by substituting loans provided by government for transfers without any immediate impact on government debt.

The "gross domestic product (GDP)" used for the compilation of the Community's own resources is also used in connection with the excessive deficit procedure. The GDP compilation procedures are monitored by a Committee established by a Council Directive of February 1989.

As from the beginning of 1994 Member States have been reporting data related to the government deficit and government debt to the European Commission at least twice a year. The Treaty gives responsibility for providing the statistical data to be used for the excessive deficit procedure to the European Commission. Against this background, the Statistical Office of the Commission (EUROSTAT) monitors the consistency of the statistical data reported in accordance with the ESA, second edition, and their comparability between Member States. Where the second edition of the ESA does not give clear guidance, EUROSTAT seeks the opinion of the Committee on Monetary, Financial and Balance of Payments Statistics (CMFB), which includes representatives of Member States' national central banks and NSIs. Taking account of the CMFB's opinion, EUROSTAT makes an independent decision on the statistical treatment to be applied by the Member States.

Exchange rates

Exchange rates vis-à-vis the ECU of the currencies of the Member States are quoted daily (the so-called 2.15 p.m. concertation) and are published in the Official Journal of the European Communities; European cross rates used throughout this Report are derived from these ECU exchange rates. For information purposes, reference is also made in this Report to nominal and real effective exchange rates on the basis of series calculated by the BIS.

Long-term interest rates

Protocol No. 6 on the convergence criteria referred to in Article 109j (1) of the Treaty establishing the European Community requires interest rate convergence to be assessed on the basis of long-term government bonds, or comparable securities, observed over a period of one year before the assessment, taking into account differences in national definitions.

While Article 5 of Protocol No. 6 assigns responsibility for providing the statistical data for the application of the Protocol to the European Commission, assistance has been provided by the EMI in defining representative long-term interest rate statistics, given its expertise in the area, and in collecting the data from the central banks for transmission to the European Commission.

Although the methodology for calculating the yields of bonds is similar across Member States, considerable differences existed in long-term interest rate statistics regarding the choice of securities, the yield formulae used, the maturities chosen, the treatment of taxation and adjustments for coupon effects. The purpose of the harmonisation exercise was to make recommendations, in particular with regard to these choices, which would be general enough to allow for differences in national markets, and yet flexible enough to allow those markets to evolve, without the comparability of data being impaired.

The harmonisation principles were that the issuer of bonds should be the central government, with fixed coupon securities of close to ten years to maturity, and that yields should be measured gross of tax. To ensure that the depth of the market is taken into account, and that no liquidity premium is carried into the yield, the representative securities should be chosen on the basis of their high liquidity. Responsibility for this choice is a matter for the Member States. At end-December 1997 eleven countries were using a benchmark bond and four a sample of bonds, using the liquidity of the market at the ten-year point as the determining factor. "Special feature" bonds (e.g. embedded option, zero coupon) are excluded from the assessment. The selection of highly liquid bonds is also seen as an effective indirect means by which to minimise the effects of different coupon values. Finally, a uniform formula was chosen from existing international standards, namely formula 6.3 from the "formulae for yield and other calculations" of the International Securities Market Association. Where there is more than one bond in the sample, the liquidity of the selected bonds warrants the use of a simple average of the yields to produce the representative rate. The aim of these changes was to focus on the statistical measurement of the perceived durability of convergence. As mentioned above, the production of the harmonised representative long-term interest rates has been implemented by the central banks, and fully harmonised data are used in this Report.

Other factors

The last paragraph of Article 109j (1) of the Treaty states that the reports of the European Commission and the EMI shall, besides the four main criteria, also take account of the development of the ECU, the results of the integration of markets, the situation and development of the balances of payments on current account and an examination of the development of unit labour costs and other price indices.

Whereas for the four main criteria Protocol No. 6 describes the data to be used in more detail and stipulates that the European Commission will provide the data to be used for the assessment of compliance with these criteria, there is no reference to these "other factors" in the Protocol. While the development of the ECU and the integration of markets relate to progress towards Economic and Monetary Union in more general terms, the analysis of the other factors is based on definitions which currently provide the most comparable results between Member States.

Chapter II

Compatibility of national legislation with the Treaty

I General observations

1.1 Introduction

Article 109j (1) and (4) of the Treaty[16] requires the EMI (as well as the Commission) to report, inter alia, on "the compatibility between each Member State's national legislation, including the statutes of its national central bank, and Articles 107 and 108 of this Treaty and the Statute of the ESCB" (in this Report also referred to as "legal convergence"). Article 108 of the Treaty, as reproduced in Article 14.1 of the Statute,[16] states in this connection that Member States shall ensure, at the latest at the date of the establishment of the ESCB, that their national legislation, including the statutes of their national central banks (NCBs), is compatible with the Treaty and the Statute.

The EMI has examined the legal situation in the Member States and the legislative measures which have been taken and/or need to be taken by the Member States with a view to achieving compatibility of their national legislation with the Treaty and the Statute. The results of this examination are presented below. The present Report draws on the EMI's previous reports on legal convergence: the 1995 and 1996 Reports on Progress towards Convergence and the legal update thereof dated October 1997.

All Member States except Denmark, whose legislation does not require adaptation, either have introduced in 1997 or in 1998, or are in an advanced process of introducing, changes in the statutes of their NCBs, following the criteria laid down in the EMI's Reports and in the EMI's opinions. The United Kingdom, which is exempt from the obligations under Article 108 of the Treaty, is in the process of introducing a new statute of its NCB which, while providing a greater level of operational central bank independence, is not expressly

intended to achieve the legal convergence as required by the EMI for full compliance with the Treaty and the Statute of the ESCB. Throughout the European Union legislators, with the above exceptions, have undertaken a legislative process intended to prepare NCBs for Stage Three of EMU.

1.2 Scope of adaptation

1.2.1 Areas of adaptation

For the purpose of identifying those areas where adaptation of national legislation is necessary, a distinction is drawn between:

- the independence of NCBs (see in particular Articles 107 of the Treaty and Articles 7 and 14.2 of the Statute);

- the legal integration of NCBs in the ESCB (see in particular Articles 12.1 and 14.3 of the Statute); and

- legislation other than statutes of NCBs.

Independence of NCBs

The Statute contemplates an important role for governors of NCBs (via their membership of the Governing Council of the ECB) with regard to the formulation of monetary policy and for the NCBs with regard to the execution of the operations of the ESCB (see Article 12.1 of the Statute, last paragraph). Thus, it will be essential for the NCBs to be independent in the performance of their ESCB-related tasks vis-à-vis external bodies.

---

[16] References to the Treaty and the Statute are references to the Treaty establishing the European Community and the Statute of the ESCB/ECB, unless otherwise indicated.

288

Legal integration of NCBs in the ESCB

Article 14.3 of the Statute states that the NCBs shall be an integral part of the ESCB, that they shall act in accordance with the guidelines and instructions of the ECB and that the Governing Council shall take the necessary steps to ensure compliance with such guidelines and instructions. Provisions in national legislation (particularly in NCB statutes) which would prevent the execution of ESCB-related tasks or compliance with decisions of the ECB would be incompatible with the effective operation of the System. Therefore, adaptations to national legislation and NCB statutes are necessary to ensure compatibility with the Treaty and the Statute.

Legislation other than statutes of NCBs

The obligation of legal convergence under Article 108 of the Treaty, which is incorporated in a chapter entitled "Monetary Policy", applies to those areas of legislation which are affected by the transition from Stage Two to Stage Three and which would be incompatible with the Treaty and Statute if they were to remain unchanged. The EMI's assessment in this field focuses in particular on laws with an impact on an NCB's performance of ESCB-related tasks and laws in the monetary area.

1.2.2 "Compatibility" versus "harmonisation"

Article 108 of the Treaty requires national legislation to be "compatible" with the Treaty and the Statute. The term "compatible" indicates that the Treaty does not require "harmonisation" of NCBs' statutes, either inter se or with that of the ECB. National particularities may continue to exist. Indeed, Article 14.4 of the Statute permits NCBs to perform functions other than those specified in the Statute, to the extent that these do not interfere with the objectives and tasks of the ESCB. Provisions enabling such additional functions would be a clear example of circumstances where differences in NCB statutes may continue. Rather, the term "compatible" implies that national legislation and the statutes of the NCBs need to be adjusted in order to eliminate inconsistencies with the Treaty and the Statute and to ensure the necessary degree of integration of the NCBs in the ESCB. In particular, while national traditions may continue to exist, all provisions which infringe on an NCB's independence as defined in the Treaty and its role as an integral part of the ESCB have to be adjusted. The Treaty and the Statute require the removal of incompatibilities with the Treaty and the Statute in national legislation. Neither the supremacy of the Treaty and the Statute over national legislation nor the nature of the incompatibility affects this obligation.

The obligation in Article 108 of the Treaty only extends to incompatibilities with Treaty and Statute provisions and not to incompatibilities with secondary Community legislation to be adopted after the selection of participating Member States and to enter into force at the beginning of Stage Three. After the start of Stage Three national legislation which is incompatible with secondary EC or ECB legislation will, of course, also have to be brought into line with such secondary legislation. This general requirement derives from the case law of the European Court of Justice.

Finally, the Treaty and the Statute do not prescribe the manner in which national legislation needs to be adapted. This may be achieved by references to the Treaty and the Statute, by the incorporation of provisions thereof, by the simple deletion of incompatibilities or by a mixture of these methods.

1.2.3 Timetable for adaptation

Article 108 of the Treaty requires national legislation to be compatible with the Treaty and the Statute "at the latest at the date of the establishment of the ESCB" (which, under Article 109l (1) of the Treaty, will be earlier than the start of Stage Three). In order to comply with Article 108, national legislative procedures must be accomplished in such a way that the compatibility of national legislation is ensured at the latest at the date of the establishment of the ESCB.

Compatibility requires that the legislative process be completed, i.e. that the respective act has been adopted by the national legislator and that all further steps, for example promulgation, have been accomplished. This applies to all legislation under Article 108. However, the distinction between different areas of legislation is important when it comes to determining the date on which legislation must enter into force.

Many decisions which the Governing Council of the ECB and the NCBs will take between the date of the ESCB's establishment and the end of 1998 will predetermine the single monetary policy and its implementation within the euro area. Therefore, incompatibilities which relate to the independence of an NCB need to be effectively removed at the date of the ESCB's establishment, which implies that the respective amendments must not only be adopted, but must also be in force at this date. Other statutory requirements relating to the legal integration of NCBs in the ESCB need only enter into force at the moment that the integration of an NCB in the ESCB becomes effective, i.e. the starting date of Stage Three or, in the case of a Member State with a derogation or a special status, the date on which it adopts the single currency.

Finally, Article 108 targets one specific point in time, i.e. the date of the establishment of the ESCB. Possible legal changes after that date, for example as a result of secondary Community legislation, do not fall within its scope. Therefore, the present Report does not, for instance, address future adaptations of national legislation relating to the introduction of the euro flowing from the EU Council Regulations on this topic, such as the replacement of national banknotes and coins by euro banknotes and coins and the legal aspects thereof.[17]

1.3 Member States with a derogation, Denmark and the United Kingdom

1.3.1 Member States with a derogation

In relation to the application of Articles 107 and 108, the Treaty and the Statute do not make a distinction between Member States with and Member States without a derogation. Also, Article 109k of the Treaty and Article 43 of the Statute do not provide for an exemption to the obligation to ensure central bank independence for Member States with a derogation. A derogation only implies, in accordance with these Articles, that the respective NCB retains its powers in the field of monetary policy and participates in the ESCB on a restricted basis until the date on which the Member State adopts the single currency.

1.3.2 Denmark

Protocol No. 12 of the Treaty on certain provisions relating to Denmark states that the Danish Government shall notify the Council of its position concerning

---

[17] See EU Council Regulation 1103/97 on certain provisions relating to the introduction of the euro and draft EU Council Regulation .../98 on the introduction of the euro.

participation in Stage Three before the Council makes its assessment under Article 109j (2) of the Treaty. Denmark has already given notification that it will not participate in Stage Three. In accordance with Article 2 of Protocol No. 12, this means that Denmark will be treated as a Member State with a derogation. Implications thereof for Denmark were elaborated in a Decision taken by the Heads of State or Government at their Edinburgh Summit meeting on 11 and 12 December 1992. This Decision states that Denmark will retain its existing powers in the field of monetary policy according to its national laws and regulations, including the powers of Danmarks Nationalbank in the field of monetary policy. As Article 107 of the Treaty, in accordance with Article 109k (3) of the Treaty, applies to Denmark, Danmarks Nationalbank has to fulfil the requirements of central bank independence.

1.3.3 United Kingdom

According to Protocol No. 11 of the Treaty on certain provisions relating to the United Kingdom of Great Britain and Northern Ireland, the United Kingdom shall be under no obligation to move to Stage Three unless it notifies the Council that it intends to do so. Pursuant to the notification given by the United Kingdom to the Council on 30 October 1997 that it does not intend to adopt the single currency on 1 January 1999, certain provisions of the Treaty (including Articles 107 and 108) and of the Statute do not apply to the United Kingdom. Accordingly, there is no current legal requirement to ensure that national legislation (including the statute of the Bank of England) is compatible with the Treaty and the Statute.

2 Independence of NCBs

2.1 General remarks

The ESCB will have the exclusive right and duty to define and implement monetary policy. Independence from political authorities will allow the System to define a monetary policy aimed at the statutory objective of price stability. Independence also requires the System to possess the powers necessary to implement monetary policy decisions.

Central bank independence is essential for the credibility of the move to Monetary Union and, thus, a prerequisite of Monetary Union. The institutional aspects of Monetary Union require monetary powers, currently held by Member States, to be exercised in a new system, the ESCB. This would not be acceptable if Member States could influence the decisions taken by the governing bodies of the ESCB.

Central bank independence finds its limits in statutes defining the objective of a central bank and the scope of its powers, as well as in the review by the judiciary of its acts.

The EMI has established a list of features of central bank independence, distinguishing between features of an institutional, personal and financial nature.[18] In doing so, the EMI made three basic assumptions:

- Central bank independence is required when exercising the powers and carrying out the tasks and duties conferred upon the ECB and the NCBs by the Treaty and the Statute. Features of central

---

[18] There is also a criterion of functional independence, but as NCBs will in Stage Three be integrated in the ESCB, this is being dealt with in the framework of the legal integration of NCBs in the ESCB (see paragraph 3 below).

bank independence should therefore be considered from that perspective.

- Such features should not be seen as a kind of secondary Community legislation, going beyond the scope of the Treaty and the Statute, but as tools to facilitate an assessment of the independence of the NCBs.

- Central bank independence is not a matter which can be expressed in arithmetical formulae or applied in a mechanical manner and the way in which it is achieved for individual NCBs is therefore assessed on a case-by-case basis.

2.2 Institutional independence

Institutional independence is a feature of central bank independence which is expressly referred to in Article 107 of the Treaty as reproduced in Article 7 of the Statute. These Articles prohibit the ECB, the NCBs and members of their decision-making bodies from seeking or taking instructions from Community institutions or bodies, from any government of a Member State or from any other body. They also prohibit Community institutions and bodies and the governments of the Member States from seeking to influence the members of the decision-making bodies of the ECB or of those decision-making bodies of the NCBs whose decisions may have an impact on the fulfilment by the NCBs of their ESCB-related tasks.

The main tasks of the ESCB are defined in Article 3 of the Statute:

- to define and implement the monetary policy of the Community;

- to conduct foreign exchange operations consistent with the provisions of Article 109 of this Treaty;

- to hold and manage the official foreign reserves of the Member States;

- to promote the smooth operation of payment systems.

The reference in Article 107 to the tasks and duties of the ESCB implies that the independence requirement refers to all ESCB-related tasks. In other fields of activity, instructions are not forbidden. This applies, for example, to NCBs in fulfilling other tasks permitted within the limitations of Article 14.4 of the Statute, which states that NCBs may perform functions other than those in the Statute, unless the Governing Council finds, by a two-thirds majority, that these interfere with the objectives and tasks of the ESCB.

The prohibition on instructions and attempts to influence covers all sources of external influence on the NCBs in relation to ESCB matters which prevent them from complying with the Treaty and the Statute.

The following rights of third parties (e.g. government or parliament) are incompatible with the Treaty and/or the Statute and therefore require adaptation.

2.2.1 A right to give instructions

Rights of third parties to give instructions to NCBs or their decision-making bodies are incompatible with the Treaty and the Statute as far as ESCB-related tasks are concerned.

2.2.2 A right to approve, suspend, annul or defer decisions

Rights of third parties to approve, suspend, annul or defer decisions of NCBs are incompatible with the Treaty and the Statute as far as ESCB-related tasks are concerned.

2.2.3 A right to censor decisions on legal grounds

A right to censor, on legal grounds, decisions relating to the performance of ESCB-related tasks is incompatible with the Treaty and the Statute as the performance of these tasks may not be obstructed at a national level. This is not only an expression of central bank independence but also of the more general requirement of the integration of NCBs in the ESCB (see Section 3 below). A right of the governor to censor decisions on legal grounds and subsequently submit them to the political authorities for final decision would, although a governor is not a "third party", be equivalent to seeking instructions from political bodies, which is incompatible with Article 107 of the Treaty.

2.2.4 A right to participate in the decision-making bodies of an NCB with a right to vote

The participation of representatives of other bodies (e.g. government or parliament) in the decision-making bodies of an NCB with a right to vote on matters concerning the performance by the NCB of ESCB-related tasks, even if this vote is not decisive, is incompatible with the Treaty and the Statute.

2.2.5 A right to be consulted (ex ante) on an NCB's decisions

An explicit statutory obligation for an NCB to consult the political authorities provides a formal mechanism to ensure that their views may influence the final decision and is therefore incompatible with the Treaty and the Statute.

It is noted that in Stage Three primary responsibility for the fulfilment of the ESCB's tasks is vested in the Governing Council of the ECB. Dialogue with political bodies will then take place mainly at the Community level (see, in particular, Article 109b of the Treaty and Article 15.3 of the Statute). However, dialogue between NCBs and their respective political authorities, even when based on statutory obligations to provide information and exchange views, is not incompatible with the Treaty and the Statute, provided that:

- this does not result in interference with the independence of the members of the decision-making bodies of NCBs;

- the ECB's competences and accountability at the Community level as well as the special status of a governor in his/her capacity as a member of its decision-making bodies are respected; and

- confidentiality requirements resulting from Statute provisions are observed.

2.3 Personal independence

Central bank independence is further substantiated by the provision of the Statute which provides for security of tenure for members of the ESCB's decision-making bodies. Article 14.2 of the Statute states that the statutes of NCBs shall, in particular, provide for a minimum term of office for a governor of five years. It also gives protection against the arbitrary dismissal of governors, by stating that a governor may be relieved from office only if he/she no longer fulfils the conditions required for the performance of his/her duties or if he/she has been guilty of serious misconduct, with the possibility of appeal to the European Court of Justice. The statutes of NCBs will need to be in conformity with this.

Against this background, the statutes of NCBs have to respect the following features of personal independence:

2.3.1 Minimum term of office for governors

The statutes of NCBs must, in accordance with Article 14.2 of the Statute, contain a minimum term of office for a governor of five years. This, of course, does not preclude longer terms of office, while an indefinite term of office does not require the adaptation of statutes if the grounds for the dismissal of a governor are in line with those of Article 14.2 of the Statute (see point 2.3.2 below). A compulsory retirement age is in itself not incompatible with the Statute requirement of a minimum term of five years.

2.3.2 Grounds for the dismissal of governors

The statutes of NCBs must ensure that a governor may not be dismissed for reasons other than those mentioned in Article 14.2 of the Statute (i.e. no longer fulfilling the conditions required for the performance of his/her duties or being guilty of serious misconduct). The purpose of this requirement is to prevent the dismissal of a governor from being at the discretion of the authorities involved in his/her appointment, particularly government or parliament. As from the date of the establishment of the ESCB, the statutes of NCBs should contain grounds for dismissal which are compatible with those laid down in Article 14.2 of the Statute or should not mention any grounds for dismissal since Article 14.2 is directly applicable.

2.3.3 Security of tenure of members of the decision-making bodies of NCBs involved in the performance of ESCB-related tasks other than governors

Personal independence could be jeopardised if the same rules for the security of tenure of office of governors were not also applied to the other members of the decision-making bodies of NCBs involved in the performance of ESCB-related tasks. A requirement to confer comparable security of tenure follows from various Treaty and Statute articles. Article 14.2 of the Statute does not restrict the security of tenure of office to governors, while Article 107 of the Treaty and Article 7 of the Statute refer to "any members of decision-making bodies of NCBs" rather than to "governors". This applies in particular where a governor is "primus inter pares" between colleagues with equivalent voting rights or where, in the case referred to in Article 10.2 of the Statute, such other members may have to deputise for the governor within the Governing Council. This general principle would not exclude a differentiation in terms of office and/or in grounds for dismissal in those cases where members of decision-making bodies and/or such bodies themselves are not involved in the performance of ESCB-related tasks.

With regard to the system of appointment of members of the decision-making bodies one particular issue merits specific attention: some statutes of NCBs provide that, when a vacancy arises, the new member is appointed for the remainder of the original term of the leaving (or deceased) member. This is aimed at ensuring a pre-established rhythm of replacements in those decision-making bodies, irrespective of unexpected early vacancies, and, in that sense, strengthens the collective independence of the decision-making bodies from political authorities. While these systems may not always ensure that each individual member of the decision-making bodies serves the minimum five years to which Article 14.2 of the Statute of the ESCB refers, the general aim pursued by such systems is not incompatible with the Treaty if the normal term of office is generally established at five years or more.[19] However, for the avoidance of doubt with respect to Article

---

[19] Such systems are foreseen in the Treaty for other independent Community institutions: the European Commission (Article 159), the European Court of Justice (Article 167) and the European Court of Auditors (Article 188b(6)).

14.2 of the Statute of the ESCB, the EMI recommends that all statutes of NCBs ensure that each individual member of a decision-making body involved in the performance of ESCB-related tasks has a minimum term of office of five years.

Such a recommendation is not warranted for transitional arrangements whereby new decision-making bodies are put in place and different expiry dates for appointees' terms of office are foreseen. These are "once and for all" schemes, aimed at ensuring different dates for the expiry of terms of office of members of decision-making bodies and, thus, achieving continuity in the management of the NCB.[20]

2.3.4 Safeguards against conflicts of interest

Personal independence also entails ensuring that no conflicts of interest arise between the duties of members of decision-making bodies of NCBs vis-à-vis their respective NCB (and of governors, additionally, vis-à-vis the ECB) and any other functions which such members of decision-making bodies involved in the performance of ESCB-related tasks may have and which may jeopardise their personal independence. As a matter of principle, membership of a decision-making body involved in the performance of ESCB-related tasks is incompatible with the exercise of other functions which might create a conflict of interest.

2.4 Financial independence

If an NCB is fully independent from an institutional and functional point of view, but at the same time unable to avail itself autonomously of the appropriate economic means to fulfil its mandate, its overall independence would nevertheless be undermined. In the EMI's opinion, NCBs should be in a position to avail themselves of the appropriate means to ensure that their ESCB-related tasks can be properly fulfilled. An ex post review of an NCB's financial accounts may be regarded as a reflection of an NCB's accountability towards its owners provided that the NCB's statute contains adequate safeguards that such a review will not infringe its independence. However, in those countries where third parties and, particularly, the government and/or parliament are in a position, directly or indirectly, to exercise influence on the determination of an NCB's budget or the distribution of profit, the relevant statutory provisions should contain a safeguard clause to ensure that this does not impede the proper performance of the NCB's ESCB-related tasks.

---

[20] Article 50 of the Statute of the ESCB provides for such a system of staggered initial appointments of the members of the Executive Board of the ECB, exclusive of the President.

3 Legal integration of NCBs in the ESCB

Another area of legal convergence concerns the legislative measures required for the legal integration of NCBs in the ESCB.[21] In particular, measures may be necessary to enable NCBs to execute tasks as members of the ESCB and in accordance with decisions by the ECB. The main areas of attention are those where statutory provisions may form an obstacle to an NCB complying with the requirements of the ESCB or to a governor fulfilling his/her duties as a member of the Governing Council of the ECB, or where statutory provisions do not respect the prerogatives of the ECB. A distinction is drawn between those areas of which statutes of NCBs are usually composed: statutory objectives, tasks, instruments, organisation and financial provisions.

3.1 Statutory objectives

The integration of NCBs in the ESCB requires that their (primary and secondary) statutory objectives are compatible with the ESCB's objectives as laid down in Article 2 of the Statute. This means, inter alia, that statutory objectives with a "national flavour", for example referring to an obligation to conduct monetary policy within the framework of the general economic policy of the Member State concerned, need to be adapted.

3.2 Tasks

In Stage Three an NCB's tasks are predominantly determined by its status as an integral part of the ESCB and, thus, by the Treaty and the Statute. In order to comply with Article 108 of the Treaty, provisions on tasks in the statutes of NCBs therefore need to be compared with the relevant Treaty and Statute provisions[22] and incompatibilities need to be removed.

This applies to any provisions which in Stage Three form an impediment to the execution of ESCB-related tasks and, in particular, to provisions which do not respect the ECB's competences under Chapter IV of its Statute.

3.3 Instruments

The statutes of many, if not all, NCBs contain provisions on monetary policy instruments. Again, national provisions on such instruments are to be compared with those contained in the Treaty and Statute and incompatibilities need to be removed in order to comply with Article 108 of the Treaty.

3.4 Organisation

In addition to the prohibition on giving, accepting or soliciting instructions, there must be no mechanisms in the statutes of NCBs which could either bind a governor in his/her voting behaviour in the Governing Council of the ECB in which he/she acts in the separate capacity as a member of that Council or prevent an NCB's decision-making bodies from complying with rules adopted at the level of the ECB.

3.5 Financial provisions

Financial provisions in the Statute, which may be of particular relevance as far as the identification of incompatibilities in the

---

[21] Article 14.3 in conjunction with Article 43.1 of the Statute implies that fully participating NCBs will become an integral part of the ESCB and that they will have to comply with guidelines and instructions from the ECB.

[22] In particular Articles 105 and 105a of the Treaty and Articles 3 to 6 of the Statute.

statutes of NCBs is concerned, may be divided into rules on accounting[23], auditing[24], capital subscriptions[25], transfer of foreign reserve assets[26] and monetary income[27]. These rules imply that NCBs need to be able to comply with their obligations under the relevant Treaty and Statute articles.

3.6 Miscellaneous

In addition to the above-mentioned issues, there may be other areas where the adaptation of the statutes of NCBs is required. For example, the obligation of professional secrecy for staff of the ECB and NCBs as laid down in Article 38 of the Statute may have an impact on similar provisions in the statutes of NCBs as well.

4 Legislation other than the statutes of NCBs

The obligation of legal convergence under Article 108 of the Treaty, which is incorporated in a chapter entitled "Monetary Policy", applies to those areas of legislation which are affected by the transition from Stage Two to Stage Three and which would be incompatible with the Treaty and the Statute if they were to remain unchanged. The EMI's assessment focuses on laws with an impact on an NCB's performance of ESCB-related tasks and laws in the monetary field. Relevant legislation requiring adaptation may in particular be found in the following areas:

4.1 Banknotes

The currency acts of a number of Member States assign the exclusive right to issue banknotes to their NCBs. These acts have to recognise the Governing Council's exclusive right to authorise the issuance of banknotes as laid down in Article 105a (1) of the Treaty and repeated in Article 16 of the Statute. In addition, provisions enabling governments to exert an influence on issues such as the denominations, production, volume and withdrawal of banknotes have to recognise the ECB's powers with regard to the euro banknotes as laid down in the above Treaty and Statute articles.

4.2 Coins

A number of Member States have laws on the issuance, production and distribution of coins. Usually, governments or, more specifically, Ministers of Finance have the exclusive right to mint coins, while NCBs are often involved in the distribution thereof. In some cases, the right to print banknotes and mint coins is combined within an NCB. Irrespective of the division of responsibilities in this field between governments and NCBs, the relevant provisions have to recognise the ECB's power of approval of the volume of issuance of coins.

4.3 Foreign reserve management

One of the main tasks of the ESCB is to hold and manage the official foreign reserves of the Member States (Article 105 (2) of the Treaty). Member States which do not transfer their official foreign reserves to their NCB do not comply with this

---

[23] Article 26 of the Statute.
[24] Article 27 of the Statute.
[25] Article 28 of the Statute.
[26] Article 30 of the Statute.
[27] Article 32 of the Statute.

requirement of the Treaty (with the exception of foreign exchange working balances, which the governments of the Member States may keep under Article 105 (3) of the Treaty). In addition, a right of a third party, for example government or parliament, to influence decisions of an NCB with regard to the management of the official foreign reserves would (under Article 105 (2) of the Treaty) not be in conformity with the Treaty. Furthermore, NCBs will have to provide the ECB with foreign reserve assets in proportion to their shares in the subscribed capital of the ECB. This means that there must be no statutory obstacles to NCBs transferring foreign reserve assets to the ECB.

4.4　Exchange rate policy

In most Member States, national legislation provides that the government is responsible for the exchange rate policy with a consultative and/or executive role for the respective NCB. Full responsibility for a Member State's exchange rate policy is only assigned to an NCB in a few cases. Provisions have to reflect the fact that

responsibility for the euro area's exchange rate policy will be transferred to the Community level in accordance with Article 109 of the Treaty, which assigns the responsibility for such policy to the EU Council in close co-operation with the ECB.

4.5　Miscellaneous

There are many other areas where legislation may have an impact on an NCB's performance of ESCB-related tasks. For example, Member States are free to organise their respective NCBs under public or private law, but provisions governing the legal status of an NCB - in the latter case, for instance, company law - may not infringe Treaty and Statute requirements for Stage Three. Furthermore, the confidentiality regime of the ESCB is governed by Article 38 of the Statute. The supremacy of Community law and rules adopted thereunder implies that national laws on access of third parties to public documents may not lead to infringements of the ESCB's confidentiality regime.

5　Country assessments

The above specification of areas of particular importance to the adaptation of statutes of NCBs and other legislation with a view to Treaty and Statute requirements for Stage Three may serve as a basis for a country-by-country assessment of the state of affairs in this respect. Such an assessment of the situation as at 24 March 1998 has been elaborated in an Annex to this Report and is summarised below.

5.1　Belgium

The statute of the National Bank of Belgium was amended to meet Treaty and Statute requirements for Stage Three with Law No. 1061/12-96/97 (the "new law"), which will progressively enter into force as from February 1998. The EMI has been consulted on a draft version of the new law, which has been amended, inter alia, in the light of the EMI's opinion.

With the adoption and entry into force of the new law, and assuming that specific provisions thereof (for which progressive adaptation through Royal Decrees is envisaged in Article 38) will enter into force on time, the statute of the National Bank of Belgium will be compatible with Treaty and Statute requirements for Stage Three.

As far as other legislation is concerned, the EMI takes note that adaptations are envisaged of the Law of 12 June 1930 creating a Monetary Fund, the Law of 28 December 1973, the Law of 23 December 1988 and Decree-Law No. 5 of 1 May 1944. The EMI is not aware of any other statutory provisions which would require adaptation under Article 108 of the Treaty.

5.2 Denmark

The statute of Danmarks Nationalbank does not contain incompatibilities in the area of central bank independence. The legal integration of the Bank in the ESCB does not need to be provided for and other legislation does not need to be adapted as long as Denmark does not adopt the single currency.

5.3 Germany

The statute of the Deutsche Bundesbank was amended to meet Treaty and Statute requirements for Stage Three with the Sixth Act amending the Deutsche Bundesbank Act dated 22 December 1997, which was published in the Federal Law Gazette on 30 December 1997 (the "new law"). The EMI has been consulted on a draft of the new law, which has been amended, inter alia, in the light of the EMI's opinion.

With the adoption and entry into force of the new law, the statute of the Deutsche Bundesbank is compatible with Treaty and Statute requirements for Stage Three.

As far as the adaptation of other legislation is concerned, the EMI takes note that adaptation of the Act on Coins is envisaged. The EMI is not aware of any other statutory provisions which would require adaptation under Article 108 of the Treaty.

5.4 Greece

The statute of the Bank of Greece was amended to meet Treaty and Statute requirements for Stage Three with Law 2548 dated 12 December 1997, which was published in the Government Gazette on 19 December 1997 (the "new law"). The EMI has been consulted on a draft of the new law, which has been amended, inter alia, in the light of the EMI's opinion.

With the adoption and entry into force of the new law, there are no remaining incompatibilities with Treaty and Statute requirements for Stage Three in the statute of the Bank of Greece. The new law addresses both the period during which the Bank of Greece is not an integral part of the ESCB as well as a situation in which Greece has adopted the single currency. There are, however, two imperfections in the new law which still require adaptation before Greece adopts the single currency. Some of the provisions of the new law will become obsolete upon the adoption by Greece of the single currency. This applies to the following provisions:

- Article 7.4 (new) on the imposition of minimum reserves and penalties in the case on non-compliance does not recognise the ECB's powers in this field.

- Article 2.4 (new) on the Bank's participation in international monetary and economic organisations does not refer to the ECB's power of approval.

As far as other legislation is concerned, the EMI is not aware of any other statutory provisions which would require adaptation under Article 108 of the Treaty.

5.5 Spain

The statute of the Banco de España was amended to meet Treaty and Statute requirements for Stage Three in the area of central bank independence with Law 66/1997 of 30 December 1997 (the "new law"). The Bank's statute is in the process of being amended to meet Treaty and Statute requirements in the area of the Bank's integration in the ESCB with a draft law (the "draft law") which is currently pending before Parliament. The EMI has been consulted on a draft of the law, which has been amended, inter alia, in the light of the EMI's opinion. The Spanish Government expects the draft law to be adopted before the date of the establishment of the ESCB.

Assuming that the draft law is adopted as it stood on 24 March 1998 and that it will enter into force on time, the statute of the Banco de España will be compatible with Treaty and Statute requirements for Stage Three.

As far as other legislation is concerned, the EMI takes note that further adaptation of Law No. 10/1975 of 12 March 1975 on Coinage is envisaged. The EMI is not aware of any other statutory provisions which would require adaptation under Article 108 of the Treaty.

5.6 France

The statute of the Banque de France is currently being adapted to meet Treaty and Statute requirements for Stage Three. The Ministry of the Economy, Finance and Industry has prepared a draft law (the "draft law") and has confirmed that the parliamentary debate on that draft will begin on 7 April 1998 and should be concluded on 30 April 1998. The EMI has been consulted on the draft law, which has been amended, inter alia, in the light of the EMI's opinion.

Assuming that the draft law is adopted as it stood on 24 March 1998 and that it will enter into force on time, the statute of the Banque de France will be compatible with Treaty and Statute requirements for Stage Three.

Article 6 (draft) states that the General Council "shall decide on issues related to the conduct of the Banque de France's activities other than those deriving from the tasks of the European System of Central Banks". In this context, it is pointed out that certain operations mentioned in Article 11 and in Chapter III of the statute of the Banque de France are to be considered as ESCB operations in the sense of Chapter IV of the Statute. This would merit clarification.

As far as the adaptation of other legislation is concerned, the EMI takes note that adaptations are envisaged of Decree No. 93-1278 of 3 December 1993 on the Banque de France, Law No. 84-46 of 24 January 1984, Decree No. 84-708 of 24 July 1984 and the Regulation on Coinage. The EMI is not aware of any other statutory provisions which would require adaptation under Article 108 of the Treaty.

5.7 Ireland

The statute of the Central Bank of Ireland was amended to meet Treaty and Statute requirements for Stage Three by the Central Bank Act 1998 (the "new law") which, in accordance with Article 1.3 thereof, will progressively enter into force through ministerial orders. The EMI has been consulted on the new law, which has been amended, inter alia, in the light of the EMI's opinion.

With the adoption and entry into force of the new law, and assuming that specific provisions thereof will enter into force on time, there will be no remaining incompatibilities with Treaty and Statute requirements for Stage Three in the statute of the Central Bank of Ireland. There are, however, two imperfections, which will not jeopardise the overall functioning of the ESCB at the start of Stage Three and which will be addressed in the context of forthcoming legislative changes.

- The Minister for Finance's ability under Article 134 (new law) to suspend in the national interest certain business transactions seems to refer to operations of entities other than the Bank and not to include the Bank's (ESCB-related) operations. However, this needs to be clarified in order to avoid any possibility of government interference in the Bank's ESCB-related operations.

- The consent of the Minister for Finance, which is required under Articles 10.1 and 13.1(b) of the Central Bank Act 1997 before the Bank may refuse to approve the rules of a payment system or subsequently revoke such approval, is unrestricted and may therefore also extend to the Bank's ESCB-related involvement in payment systems.

As far as other legislation is concerned, the Decimal Currency Act has also been adapted through the new law. The EMI is not aware of any other statutory provisions which would require adaptation under Article 108 of the Treaty.

5.8   Italy

The statutory provisions governing the Banca d'Italia, which are contained in various laws and decrees, have been amended to meet Treaty and Statute requirements for Stage Three. Law No. 433 of 17 December 1997 empowered the Government to bring Italian legislation into line with Article 108 of the Treaty through a legislative decree. Subsequently, the EMI was consulted on a draft legislative decree submitted to it by the Italian Government. This legislative decree (No. 43 dated 10 March 1998; the "legislative decree") was published in the Official Gazette of 14 March 1998. It amends various laws and also provides for amendments to the Statute of the Banca d'Italia (the "By-Laws"). The amendments of the Bank's By-Laws, on which the EMI was consulted, were adopted by the Bank's General Meeting of Shareholders on 19 March 1998 and will enter into force upon approval by a Presidential Decree. The Government expects this to take place in the first half of April 1998.

Assuming that the amendments to the Bank's By-Laws adopted by the General Meeting of Shareholders are approved by a Presidential Decree and that they will enter into force on time, and assuming that the provisions referred to in Article 11.1 of Legislative Decree No. 43 dated 10 March 1998 will enter into force on the date of the establishment of the ESCB at the latest, the statute of the Banca d'Italia will be compatible with Treaty and Statute requirements for Stage Three.

As far as other legislation is concerned, the EMI is not aware of any other statutory provisions which would require adaptation under Article 108 of the Treaty.

5.9   Luxembourg

The Law of 20 May 1983 establishing the Institut Monétaire Luxembourgeois ("IML") as amended and the Law of 15 March 1979 on the monetary status of Luxembourg are currently being amended to meet Treaty and Statute requirements for Stage Three with Law No. 3862 (the "draft law"). The Government expects the draft law to be adopted by Parliament before April 1998 so that it may enter into force on 1 May 1998.

In February 1994 the EMI was consulted on an initial draft.

Assuming that the draft law is adopted as it stood on 24 March 1998 and that it will enter into force on time, there will be no remaining incompatibilities with Treaty and Statute requirements for Stage Three in the statute of the IML, although there are various imperfections which will, however, not jeopardise the overall functioning of the ESCB at the start of Stage Three:

- Article 2.2, first indent, and Article 6 lit. a (draft) state that the IML's Council shall "define and implement monetary policy at a national level"; this is inconsistent with Article 2A)(3) and (4) (draft), which states that the IML becomes a part of the ESCB and fulfils its missions within the framework of international monetary treaties to which Luxembourg is a party. In addition, the Bank's Council is largely composed of members who will not fulfil their duties vis-à-vis the IML on the basis of professional exclusivity while, at the same time, no explicit rules ensure that conflicts of interest might not arise from other functions of the IML's Council members. These inconsistencies should be corrected urgently.

- The IML's statutory objective as laid down in Article 2.1 (draft) does not unambiguously reflect the primacy of the ESCB's secondary statutory objective.

- Article 2.2, fifth indent, and Article 17 (draft) state that the IML shall issue monetary tokens, which without recognising the competences of the ECB in this field.

- Article 25 (draft) states that the IML may provide credit facilities to ensure the stability of payment systems without recognising the competences of the ECB in this domain.

As far as other legislation is concerned, the EMI is not aware of any other statutory provisions which would require adaptation under Article 108 of the Statute.

5.10 Netherlands

The statute of De Nederlandsche Bank is currently being amended to meet Treaty and Statute requirements for Stage Three. The EMI has been consulted on a draft law (the "draft law"), which has been amended, inter alia, in the light of the EMI's opinion. The draft law was endorsed by the Second Chamber of Parliament on 17 February 1998 and is currently pending before the First Chamber of Parliament, which can only reject or endorse the draft law in its entirety. The Government expects the draft law to be endorsed by the First Chamber of Parliament on 24 March 1998 and published in the Government Gazette on 25 March 1998.

Assuming that the draft law is adopted as it stood on 24 March 1998 and that it will enter into force on time, there will be no remaining incompatibilities with Treaty and Statute requirements for Stage Three in the statute of De Nederlandsche Bank, although there is one imperfection, which will, however, not jeopardise the overall functioning of the ESCB at the start of Stage Three: Article 3 (draft) states that "the Bank" shall "co-define" the ESCB's monetary policy, whereas it is the Bank's Governor who will do so in his/her capacity as a member of the Governing Council of the ECB.

As far as other legislation is concerned, the EMI takes note that adaptations are envisaged of the Coinage Act, the Act on the exchange rate of the guilder, the Act on external financial relations 1994, the Act on the supervision of securities trade 1995, the Archives Act 1995, and Royal Decrees adopted under the Act on public access to Government documents as well as under the Ombudsman Act. The EMI is not aware of any other statutory provisions which would require adaptation under Article 108 of the Treaty.

5.11 Austria

The statute of the Oesterreichische Nationalbank is currently being adapted to meet Treaty and Statute requirements for Stage Three. A draft law (the "draft law") has been submitted to Parliament and the Government expects the draft law to be adopted in the course of April 1998. The EMI has been consulted on the draft law, which has been amended, inter alia, in the light of the EMI's opinion.

Assuming that the draft law is adopted as it stood on 24 March 1998 and that it will enter into force on time, the statute of the Oesterreichische Nationalbank will be compatible with Treaty and Statute requirements for Stage Three.

As far as other legislation is concerned, the EMI takes note that adaptation of the Foreign Exchange Act is envisaged. The EMI is not aware of any other statutory provisions which would require adaptation under Article 108 of the Treaty.

5.12 Portugal

The statute of the Banco de Portugal was amended to meet Treaty and Statute requirements for Stage Three, following a consultation with the EMI, as follows.

- Article 105 of the Constitution was adapted by means of the Constitutional Law No. 1/97 of 20 September 1997. The new article (renumbered Article 102) now states that the Bank is the national central bank of Portugal and performs its functions in accordance with the law and with the international norms binding upon the Portuguese

State. This reference to "international norms" intends to cover in particular the Treaty and the Statute.

- The Organic Law of the Banco de Portugal of 30 October 1990 as amended was changed with Law No. 5/98 of 31 January 1998 (the "new law").

With the adoption and the entry into force of the Constitutional Law No. 1/97 and the new law, the statute of the Banco de Portugal is compatible with Treaty and Statute requirements for Stage Three.

As far as other legislation is concerned, the EMI takes notes that adaptations are envisaged of Decree-Law No. 333/81 of 7 December 1981, Decree-Law No. 293/86 of 12 September 1986, Decree-Law No. 178/88 of 19 May 1988 and Decree-Law No. 13/90 of 8 January 1990. The EMI is not aware of any other statutory provisions which would require adaptation under Article 108 of the Treaty.

5.13 Finland

The statute of Suomen Pankki was amended to meet Treaty and Statute requirements for Stage Three by means of a revised Act on the Bank of Finland (the "revised law"), which entered into force on 1 January 1998. The revised law has, again, been adapted through a new law (the "new law") in order to bring the Bank's statute fully into line with the Treaty and the Statute. The new law was adopted by Parliament on 20 March 1998 and is expected to be promulgated on 27 March 1998. The new law will enter into force, in respect of the provisions on independence, immediately after its promulgation and, in respect of the provisions on the Bank's legal integration in the ESCB, on 1 January 1999. The EMI has been consulted on both the revised law and the new law in their draft versions, and both have been amended, inter alia, in the light of the EMI's opinion.

With the adoption of the new law, the statute of Suomen Pankki will be compatible with Treaty and Statute requirements for Stage Three.

As far as other legislation is concerned, the EMI takes note that adaptations of the Currency Act and the Act on Coins have been completed. The EMI is not aware of any other statutory provisions which would require adaptation under Article 108 of the Treaty.

5.14 Sweden

The Constitution Act, the Riksdag Act and the Sveriges Riksbank Act are currently being adapted to meet Treaty and Statute requirements for the independence of Sveriges Riksbank. A draft law (the "draft law") is currently pending before Parliament. An adaptation of the Constitution Act requires the approval of two consecutive Parliaments, the next Parliament coming into being after the general election in September 1998. A first approval of amendments to the Constitution Act and the Riksdag Act by Parliament was given on 4 March 1998 and a second approval is expected to be given in October 1998, when the Sveriges Riksbank Act is also expected to be adopted in accordance with the Constitution Act as amended. All adaptations are envisaged to enter into force as from 1 January 1999. The EMI has been consulted on the envisaged changes to the above-mentioned Acts, which have been amended, inter alia, in the light of the EMI's opinion.

Assuming that the draft law is adopted as it stood on 24 March 1998, there are two remaining incompatibilities with Treaty and Statute requirements for Stage Three in the statute of Sveriges Riksbank:

- The timetable for adaptation (see above) is incompatible with Article 108 of the Treaty, which requires adaptations in the area of central bank independence to become effective at the date of the establishment of the ESCB at the latest.

- The draft law does not anticipate the Bank's legal integration in the ESCB, although Sweden is not a Member State with a special status and must therefore comply with all adaptation requirements under Article 108 of the Treaty. This affects a number of provisions in the Bank's statute.

As far as other legislation is concerned, the EMI notes that legislation on access to public documents and the law on secrecy need to be reviewed in the light of the confidentiality regime under Article 38 of the Statute. The EMI is not aware of any other statutory provisions which would require adaptation under Article 108 of the Treaty.

5.15 United Kingdom

Since the United Kingdom has notified the Council that it does not intend to adopt the single currency on 1 January 1999, there is no current legal requirement to ensure that national legislation (including the statute of the Bank of England) is compatible with the Treaty and the Statute. The EMI notes, however, that the United Kingdom is in the process of adopting several reforms covering its monetary policy framework. Further legislation would be required if the United Kingdom were to notify the Council that it intended to adopt the single currency.

Annex

Compatibility of national legislation, including the statutes of national central banks ("NCBs"), with the Treaty/Statute, with particular emphasis on adaptations under Article 108 of the Treaty in view of Stage Three

This Annex contains an assessment of the compatibility of national legislation, including the statutes of the individual NCBs, in the Member States of the European Union with the Treaty and the Statute. It pays particular attention to completed and/or planned adaptations of such legislation under Article 108 of the Treaty. Issues listed in this Annex follow the sequence of topics addressed in Chapter II of the present Report.

For the sake of brevity, the content of this Annex is deliberately condensed and should be read in conjunction with the relevant parts of the present Report and the EMI's previous reports on legal convergence in the EU Member States for further clarification. Likewise, no reference is made to opinions on the adaptation of national legislation which the EMI has delivered in accordance with the consultation procedures under Article 109f (6) of the Treaty and Article 5.3 of its Statute, unless there is a specific reason to do so.

References to articles relate to those of the statute of the NCB concerned, unless otherwise indicated. References to articles in the Treaty and the Statute relate to those in the Treaty establishing the European Community and the Statute of the ESCB/ECB respectively.

BELGIUM

1 Legislation within the scope of Article 108 of the Treaty

The following legislation required adaptation under Article 108 of the Treaty:

- the Organic Law on the National Bank of Belgium of 24 August 1939 as amended (the "old law");

- the Law of 12 June 1930 creating a Monetary Fund;

- the Law of 28 December 1973;

- the Law of 23 December 1988;

- Decree-Law No. 5 of 1 May 1944.

2 Adaptation of the statute of the National Bank of Belgium

The statute of the National Bank of Belgium was amended to meet Treaty and Statute requirements for Stage Three with Law No. 1061/12-96/97 (the "new law"), which will progressively enter into force as from February 1998. The EMI has been consulted on a draft version of the new law, which has been amended, inter alia, in the light of the EMI's opinion.

2.1 Independence

With regard to the Bank's independence, the following adaptations of the old law have been made in the new law with effect from the date of the establishment of the ESCB at the latest.

2.1.1 Institutional independence

Article 29 (old) gave the Minister for Finance and Foreign Trade the right to oppose the execution of any measure adopted by the Bank which would be contrary to the law, statutes or interests of the State. In addition, Article 30 (old) gave the Government Commissioner the right to suspend any decision by the Bank that would be contrary to the law, statutes or interests of the State. These articles were already amended by the Law of 22 March 1993, but the possibility for the Minister for Finance and Foreign Trade or the Government Commissioner to challenge decisions of the Bank on legal grounds, which could potentially also extend to decisions on ESCB-related tasks, was maintained. This possibility has now been restricted by Article 22 (new) to the Bank's non-ESCB related tasks.

In addition, whereas under the old law the Council of Regency was competent to take certain monetary policy decisions, Article 20 (new) restricts the Council of Regency's involvement to an advisory role without an ex ante right of consultation. However, the provisions of the old law concerning the competences of the Council of Regency will be abrogated on a date to be decided by the King, at the latest on the day of introduction of the euro (Article 38(1) and (3) of the new law). As the Council of Regency does not fulfil the requirements of the Treaty and the Statute on independence and provisions on independence need to be effective at the date of the establishment of the ESCB at the latest, the Government envisages an adaptation in this respect to take effect at the date of establishment of the ESCB at the latest.

2.1.2 Personal independence

Under Article 44 of the present Articles of Association of the Bank, the Governor could be suspended or dismissed by the King without indication of a reason. This incompatibility with Article 14.2 of the Statute has been resolved in Article 25 (new), in which the grounds for dismissal are reproduced as laid down in Article 14.2.

2.2 Legal integration in the ESCB

With regard to the Bank's legal integration, the following adaptations have been made with effect from the date on which Belgium adopts the single currency.

2.2.1 Statutory objective

The old law neither reflected the primacy of the ESCB's statutory objective nor anticipated the Bank's integration in the ESCB. This has been resolved in the new law through the fact that the Bank's statutory objective in Stage Three will be determined by directly applicable Community law and in particular Article 105 (1) of the Treaty and Article 2 of the Statute and through Article 2 (new), which explicitly acknowledges the Bank's integration in the ESCB.

2.2.2 Tasks

Articles 6 to 9 (old) on the issuance, design, text, replacement and withdrawal of banknotes did not recognise the ECB's powers in this field. This has been resolved in Article 2 (new) through the general reference to the Bank's status as an integral part of the ESCB. In addition, Articles 11 to 19 (old), which listed inter alia the Bank's tasks, have been adapted in Chapter II, Articles 5 to 9 (new), which bring the description of the Bank's tasks into line

with the Treaty and the Statute as far as ESCB-related tasks are concerned.

2.2.3 Instruments

Articles 11 to 19 (old), which established inter alia the instruments which the Bank was empowered to apply in carrying out its tasks, have been adapted in Chapter II, Articles 5 to 9 (new) so as to be in line with the Treaty and the Statute in this respect.

2.2.4 Organisation

Whereas under the old law the Council of Regency had the competence to take certain monetary policy decisions, in Article 20 (new) its role has been restricted to advisory tasks.

3 Adaptation of other legislation

3.1 Law of 12 June 1930 creating a Monetary Fund

Article 1 of this law, which sets a limit on the volume of divisionary monies which may be issued by the Treasury (which may be extended by Royal Decree), does not recognise the ECB's power of approval of the volume of issuance as laid down in Article 105a (2) of the Treaty. The so-called "euro legislation" which is in the process of being adopted will remove this incompatibility.

3.2 Law of 28 December 1973

Articles 1 to 3 of this law relating to budget proposals for 1973 and 1974, which are the legal basis for the imposition of minimum reserves on credit institutions by the Bank, do not respect the ECB's competences in this field. According to

Article 38(4), third paragraph, of the new law, the above provisions will be repealed with effect from the date on which Belgium adopts the single currency.

3.3 Law of 23 December 1988

Article 2 of this law, which authorises the Government to determine the exchange rate of the Belgian franc without prejudice to international obligations applicable to the Belgian State, neither envisages the introduction of the euro nor recognises the Community's powers in the field of exchange rates. According to Article 38(4), fourth paragraph, of the new law, the above article will be repealed with effect from the date on which Belgium adopts the single currency. The same applies to Article 3 of this law, which entrusts a special regulatory power to the Minister for Finance and Foreign Trade with regard to the application of Royal Decrees relating to the Government's power to determine the exchange rate for the Belgian franc. According to Article 38(4), fourth paragraph, of the new law, Article 3 of the Law of 23 December 1988 is repealed with effect from the date on which Belgium adopts the single currency.

3.4 Decree-Law No. 5 of 1 May 1944

This Decree-Law is incompatible with the Treaty and the Statute to the extent that it relates to the execution of international payment, exchange and compensation agreements entered into by the Bank for the account of the State and to the extent that it relates to credit activities exercised by the Bank outside the scope of monetary policy such as bilateral payment agreements with foreign states. According to Article 38(4), second paragraph, of the new law, this Decree-Law will be repealed with effect from the date on which Belgium adopts the single currency.

4 Assessment of compatibility

With the adoption and entry into force of the new law, and assuming that specific provisions thereof (for which progressive adaptation through Royal Decrees is envisaged in Article 38) will enter into force on time, the statute of the National Bank of Belgium will be compatible with Treaty and Statute requirements for Stage Three.

As far as other legislation is concerned, the EMI takes note that adaptations are envisaged of the Law of 12 June 1930 creating a Monetary Fund, the Law of 28 December 1973, the Law of 23 December 1988 and Decree-Law No. 5 of 1 May 1944. The EMI is not aware of any other statutory provisions which would require adaptation under Article 108 of the Treaty.

DENMARK

1 Legislation within the scope of Article 108 of the Treaty

National Bank of Denmark Act (Act No. 116) of 7 April 1936 as amended.

2, 3 Adaptation of the statute of Danmarks Nationalbank and other legislation

Protocol No. 12 of the Treaty on certain provisions relating to Denmark states that the Danish Government shall notify the Council of its position concerning participation in Stage Three before the Council makes its assessment under Article 109j (2) of the Treaty. Denmark has already given notification that it will not participate in Stage Three and, in accordance with Article 2 of Protocol No. 12, this means that Denmark will be treated as a Member State with a derogation. Implications of this were elaborated in a Decision taken by the Heads of State or Government at their Edinburgh summit meeting on 11 and 12 December 1992. The Decision states that Denmark will retain its existing powers in the field of monetary policy according to its national laws and regulations, including the powers of Danmarks Nationalbank in the field of monetary policy. In the light of this situation, no adaptation of the Bank's statute in the area of its legal integration in the ESCB nor any other legislation is envisaged in view of Stage Three. Finally, there are no incompatibilities in the area of central bank independence in the Bank's statute which would require adaptation under Article 108 of the Treaty in conjunction with Articles 109k (3) and 107 thereof.

4 Assessment of compatibility

The statute of Danmarks Nationalbank does not contain incompatibilities in the area of central bank independence which would require adaptation under Article 108 of the Treaty. The legal integration of the Bank in the ESCB does not need to be provided for and other legislation does not need to be adapted as long as Denmark does not adopt the single currency.

GERMANY

1 Legislation within the scope of Article 108 of the Treaty

The following legislation required adaptation under Article 108 of the Treaty:

- the Bundesbank Act of 26 July 1957, as amended by the Fifth Act amending the Deutsche Bundesbank Act dated 8 July 1994 (the "old law");

- the Act on Coins.

2 Adaptation of the statute of the Deutsche Bundesbank

The statute of the Deutsche Bundesbank was amended to meet Treaty and Statute requirements for Stage Three with the Sixth Act amending the Deutsche Bundesbank Act dated 22 December 1997, which was published in the Federal Law Gazette on 30 December 1997 (the "new law"). The EMI has been consulted on the draft of the new law, which has been amended, inter alia, in the light of the EMI's opinion.

2.1 Independence

With regard to the Bank's independence, the following adaptations were made with effect from 31 December 1997.

2.1.1 Institutional independence

Article 13.2 (old), which gave the German Government the right to defer a decision of the Central Bank Council for up to two weeks, was incompatible with Treaty and Statute requirements on central bank independence. This provision has been repealed in the new law.

2.1.2 Personal independence

The fact that there used to be no guaranteed minimum five-year term of office for members of the Bank's decision-making bodies was incompatible with Article 14.2 of the Statute. Articles 7 and 8 (new) have increased the minimum term of office of the Bank's President, the other members of the Board and the Presidents of the Land Central Banks from two to five years.

2.2 Legal integration in the ESCB

With regard to the Bank's legal integration in the ESCB, the following adaptations have been made with effect from the date on which Germany adopts the single currency.

2.2.1 Statutory objective

Article 3 (old), which contained the Bank's statutory objective, neither reflected the primacy of the ESCB's statutory objective nor anticipated the Bank's integration in the ESCB in Stage Three. Article 3 (new) introduces an explicit reference to the Bank's integration in the ESCB. In addition, following a suggestion made by the EMI when it was consulted by the Federal Government on its draft legislation, Article 12 (old) has been altered to state explicitly that the Bank may only support national economic policy if this is compatible with the objectives and tasks of the ESCB.

2.2.2 Tasks

Article 14.1 (old), which established the Bank's exclusive right to issue banknotes, did not recognise the ECB's competence in this field. Article 14.1 (new), first sentence, introduces an explicit reference to the ECB's right of approval with regard to the issuance of banknotes as laid down in Article 105a (1) of the Treaty and repeated in Article 16 of the Statute.

2.2.3 Instruments

Articles 15 and 16 (old), which listed the Bank's monetary policy instruments (discount, lending and open market policies and minimum reserve policy), did not recognise the ECB's competences in this field. These provisions have been repealed in the new law.

2.2.4 Organisation

Article 6.1 (old), first sentence, which provided for the Central Bank Council's competence to determine the monetary policy of the Bank, did not reflect the ECB's competences in this field. Article 6.1 (new), first sentence, explicitly states that (a) the responsibility for the definition of monetary policy in Stage Three will pass to the Governing Council of ECB; (b) the Bank will need to comply with guidelines and instructions from the ECB in the performance of ESCB-related tasks; and (c) the Bank's President, in his/her capacity as a member of the Governing Council, is independent of instructions from the Central Bank Council.

2.2.5 Participation in international monetary institutions

Following a suggestion made by the EMI when it was consulted by the Federal Government on its draft legislation, Article 4 has been amended. An insertion into this provision makes it clear that the Bank's power to participate in international monetary institutions will be subject to the ECB's approval.

3   Adaptation of other legislation

It is envisaged that the Act on Coins will be amended in order to give explicit recognition to the competence of the ECB under Article 105a (2), first sentence, of the Treaty. This amendment will be part of the Act on the introduction of the euro and will enter into force on the date on which Germany adopts the single currency.

4   Assessment of compatibility

With the adoption and entry into force of the new law, the statute of the Deutsche Bundesbank is compatible with Treaty and Statute requirements for Stage Three.

As far as the adaptation of other legislation is concerned, the EMI takes note that adaptation of the Act on Coins is envisaged. The EMI is not aware of any other statutory provisions which would require adaptation under Article 108 of the Treaty.

GREECE

I Legislation within the scope of Article 108 of the Treaty

The statute of the Bank of Greece of 1927 as amended (the "old law") required adaptation under Article 108 of the Treaty.

2 Adaptation of the statute of the Bank of Greece

The statute of the Bank of Greece was amended to meet Treaty and Statute requirements for Stage Three with Law 2548 dated 12 December 1997, which was published in the Government Gazette on 19 December 1997 (the "new law"). The EMI has been consulted on a draft of the new law, which has been amended, inter alia, in the light of the EMI's opinion.

2.1 Independence

With regard to the Bank's independence, the following adaptations were made with effect from 19 December 1997.

2.1.1 Institutional independence

Article 47 (old), which established the Government Commissioner's power to veto decisions of the General Council on the grounds of legality, was incompatible with Treaty and Statute requirements on central bank independence. This incompatibility has been resolved by means of Article 6 of the new law, which makes a newly established Monetary Policy Council responsible for the Bank's ESCB-related tasks, the decisions of which may not be vetoed by the Government Commissioner. In addition, the subordination of the Bank's monetary policy decisions to the Government's macroeconomic objectives was incompatible with Treaty and Statute requirements on central bank independence. Article 1 (new) on the Bank's statutory objective remedies this situation (see also paragraph 2.2.1 below).

2.1.2 Personal independence

Article 29 (old) did not contain a minimum five-year term of office for the Bank's Governor (or for the other members of the General Council) and was therefore incompatible with Article 14.2 of the Statute. Articles 5(3) and 6(3) (new) fix the term of office of the Governor, the Deputy Governors and the other members of the Monetary Policy Council at six years. All the members of the Monetary Policy Council are required to devote their professional activities exclusively to the Bank, with only a few minor exceptions (such as academic positions) which cannot give rise to potential conflicts of interest.

2.2 Legal integration in the ESCB

With regard to the Bank's legal integration in the ESCB, a number of adaptations have been made with effect from the date on which Greece adopts the single currency. In general, the new law acknowledges in Articles 1.2 and 2.3 that the Bank will become an integral part of the ESCB and will need to comply with the ECB's guidelines and instructions. In addition, Article 12.17 (new) states that any provision of the new law which is incompatible with primary or secondary Community law governing the Bank's ESCB-related tasks is to be deemed to be abolished as from the date on which Greece adopts the single currency. Thus, the new law addresses both a situation in which Greece is a Member State with a derogation as well as a situation in which Greece has adopted the single currency. However, some of the provisions of the new law will nevertheless become obsolete upon the adoption by Greece of the single currency and the statute of the Bank must then, for reasons of legal clarity and certainty, be further adapted in the area of the Bank's integration in the ESCB. This applies to Articles 2.4 and 7.4 (see paragraphs 2.2.4 and 2.2.3 below).

2.2.1 Statutory objective

The Bank's statutory objective neither reflected the primacy of the ESCB's statutory objective nor anticipated the Bank's legal integration in the ESCB. Article 1 (new) remedied this situation through a reference to the primacy of maintaining price stability (in Article 1.1), through an explicit recognition of the Bank's legal integration in the ESCB and through a reference to the ESCB's statutory objective in the event of Greece adopting the single currency (in Article 1.2).

2.2.2 Tasks

Article 2.1 (new) states that the main tasks of the Bank shall be to define and implement monetary policy and to conduct the policy with regard to the exchange rate of the Greek drachma against other currencies within the framework of the exchange rate policy chosen by the Government following consultation from the Bank. In addition, Article 2.3 (new) recognises the Bank's legal integration in the ESCB once Greece adopts the single currency and the fact that the Bank from that moment onwards will have to perform the above tasks within the framework of the ESCB. Furthermore, Article 12.2 (new) states that the Bank shall conduct exchange rate policy in accordance with the instructions and guidelines of the ECB as from the date on which Greece adopts the single currency.

2.2.3 Instruments

Article 7.4 (new) on the imposition of minimum reserves and penalties in the case of non-compliance does not recognise the ECB's powers in this field under Article 19 of the Statute. This is an imperfection in the new law which still requires adaptation with effect from the date on which Greece adopts the single currency.

2.2.4 Participation in international monetary and economic organisations

Article 2.4 (new) states that the Bank may participate in international monetary and economic organisations. This Article does not reflect the ECB's right to approve such participation as laid down in Article 6.2 of the Statute. This is an imperfection in the new law which still requires adaptation with effect from the date on which Greece adopts the single currency.

3 Adaptation of other legislation

The EMI is not aware of any other statutory provisions which would require adaptation under Article 108 of the Treaty.

4 Assessment of compatibility

With the adoption and entry into force of the new law, there are no remaining incompatibilities with Treaty and Statute requirements for Stage Three in the statute of the Bank of Greece. The new law addresses both the period during which the Bank of Greece is not an integral part of the ESCB as well as a situation in which Greece has adopted the single currency. There are, however, two imperfections in the new law which still require adaptation before Greece adopts the single currency. Some of the provisions of the new law will become obsolete upon the adoption by

Greece of the single currency. This applies to the following provisions:

- Article 7.4 (new) on the imposition of minimum reserves and penalties in the case of non-compliance does not recognise the ECB's powers in this field.

- Article 2.4 (new) on the Bank's participation in international monetary and economic organisations does not refer to the ECB's power of approval.

As far as other legislation is concerned, the EMI is not aware of any other statutory provisions which would require adaptation under Article 108 of the Treaty.

SPAIN

1 Legislation within the scope of Article 108 of the Treaty

The following legislation required adaptation under Article 108 of the Treaty:

- Law 13/1994 dated 1 June 1994 on the "Autonomy of the Banco de España" as amended (the "old law");

- Law 10/1975 of 12 March 1975 on Coinage.

2 Adaptation of the statute of the Banco de España

The statute of the Banco de España was amended to meet Treaty and Statute requirements for Stage Three in the area of central bank independence with Law 66/1997 of 30 December 1997 (the "new law"). The statute of the Bank is in the process of being amended to meet Treaty and Statute requirements in the area of the Bank's integration in the ESCB with a draft law (the "draft law") which is currently pending before Parliament. The EMI has been consulted on a draft of the law, which has been amended, inter alia, in the light of the EMI's opinion. The Spanish Government expects the draft law to be adopted before the date of the establishment of the ESCB.

2.1 Independence

With regard to the Bank's independence, the new law contains the following adaptations which will enter into force on the date of the establishment of the ESCB/ECB.

2.1.1 Institutional independence

Article 20.3 (old), which excluded voting rights for the Director-General of the Treasury and Financial Policy and the Vice-President of the National Stock Market Commission, applied to monetary policy issues but not to all ESCB-related tasks and was therefore incompatible with Treaty and Statute requirements on central bank independence. This Article has been adapted by the new law, which extends the exclusion of voting rights described above to cover all ESCB-related tasks.

2.1.2 Personal independence

Article 25.2 (old), which contained a term of office for members of the Governing Council other than the Governor and the Deputy Governor of four years rather than a minimum of five years, was incompatible with Article 14.2 of the Statute. This Article has been adapted by the new law, which extends the term of office of such members to six years.

2.2 Legal integration in the ESCB

With regard to the Bank's legal integration in the ESCB, the following adaptations are envisaged in the draft law with effect from the date on which Spain adopts the single currency.

2.2.1 Statutory objective

Article 7 (old):

- The Bank's powers to define and implement monetary policy do not recognise the ECB's powers in this field.

- The Bank's secondary objective to support the general economic policy of the Spanish

Government is not in conformity with the ESCB's statutory objective.

Article 7.2 (draft) provides for an amendment of Article 7 which would be compatible with Treaty and Statute requirements for Stage Three.

2.2.2 Tasks

- *Issuance of banknotes*
  Article 7.3 (c) and (d) and Article 15, which establish the Bank's exclusive right to issue banknotes and to determine the volume of coins issued, do not recognise the ECB's competences in this field.

- *Monetary policy*
  Articles 8 and 9, which lay down the Bank's powers with regard to the formulation and implementation of monetary policy, do not acknowledge the ECB's powers in this field.

- *Foreign exchange policy*
  Article 11, which specifies the power of the Spanish Government to adapt the exchange rate system and the parity of the Spanish peseta against other currencies, does not recognise the Community's competence in exchange rate arrangements and does not envisage the introduction of the euro.

The draft law provides for amendments to the above articles which would make them compatible with Treaty and Statute requirements for Stage Three.

2.2.3 Instruments

- Article 9, which contains rules on minimum reserves, does not acknowledge the fact that their content will be determined by the ECB.

- Article 12, which establishes the Bank's competence to implement the Government's exchange rate system, does not recognise the ECB's competence in this field.

The draft law provides for amendments to the above articles which would make them compatible with Treaty and Statute requirements for Stage Three.

3 Adaptation of other legislation

3.1 Law 10/1975 of 12 March 1975 on Coinage

This law establishes a regime for minting coins in a manner that does not recognise the competences of the ECB under Article 105a (2) of the Treaty. The draft law provides for an amendment of Article 4 of Law 10/1975 of 12 March 1975 on Coinage which would make it compatible with Treaty and Statute requirements for Stage Three.

4 Assessment of compatibility

Assuming that the draft law is adopted as it stood on 24 March 1998 and that it will enter into force on time, the statute of the Banco de España will be compatible with Treaty and Statute requirements for Stage Three.

As far as other legislation is concerned, the EMI takes note that further adaptation of Law No. 10/1975 of 12 March 1975 on Coinage is envisaged. The EMI is not aware of any other statutory provisions which would require adaptation under Article 108 of the Treaty.

FRANCE

1 Legislation within the scope of Article 108 of the Treaty

The following legislation required adaptation under Article 108 of the Treaty:

- Law No. 93-980 of 4 August 1993 on the status of the Banque de France and the activities and supervision of credit institutions as amended;

- Decree No. 93-1278 of 3 December 1993 on the Banque de France;

- Law No. 84-46 of 24 January 1984;

- Decree No. 84-708 of 24 July 1984.

2 Adaptation of the statute of the Banque de France

The statute of the Banque de France is currently being adapted to meet Treaty and Statute requirements for Stage Three. The Ministry of the Economy, Finance and Industry has prepared a draft law and has confirmed that the parliamentary debate on that draft will begin on 7 April 1998 and should be concluded on 30 April 1998. The EMI has been consulted on the draft law, which has been amended, inter alia, in the light of the EMI's opinion.

2.1 Independence

With regard to the Bank's institutional independence, the following adaptations are envisaged in the draft law with effect from the date on which France participates in the appointment of members of the Executive Board of the ECB.

- Article 1 of the current statute, which contains a prohibition on external influence, is restricted in its application to the Governor, Deputy Governors and the members of the Monetary Policy Council, which is responsible only for monetary policy issues. Consequently, it does not extend to all ESCB-related tasks. Article 1 (draft), third paragraph, extends the prohibition on external influence to all ESCB-related issues, while Article 5 (draft) recognises the independence of the Bank's President in his/her capacity as a member of the Governing Council of the ESCB/ECB.

- Article 2, third paragraph, states that the Bank shall hold and manage the State's gold and foreign exchange reserves, which shall be recorded as assets in its balance sheet. The same Article also states that these provisions shall be applied in accordance with a formal agreement between the State and the Bank, which shall be subject to approval by Parliament. Article 2.II (draft) amends Article 2, third paragraph, in such a manner that the Bank shall hold and manage the above reserves under the conditions laid down in the Statute and, as in the past, the reserves shall be recorded as assets in the Bank's balance sheet according to modalities laid down in a formal agreement between the State and the Bank. The EMI takes note that the French Government has committed itself to submitting the above agreement to the ECB for its approval.

- Article 19 provides for an obligation for the Bank's Governor to report at least once a year to the President of the Republic and Parliament on the Bank's activities, monetary policy and its prospects and states in a second paragraph that the Governor may be asked, and may him/herself ask, to appear before the Finance Committees of the two Chambers of Parliament. Article 7 (draft) envisages amendment of Article 19, second paragraph, adding that this is without prejudice to Article 107 of the Treaty and the ECB's secrecy rules.

2.2 Legal integration in the ESCB

With regard to the Bank's legal integration in the ESCB, the following adaptations are envisaged in the draft law with effect as from 1 January 1999 or, alternatively, as from the date on which France adopts the single currency if that were to be a later date.

2.2.1 Statutory objective

Article 1, which contains the Bank's statutory objective, reflects neither the ESCB's statutory objective nor the Bank's legal integration in the ESCB in Stage Three. Article 1 (draft) envisages accommodating this point through an explicit recognition of the Bank's status as an integral part of the ESCB in Stage Three and a reference to the ESCB's statutory objective.

2.2.2 Tasks

- *Issuance of banknotes (Article 5)*
  The Bank's exclusive right to issue banknotes does not recognise the ECB's competence in this field. While Article 3.1 (draft) on the issuance of banknotes refers explicitly to Article 105a of the Treaty, it also states that the Bank shall have the sole right to issue banknotes with legal tender status within metropolitan France in the départements d'outre-mer and in the territorial collectivities of Saint Pierre et Miquelon and Mayotte. Banknotes issued in the départements d'outre-mer and the above territorial collectivities are put into circulation by the Institut d'émission des départements d'outre-mer (IEDOM) on behalf of the Bank. The EMI takes note that the French Government is currently examining the consistency of the arrangements between the Bank and the IEDOM with the Bank's status as an integral part of the ESCB and

the constraints derived from that status, which is expected to lead to a revision of the statutes of the IEDOM.

- *Monetary policy (Article 7)*
  The power of the Monetary Policy Council to define (the terms and conditions of) monetary policy operations does not recognise the ECB's powers in this field. Article 4 (draft) envisages the amendment of Article 7 in such a manner that it will explicitly be recognised that the ECB's Governing Council, and not the Bank's Monetary Policy Council, will define monetary policy.

- *Foreign exchange policy (Article 2)*
  The Government's powers to determine the exchange rate regime and the parity of the French franc, as laid down in Article 2, first paragraph, and the task of the Bank to regulate the exchange rates between the franc and other currencies both on behalf of the Government and within the framework of the general exchange rate policy guidelines formulated by the Minister of the Economy, Finance and Industry, as laid down in Article 2, second paragraph, do not envisage the introduction of the euro and do not recognise the Community's competence in exchange rate matters. It is envisaged in Article 2.I (draft) that the above paragraphs will be repealed.

The Bank's right to participate in international monetary agreements with the permission of the Minister of the Economy, Finance and Industry does not recognise the Community's competences in this field. Article 2.III (draft) amends Article 2 in such a manner that the ECB's and Community's competences will be recognised through explicit references to Article 6.2 of the Statue and Article 109 of the Treaty.

2.2.3 Instruments

■ Article 2, third paragraph, and Article 7, second and third paragraphs, on the Bank's instruments to conduct foreign exchange rate policy and monetary policy, respectively, do not recognise the ECB's competences in this field. Article 2.II (draft) envisages amendment of Article 2, third paragraph (see paragraph 2.I, second indent, above), while Articles 4.I and 4.II (draft) amend Article 7, second and third paragraphs, in such a manner that the second paragraph on open market and credit operations will explicitly recognise that such operations will be conducted within the framework of the ESCB and in accordance with the guidelines and instructions of the ECB, while references to the Bank's power to impose minimum reserves (third paragraph) will be repealed.

■ Article 18 establishes the Bank's right to enter into financial operations. This right must be without prejudice to the Bank's ESCB-related obligations and particularly ECB approval and collateral requirements. It is envisaged to accommodate this concern through Article 1 (draft), which states that the Bank participates in carrying out the tasks and achieving the objectives of the ESCB conferred upon it by the Treaty. In addition, where the tasks of the Monetary Policy Council are concerned, the draft law respects the exclusive competences of the Governing Council of the ECB (for example, Article 4.I (draft) states that the Monetary Policy Council "examines" monetary policy developments, "analyses" the implications of the ESCB's monetary policy and "specifies" within the framework of the ECB's guidelines and instructions the nature and scope of collateral accepted by the Banque de France).

2.2.4 Organisation

The Bank's General Council is, in accordance with Article 11, second paragraph, in charge of the Bank's activities other than those directly related to monetary policy. As the General Council cannot, in view of its composition, which includes government representatives with a right to vote, be considered to fulfil Treaty and Statute requirements for Stage Three on independence, adaptation is required as far as ESCB-related tasks are concerned. Therefore, Article 6 (draft) states that the General Council shall decide on issues related to the conduct of the Bank's activities other than those deriving from the tasks of the ESCB. In this context, it is pointed out that certain operations mentioned in Article 11, fourth paragraph, and in Chapter III, Articles 15.2, 17 and 18 of the Bank's statute are to be considered as ESCB operations in the sense of Chapter IV of the Statute. This would merit clarification.

3 Adaptation of other legislation

3.1 Decree No. 93-1278 of 3 December 1993 on the Banque de France

This decree stipulates the application procedures for Law No. 93-980 of 4 August 1993 on the status of the Banque de France and the activities and supervision of credit institutions as amended.

It lays down the procedures for:

■ appointing and remunerating the members of the Monetary Policy Council and of the General Council;

■ the functioning of the Monetary Policy Council and of the General Council;

■ electing the representative of the Bank's staff on the General Council;

- drawing up the Bank's annual budget, which is submitted to the General Council;

- the presentation and approval of the accounts, including the distribution of profits.

It also establishes the rules governing the drawing-up of the Bank's accounts and the auditing of these accounts by external auditors.

Responsibility for the budget, the accounts, the profit allocation proposal and the audit belongs to the competence of the General Council. As a consequence of Article 6 (draft), adaptation would be required for the legal integration of the Bank in the ESCB.

3.2 Law No. 84-46 of 24 January 1984

Article 33(8) of Law No. 84-46 of 24 January 1984 empowers the Committee on banking and financial regulations to adopt, without prejudice to the competences of the Monetary Policy Council, instruments and rules on credit. This Article does not recognise the ECB's power in this field. Article 8 (draft) states that the Monetary Policy Council shall adopt "subject to the tasks conferred upon the ESCB by Article 105(2) of the Treaty establishing the European Community, the instruments and rules of credit policy".

3.3 Decree No. 84-708 of 24 July 1984

Article 13 of this decree entitles the Bank to delegate its competences in the field of minimum reserves to the IEDOM and the Institut d'émission d'outre-mer (IEOM), which act under its authority and for its account. Article 4 (draft) abrogates the Bank's competences with respect to minimum reserves, and therefore the entitlement to delegate these functions also disappears.

4 Assessment of compatibility

Assuming that the draft law is adopted as it stood on 24 March 1998 and that it will enter into force on time, the statute of the Banque de France will be compatible with Treaty and Statute requirements for Stage Three.

Article 6 (draft) states that the General Council "shall decide on issues related to the conduct of the Banque de France's activities other than those deriving from the tasks of the European System of Central Banks". In this context, it is pointed out that certain operations mentioned in Article 11 and in Chapter III of the statute of the Banque de France are to be considered as ESCB operations in the sense of Chapter IV of the Statute. This would merit clarification.

As far as the adaptation of other legislation is concerned, the EMI notes that adaptations are envisaged of Decree No. 93-1278 of 3 December 1993 on the Banque de France, Law No. 84-46 of 24 January 1984, Decree No. 84-708 of 24 July 1984 and the Regulation on Coinage. The EMI is not aware of any other statutory provisions which would require adaptation under Article 108 of the Treaty.

IRELAND

1 Legislation within the scope of Article 108 of the Treaty

The Central Bank Acts 1942-1997 and legislation relating to coinage required adaptation under Article 108 of the Treaty.

2 Adaptation of the statute of the Central Bank of Ireland

The statute of the Central Bank of Ireland was amended to meet Treaty and Statute requirements for Stage Three by the Central Bank Act 1998 (the "new law") which, in accordance with Article 1.3 thereof, will progressively enter into force through ministerial orders. The EMI has been consulted on the new law, which has been amended, inter alia, in the light of the EMI's opinion.

2.1 Independence

With regard to the Bank's independence, the following adaptations were made and are expected to be brought into operation from the date of the establishment of the ESCB/ECB.

2.1.1 Institutional independence

Article 5.3 of the Central Bank Act 1942, which contained the right of Service Directors to participate in meetings of the Board of Directors with a right to vote, was incompatible with Treaty and Statute requirements on central bank independence. The new law overcomes this by means of the provision in Article 4 that sole authority and responsibility for the performance and exercise of any of the Bank's functions, duties or powers under the Treaty or the Statute shall be vested in the Governor or, in his/her absence, the Director General of the Bank.

Article 6.2 of the Central Bank Act 1942, which imposed the obligation on the Governor or the Board of Directors to consult the Minister for Finance if requested, was an explicit statutory mechanism which could be used to influence the decision-making process within the Bank and was, therefore, incompatible with Treaty and Statute requirements on central bank independence. The new law overcomes this by means of Article 5, which requires the Governor and the Board of Directors to consult the Minister for Finance only with regard to functions and duties other than those imposed by the Treaty and the Statute. In addition, while the Minister may request that the Governor or the Board of Directors informs him/her with regard to the pursuit of the Bank's primary objective to maintain price stability, this power is subject to Treaty and Statute requirements (Article 5 of the new law).

According to Article 24 of the Central Bank Act 1997, the Governor was required to attend the meeting of a Select Committee of Dáil Éireann. This obligation would only have been compatible with the Treaty and the Statute if it (a) respected the independence of the Governor in his/her capacity as a member of the Governing Council/General Council of the ECB; (b) only applied to ex post information; and (c) was without prejudice to the confidentiality regime of Article 38 of the Statute. The new law addresses this issue in Article 17 by means of a provision which states that the Governor's attendance is to be subject to Treaty and Statute requirements.

The Minister for Finance's power under Article 134 (new law) to suspend in the national interest certain business transactions after consulting the Bank seems to refer to operations of entities other than the Bank and not to include the Bank's (ESCB-related) operations. However, this lack of legal clarity is an imperfection in the new law which merits further consideration in order to rule out any possibility of government interference in the Bank's ESCB-related operations. The EMI takes note that the Irish Government intends to do this in the context of forthcoming legislative changes.

Articles 10.1 and 13.1(b) of the Central Bank Act 1997 require the consent of the Minister for Finance before the Bank may refuse to approve the rules of a payment system or subsequently revoke such approval. This requirement is unrestricted and may therefore also extend to the Bank's ESCB-related involvement in payment systems which would not be in line with Treaty and Statute requirements for Stage Three. This lack of legal clarity is an imperfection in the new law which the Irish Government intends to address in the context of forthcoming legislative changes.

2.1.2 Personal independence

Article 21 of the Central Bank Act 1942 was not fully in line with the grounds specified in Article 14.2 of the Statute with regard to the grounds for dismissal of the Governor, who may be dismissed "for cause stated". Article 7 (new law) addresses this issue by making express reference to "serious misconduct" as a ground for dismissal and by including a provision which states that any decision to remove the Governor is subject to referral to the European Court of Justice in such a manner and for such reasons as are consistent with Article 14.2 of the Statute.

In relation to the Bank's non-executive Directors, there were no arrangements in place to ensure that no conflicts of interest could arise in their performance of ESCB-related tasks. Article 4 (new law) overcomes this by providing that sole authority and responsibility for the performance and exercise of any of the Bank's functions, duties or powers under the Treaty or the Statute shall

be vested in the Governor or, in his/her absence, the Director General of the Bank.

2.1.3 Financial independence

The power of the Minister for Finance under Article 23 of the Central Bank Act 1989 to regulate the periodical determination and distribution of surplus income needed to be adapted by means of the addition of a safeguard clause to prevent it from impeding the proper performance of ESCB-related tasks. Article 12 (new law) adapts this power of the Minister by requiring him/her to have regard to the Bank's powers, functions and duties under the Treaty and the Statute.

2.2 Legal integration in the ESCB

With regard to the Bank's legal integration, the following adaptations have been made.

2.2.1 Statutory objective

The Bank's statutory objective neither reflected the primacy of the ESCB's statutory objective nor anticipated the Bank's integration in the ESCB. Article 5 (new law) addresses this point by expressly providing that the primary objective of the Bank, in discharging its functions as part of the ESCB, shall be to maintain price stability.

2.2.2 Tasks

It was necessary to confer specific new powers on the Bank in order to enable it to participate in the ESCB and fulfil the obligations laid down in the Treaty. Articles 4 and 5 (new law) contain provisions to enable this to be achieved.

2.2.3 Issuance of banknotes

The Bank's exclusive right to issue banknotes did not recognise the ECB's competences in this field. Article 16 (new law) addresses this point by providing that it shall be lawful for the Bank, with the authorisation of the ECB, to issue legal tender banknotes denominated in Irish pounds and any other denomination for which the ECB has authorised the issuance. In addition, Article 16 expressly provides that such banknotes and banknotes issued by the ECB in accordance with Article 105a of the Treaty shall be legal tender in Ireland for payments of any amount.

2.2.4 Foreign exchange policy

Provisions in the Central Bank Acts 1942 and 1989 gave powers to the Minister for Finance to set exchange rates which do not recognise Community competences in this field in Stage Three. Article 13 (new law) repealed these provisions.

3 Adaptation of other legislation

3.1 Decimal Currency Act

The rights of the Ministry of Finance with respect to coinage did not recognise the ECB's competences in this field. Article 14 (new law) addresses this issue by amending the Decimal Currency Act 1969, so as to provide that the issuance of coins by the Minister for Finance through the Bank is subject to the ECB's approval of the volume of coins issued.

4 Assessment of compatibility

With the adoption and entry into force of the new law, and assuming that specific provisions thereof (for which progressive adaptation through ministerial orders is envisaged in Article 1.3) will enter into force on time, there will be no remaining incompatibilities with Treaty and Statute requirements for Stage Three in the statute of the Central Bank of Ireland. There are, however, two imperfections, which will not jeopardise the overall functioning of the ESCB at the start of Stage Three and which will be addressed in the context of forthcoming legislative changes.

- The Minister for Finance's ability under Article 134 (new law) to suspend in the national interest certain business transactions seems to refer to operations of entities other than the Bank and not to include the Bank's (ESCB-related) operations. However, this needs to be clarified in order to avoid any possibility of government interference in the Bank's ESCB-related operations.

- The consent of the Minister for Finance, which is required under Articles 10.1 and 13.1(b) of the Central Bank Act 1997 before the Bank may refuse to approve the rules of a payment system or subsequently revoke such approval, is unrestricted and may therefore also extend to the Bank's ESCB-related involvement in payment systems.

As far as other legislation is concerned, the Decimal Currency Act has also been adapted through the new law. The EMI is not aware of any other statutory provisions which would require adaptation under Article 108 of the Treaty.

ITALY

1 Legislation within the scope of Article 108 of the Treaty

The following legislation required adaptation under Article 108 of the Treaty:

- statute of the Banca d'Italia (Royal Decree No. 1067 of 11 June 1936 as amended);

- the 1910 codified law on the Banks of Issue (Royal Decree No. 204 of 28 April 1910 as amended);

- Title III of the 1936 Banking Law (Royal Decree Law No. 375 of 12 March 1936 as amended);

- Royal Decree Law No. 1284 of 23 November 1914;

- Royal Decree No. 1377 of 17 June 1928;

- Presidential Decree No. 811 of 9 October 1981;

- Presidential Decree No. 148 of 31 March 1988;

- Law No. 82 of 7 February 1992;

- Law No. 483 of 26 November 1993.

2 Adaptation of statutory provisions governing the Banca d'Italia

The statutory provisions governing the Banca d'Italia, which are contained in various laws and decrees, have been amended to meet Treaty and Statute requirements for Stage Three. Law No. 433 of 17 December 1997 empowered the Government to bring Italian legislation into line with Article 108 of the Treaty through a legislative decree.

Subsequently, the EMI was consulted on a draft legislative decree submitted to it by the Italian Government. This legislative decree (No. 43 dated 10 March 1998; the "legislative decree") was published in the Official Gazette of 14 March 1998. It amends various laws and also provides for amendments to the statute of the Banca d'Italia (the "By-Laws"). The amendments of the Bank's By-Laws, on which the EMI was consulted, were adopted by the Bank's General Meeting of Shareholders on 19 March 1998 and will enter into force upon approval by a Presidential Decree. The Government expects this to take place in the first half of April 1998.

2.1 Independence

With regard to the Bank's independence, the following adaptations were made with effect from 14 March 1998.

2.1.1 Institutional independence

- Article 2 of Royal Decree Law No. 1284 of 23 November 1914 and Article 5 of Royal Decree No. 1377 of 17 June 1928, which established the power of the Minister of the Treasury, Budget and Economic Planning to set interest rates on certain interest-bearing current account deposits with the Bank (with the exception of those on compulsory reserves), were incompatible with Treaty and Statute requirements on central bank independence. Article 3, first paragraph, of the legislative decree provides for the repeal of these provisions. Furthermore, pursuant to Article 3 of the legislative decree, the power of the Minister is transferred to the Governor until the adoption by Italy of the single currency. Subsequently, decisions shall be taken in accordance with the Treaty and the Statute.

■ The Board of Directors decides on the issuance of banknotes and the rules and conditions for the Bank's operations. The term of office of its members was three years, which did not comply with Article 14.2 of the Statute. Article 3, second paragraph, of the legislative decree, which is intended to replace Article 22, second paragraph, of the 1936 Banking Law, raises the term of office of the members of the Board to five years. A corresponding amendment of Article 17 of the Bank's statute is provided for by the amendment of the Bank's By-Laws.

■ The 1910 codified law on the Banks of Issue provided for the power of the Treasury to suspend or annul resolutions adopted by the Board of Directors of the Bank on grounds of legitimacy. This was incompatible with Treaty and Statute requirements on institutional independence. Article 3.3 of the legislative decree foresees that the power of the Minister of the Treasury, Budget and Economic Planning to suspend or annul deliberations of the Board of Directors for legal reasons shall not apply to resolutions adopted by the Board that relate to matters within the scope of the authority of the ESCB and, in particular, to those involving banknotes denominated in lira, the rules and conditions for the Bank's operations and the appointment of the Bank's correspondents in Italy and abroad. This removes the incompatibility.

■ The Italian foreign reserves are currently managed by the Ufficio italiano dei cambi (UIC) and the Bank, which is incompatible with Article 105 (2), third indent, of the Treaty, which states that one of the tasks of the ESCB is to hold and manage the official foreign reserves of the Member States. It is assumed that, according to Articles 7.2 and 11.1

of the legislative decree, the Bank will independently manage the official foreign exchange reserves in conformity with Article 31 of the Statute as from the date of the establishment of the ESCB.

2.1.2 Personal independence

The Board of Directors has some limited competence in certain ESCB-related matters other than monetary policy. All of its component members, with the exception of the Governor, are non-executive members. In order to achieve full compliance with the requirements on personal independence concerning the need to avoid conflicts of interest arising from other functions, the amendment of the Bank's By-Laws provides for an amendment of Article 60, according to which existing cases of incompatibilities are broadened and a general clause is inserted which excludes from membership of the Board all persons having a conflict of interest with the Bank.

2.2 Legal integration in the ESCB

With regard to the Bank's legal integration in the ESCB, the following adaptations are envisaged with effect from the date on which Italy adopts the single currency.

2.2.1 Tasks

■ *Issuance of banknotes*
Various articles (Article 1 and Article 20, second paragraph, points 1 and 2, of the statute of the Bank; Articles 4 and 142 of the 1910 codified law on the Banks of Issue; Presidential Decree No. 811 of 9 October 1981) did not recognise the ECB's competences in this field. Article 4 of the legislative decree states that the Bank shall issue banknotes in accordance with the Treaty and the Statute.

- *Control of the amount of banknotes and coins held by the Bank*

  Article 110, Article 111, first paragraph, point 1, and Article 111, last paragraph, of the 1910 codified law on the Banks of Issue, which stated the consultative duties assigned to a parliamentary committee chaired by the Minister of the Treasury, Budget and Economic Planning in matters concerning the control of the currency issued by the Treasury and the Bank, did not recognise the ECB's powers in this field. Article 4 of the legislative decree provides for the repeal of Article 111 and an amendment of Article 110 so that the control of the currency is no longer extended to banknotes in circulation.

  Articles 120, 122 and 124(b) of the 1910 codified law on the Banks of Issue on the power of the Minister of the Treasury, Budget and Economic Planning to control, inter alia by means of inspections, compliance with the rules governing the movement of banknotes, the amount of banknotes and coins held by the Bank, the actual quantity of banknotes in circulation, held by the Bank's cashier's department and in stock and the quantity of those which are withdrawn because they are worn but have yet to be destroyed did not recognise the ECB's competence in this field. Article 4 of the legislative decree provides for the repeal of the above provisions.

  Article 130 of the 1910 codified law on the Banks of Issue, which contained an obligation for the Minister of the Treasury, Budget and Economic Planning to submit a report to Parliament on the issuance of banknotes in the previous year, did not recognise the ECB's powers in this field. Article 4 of the legislative decree provides for the repeal of Article 130 of the 1910 codified law on the Banks of Issue.

- *Formulation and implementation of monetary policy*

  Law No. 82 of 7 February 1992, which established the power of the Governor of the Bank to change the official discount rate and the rate on fixed term advances for the purpose of controlling market liquidity, did not recognise the ECB's powers in this field.

  Article 10 of Law No. 483 of 26 November 1993, which laid down the power of the Bank to establish reserve requirements for banks and related rules, did not recognise the ECB's powers in this field.

  According to Article 6.1 of the legislative decree, the above powers are no longer exercised at the national level as they fall within the scope of Chapter IV of the Statute of the ESCB. The amendment of the Bank's By-Laws amends Article 25.4 thereof accordingly.

- *Dealing in foreign exchange and the management of official foreign exchange reserves*

  Article 4, first and second paragraphs, of the Presidential Decree No. 148 of 31 March 1988, which established the power of the Bank and the UIC to manage the official foreign exchange reserves and to conduct foreign exchange operations in pursuit of their institutional aims on the basis of the powers assigned to them, did not envisage the transfer of such reserves to the ESCB and did not recognise the ECB's powers in this field. Article 7 of the legislative decree provides that the Bank is required to transfer foreign exchange reserves to the ECB in compliance with Article 30 of the Statute. In addition, the Bank is empowered to manage the official foreign exchange reserves in conformity with Article 31 of the Statute.

2.2.2 Instruments

- Articles 26, 27, 29, 60 and 62 of the 1910 codified law on the Banks of Issue and Articles 41, 42 and 45(2) to 53 of the Bank's By-Laws, as well as various other laws on securities which specified and regulated the operations, classified by type, in which the Bank could engage and the securities which it could accept on an exhaustive basis, did not recognise the ECB's powers in this field. Articles 6.2 and 6.3 of the legislative decree provide for the repeal of the above provisions of the 1910 codified law on the Banks of Issue and the other laws which established the eligibility of certain types of instruments to be used as security for advances. Articles 6.2 and 6.3 of the legislative decree foresee that the Bank's operations are subject to the Statute and to the provisions adopted by the ECB in the implementation of its Statute. The amendment of the Bank's By-Laws provides for the repeal of Articles 45 to 52 and an amendment of Articles 41 and 42 in accordance with Articles 6.2 and 6.5 of the legislative decree.

- Article 20, second paragraph, points 3 and 5, of the Bank's By-Laws, which describes the power of the Board of Directors to establish rules and terms for the Bank's operations and to appoint the Bank's domestic and foreign correspondents, did not recognise the ECB's powers in this field. Article 6.4 of the legislative decree states that the above powers of the Board of Directors are subject to the Statute and to the provisions adopted by the ECB in the implementation of its Statute. In compliance with these provisions, the amendment of the Bank's By-Laws provides for a corresponding amendment of its Article 20.

- Articles 124(e), 128 and 131 of the 1910 codified law on the Banks of Issue, which established the power of the Minister of the Treasury, Budget and Economic Planning to control compliance with the binding restrictions on the operations conducted by the Bank and the application of the official rate for such operations, did not recognise the ECB's powers in this field. Article 6.2 of the legislative decree provides for the repeal of these provisions.

2.2.3 Financial provisions

Article 11 of Law No. 483 of 26 November 1993, which contained an obligation for the Bank to pay a contribution to the Ministry of the Treasury, Budget and Economic Planning related to the income accruing from the management of compulsory reserves, did not recognise the ECB's powers in this field. Article 8.4 of the legislative decree provides for the repeal of this provision. Moreover, for the purpose of the integration of the Bank in the ESCB, Article 8.1 of the legislative decree provides that, in drawing up its annual accounts, the Bank may harmonise its accounting and financial reporting methods with the corresponding rules and recommendations issued by the ECB.

3 Adaptation of other legislation

See Section 2.

4 Assessment of compatibility

Assuming that the amendments to the Bank's By-Laws adopted by the General Meeting of Shareholders are approved by a Presidential Decree and that they will enter into force on time, and assuming that the provisions referred to in Article 11.1 of the Legislative Decree No. 43 dated 10 March 1998 will enter into force on the date of the establishment of the ESCB at the latest, the statute of the Banca d'Italia will be compatible with Treaty and Statute requirements for Stage Three.

As far as other legislation is concerned, the EMI is not aware of any other statutory provisions which would require adaptation under Article 108 of the Treaty.

LUXEMBOURG

1 Legislation within the scope of Article 108 of the Treaty

The following legislation required adaptation under Article 108 of the Treaty:

- the Law of 20 May 1983 establishing the Institut Monétaire Luxembourgeois as amended;

- the Law of 15 March 1979 on the monetary status of Luxembourg.

2 Adaptation of the statute of the Institut Monétaire Luxembourgeois

The Law of 20 May 1983 establishing the Institut Monétaire Luxembourgeois as amended and the Law of 15 March 1979 on the monetary status of Luxembourg are currently being amended to meet Treaty and Statute requirements for Stage Three with Law No. 3862 (the "draft law"). The Government expects the draft law to be adopted by Parliament before April 1998 so that it may enter into force on 1 May 1998. In February 1994 the EMI was consulted on an initial draft. The draft law provides that the name of the IML will be changed to the "Central Bank of Luxembourg" at the date of the establishment of the ESCB.

2.1 Independence

With regard to the independence of the IML, the following adaptations are envisaged in the draft law.

2.1.1 Institutional independence

Under the present law, the "last word" in monetary policy decisions belongs to the Government, a situation which is incompatible with Treaty and Statute requirements on central bank independence. Articles 5 and 6 (draft), which reproduce the first part of the prohibition on seeking or taking instructions as laid down in Article 107 of the Treaty, vests responsibility for decisions in the monetary domain at the national level in the Council of the IML.

2.1.2 Personal independence

- Article 12.3 states that, if there is a fundamental disagreement between the Government and the Management on the IML's policy and the execution of its tasks, the Government, with the consent of the Council of the IML, may propose to the Grand-Duke the collective, and only the collective, dismissal of the Management. "Fundamental disagreement" is a ground for dismissal which is incompatible with Article 14.2 of the Statute and this is now intended to be remedied in Article 12.3 of the draft law, which reproduces the literal grounds for dismissal as laid down in the Statute.

- According to Article 6 (draft), the Council shall be the highest decision-making body within the IML. The Council is largely composed of members who will not fulfil their duties for the IML on the basis of professional exclusivity, while, at the same time, no explicit rules ensure that conflicts of interest might not arise from other functions of the IML's Council members. This is an inconsistency in the draft law which should be corrected urgently.

2.2 Legal integration in the ESCB

With regard to the IML's legal integration in the ESCB, the following adaptations are envisaged in the draft law.

2.2.1 Statutory objective

Article 2.2, which states that the IML is responsible for promoting the stability of the currency, neither reflects the primacy of the ESCB's statutory objective nor anticipates the integration of the IML in the ESCB. Article 2.1(1) (draft) states explicitly that the IML's primary objective shall be to maintain price stability and Articles 2.3 and 2.4 (draft) provide that the IML shall become an integral part of the ESCB as the Central Bank of Luxembourg and that it will have to perform its tasks within the framework of international agreements in the monetary field entered into by Luxembourg, such as the Treaty. There is, however, a lack of legal clarity in the secondary objectives of the IML as set out in the draft law: Article 2.1 (draft) states that without prejudice to the objective of price stability, the IML supports the general economic policy. This implies that the IML may have to support the economic policy of the Luxembourg Government rather than the general economic policies in the Community as laid down in Article 105(1) a of the Treaty, although a national economic policy can only be supported by an NCB insofar as this is compatible with its obligations as an integral part of the ESCB. This lack of legal clarity is an imperfection in the draft law which merits further consideration.

2.2.2 Tasks

Article 2, which lists the IML's activities, does not respect the ECB's competences with regard to a number of the IML's activities in Stage Three. According to Article 2.2, first indent, and Article 6 lit. a of the draft law, the Council of the IML shall have the task to "define and implement monetary policy at a national level". It is recognised that Articles 2.3 and 2.4 (draft) explicitly state that the IML will become an integral part of the ESCB as the Central Bank of Luxembourg and that it will have to perform its tasks within the framework of international agreements in the monetary field entered into by Luxembourg, such as the Treaty. However, as monetary policy in Stage Three will be defined by the Governing Council of the ECB and implemented by the Executive Board of the ECB, any allocation of competences beyond the scope of the execution of monetary policy to the IML's Council is an inconsistency in the draft law which should be corrected urgently.

Pursuant to Article 2.2, fifth indent, and Article 17 (draft), the IML shall issue monetary tokens. These provisions recognise neither the competences of the ECB under Article 105a (1) of the Treaty with regard to banknotes nor its competences under Article 105a (2), first sentence, of the Treaty with respect to coins. Again (see also above), although Articles 2.3 and 2.4 (draft) explicitly state that the IML will become an integral part of the ESCB as the Central Bank of Luxembourg and that it will have to perform its tasks within the framework of international agreements in the monetary field entered into by Luxembourg, such as the Treaty, there is still a lack of clarity which merits further consideration.

2.2.3 Instruments

Articles 21 to 29 on the IML's instruments in the monetary field are incompatible with the Treaty and Statute as they do not respect the ECB's competences in this field. Articles 21 to 27 (draft) provide for amendments of the former articles so as to reproduce, where appropriate, the relevant Articles of the Statute.

Article 25 (draft) states that the IML may provide credit facilities to ensure the stability of payment systems without recognising the ECB's competences in this field. This is an imperfection in the draft law which merits further consideration.

3 Adaptation of other legislation

3.1 The Law of 15 March 1979 on the monetary status of Luxembourg

This law lays down provisions on the issuance and distribution of banknotes and coins (Article 3) which do not recognise the ECB's and the EU Council's powers in this field as laid down in Article 105a (2) of the Treaty. Furthermore, the law attributes exclusive competence for the exchange rate policy with regard to the Luxembourg franc to the Government (Article 2), which neither envisages the introduction of the euro nor recognises the Community's powers in the field of exchange rates.

The draft law on the monetary status of Luxembourg addresses these issues. However, Article 2.1 (draft) states that the Government may formulate general orientations for the exchange rate policy of the Luxembourg franc in relation to other currencies. Although this prima facie may not seem to be in line with the Treaty and the Statute, it is understood that once the Luxembourg franc has disappeared as a currency in its own right, i.e. from the date on which Luxembourg adopts the single currency onwards, the above provisions lose their applicability.

4 Assessment of compatibility

Assuming that the draft law is adopted as it stood on 24 March 1998 and that it will enter into force on time, there will be no remaining incompatibilities in the statute of the Institut Monétaire Luxembourgeois, although there are various imperfections which will, however, not jeopardise the overall functioning of the ESCB at the start of Stage Three.

- Article 2.2, first indent, and Article 6 lit. a (draft) state that the IML's Council shall "define and implement monetary policy at a national level"; this is inconsistent with Article 2A)(3) and (4) (draft), which states that the IML becomes a part of the ESCB and fulfils its missions within the framework of international monetary treaties to which Luxembourg is a party. In addition, the Bank's Council is largely composed of members who will not fulfil their duties vis-à-vis the IML on the basis of professional exclusivity, while, at the same time, no explicit rules ensure that conflicts of interest might not arise from other functions of the IML's Council members. These inconsistencies should be corrected urgently.

- The IML's statutory objective as laid down in Article 2.1 (draft) does not unambiguously reflect the primacy of the ESCB's secondary statutory objective.

- Article 2.2, fifth indent, and Article 17 (draft) state that the IML shall issue monetary tokens, without recognising the competences of the ECB in this field.

- Article 25 (draft) states that the IML may provide credit facilities to ensure the stability of payment systems without recognising the competences of the ECB in this domain.

As far as other legislation is concerned, the EMI is not aware of any other statutory provisions which would require adaptation under Article 108 of the Statute.

NETHERLANDS

1 Legislation within the scope of Article 108 of the Treaty

The following legislation required adaptation under Article 108 of the Treaty:

- the Bank Act 1948 as amended;

- the Coinage Act;

- the Act on the exchange rate of the guilder;

- the Act on external financial relations 1994;

- the Act on the supervision of securities trade 1995;

- the Archives Act 1995;

- statutory instruments pursuant to the Act on public access to Government documents and the Ombudsman Act.

2 Adaptation of the statute of De Nederlandsche Bank

The statute of De Nederlandsche Bank is currently being amended to meet Treaty and Statute requirements for Stage Three. The EMI has been consulted on a draft law (the "draft law"), which has been amended, inter alia, in the light of the EMI's opinion. The draft law was endorsed by the Second Chamber of Parliament on 17 February 1998 and is currently pending before the First Chamber of Parliament, which can only reject or endorse the draft law in its entirety. The Government expects the draft law to be endorsed by the First Chamber of Parliament on 24 March 1998 and published in the Official Bulletin on 25 March 1998.

2.1 Independence

With regard to the Bank's independence, the following adaptations are envisaged in the draft law with effect from May 1998.

2.1.1 Institutional independence

Article 26, which contains a right of the Minister for Finance to give instructions to the Bank, is incompatible with Treaty and Statute requirements on central bank independence. The supervisory role of the Royal Commissioner, as currently elaborated in the Bank's statute, is also incompatible with Treaty and Statute requirements on central bank independence. According to the draft law, the right of instruction of the Minister for Finance will be abolished. In addition, Article 3.3 of the draft law states that the Bank's Governing Board can only be bound by the ECB's guidelines, decisions or instructions. Furthermore, according to the draft law, the office of the Royal Commissioner will be abolished. Instead, it is envisaged in the draft law that the Government will have the right to appoint one special member to the Bank's Supervisory Board (see also paragraph 2.2.4 below).

2.1.2 Personal independence

Article 23.5, which makes non-compliance with instructions from the Minister for Finance a ground for dismissal, is incompatible with the grounds for dismissal listed in Article 14.2 of the Statute. Article 11.3 of the draft law states that the members of the Governing Board can only be relieved from office on the grounds mentioned in Article 14.2 of the Statute.

2.2 Legal integration in the ESCB

With regard to the Bank's legal integration in the ESCB, the following adaptations are envisaged in the draft law with effect from the date on which the Netherlands adopts the single currency.

2.2.1 Statutory objective

Article 9.1, which contains the statutory objective of the Bank, reflects neither the primacy of the ESCB's statutory objective nor the Bank's legal integration in the ESCB. Article 2 (draft) copies the statutory objective of the ESCB into the statute of the Bank and states explicitly that the Bank will become an integral part of the ESCB upon adoption of the single currency by the Netherlands.

2.2.2 Tasks

Chapter II of the present statute of the Bank on its activities does not envisage the Bank's ESCB-related tasks in Stage Three. Article 3 (draft) enumerates the ESCB-related tasks of the Bank, including the issuance of banknotes, and also clarifies the fact that the Bank will exercise these tasks within the framework of the ESCB and the implementation of the Treaty.

2.2.3 Instruments

Chapter II of the present statute of the Bank does not envisage the introduction of the ECB's monetary policy instruments. Articles 2 and 3 (draft) provide for the integration of the Bank in the ESCB and enumerate the Bank's ESCB-related tasks.

2.2.4 Organisation

- It is envisaged in the draft law that the Government representative on the Supervisory Board will only have the power to request "information" about non-ESCB-related and ESCB-related activities of the Bank, a request which, in accordance with Article 13 (draft), may be rejected if the information requested is confidential, either on the basis of the Statute or on the basis of national legislation. It is also envisaged in the draft law that the Government representative will be subject to the prohibition on receiving or soliciting instructions as laid down in Article 107 of the Treaty.

- Article 3 (draft) states that "the Bank" shall "co-define" (and execute) the ESCB's monetary policy in the implementation of the Treaty and within the framework of the ESCB. As it is the Bank's Governor, and not the Bank itself, who will participate in the definition of the ESCB's monetary policy in his/her capacity as a member of the Governing Council of the ECB, the word "co-define" in combination with the words "the Bank" in Article 3 (draft) would not seem to be in line with the Treaty and the Statute. However, on the following grounds it could be argued that this is not a major problem. First, the "umbrella provision" of Article 2 (draft) on the Bank's status as an integral part of the ESCB already defines the Bank's position in Stage Three as well as the legal perspective from which the law, once in force, will have to be applied. Second, Article 3 (draft) only enumerates the Bank's ESCB-related tasks and does not address the question as to which organ of the Bank will be given specific responsibility for executing these tasks. This question is addressed in Article 7 of the (draft) Articles of Association of the Bank, which, with reference to the Statute, explicitly recognises that the Governor - but only the Governor - has a dual capacity: as President of the Bank and, as such, as a member of the ESCB's decision-making body on, inter alia, monetary policy matters, the Governing Council of the ECB. Moreover, "co-define" might be understood as meaning a "co-decision", which does not correspond to the rules for decision-making in the ESCB. On the above grounds, the combination of the words "the Bank" and "co-define" is considered as an imperfection which will, however, not jeopardise the overall functioning of the ESCB at the start of Stage Three.

3 Adaptation of other legislation

3.1 Coinage Act

The Coinage Act contains the Minister for Finance's competence to issue guilder coins and lower-denomination coins. This power does not recognise the ECB's power to approve the volume of issuance of coins and the EU Council's competences with regard to the denomination and technical specifications of coins as laid down in Article 105a (2) of the Treaty. However, Article 23 of the draft law adapting the statute of the Bank introduces a provision to the effect that these national competences will have to be exercised with due regard to the ECB's and the EU Council's powers in this field. The Government envisages that this provision will be adopted in March 1998 and enter into force as from the date on which the Netherlands adopts the single currency.

3.2 Act on the exchange rate of the guilder

This Act does not envisage the introduction of the euro or the transfer of competences in exchange rate matters to the Community level. It is envisaged that this Act will be replaced by a legislative provision authorising the Minister for Finance to conclude, on behalf of the Netherlands and jointly with the Member States of the future euro area, arrangements on the exchange rate of the euro in relation to the currencies of those Member States which do not adopt the single currency from the outset. A draft law to this effect is pending before the First Chamber of Parliament. The Government expects this law to enter into force as from the date on which the Netherlands adopts the single currency.

3.3 Act on external financial relations 1994

This Act does not envisage the introduction of the euro or the Bank's integration in the ESCB. It is envisaged that this Act will be amended in order to ensure that the obligations on De Nederlandsche Bank to comply with general guidelines from the Minister for Finance and to exchange information with the Minister do not contravene the Bank's Treaty obligations, and in order to ensure that the Bank is able to exchange information with the ECB. A draft law to this effect is pending before the First Chamber of Parliament. The Government expects this law to enter into force on the date of the establishment of the ESCB.

3.4 Act on the supervision of securities trade 1995

This Act does not envisage the monetary policy functions of the ECB in Stage Three. It is envisaged that this Act will be amended so as to ensure that the ECB, as De Nederlandsche Bank, will not be subject to the supervisory regime applicable to securities institutions. A draft law to this effect is pending before the First Chamber of Parliament. The Government expects the draft law to enter into force as from the date on which the Netherlands adopts the single currency.

3.5 Archives Act 1995

This Act grants citizens the right of access, subject to certain restrictions and conditions, to information contained in the archives of public bodies and entities. The Act is also applicable to the Bank in view of its public function and is therefore currently being reviewed in the light of the confidentiality regime within the ESCB under Article 38 of the Statute.

3.6 Act on public access to Government documents and the Ombudsman Act

The Act on public access to Government documents and the Ombudsman Act are applicable to the Bank with the exception of its activities in the fields of monetary policy and prudential supervision. These Acts contain provisions enabling third parties to gain access (subject to certain well-defined restrictions) to Bank documents. This does not respect the ESCB's confidentiality regime. The Government therefore envisages that secondary legislation will ensure that documents containing confidential information relating to the Bank's ESCB-related tasks will be exempt from these Acts. Furthermore, the draft law adapting the statute of the Bank also explicitly provides for adherence to the ESCB's confidentiality regime (Articles 18, 19 and 20 of the draft law).

4 Assessment of compatibility

Assuming that the draft law is adopted as it stood on 24 March 1998 and that it will enter into force on time, there will be no remaining incompatibilities with Treaty and Statute requirements for Stage Three in the statute of De Nederlandsche Bank, although there is one imperfection which will, however, not jeopardise the overall functioning of the ESCB at the start of Stage Three: Article 3 (draft) states that "the Bank" shall "co-define" the ESCB's monetary policy, whereas it is the Bank's Governor in his/her capacity as a member of the Governing Council of the ECB who will do so.

As far as other legislation is concerned, the EMI takes note that adaptations are envisaged of the Coinage Act, the Act on the exchange rate of the guilder, the Act on external financial relations 1994, the Act on the supervision of securities trade 1995, the Archives Act 1995, and Royal Decrees adopted under the Act on public access to Government documents as well as under the Ombudsman Act. The EMI is not aware of any other statutory provisions which would require adaptation under Article 108 of the Treaty.

AUSTRIA

1 Legislation within the scope of Article 108 of the Treaty

The following legislation required adaptation under Article 108 of the Treaty:

- the National Bank Act 1984 of 20 January 1984 as amended;

- the Foreign Exchange Act.

2 Adaptation of the statute of the Oesterreichische Nationalbank

The statute of the Oesterreichische Nationalbank is currently being adapted to meet Treaty and Statute requirements for Stage Three. A draft law (the "draft law") has been submitted to Parliament and the Government expects the draft law to be adopted in the course of April 1998. The EMI has been consulted on the draft law, which has been amended, inter alia, in the light of the EMI's opinion.

2.1 Independence

With regard to the Bank's independence, the following adaptations are envisaged in the draft law with effect from the date of the decision by the EU Council - in the composition of Heads of State or Government in accordance with Article 109j (4) of the Treaty - as to which Member States qualify for adoption of the single currency.

2.1.1 Institutional independence

Article 22.3 states that the General Council, which is a decision-making body in monetary policy matters, is largely composed of representatives of various branches of industry who fulfil their duties towards the Bank on a non-exclusive basis. This combination of responsibility for monetary policy, on the one hand, and the representation of the interests of third parties, on the other, creates a potential for conflicts of interest and is, therefore, incompatible with the Treaty and the Statute. According to the draft law, the General Council of the Bank will remain its decision-making body in the field of monetary policy until Austria adopts the single currency. As NCBs will have to take important decisions between the date of the establishment of the ESCB and the start of Stage Three, decision-making bodies of NCBs have to fulfil the independence requirements of the Treaty and the Statute on the date of the establishment of the ESCB at the latest. This is accomplished through: Article 34.1 (draft), which states that the Governor shall be independent in his/her capacity as a member of the Governing Council of the ECB; Article 21.5 (draft), which states that the General Council may not take any decisions which could impede the performance of the Bank's ESCB-related tasks; and Article 88.2 (5) (draft), which adds that the Board of Executive Directors is responsible for the implementation of preparatory measures for Stage Three rather than the General Council, which may not give instructions in this field or otherwise take measures which could obstruct such implementation.

Article 45.4, which gives the State Commissioner the right to raise - with suspensive effect - objections to a decision of the General Council, is incompatible with Treaty and Statute requirements on central bank independence. The draft law envisages that, as a government representative, the State Commissioner will in future be entitled to attend the meetings of the General Council of the Bank, albeit in an advisory capacity.

2.1.2 Personal independence

Article 21.14, which implies that the members of the Board of Executive Directors do not have a minimum term of office of five years, is incompatible with Treaty and Statute requirements on central bank independence. Chapter I, Article 33, of the draft law envisages the appointment of the members of the Board of Executive Directors for a five-year period.

2.2 Legal integration in the ESCB

With regard to the Bank's legal integration in the ESCB, the following adaptations are envisaged in the draft law with effect from the date on which Austria adopts the single currency.

2.2.1 Statutory objective

The Bank's statutory objective reflects neither the primacy of the ESCB's statutory objective nor the Bank's legal integration in the ESCB. According to the draft law, this provision will be abolished. Chapter I, Article 2.2, of the draft law states that, according to Article 105 of the Treaty and Article 2 of the Statute, the Bank has to ensure the fulfilment of the objective of price stability and that, only insofar as this is possible without interfering with the objective of maintaining price stability, the Bank has to take into account the macroeconomic requirements with regard to economic growth and employment trends.

2.2.2 Tasks

Article 3, which contains a provision relating to the Bank's participation in international monetary institutions, does not recognise the ECB's competence in this field. Article 3 (draft) explicitly acknowledges the ECB's right to approve such participation as laid down in Article 6 of the Statute.

2.2.3 Instruments

- Article 61, which establishes the Bank's exclusive right to issue banknotes and requires the Federal Minister for Finance to approve the face value of the banknotes, does not recognise the ECB's competence in this field.

- Article 41, which contains a provision that public authorities are prohibited from drawing on the funds of the Bank without providing the countervalue, an exception being made with regard to the discount of short-term Federal Treasury certificates, is in contradiction with Article 104 of the Treaty.

- Article 43 on minimum reserve requirements does not acknowledge the ECB's powers in this field.

- Articles 47 to 60 on the operations in which the Bank may be involved do not recognise the ECB's powers in this field.

The draft law provides for amendments to the above Articles which would be compatible with the Treaty and the Statute.

2.2.4 ERP financial operations

According to Article 83 of the draft law, ERP financial operations may be entered into by the Bank outside the framework of the "General Documentation on ESCB monetary policy instruments and procedures" ("General Documentation"), whereas such operations will not be subject to the collateral requirements of the General Documentation. The continuation of such operations and the terms under which such operations are entered into will have to be examined in the light of the Bank's integration in the ESCB and the possible constraints which may be derived from the Statute in this respect.

3 Adaptation of other legislation

3.1 Foreign Exchange Act

Articles 2.5 and 2.6 of this Act contain provisions on exchange rates which do not reflect the Community's powers in this field. The EMI takes note that the abolition of these two provisions is envisaged in the framework of the draft law and is expected to enter into force from the date on which Austria adopts the single currency.

4 Assessment of compatibility

Assuming that the draft law is adopted as it stood on 24 March 1998 and that it will enter into force on time, the statute of the Oesterreichische Nationalbank will be compatible with Treaty and Statute requirements for Stage Three.

As far as other legislation is concerned, the EMI takes note that further adaptation of the Foreign Exchange Act is envisaged. The EMI is not aware of any other statutory provisions which would require adaptation under Article 108 of the Treaty.

PORTUGAL

1 Legislation within the scope of Article 108 of the Treaty

The following legislation required adaptation under Article 108 of the Treaty:

- Article 105 of the Constitution referring to the Banco de Portugal;

- the Organic Law of the Banco de Portugal approved by Decree-Law No. 337/90 of 30 October 1990 and amended by Decree-Law No. 231/95 of 12 September 1995 and by Law No. 3/96 of 5 February 1996 (the "old law");

- Decree-Law No. 333/81 of 7 December 1981;

- Decree-Law No. 293/86 of 12 September 1986;

- Decree-Law No. 178/88 of 19 May 1988;

- Decree-Law No. 13/90 of 8 January 1990.

2 Adaptation of the statute of the Banco de Portugal

The statute of the Banco de Portugal was amended to meet Treaty and Statute requirements for Stage Three, following consultation of the EMI, as follows.

- Article 105 of the Constitution was adapted by means of the Constitutional Law 1/97 of 20 September 1997. The new article (renumbered Article 102) now states that the Bank is the national central bank of Portugal and performs its functions in accordance with the law and the international norms binding upon the Portuguese State. This

reference to "international norms" intends to cover in particular the Treaty and the Statute.

- The old law was amended with Law No. 5/98 of 31 January 1998 (the "new law").

2.1 Independence

With regard to the Bank's institutional independence, the following adaptations have been made with effect from 2 February 1998:

- Notwithstanding the fact that the old law empowered the Bank to conduct monetary policy, the Minister of Finance used to sign the Bank's "Avisos" relating to some features of the reserve requirements framework and the discount rate. This was incompatible with Treaty and Statute requirements on central bank independence and the Minister of Finance's involvement has been abolished by means of the new law.

- The need to submit to the Government the vetoes of the Governor suspending decisions of the Board of Directors could have been regarded as a form of seeking instructions which would have been incompatible with the Treaty and the Statute and has been abolished in the new law.

2.2 Legal integration in the ESCB

With regard to the Bank's legal integration in the ESCB, the following adaptations have been made with effect from the date on which Portugal adopts the single currency.

2.2.1 Statutory objectives

Under Article 3 (old), the Bank's statutory objective did not anticipate the Bank's legal integration in the ESCB. Article 3 (new) makes an explicit reference to the Bank as an integral part of the ESCB, pursuing the ESCB's objectives, participating in the performance of its tasks and, subject to the provisions of the Statute, acting in accordance with its guidelines and instructions.

2.2.2 Tasks

- Under the old law, Articles 6 (exclusive right to issue banknotes), 7, 8 (definition and specifications of banknotes and coins), 12 (imitation and reproduction of banknotes), 15, 16 and 17 (currency issues) did not recognise the ECB's powers in respect of banknotes and coins. In the new law, Article 6 contains an explicit reference to the ECB's right of approval with regard to the issuance of banknotes. Articles 7 and 8 have been removed, remaining in force only in relation to banknotes and coins denominated in escudos and until the date on which they will lose their legal tender status. Article 9 of the new law (corresponding to the old Article 12) refers only to banknotes denominated in escudos, while Articles 15, 16 and 17 have been removed.

- Articles 18.1 (conduct of monetary policy) and 21 (implementation of monetary and foreign exchange policies) of the old law did not recognise the ECB's powers in these fields. In the new law, Article 12 (corresponding to the old Article 18) no longer makes any reference to the conduct of monetary policy, and Article 15 (corresponding to the old Article 21) states that the duties of the Bank regarding money and foreign exchange markets must be performed within the scope of its participation in the ESCB.

- Under Article 22.1(a) and (c) of the old law, the Bank's competence to direct the money and foreign exchange markets and to define and impose minimum reserves did not recognise the ECB's powers in these fields, while the reference to the national economic policy objectives did not correspond to the statutory objective of the ESCB. In the new law, Article 16 (corresponding to the old Article 22) explicitly states that the Bank will act pursuant to the rules adopted by the ECB, co-operating in the implementation of minimum reserve requirements and other operational monetary control methods to which the ECB decides to resort, while the reference to the national economic policy objectives has been deleted.

- According to Article 32 (old), the Bank was responsible for licensing external payments whenever required. Under Article 21 of the new law (corresponding to the old Article 32), such responsibility may only be assumed whenever required in accordance with the Treaty.

2.2.3 Instruments

Article 35 (old) on the Bank's monetary policy operations did not recognise the ECB's powers in this field. Article 24 of the new law (corresponding to the old Article 35) explicitly states that such operations will be carried out in order to meet the ESCB's objectives and to perform ESCB-related tasks.

2.2.4 Organisation

Article 46 has been inserted into the new law. It states that, without prejudice to the powers of the Board of Auditors, the accounts of the Bank will also be audited by external auditors.

2.2.5 Participation in international monetary institutions

An insertion into Article 23 (new) makes it clear that the Bank's power to participate in international monetary institutions will be subject to the ECB's approval.

3 Adaptation of other legislation

Portugal is currently amending various laws with a view to Stage Three. The EMI has been consulted on draft amendments to all the legislation listed below.

3.1 Decree-Law No. 333/81 of 7 December 1981

This Decree-Law gives Imprensa Nacional - Casa de Moeda (the national mint) the exclusive right to produce coins and does not recognise the ECB's powers in this field. The Government envisages that this Decree-Law will be amended so that such a right will be exercised without prejudice to Article 105a (2) of the Treaty. A draft law amending this Decree-Law has been approved by the Government. The Government envisages that the draft law will enter into force on the date on which Portugal adopts the single currency.

3.2 Decree-Law No. 293/86 of 12 September 1986

This Decree-Law establishes the legal system with regard to the legal tender status of coins and some of its provisions, in particular Article 9, which deals with legal acts authorising the minting of commemorative coins (which are legal tender according to Article 12 of the same Decree-Law) and defines their technical characteristics, designs, volume of issuance and liberatory power, do not recognise the ECB's powers in this field. The Government

envisages that this Decree-Law will be amended in order to state that, as from the date on which Portugal adopts the single currency, the volume of issuance will be subject to the ECB's approval and minting will be done in accordance with any measures adopted by the EU Council under Article 105a (2) of the Treaty. A draft law amending this Decree-Law has been approved by the Government.

3.3 Decree-Law No. 178/88 of 19 May 1988

This Decree-Law contains one provision (Article 4) which reproduces Article 9 of Decree-Law No. 293/86 and, as stated above, does not recognise the ECB's powers in respect of coins. The same solution as for Decree-Law No. 293/86 is foreseen by the Government.

3.4 Decree-Law No. 13/90 of 8 January 1990

This Decree-Law deals with rules on foreign exchange operations which will have to be reviewed in the light of the introduction of the euro. For example, the definition of "foreign currency" in Article 5.3, which includes "banknotes and coins which are legal tender in foreign countries", does not anticipate the fact that euro banknotes and coins, notwithstanding their status as legal tender in all participating Member States, will not be a "foreign" currency. The Government envisages that this Decree-Law will be amended in such a way that it will be made clear that, on the one hand, any references to "foreign currency" or to "banknotes and coins which are legal tender in foreign countries" do not relate to the euro and, on the other, all references to the ECU as a "basket" currency (as distinct from the national currency) will disappear, with the result that the euro will be treated as the national currency in its own right. A draft law amending the Decree-Law, which is to enter into force as from the date on which Portugal adopts the single currency, has been approved by the Government.

4   Assessment of compatibility

With the adoption and the entry into force of the Constitutional Law No. 1/97 and the new law, the statute of the Banco de Portugal is compatible with Treaty and Statute requirements for Stage Three.

As far as other legislation is concerned, the EMI takes note that adaptations are envisaged of Decree-Law No. 333/81 of 7 December 1981, Decree-Law No. 293/86 of 12 September 1986, Decree-Law No. 178/88 of 19 May 1988 and Decree-Law No. 13/90 of 8 January 1990. The EMI is not aware of any other statutory provisions which would require adaptation under Article 108 of the Treaty.

FINLAND

1 Legislation within the scope of Article 108 of the Treaty

The following legislation required adaptation under Article 108 of the Treaty:

- the Act on the Bank of Finland of 21 December 1925 as amended (the "old law");

- the Currency Act;

- the Act on Coins.

2 Adaptation of the statute of Suomen Pankki

The statute of Suomen Pankki was amended to meet Treaty and Statute requirements for Stage Three by means of a revised Act on the Bank of Finland (the "revised law"), which entered into force on 1 January 1998. The revised law has, again, been adapted through a new law (the "new law") in order to bring the Bank's statute fully into line with the Treaty and the Statute. The new law was adopted by Parliament on 20 March 1998 and is expected to be promulgated on 27 March 1998. The new law will enter into force, in respect of the provisions on independence (see paragraphs 2.1.1 and 2.1.2 below), immediately after its promulgation and, in respect of the provisions on the Bank's legal integration in the ESCB (see paragraph 2.2 below), on 1 January 1999. The EMI has been consulted on both the revised law and the new law in their draft versions, and both have been amended, inter alia, in the light of the EMI's opinion.

2.1 Independence

With regard to the Bank's independence, the following adaptations were made with effect from 1 January 1998 (for the revised law) and with effect from the date of the new law's promulgation (for the new law).

2.1.1 Institutional independence

- The Bank's institutional independence has been enhanced in the revised and the new law. Article 1 (revised) stated that the Bank is an independent institution. Furthermore, Article 5 (revised) introduced a prohibition on seeking or taking instructions in the monetary field, while Article 4 (new) provides for an extension to all ESCB-related tasks. The latter Article also states that such a prohibition is to apply to the Bank as well as to the members of its decision-making bodies, but that it does not, at the same time, apply to instructions issued by the ECB. Finally, Article 13 (revised) attributed responsibility for supervising the administration of the Bank to the Parliamentary Supervisory Council, while Article 16 (revised) made the Board responsible for the fulfilment of the Bank's mandate and for the administration of the Bank.

- The new law contains various articles with extensive possibilities for obtaining and obligations to provide information about the Bank's activities. See, for example, Article 11, paragraph 1, section 5 (Parliamentary Supervisory Council vis-à-vis Parliament); Article 11, paragraph 3, last sentence; Article 14 (Board vis-à-vis Parliamentary Supervisory Council); and Article 27 (Bank vis-à-vis Parliament). Such provisions are only compatible with

Treaty and Statute requirements on institutional independence if they do not lead de facto to ex ante consultations of third parties on the Bank's ESCB-related tasks.

2.1.2 Personal independence

While under the old law the Governor and the other members of the Board could be dismissed by the President of the Republic at his/her considered discretion, Articles 18 and 19 (revised) stated that the President of the Republic could remove the Governor or other members of the Board from office if the Governor or such a member was guilty of misconduct in office, if his/her performance had otherwise shown that he/she was not suited to continue in office or if he/she no longer fulfilled the conditions required for the performance of his/her duties. These grounds for dismissal did not correspond to the grounds for dismissal as laid down in Article 14.2 of the Statute. The new law addresses this incompatibility for members of the Board in Article 16 by reproducing the grounds for dismissal as laid down in Article 14.2 of the Statute and by recognising the fact that the possibility for the Governor to appeal is governed by the Statute. As the Parliamentary Supervisory Council will not be involved in the performance of ESCB-related tasks, such adaptations are not required for its members.

2.1.3 Financial independence

Article 21, paragraph 2, of the new law provides for objective criteria with regard to the distribution of profit to the State from which the Parliamentary Supervisory Council may only deviate if this can be justified on the basis of either the Bank's financial position or the size of its reserve fund. As such a deviation may have an impact on the means available to the Bank for it to perform its ESCB-related tasks,

this provision must be accompanied by a safeguard clause to ensure that it will not impede the proper performance of the Bank's ESCB-related tasks. Such a safeguard clause is contained in the Explanatory Memorandum to the new law, which in Scandinavian legal systems tends to have almost the same status as the law itself.

2.2 Legal integration in the ESCB

With regard to the Bank's legal integration in the ESCB, the following adaptations were made with effect from 1 January 1998 (for the revised law) and with effect from 1 January 1999 (for the new law).

2.2.1 Statutory objective

Article 2 (revised), which contained the Bank's statutory objective, neither reflected the primacy of the ESCB's statutory objective nor anticipated the Bank's legal integration in the ESCB. Article 1 of the new law overcomes this through explicit recognition of the Bank's integration in the ESCB and the obligation to perform its ESCB-related tasks in accordance with the ECB's guidelines and instructions, as well as through Article 2 of the new law, which brings the Bank's statutory objective into line with that of the ESCB.

2.2.2 Tasks

■ *Issuance of banknotes*
Article 4 (revised), which established the Bank's exclusive right to issue banknotes, did not recognise the ECB's competence in this field.

■ *Monetary policy*
Articles 3 and 6 (revised), which established the Bank's powers to define and implement monetary policy, did not acknowledge the ECB's competence in this field.

- *Foreign exchange policy*
  Article 3 (revised), which established the Bank's competence to manage and invest Finland's foreign exchange reserves and to take other measures necessary to support the country's external liquidity, did not recognise the ECB's powers in this field.

The new law overcomes all the above points by recognising in the wording of Article 3 (new) that the execution of the Bank's tasks will take place within the framework of the ESCB (i.e. the Bank will "contribute" to the execution of monetary policy as defined by the Governing Council of the ECB, to the issuance of banknotes and to the holding and management of foreign exchange reserves).

2.2.3 Instruments

- Article 6 (revised), which listed the Bank's instruments, did not recognise the ECB's competence in this field. Article 5 of the new law overcomes this point through adaptation of Article 6 (revised) which has to be read in conjunction with Article 3 of the new law; the latter Article recognises that the Bank's tasks will be executed, and its instruments thus applied, within the framework of the ESCB.

- Article 7 (revised) on minimum reserves did not recognise the ECB's competence in this field. It is resolved in the new law by deleting all references to minimum reserves; the power to impose such reserves will be derived directly from the Statute (Article 19) in conjunction with references in the new law to the framework of the ESCB, of which the Bank will form part, and to Articles 1 and 3 (revised) in particular.

- Article 9 (revised) stated that the Bank was required to obtain adequate collateral when granting credit, but that

with exceptionally good reason the Bank could temporarily rescind this collateral requirement. This exception was not in line with Article 18 of the Statute and has therefore been deleted from the Bank's statute in Article 7 of the new law.

2.2.4 Organisation

Article 17 (old) defined the Parliamentary Supervisory Council's responsibilities in such a way that they also extended to monetary policy issues which, in the light of the Council's composition, was incompatible with the Treaty. Article 13 (revised) remedied this situation through the attribution to the Council of supervisory responsibilities with regard to the administration of the Bank, while Article 16 (revised) made the Board responsible for the fulfilment of the Bank's mandate and for the administration of the Bank. This division of responsibilities is maintained in Articles 11 and 14 (new), whereby the Board's responsibilities extend to ESCB-related tasks.

2.2.5 Confidentiality

Article 36 (revised), which contained an obligation to maintain secrecy, did not reflect the fact that the confidentiality regime with regard to ESCB-related information will be governed by Article 38 of the Statute. Article 26 (new) explicitly recognises the above regime.

3 Adaptation of other legislation

3.1 Currency Act

The Government's competence with regard to the exchange rate of the Finnish markka and the Bank's involvement in this matter, as stipulated in the Currency Act, did not recognise the Community's competence in exchange rate matters and did not envisage the introduction of the euro. The Currency Act has been repealed by the Currency Repeal Act, all necessary provisions relating to the use of the Finnish markka and penni as legal tender during the transitional period have been incorporated in transitional provisions, and the provision on decision-making concerning the external value of the Finnish markka has been repealed.

3.2 Act on Coins

In connection with the Currency Repeal Act, a new Coins Act has been enacted to supplement the European Community legislation on coins.

4 Assessment of compatibility

With the adoption of the new law, and assuming that it will enter into force on time, the statute of Suomen Pankki will be compatible with Treaty and Statute requirements for Stage Three.

As far as other legislation is concerned, the EMI notes that adaptations of the Currency Act and the Act on Coins have been completed. The EMI is not aware of any other statutory provisions which would require adaptation under Article 108 of the Treaty.

SWEDEN

1 Legislation within the scope of Article 108 of the Treaty

The following legislation required adaptation under Article 108 of the Treaty:

- the Constitution Act;

- the Riksdag Act;

- the Sveriges Riksbank Act (1988:1385) as amended.

2 Adaptation of the statute of Sveriges Riksbank

The Constitution Act, the Riksdag Act and the Sveriges Riksbank Act are currently being adapted to meet Treaty and Statute requirements for the independence of Sveriges Riksbank. A draft law (the "draft law") is currently pending before Parliament. An adaptation of the Constitution Act requires the approval of two consecutive Parliaments, the next Parliament coming into being after the general election in September 1998. A first approval of amendments to the Constitution Act and the Riksdag Act by Parliament was given on 4 March 1998 and a second approval is expected to be given in October 1998, when the Sveriges Riksbank Act is also expected to be adopted in accordance with the Constitution Act as amended. All adaptations are envisaged to enter into force as from 1 January 1999. The EMI has been consulted on the envisaged changes to the above-mentioned Acts, which have been amended, inter alia, in the light of the EMI's opinion.

2.1 Independence

With regard to the Bank's independence, the following adaptations are envisaged in the draft law.

2.1.1 Institutional independence

Article 42 of the Sveriges Riksbank Act, which contains the provision that the Minister of Finance has to be consulted prior to the Riksbank making a monetary policy decision of major importance, is incompatible with Treaty and Statute requirements on central bank independence. The draft law proposes that Article 42 of the Act be reformulated to make provision for the Riksbank, prior to every monetary policy decision of importance, to inform the Minister of Finance. This is not incompatible with Treaty and Statute requirements on institutional independence, provided that it does not interfere with the independence of the members of the Bank's Executive Board, respects the competence and accountability of the ECB and the members of its decision-making bodies, and observes the confidentiality requirements of the Statute.

2.1.2 Personal independence

- Chapter 9, Article 12, of the Constitution Act, which implies that a refusal to discharge a Board member from his/her responsibility may be used as a ground for dismissal and that Board members may remove the Governor from his/her position without specifying the reasons for his/her dismissal, is not in conformity with Article 14.2 of the Statute. The draft law remedies this by reproducing the literal grounds for dismissal as laid down in Article 14.2 of the Statute and in Chapter 9, Article 12, of the Constitution Act.

- Chapter 8, Article 6, of the Riksdag Act provides that the term of office of members of the Bank's Governing Board other than the Governor will be four years, while Chapter 9, Article 12, of the Constitution Act allows members of Parliament to be members of the Bank's Governing Board. This is incompatible both with the term of office stipulated in Article 14.2 of the Statute and with the prohibition on external influence as laid down in Article 107 of the Treaty, since the Bank's Governing Board is a decision-making body involved in monetary policy matters (for as long as Sweden does not adopt the single currency) or in the performance of ESCB-related tasks. Article 41 of the draft law envisages vesting responsibility for monetary policy matters and, eventually, the performance of ESCB-related tasks in the Bank's Executive Board. Thus, there would be no need for any further adaptation.

2.1.3 Financial independence

Article 49 (draft) states that Parliament will determine the distribution of profit. In this respect, if Parliament were to deviate from the objective criteria to which it has adhered in the past, this could affect the Bank's financial independence. A statutory safeguard clause should therefore be considered in order to ensure that Parliament's power may not impede the proper performance of the Bank's ESCB-related tasks. It is envisaged that this will be accomplished through a reference in the Explanatory Memorandum to the above-mentioned laws, which in Scandinavian legal systems has almost the same status as the law itself. This reference entails that the distribution of profit will continue to be determined according to the established objective criteria.

2.2 Legal integration in the ESCB

Sweden is not a Member State with a special status. Thus, Article 108 of the Treaty is applicable to Sweden as well and requires adaptations of Swedish legislation necessary for the Bank's legal integration in the ESCB to be prepared and adopted by the date of the establishment of the ESCB in order to become effective as from the date on which Sweden adopts the single currency. The following provisions are incompatible with the Treaty and the Statute.

2.2.1 Statutory objective

Article 4 of the Sveriges Riksbank Act, which contains the Bank's statutory objective, does not unambiguously reflect the primacy of maintaining price stability. Article 4 (draft) would remove this incompatibility with the Treaty and Statute requirements on the Bank's legal integration in the ESCB.

2.2.2 Tasks

- *Monetary policy*
  Chapter 9, Article 12, of the Constitution Act and Article 4 of the Sveriges Riksbank Act, which establish the Bank's powers in this field, do not recognise the ECB's powers in this field.

- *Exchange rate policy*
  Chapter 9, Article 12, of the Constitution Act and Article 4 of the Sveriges Riksbank Act, which establish the Bank's powers in this field, do not acknowledge the Community's and the ECB's competence in this field.

- *Issuance of banknotes*
  Chapter 9, Article 13, of the Constitution Act and Article 5 of the Sveriges Riksbank Act, which establish the Bank's exclusive right to issue banknotes and

coins, do not recognise the ECB's competence in this field.

2.2.3 Instruments

Article 20 of the Sveriges Riksbank Act, which deals with the imposition of minimum reserves on credit institutions, does not respect the ECB's competence in this field.

2.2.4 Exchange rate policy

Chapter 9, Article 12, of the Constitution Act, and Article 4 of the Sveriges Riksbank Act do not recognise the powers of the EU Council and the ECB in the field of exchange rate matters.

3 Adaptation of other legislation

Sweden is not a Member State with a special status. Thus, Article 108 of the Treaty is applicable to Sweden as well and requires adaptations of Swedish legislation necessary in the area of other legislation to be prepared and adopted by the date of the establishment of the ESCB. This applies in particular to legislation on access to public documents and the law on secrecy, which need to be reviewed in the light of the confidentiality regime under Article 38 of the Statute.

4 Assessment of compatibility

Assuming that the draft law is adopted as it stood on 24 March 1998, there are two remaining incompatibilities with Treaty and Statute requirements for Stage Three in the statute of Sveriges Riksbank.

- The timetable for adaptation (see above, section 2, first paragraph) is incompatible with Article 108 of the Treaty, which requires adaptations in the area of central bank independence to become effective at the date of the establishment of the ESCB at the latest.

- The draft law does not anticipate the Bank's legal integration in the ESCB, although Sweden is not a Member State with a special status and must therefore comply with all adaptation requirements under Article 108 of the Treaty. This affects a number of provisions in the Bank's statute.

As far as other legislation is concerned, the EMI notes that legislation on access to public documents and the law on secrecy need to be reviewed in the light of the confidentiality regime under Article 38 of the Statute. The EMI is not aware of any other statutory provisions which would require adaptation under Article 108 of the Treaty.

UNITED KINGDOM

According to Protocol No. 11 of the Treaty on certain provisions relating to the United Kingdom of Great Britain and Northern Ireland, the United Kingdom will be under no obligation to move to Stage Three unless it notifies the Council that it intends to do so. Pursuant to the notification given by the United Kingdom to the Council on 30 October 1997 that it does not intend to move to Stage Three of EMU on 1 January 1999, certain provisions of the Treaty (including Articles 107 and 108) and of the Statute do not apply to the United Kingdom. Accordingly, there is no current legal requirement to ensure that national legislation (including the statute of the Bank of England) is compatible with the Treaty and the Statute.

Glossary

Glossary

Bilateral central rate: the official exchange rate between any pair of **ERM** member currencies, around which the **ERM fluctuation margins** are defined.

Convergence criteria: criteria established in Article 109j (1) of the **Treaty** (and developed further in Protocol No. 6). They relate to the performance with respect to price stability, government financial positions, exchange rates and long-term interest rates. The reports produced under Article 109j (1) by the **European Commission** and the EMI shall examine the achievement of a high degree of sustainable convergence by reference to the fulfilment by each Member State of these criteria.

Convergence programmes: medium-term government plans and assumptions regarding the development of key economic variables towards the achievement of **reference values** indicated in the **Treaty**. Regarding budgetary positions, measures to consolidate fiscal balances as well as underlying economic scenarios are highlighted. Convergence programmes normally cover the next three to four years, but are regularly updated during that time. They are examined by the **European Commission** and the **Monetary Committee**. Their reports serve as the basis for an assessment by the **ECOFIN** Council. After the start of Stage Three of **Economic and Monetary Union**, Member States with a derogation will continue to submit convergence programmes, while countries which are members of the euro area will have annual *stability programmes,* in accordance with the **Stability and Growth Pact**.

Council (of the European Union): is made up of representatives of the Governments of the Member States, normally the Ministers responsible for the matters under consideration (therefore often referred to as the *EU Council* or *Council of Ministers*). The Council meeting in the composition of the Ministers of Finance and Economy is often referred to as the *ECOFIN Council*. In addition, the Council may meet in the composition of the Heads of State or of Government. See also **European Council**.

Current transfers: government transfers to enterprises, households and the rest of the world, net of transfers received from the rest of the world, that are not related to capital expenditure; they comprise, among other operations, production and import subsidies, social benefits and transfers to EC institutions.

Cyclical component of the budget balance: shows the effect on the budget balance of the **output gap**, as estimated by the **European Commission**.

Debt ratio: the subject of one of the fiscal **convergence criteria** laid down in **Treaty** Article 104c (2). It is defined as the ratio of government debt to gross domestic product at current market prices, where government debt is defined in Protocol No. 5 (on the **excessive deficit procedure**) as *"total gross debt at nominal value outstanding at the end of the year and consolidated between and within the sectors of general government".* General government is as defined in the **European System of Integrated Economic Accounts**

Deficit ratio: the subject of one of the fiscal **convergence criteria** named in **Treaty** Article 104c (2). Defined as *"the ratio of the planned or actual government deficit to gross domestic product"* at current market prices, where the government deficit is defined in Protocol No. 5 (on the **excessive deficit procedure**) as net borrowing of the **general government.** General government is as defined in the **European System of Integrated Economic Accounts**

ECB (European Central Bank): the ECB will have legal personality. It will ensure that the tasks conferred upon the **ESCB** are implemented either by its own activities pursuant to its Statute or through the national central banks.

ECOFIN: see **Council (of the European Union)**.

Economic and Financial Committee: a consultative Community body to be set up at the start of Stage Three, when the **Monetary Committee** will be dissolved. The Member States, the **European Commission** and the **ECB** shall each appoint no more than two members of the Committee. Article 109c (2) of the **Treaty** contains a list of the tasks of the Economic and Financial Committee, including the review of the economic and financial situation of the Member States and of the Community.

Economic and Monetary Union (EMU): the **Treaty** describes the process of achieving economic and monetary union in the EU in three stages. *Stage One* of EMU started in July 1990 and ended on 31 December 1993: it was mainly characterised by the dismantling of all internal barriers to the free movement of capital within the EU. *Stage Two* of EMU began on 1 January 1994. It provided for, inter alia, the establishment of the European Monetary Institute, the prohibition of monetary financing of and privileged access to financial institutions for the public sector and the avoidance of excessive deficits. *Stage Three* will start on 1 January 1999 in accordance with the decision pursuant to Article 109j (4), with the transfer of monetary competence to the **ESCB** and the introduction of the **euro**.

ECU (European Currency Unit): in its present definition (Council Regulation No. 3320/94 of 20 December 1994), the ECU is a basket made up of the sum of fixed amounts of twelve out of the fifteen currencies of the Member States. Article 109g of the **Treaty** states that this composition shall not be changed until the start of Stage Three. The value of the ECU is calculated as a weighted average of the value of its component currencies. As official ECU, it serves, inter alia, as the numeraire of the **ERM** and as a reserve asset for central banks. Official ECUs are created by the EMI through three-month swap operations against one-fifth of the US dollar and gold assets held by the fifteen EU central banks. Private ECUs are ECU-denominated financial instruments (e.g. bank deposits or securities) which are based on contracts which, as a rule, make reference to the official ECU. The "theoretical" value of the private ECU is defined on the basis of the value of the individual components of the ECU basket. However, the use of the private ECU is different from that of the official ECU and in practice the market value of the private ECU may diverge from its "theoretical" basket value. The replacement of the private ECU by the **euro** at the rate of one to one is laid down in Article 2 of the Council Regulation on certain provisions relating to the introduction of the euro, see (EC) No. 1103/97 of June 1997.

Effective (nominal/real) exchange rates: in their *nominal* version, effective exchange rates consist of a weighted average of various bilateral exchange rates. *Real* effective exchange rates are nominal effective exchange rates deflated by a weighted average of foreign prices or costs relative to domestic ones. They are thus measures of a country's price and cost competitiveness. The choice of currencies and weights reflects the economic issue being analysed. The most commonly used measures of effective exchange rates employ trade weights.

Elderly dependency ratio: shows the proportion of the population of a country aged 65 and over in comparison with the population aged 15-64; it thereby indicates approximately how many elderly persons' unfunded social benefits have to be financed on average by each member of the generation that is still below retirement age.

EMS (European Monetary System): established in 1979 in accordance with the Resolution of the **European Council** on the establishment of the EMS and related matters of 5 December 1978. The Agreement of 13 March 1979 between the central banks of the Member States of the European Economic Community lays down the operating procedures for the EMS. The objective is to create closer monetary policy co-operation between Community countries leading to a zone of monetary stability in Europe. The main components of the EMS are: the **ECU**; the exchange rate and intervention mechanism (**ERM**); and various credit mechanisms.

EMU: see **Economic and Monetary Union**.

ERM (Exchange Rate Mechanism): the exchange rate and intervention mechanism of the **EMS** defines the exchange rate of participating currencies in terms of a central rate vis-à-vis the **ECU**. These central rates are used to establish a grid of bilateral exchange rates between participating currencies. Exchange rates are allowed to fluctuate around **bilateral central rates** within the **ERM fluctuation margins**. In August 1993 the decision was taken to widen the fluctuation margins to ±15%. Pursuant to a bilateral agreement between Germany and the Netherlands, fluctuation margins between the Deutsche Mark and the Dutch guilder are maintained at ±2.25%. Adjustments of central rates are subject to mutual agreement between all countries participating in the ERM (see also **realignment**).

ERM fluctuation margins: floor and ceiling of bilateral exchange rates, within which **ERM** currencies are allowed to fluctuate.

ESCB (European System of Central Banks): the ESCB will be composed of the **ECB** and the national central banks of the Member States. Its primary objective will be to maintain price stability. Its basic tasks will be to define and implement the monetary policy of the **euro area**, to hold and manage the official reserves of the participating Member States and conduct foreign exchange operations and to promote the smooth operation of payment systems in the euro area. The ESCB will also contribute to the smooth conduct of policies pursued by the competent authorities relating to the prudential supervision of credit institutions and the stability of the financial system.

euro: the name of the European currency adopted by the **European Council** at its meeting in Madrid on 15 and 16 December 1995 and used instead of the generic term "**ECU**" used by the **Treaty** to refer to the European Currency Unit.

euro area: area encompassing those Member States where the **euro** will be adopted as the single currency in accordance with the **Treaty** and in which a single monetary policy will be conducted under the responsibility of the relevant decision-making bodies of the **ECB**.

European Commission: institution of the European Community which ensures the application of the provisions of the **Treaty**, takes initiatives for Community policies, proposes Community legislation and exercises powers in specific areas. In the economic policy area, the Commission recommends broad guidelines for the economic policies in the Community and reports to the **Council** on economic developments and policies. It monitors public finances and initiates the procedure on excessive deficits. It consists of twenty members and includes two nationals from Germany, Spain, France, Italy and the United Kingdom, and one from each of the other Member States. *EUROSTAT* is the Directorate General of the Commission responsible for the production of Community statistics through the collection and systematic processing of data, produced mainly by the national authorities, within the framework of comprehensive five-yearly Community statistical programmes.

European Council: provides the European Union with the necessary impetus for its development and defines the general political guidelines thereof. It brings together the Heads of State or of Government of the Member States and the President of the **European Commission**. See also **Council**.

European Parliament: consists of 626 representatives of the citizens of the Member States. It is a part of the legislative process, though with different prerogatives according to the procedures through which EU law is to be enacted. In the framework of **EMU**, the Parliament will have mainly consultative powers. However, the **Treaty** establishes certain procedures for democratic accountability of the **ECB** to the Parliament (presentation of the annual report, general debate on the monetary policy, hearings to the competent parliamentary committees).

European System of Integrated Economic Accounts (ESA): represents a system of uniform statistical definitions and classifications aiming at a coherent quantitative description of the economies of EU Member States. The ESA is the Community's version of the United Nations' revised System of National Accounts. The respective definitions are, inter alia, the basis for calculating the fiscal **convergence criteria** laid down in the **Treaty**.

EUROSTAT: see **European Commission**.

Excessive deficit procedure: the **Treaty** provision (defined in Article 104c and specified in Protocol No. 5) that requires EU Member States to maintain budgetary discipline, defines the conditions for a budgetary position to be judged as satisfactory and regulates the steps to be taken following the observation that these conditions are not fulfilled. In particular, the fiscal **convergence criteria** (government **deficit ratio** and **debt ratio**) are specified, the procedure that may result from the **Council's** decision that an excessive deficit exists in a certain Member State is described and further steps to be taken in the event that an excessive deficit situation persists are identified.

Exchange rate volatility: a measure of the variability of exchange rates, it is usually calculated using the standard deviation of daily percentage changes.

Funded and unfunded pensions: a funded pension scheme is one where pension commitments are covered by real or financial assets, as opposed to an unfunded, or pay-as-you-go, form of pension scheme in which current contributions of employers and employees are relied upon to pay current pensions directly.

General government: aggregation of central government, regional or local government and social security funds, with the exclusion of commercial operations, as defined in the **European System of Integrated Economic Accounts** (Protocol No. 5 on the **excessive deficit procedure**).

Growth-interest differential: the difference between the annual change in nominal GDP and the nominal average interest rate paid on outstanding government debt (the "effective" interest rate). It is one of the determinants of changes in the government debt ratio.

Harmonised Index of Consumer Prices (HICP): Protocol No. 6 on the **convergence criteria** referred to in Article 109j (1) of the **Treaty** establishing the European Community requires price convergence to be measured by means of the consumer price index on a comparable basis, taking into account differences in national definitions. Although current consumer price statistics in the Member States are largely based on similar principles, there are considerable differences of detail and these affect the comparability of the national results. In order to fulfil the Treaty requirement the **European Commission** (EUROSTAT), in close liaison with the National Statistical Institutes and the EMI, has carried out conceptual work on the harmonisation of consumer price statistics. The Harmonised Index of Consumer Prices is the outcome of these efforts.

Harmonised long-term interest rates: Protocol No. 6 on the **convergence criteria** referred to in Article 109j (1) of the **Treaty** establishing the European Community requires interest rate convergence to be measured by means of interest rates on long-term government bonds or comparable government securities, taking into account differences in national definitions. In order to fulfil the Treaty requirement the EMI has carried out conceptual work on the harmonisation of long-term interest rate statistics and regularly collects the data from national central banks, on behalf of the **European Commission** (EUROSTAT). Fully harmonised data are used in this report.

Intervention at the limits: compulsory intervention carried out by central banks, the currencies of which are respectively at the floor and ceiling of their **ERM fluctuation margins**.

Intra-marginal intervention: intervention carried out by a central bank to influence the exchange rate of its currency within its **ERM fluctuation margins**.

Investment: gross fixed capital formation as defined in the **European System of Integrated Economic Accounts**.

Measures with a temporary effect: comprise all non-cyclical effects on fiscal variables which (i) reduce (or increase) the **general government** deficit or gross debt (**debt ratio**, **deficit ratio**) in a specified period only ("one-off" effects) or (ii) improve (or worsen) the budgetary situation in a specified period at the expense (or to the benefit) of future budgetary situations ("self-reversing" effects).

Monetary Committee: a consultative Community body, composed of two representatives from each Member State in a personal capacity (normally, one from the government and one from the central bank) and two representatives of the **European Commission**. It was created in 1958 on the basis of Article 105 of the EEC **Treaty**. In order to promote co-ordination of the policies of Member States to the full extent needed for the functioning of the internal market, Article 109c of the Treaty lists a set of areas where the Monetary Committee contributes to the preparation of the work of the **Council**. At the start of Stage Three of **Economic and Monetary Union**, the Monetary Committee will be dissolved and an **Economic and Financial Committee** will be created instead.

Net capital expenditure: comprises a government's final capital expenditure (i.e. gross fixed capital formation, plus net purchases of land and intangible assets, plus changes in stocks) and net capital transfers paid (i.e. investment grants, plus unrequited transfers paid by the general government to finance specific items of gross fixed capital formation by other sectors, minus capital taxes and other capital transfers received by the general government).

358

Net external asset or liability position: or the International Investment Position (IIP) - the statistical statement of the value and composition of the stock of an economy's financial assets or financial claims on the rest of the world, less an economy's financial liabilities to the rest of the world.

Nominal effective exchange rates: see **effective (nominal/real) exchange rates**.

Non-cyclical factors: indicate influences on the government's budget balances that are not due to cyclical fluctuations (the **cyclical component of the budget balance**). They can therefore result from either structural, that is permanent, changes in budgetary policies or from measures with a "temporary effect" (see also **measures with a temporary effect**).

Output gap: is defined as the difference between the actual and potential output level of an economy as a percentage of the potential output. Potential output is calculated on the basis of the trend rate of growth of the economy, as estimated by the **European Commission**. A positive (negative) output gap means that actual output is above (below) the trend or potential level of output, and suggests the possible emergence (absence) of inflationary pressures.

Primary balance: government net borrowing or net lending excluding interest payments on government liabilities.

Real effective exchange rates: see **effective (nominal/real) exchange rates**.

Realignment: change in the **ECU** central rate and **bilateral central rates** of one or more currencies participating in the **ERM**.

Reference period: time intervals specified in Article 104c (2a) of the **Treaty** and in Protocol No. 6 on the **convergence criteria** for examining progress towards convergence.

Reference value: Protocol No. 5 of the **Treaty** on the excessive deficit procedure sets explicit reference values for the deficit ratio (3% of GDP) and the debt ratio (60% of GDP), whereas Protocol No. 6 on the **convergence criteria** specifies the methodology for the computation of the reference values relevant for the examination of price and long-term interest rate convergence.

Stability and Growth Pact: consists of two **European Council** Regulations on the "strengthening of the surveillance of budgetary positions and the surveillance and co-ordination of economic policies" and on "speeding up and clarifying the implementation of the **excessive deficit procedure**" and of a European Council Resolution on the Stability and Growth Pact adopted at the Amsterdam summit on 17 June 1997. It is intended to serve as a means of safeguarding sound government finances in Stage Three of **EMU** in order to strengthen the conditions for price stability and for strong sustainable growth conducive to employment creation. More specifically, budgetary positions close to balance or in surplus are mentioned as a condition for Member States to deal with normal cyclical fluctuations, while keeping the government deficit below the **reference value** of 3% of GDP. In accordance with the Stability and Growth Pact, countries participating in Monetary Union will report *stability programmes*, while countries with a derogation will continue to have **convergence programmes**.

Stock-flow adjustments: a statistical concept that ensures consistency between the government deficit (defined as net borrowing or net lending) and the annual variation of the stock of government gross debt. It comprises the government's accumulation of financial assets, the change in the value of the debt denominated in foreign currency, the government's privatisation receipts used for the repayment of debt, the change in the consolidated amount of general government debt and remaining statistical adjustments.

Treaty: refers to the Treaty establishing the European Community. The Treaty was signed in Rome on 25 March 1957 and entered into force on 1 January 1958. It established the *European Economic Community (EEC)* and was often referred to as the "Treaty of Rome". The Treaty on European Union was signed in Maastricht (therefore often referred to as the "Maastricht Treaty") on 7 February 1992 and entered into force on 1 November 1993. It amended the EEC Treaty, which is now referred to as the Treaty establishing the *European Community*. The Treaty on European Union will be amended by the "Amsterdam Treaty", which was signed in Amsterdam on 2 October 1997 and is in the process of being ratified.